# Plywood

# Plywood

## A Material Story

**Christopher Wilk**

with Elizabeth Bisley

Thames & Hudson

(frontispiece)

Skating shelters, Winnipeg, Canada
Designed by Patkau Architects, 2011
(see p. 202).

Front cover

(top left) Workman carrying a complete Deperdussin monocoque fuselage (see p. 81).

(top right) Skating shelters, Winnipeg, Canada (see p. 201).

(centre) Gunnison Homes advertising brochure (see p. 134).

(bottom left) Long Chair, birch plywood seat with laminated plywood frame
Designed by Marcel Breuer, manufactured by Isokon Furniture Company, London, 1936.

(bottom right) Metropol Parasol, Seville, Spain (see p. 204).

Back cover

(top left) Skateboarding ramp, California (see p. 178).

(top right) Plywood hatboxes, manufactured in Russia and the US (see p. 45).

(centre) Cover of Puutalo Oy catalogue (see p. 126).

(bottom left) Method of cutting veneers, late 18th century (see p. 39).

(bottom right) Cutting veneers on a rotary lathe (see p. 12).

First published in the United Kingdom in 2017 by Thames & Hudson in association with the Victoria and Albert Museum.


Designed by Roger Fawcett-Tang



British Library Cataloguing-in-Publication Data

A catalogue record for this book is available from the British Library

ISBN 978-0-500-51940-0

Printed and bound in Slovenia by DZS-Grafik d.o.o.



**V&A Publishing**

Supporting the world's leading museum of art and design, the Victoria and Albert Museum, London

This publication accompanies the exhibition 'Plywood: Material of the Modern World' at the Victoria and Albert Museum from 15 July to 12 November 2017.

Exhibition sponsored by

**MADE.COM**

Supported by

**The American Friends of the V&A**

# Contents

1 (above)

**Rotary lathe cutting veneer from kauri logs**
R. Emerson Curtis, Australia, 1945

# Introduction

Plywood is a material that is widely known yet, remarkably, little understood. Seen in the public imagination as both a mundane and ubiquitous material of building sites and domestic do-it-yourself (DIY) projects, and also as a material of high-style architecture and design, plywood has a long history that is largely unknown and has been little researched.

This book focuses on the period from about 1850 to the present day, looking at moments in which plywood has been particularly important or influential, where it has been shaped by change in technology or use, and where cultural attitudes to the material can reveal something about its wider social and technological history. Rather than attempting a complete account of plywood's use, the book instead offers a series of episodes from the history of the material, highlighting points at which plywood has played a particularly significant role in determining the shape of contemporary design.

### What is plywood?

Plywood is made from a stack of thin sheets (plies) of wood called veneers, invariably odd in number, and glued together with the grain of each layer running perpendicular to the next (figs 2–4). This cross-graining creates maximum strength and stability in the material. The building-up of cross-grained layers of veneer was a constructional technique first used in the ancient world, although it was then rarely used until the mid-eighteenth century (see pp. 17–20). In the mid-nineteenth century it was patented both as a highly successful technique for making moulded chair seats and backs (for commercial and domestic use) and also as a wood product with myriad applications, both moulded and flat. It has always been assumed that the history of plywood was mainly that of the flat board. This book demonstrates, however, that between 1850 and the 1890s, moulded plywood was the most common form of the material and furniture design the driver of innovation in its use.

By 1890 the flat plywood board was first mass produced for sale to manufacturers. The board form enabled increasingly standardized design, easy transportation and simpler handling of a square

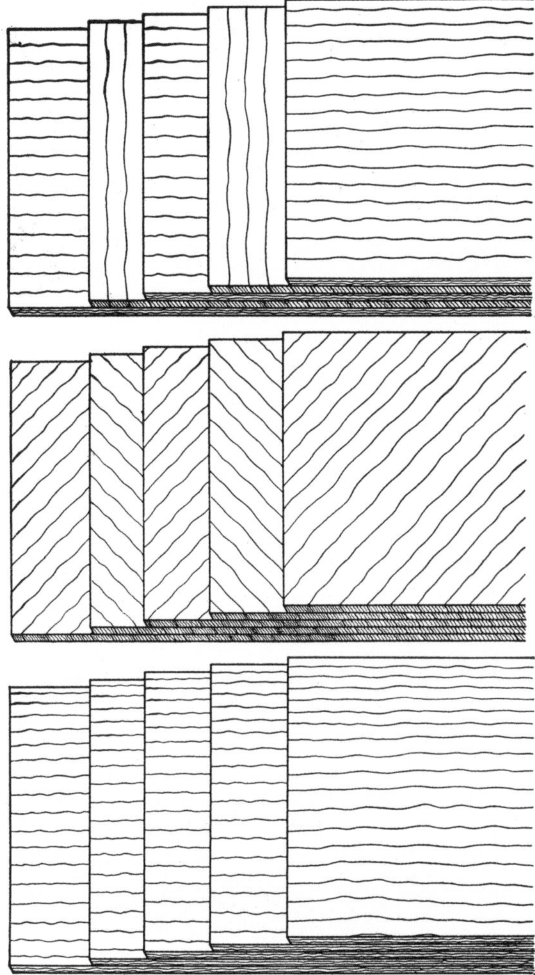

2 (left)

**Top: standard cross-grained plywood construction**

**Middle: diagonal cross-grained plywood construction used in aeroplanes and boats**

**Bottom: laminated construction, with all grain running in the same direction**

From Louis H. Meyer, *Plywood: What It Is – What It Does* (New York 1947), p. 6

3 equal ply construction.

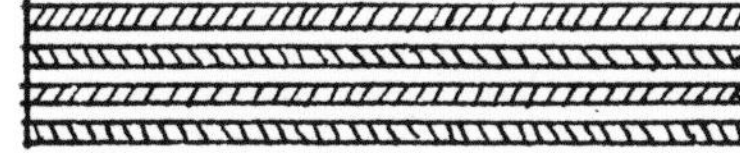

7-ply construction.

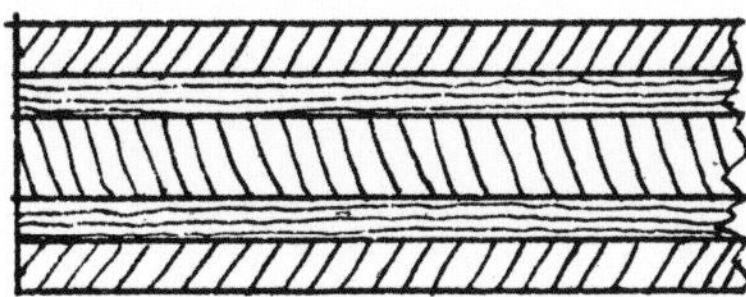

¾-in. 5-ply construction.

3 (left)

**Typical plywood construction**

From Andrew Dick Wood and Thomas Gray Linn, *Plywoods, Their Development, Manufacture and Application* (Edinburgh and London 1942), fig. 1, p. 10

metreage of wood that was, as pieces of solid wood, more expensive to transport or to make use of. One of the largest applications of plywood boards from the 1890s until at least the 1930s was for making collapsible chests used to transport tea from Britain's colonies to global markets. Boards were also used in World War I aircraft, but less well known was plywood's crucially important use in moulded aeroplanes from about 1911 to 1930 and then, more famously, during a period of metals shortages around World War II. It was largely this extraordinary application, viewed as a major technological contribution to the war effort, together with the 1930s adoption of plywood for architectural use, which contributed to raising the status of the material. In the post-war era plywood became a common material on the building site, for higher-style rather than only mass-market furniture and, notably, for an endless array of DIY projects, from boat building to home improvement.

Sales of plywood suffered from the 1960s, as cheaper board materials were introduced and, later, as plywood's reputation was increasingly tarnished by health and environmental concerns. Since the late 1980s, plywood has benefited from the renewed popularity of wood over less sustainable materials. It has also found new life as a material especially suitable for manufacturing and making using digital platforms and technologies. Despite this interest in plywood as an accessible and, depending upon its sourcing and manufacture, 'green' material, the vast majority of plywood currently manufactured is used for construction – often disposable, cheap and highly polluting. Plywood's networks of production and consumption have often covered both the cutting edge of manufacture and design, and extreme poverty of materials and environment.

The earliest development of plywood was almost certainly an attempt to deal with solid wood's inevitable and often irreversible reaction to changing or extreme atmospheric conditions. In an environment of low relative humidity wood shrinks and splits; with excessive relative humidity it expands.[1] Such movement can result in deformations that include shrinkage, warping and splitting. Plywood has repeatedly been used to solve this essential challenge of woodworking. Its laminated (i.e. layered and glued), cross-grained structure mitigates such movement, creates structural (dimensional) stability and is, in terms of strength, more resistant to stresses.

It would be a mistake to approach plywood's history as the 'invention' of a material, or even one mainly to do with technological innovation. It may be more useful to describe plywood's history as being one in which a relatively simple composite material was created out of existing ones (veneers and glue) in order to solve specific design, labour or cost problems. Within that story there were certainly moments when key advances were made (for example the development of synthetic glues). But this is not a story in which a brand new material was born at a particular moment. Instead, it is the adaptation and reuse of a long-understood construction technique in an increasingly broad range of applications. Across this long history, plywood was regularly represented as a new material: a promotional strategy that relied not only on its often hidden presence in existing products, but also on innovative plywood designs or on new methods of gluing or manufacturing (especially moulding).

While plywood is laminated, not all laminated wood is plywood. For example, laminated wood (fig. 2) – used variously in the early twentieth century to make propellers or chair arms and legs, or more recently in giant architectural elements – can have the grains of all layers running in the same direction and can be made from solid wood rather than veneers. In general, though not universally, when people refer to laminated wood today they are distinguishing it from plywood with reference to this single-grain direction of the laminate layers. This book is about plywood as a

4 (below)
**A: Alternative form of plywood with batten or board core variously called 'laminboard', 'battenboard' or 'blockboard'**
**B: Plywood was sometimes made with a thicker veneer core**
From Thomas D. Perry, *Modern Plywood* (New York 1942), p. 38

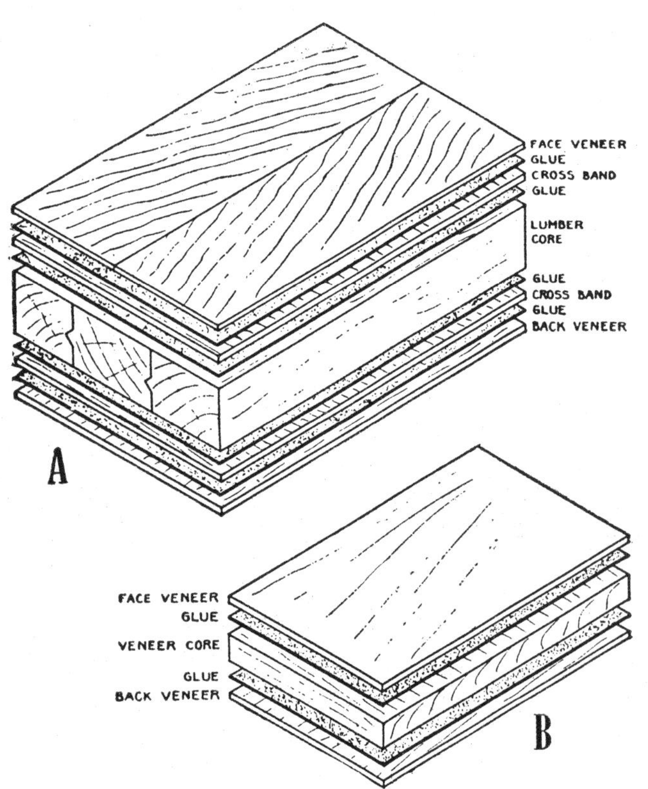

material of cross-grained laminated veneers and does not include substantial discussion of other laminated wood products.

The language used to describe plywood and the veneers from which it was made is an important, even crucial, part of its history. The material that we now call plywood has been variously named in its long history of production and use in the English-speaking world. In the late eighteenth century plywood appears to have been termed 'glued up panels' or 'pasteboards'. In the nineteenth century it was named 'pressed work', 'built-up work', 'veneers' or 'veneer work' and, at the very end of the century, '3-ply' or 'three-ply'. In the very early twentieth century the word 'ply wood' (fig. 75) first appeared, even though older terminology remained in use well into the 1920s and 1930s.

### Histories of plywood

While plywood has an important place in the history of materials, even more significant is the story of how it was perceived, how its value and identity were negotiated, and how it was positioned and repositioned in the public imagination. Expensive and highly valued in the seventeenth and eighteenth centuries, veneers came to be seen by nineteenth-century consumers as cheap and dishonest – a showy surface layer hiding a sham interior. This profound shift in perception was linked to technological developments of the late eighteenth and early nineteenth centuries, in which new machinery suddenly allowed for the mass production of machine-cut veneers. Veneers, and veneered or 'built-up' furniture, consequently became associated with cheapness, poor quality and deception. This attitude has, in some markets, shaped perceptions of plywood to the present day.

This book approaches the history of plywood, in part, as a cultural one, looking especially closely at the material in relation to dramatic shifts in its reputation. Plywood is perhaps unique among materials in its capacity to shift over time between an association with cheapness and shoddiness, and with valued, technological sophistication. This suggests that plywood deserves attention for its role in shaping social values as well as economic ones – its economic, social and industrial history is mirrored in the material's shifts in status between 'low' and 'high' aesthetic or technical value. Plywood's cultural history is here built through a careful study of its reception by consumers (including manufacturers), which makes clear that plywood was redefined, mainly during the years 1925–45, from a largely hidden and cheap material to a truly modern one, taking its place with genuinely newly exploited materials such as aluminium and plastic.[2]

Questions about the place and meaning of plywood in the designed world are explored here, especially in areas where materials have been too little explained as part of a broader design history. For example, although plywood has a highly significant place in the history of architecture and design (in the widest sense, from furniture to aircraft), many of the products in this book have not been much discussed in the context of their material. Most books on aircraft, the central topic of chapter 4, are surprisingly little concerned with materials, and even in specialist monographs on individual makers or models the emphasis is firmly on speed or altitude records, famous pilots and tales of derring-do.[3]

The intention here is also to cast a useful light on accepted histories of modernism. In the early twentieth century plywood became a material of choice for modernism's leading architects and designers in Germany, the Netherlands and the US. Plywood was not alone in this – it sat alongside other industrial materials, especially steel and, later, aluminium, which were adopted for high-end design. Histories of modernism have tended to avoid an in-depth analysis of materials, focusing instead on the moment of a material's adoption as a kind of cipher for engagement with modernity. On the one hand, this book discusses the industrial imperative that drove the development and use of plywood over a much longer time frame. On the other, it provides an alternative to numerous otherwise informative accounts of leading designers who became closely associated with plywood, such as Alvar Aalto, Marcel Breuer or Ray and Charles Eames, where a narrow disciplinary context avoids both longer histories of the material and the (then) contemporary breadth of its application.

### The geography of plywood

This book does not claim to be the last word on plywood – while every attempt has been made to signal developments in and connections with international centres of production elsewhere (especially Russia, Finland and Germany), the focus is largely on the US and Britain. The US was one of the world's largest producers of wood and plywood in the nineteenth and twentieth centuries, one with a well-documented trade history (despite the frustrating shortage of records of major plywood companies), and the home of the world's longest-running research facility for wood products, the Forest Products Laboratory (FPL), in Madison,

Wisconsin.[4] In Europe, Britain was the world's largest importer of plywood from the late nineteenth to the first half of the twentieth century. The Russian Empire clearly played a key role in the development of plywood as an industrial product but, unfortunately, much of that history still remains hidden. Aspects of it are included here as are references to Finland, a country that, in terms of its national identity, has been closely associated with plywood design and manufacturing since about 1930. Germany's place in plywood history is important and still under-researched. Sweden and Denmark's association with plywood products arises mainly in the post-World War II era. Whereas the US and Finland were dominant producers of plywood in the mid-twentieth century (the latter country exporting a significant percentage of its production), since the early 1990s that role has been taken over by manufacturers in Asia: Indonesia, Japan and Malaysia, and most recently mainly by China. Much as different plywood-producing nations in the twentieth century were known for particular qualities and types of plywood (e.g. the highest-quality birch plywood was – and still is – made in Finland),today's market is similarly segmented across many countries, albeit with a much wider geography.

**Approaches to a material**

Plywood has had its own chroniclers. The first English-language books on plywood (published 1927–42) concentrated on the constructional and technical aspects of the material (figs 2–4), its methods of manufacture and its use. These books were published at a moment of intense efforts by the plywood industry to raise the status of the material, and must be seen in this context. For this reason most of them offer a fanciful account of its history based on its use in furniture alone. Despite this, they remain much mined sources of information today.[5] This book provides a broad chronological explanation of how plywood was created, adapted and developed between 1850 and the present using specific case studies to invite a deeper analysis of certain, highly significant moments in plywood's history.

This narrative about plywood relies on a multiplicity of archival sources, trade literature, patent records, the popular press and literary sources, commercial advertising, and consumer and cultural responses. Material and textual sources, generated by people and institutions with diverse (sometimes vested) interests in plywood, together allow the material to be seen and understood from a range of different perspectives. Indeed, this book is unusual in integrating documentary research and a cultural history narrative with a close study of the physical evidence of plywood in historical and contemporary objects – an approach that arose directly from the project's inception as a museum exhibition.

The different chapters concentrate on particular types of product and therefore tend to draw upon specific source types (while all draw upon secondary literature where it exists). Chapter 1, on the historical beginnings of plywood, focuses mainly on patents as a form of documentation, especially appropriate when dealing with the creation of a language for a material perceived as 'new'. Chapter 2, on early plywood technology and manufacturing, draws upon patents and descriptions of wood-cutting machinery, and on nineteenth- and very early twentieth-century books and magazines. Chapter 3, concerned with the nineteenth-century cultural history of plywood, and the legacy of this in the twentieth century, relies upon a wide range of popular literature, fiction (novels, short stories and plays) as well as non-fiction (newspaper and magazine articles on a range of topics). It is also concerned with how culturally informed, prejudicial attitudes to veneer and plywood were reflected in court cases and government regulatory hearings. Such proceedings, where individuals testified and were cross-examined under oath, are especially useful in revealing details of language as well as manufacturing and marketing techniques, which are otherwise rarely represented in the historical record.

Chapter 4 changes gear by introducing a case study on the important and influential use of plywood in aircraft, focusing largely on monocoque fuselages. It makes use of aircraft patents and trade journals, published and unpublished reports from the FPL and from private firms, as well as secondary literature. Chapter 5 focuses on architecture and building – an arena where plywood became highly visible to the public, starting in the 1930s. Plywood's use in architecture was actively promoted by trade associations and the chapter draws upon wood trade, building and architectural journals, as well as the contemporary popular press and later monographs. Chapter 6 uses contemporary press articles, archival material, and trade and secondary literature to document how wartime use of plywood raised its status after 1945, and saw it accepted as a modern and reliable material for home and industrial use. The last chapter makes use of international trade data; reports from government regulatory agencies, government and non-governmental scientific organizations, and environmental and trade groups; press accounts; and interviews with design and trade professionals to chart both the 'fall' of plywood's reputation in the late 1960s, and its later revival as a material in particular for design using digital platforms. The focus here is not products but the way in which plywood has found new life in systems of production and use, and also some notable technical innovations.

In highlighting important episodes in the history of the plywood, others are necessarily excluded. For example, aircraft in the first half of the twentieth century are discussed in chapter 4 rather than the closely related field of boat design and construction in the same period. The choice to explore architecture in the period from 1930 to 1945 focuses on an era of experimentation and formative development, rather than the much more common use of plywood in homes in the post-war era. And, among other topics, there was, unfortunately, insufficient space to mention the fascinating experiments in plywood conducted at the New Bauhaus school of design in Chicago in the 1940s.

A book on plywood seems especially relevant owing to its marked popularity for everyday and industrial uses. Among the various reasons for this are a growing interest in the nature and functionality of materials, and a great resurgence in making of all kinds.[6] Still easily accessible and workable with minimum technology, plywood is also highly valued as one of the most important materials in digital design and manufacturing, both in small community or commercial workshops and also on an industrial scale. The working of plywood using digitally controlled cutting machines has become so common a part of the landscape of making today that the leap to such new technology from traditional and mechanized saws is no longer much commented upon. As long as close attention is paid to the manner in which plywood is sourced and manufactured, it remains a material with a secure future.

## How plywood is made

The following sequence of plates (figs 5–13) explains how plywood was made in the early and mid-twentieth century. The basic steps remain the same today, although digital technology (see chapter 7) is now employed in many of the stages. Increasing use of digital technology has meant that the production of plywood is faster and involves fewer workers than in the past.

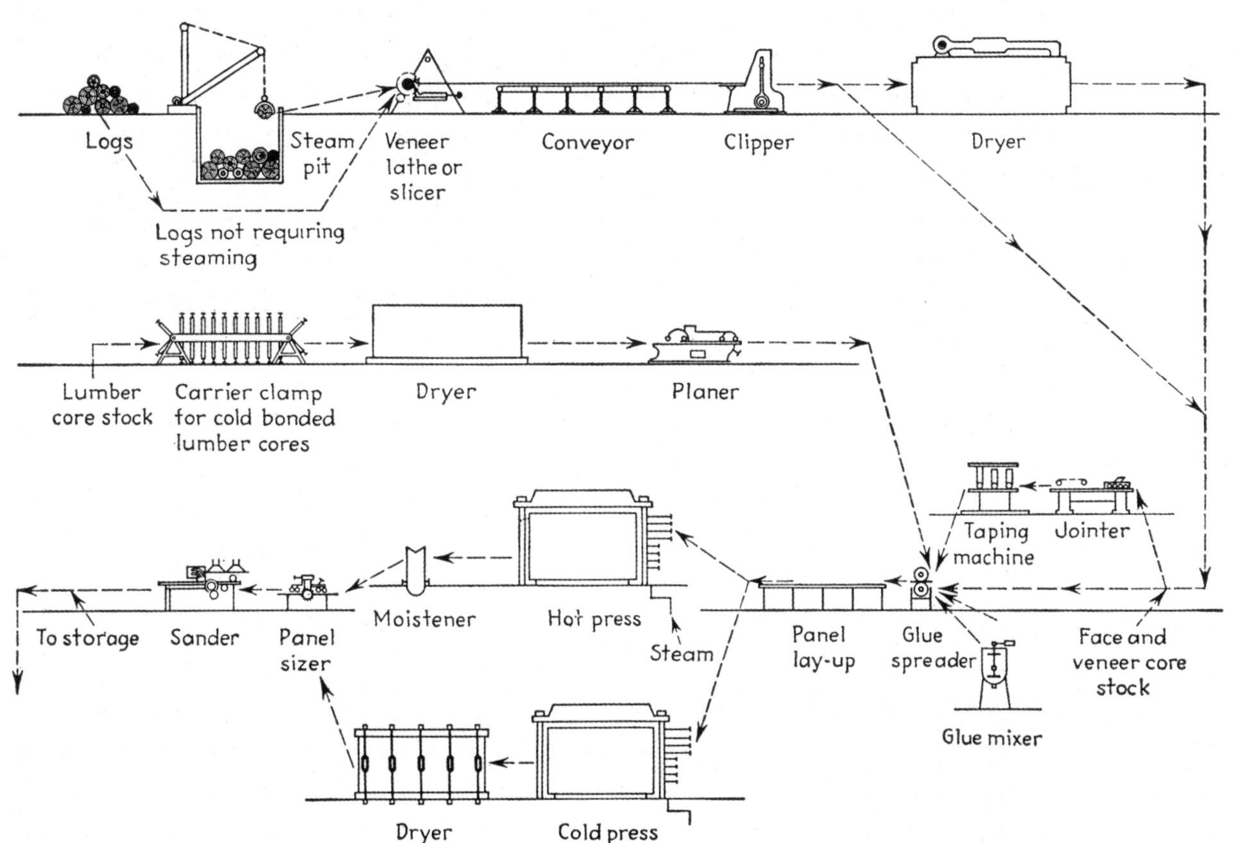


5 (below)
**Diagram showing stages of manufacture of plywood**
From Louis H. Meyer, *Plywood: What It Is – What It Does* (New York 1947), p. 6

6 (right)

**Barker (or de-barker) peels bark off a log that has been previously soaked, steamed or sprayed to soften the bark and consistently moisten the wood for easiest cutting (Oregon, US)**

7 (right)

**Veneers are cut by knife in a peeling action on a rotary lathe. The veneer is then cut (or 'clipped') into the desired sizes (Washington State, US)**

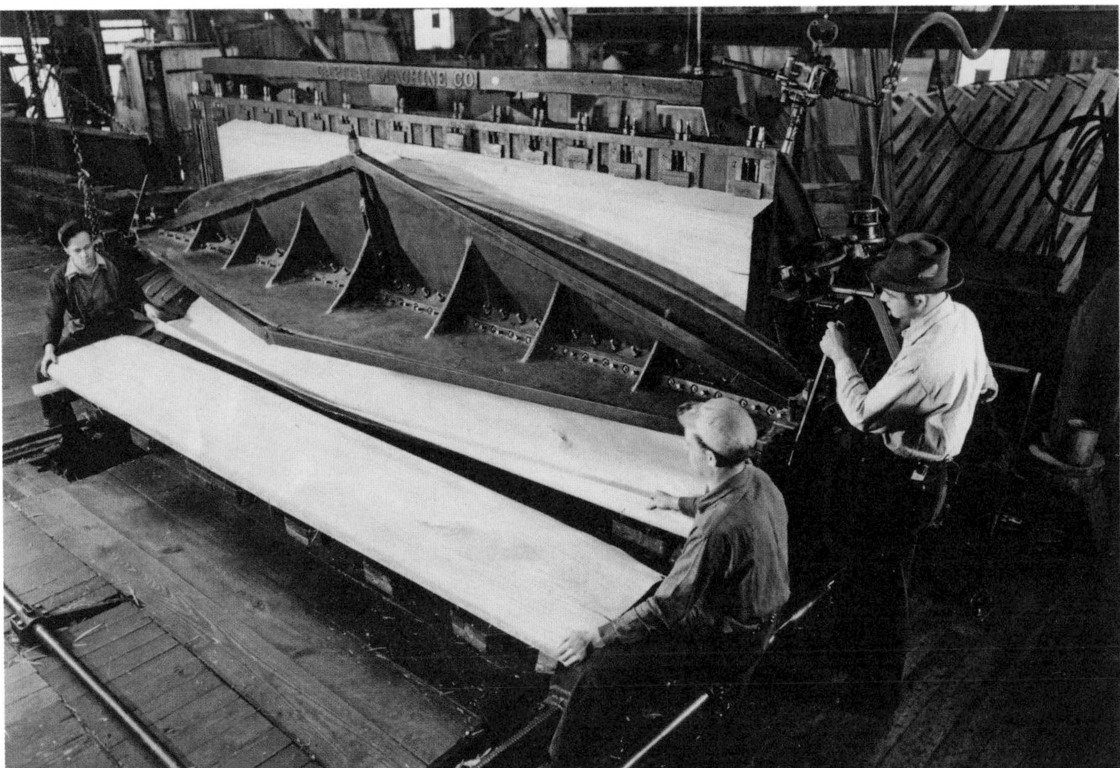


8 (left)

**Higher-quality woods are flat-sliced from a large piece of timber (or 'flitch') to achieve the most decorative grain appearance (Southern US)**

9 (left)

**Veneers are removed from a hot-air dryer, where optimum moisture content for gluing has been achieved (Oregon or Washington State, US)**

10 (right)

**Patches or plugs are placed in imperfections (such as knots or damage) and adhered using heat and pressure (Southern US)**

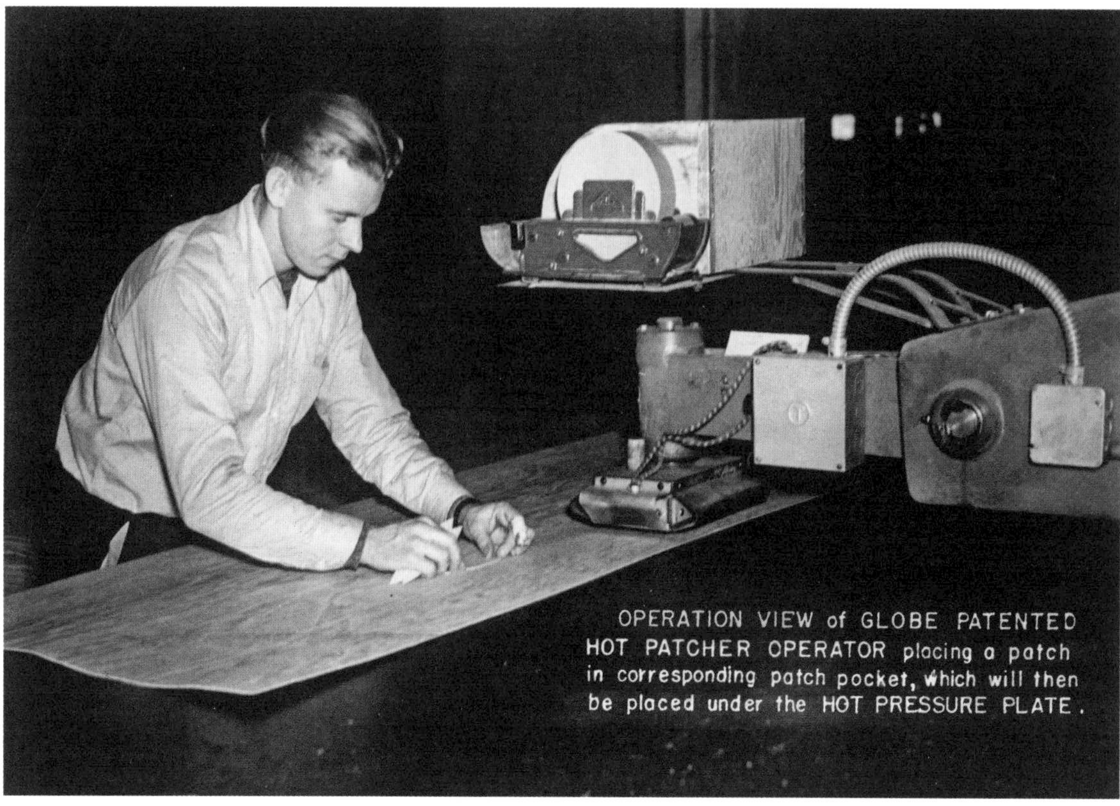

OPERATION VIEW of GLOBE PATENTED
HOT PATCHER OPERATOR placing a patch
in corresponding patch pocket, which will then
be placed under the HOT PRESSURE PLATE.


11 (right)

**Veneer pieces are taped together into large sheets before gluing (Oregon or Washington State, US)**

12 (left)

**Veneer samples are put through a glue spreader and glue is applied on both sides (at the US Forest Products Laboratory, c. 1917). In board production the veneers would then be stacked one on top of the other with their grain in alternate directions**

13 (left)

**The assembled ('layed-up') stack of veneers would then be pressed (sometimes pre-pressed cold to ensure best spread of glue and easier handling) into a multi-opening, heated hydraulic press. Plywood boards are here removed from the hot press. They are then sanded, graded and packed (Southern US)**

# 1 Plywood Becomes Plywood
## (antiquity–c. 1900)

The word plywood, or ply wood, was first recorded no later than 1906 (see p. 63) although it did not enter common use in the English-speaking world until the 1920s. By this time plywood was used mainly in the form of boards, commonly called panels, but also in moulded shapes. It was, by and large, the product of the factory; it might be made and worked in a single factory or produced in one for use or finishing in another.

However, if we take plywood to refer to the technique of gluing together a stack of veneers, with the grain of each layer running in a perpendicular direction to the adjacent one, then its use dates back centuries. From ancient times until the mid- to late nineteenth century the plywood technique was employed exclusively by small workshops and the material was produced in very small quantities, both as a board or in moulded form, for immediate use. Throughout its history the making of such layered wood boards was necessarily closely linked to the form of wood used: veneers.[1] Accordingly, the history of plywood development and technology must be told in tandem with that of the cutting, gluing and application of veneers. Professional woodworkers and, eventually, cabinetmakers cut veneers for largely ornamental but also practical reasons. Their artisanal knowledge of the material and how it functioned would have given them a deep understanding of how the grain structure functioned when veneer was used on its own and when glued together in layers.

Tracing the history of plywood before the late eighteenth century is challenging. Written descriptions of the material, although rare, appear to date only from this time, becoming more common in the mid-nineteenth century. Before then we can only speculate on why or in what form plywood was used based on surviving historic objects. Building a picture of the early history of plywood is also difficult, however, because the traditional purpose of veneering (including veneers used as the outside layers of plywood) was both to decorate a surface and to hide what lay beneath.

### The ancient world

The use of veneers in ancient Egypt is documented not only in surviving objects but also in wall carvings depicting woodworkers (fig. 15), tools, working methods and finished objects veneered in wood, including furniture and jewelry boxes. For such objects a tool later called a veneer hammer would be used to press glued veneer onto a structure of solid wood, with pressure applied until the glue dried. Generally, the grain direction of veneer and solid wood would be the same. Examples of objects made of plywood (i.e. cross-grained) construction are much rarer but there is evidence of the use of this technique from as early as the Third Dynasty (c. 2649–2575 BCE), in a coffin made from panels of six-ply wood joined with wooden pegs, which was found in the Step Pyramid at Saqqara.[2] Such use would suggest that the woodworkers who first

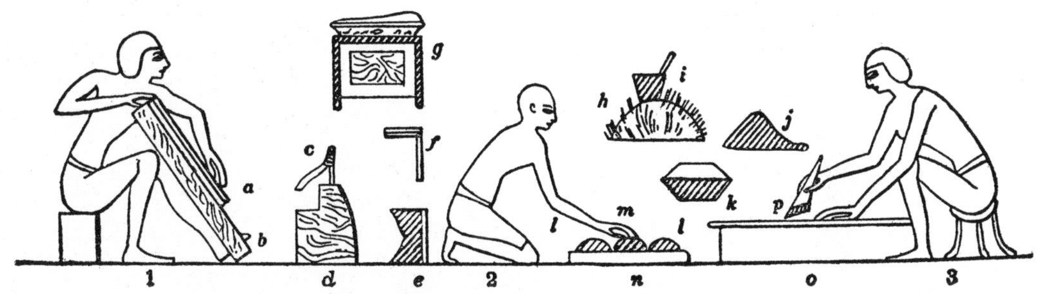

VENEERING AND THE USE OF GLUE.
Thebes.
a, a piece of dark wood applied to one of ordinary quality, b.
c, adze, fixed into a block of wood of the same colour as b.
e, a ruler; and f, a right angle, similar to those used by our carpenters.
g, a box. i, a glue pot on the fire. j, a piece of glue.
Fig. 2 is grinding something. Fig. 3 is applying the glue with a brush, p.
Illustration 1. Mural Record of Veneering, discovered in the Sculpture of Thebes and dated as early as the time of the Third Thothmes.
Reproduced from line drawing in "The Manners and Customs of the Ancient Egyptians," by Sir J. Gardner Wilkinson.


14 (opposite)
**Detail of mahogany chair showing three-ply back**
Possibly by William Linnell and John Linnell, London, c. 1760

15 (left)
**Nineteenth-century drawing of an ancient wall carving in Thebes, Egypt, showing veneering and the use of glue**
From J.G. Wilkinson, *Manners and Customs of the Ancient Egyptians* (New York 1878). Reproduced in Knight and Wulpi, *Veneers and Plywood* (New York 1927)

employed laminated, cross-grained veneers knew that such a combination of materials would be stronger than solid wood. The idea, frequently suggested in general literature, that plywood was always cheaper than solid wood did not necessarily apply before the nineteenth century. Until then plywood most likely would have been chosen, primarily, as a means of mitigating the expansion or contraction of the wood in conditions of very high or low relative humidity and, secondarily, for its strength.

While limited evidence survives of the use of veneer in ancient Greece, the Roman author Pliny the Elder not only mentioned veneered furniture but devoted a full chapter to the subject in his *Natural History* (77 CE). While Pliny describes the cutting and gluing of wood for decorative veneers, there is no mention of laminating layers of wood (beyond a veneered top layer) or of plywood construction.[3]

As a technique in furniture production or, for that matter, in any other field of making, plywood construction seems not to have appeared in Europe until the eighteenth century. Wood veneer was used for decorating solid, joined furniture from the sixteenth century and during the seventeenth century, encouraged by the import of expensive, tropical woods, the technique of marquetry (in which both ground and detail of design were cut in veneer) was developed. By the turn of the eighteenth century it had become fashionable at the highest levels of European society, in cities such as Paris, Amsterdam and Antwerp, and later in London, to commission highly elaborate cabinets with increasingly large, veneered surfaces. But it was not until the

16 and 17
(above and right)

**Mahogany chair, with detail showing three-ply back**
Possibly by William Linnell and John Linnell, London, c. 1760

middle of the eighteenth century that furniture makers in Britain, having gained experience at working with veneers, appear to have used plywood construction for specialist tasks. This coincided with and may have been spurred by the need to fulfil a demand for objects with cut-out lattice or trellis patterns, which contemporaries considered to be in the Chinese or Gothic taste.

A noteworthy example of such plywood use, one in which the structural demands of the design were best suited to cross-laminated rather than solid wood, were large, rectilinear trellis patterns that formed chair backs (figs 16–17). To make the chair back illustrated here the maker would have glued together three sheets of thick veneer – each 3–5 mm (⅛–¼ in.) – allowed them to dry until a solid board was formed, and then set about cutting the pattern using a highly adjustable fret saw with a fine blade that could be passed through holes drilled into the board. Cabinetmakers could have used small pieces of solid wood for such backs but jointing these is a delicate business potentially wasteful of expensive wood.[4] The use of the glued stack of three veneers, with the grain of each layer running perpendicular to the next, meant that the wood would not shrink or split as readily despite the amount of wood cut away. Smaller pierced, fretsawn galleries fitted to the top edges of contemporary and later tables (fig. 18), to sideboards and as fretted cresting for bookcases also employed workshop-made plywood sheets. The protection against splitting that plywood gave meant that ever finer frets could be cut, compared with those cut from a solid board or made from solid pieces joined together.

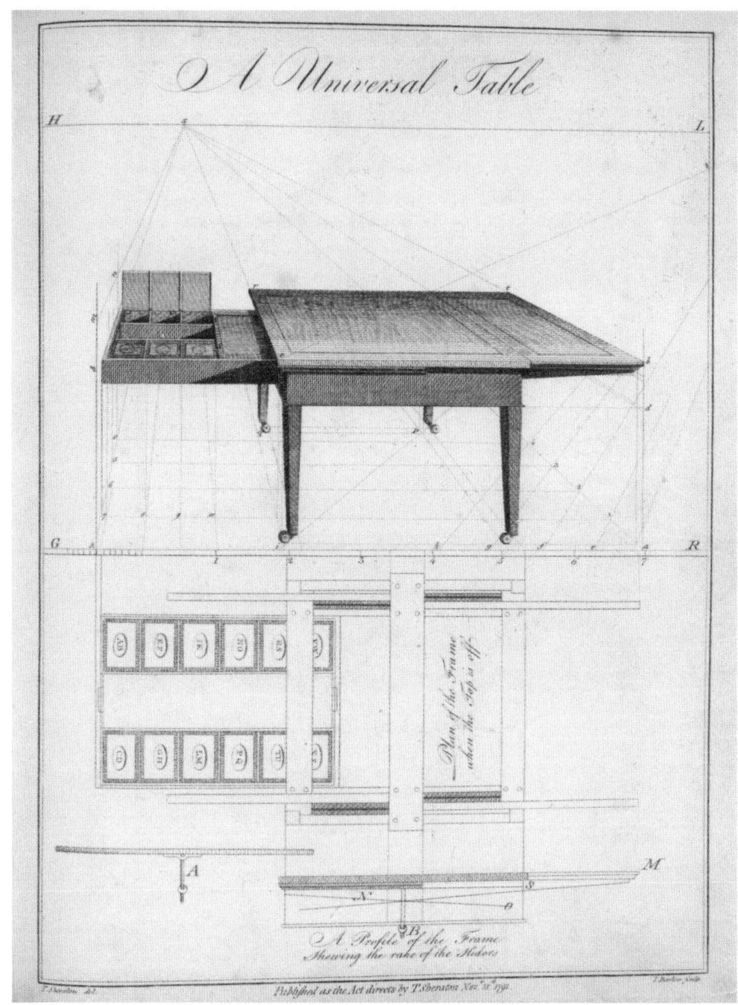

A valuable written description of the use of plywood for table tops was published by the English furniture designer and author Thomas Sheraton (1751–1806) in 1791 (fig. 19). His 'Universal Table' was a dining table suitable for two, five or eight people with a central surface, from under which two smaller leaves (described as 'flaps') slid out: 'the panels are sometimes glued up in three thicknesses, the middle piece being laid with the grain across, and the other two lengthways of the panel, to prevent warping'. He described the largest, central table surface, or 'bed', as being composed of two panels of plywood or, if the client preferred, solid wood, set within a frame of 3-in. (76-mm) wide boards. That each panel was three-ply suggests that the veneers were relatively thick, assuming an overall panel thickness of about 20 mm. In addition, Sheraton's instruction that the gaps between frame and panel were to be filled in with 'a white string' (an inlay of light-coloured wood) suggests that the entire surface was to be left as described, rather than covered with a thinner layer of veneer, as was often the case with such frame-and-panel construction at this time.[5]

18 (left)

**Mahogany table with fretsawn three-ply gallery, 1760s**

19 (above)

**'Universal Table', showing 'glued up' panels**

From Thomas Sheraton, *The Cabinet-Maker and Upholsterer's Drawing Book* (London 1791), pl. 25

Sheraton offers no suggestion that his use of 'glued up' panels represents a new technique for table tops. As a cabinetmaker experienced in the use of veneers, he, like his peers, would have known that gluing an odd number of veneers together with the grain of each layer perpendicular to the adjacent one would result in less shrinkage, hence limited movement of the panels within the frame and an evenness of stress (but also strength) across the resulting surface.

Sheraton's use of the term 'glued up' marked the beginning of an era during which a terminology for describing plywood was gradually developed as use of the material increased. Of some significance to naming it must have been the increasing number of publications describing furniture designs (pattern books especially), and the dawning of the era of widespread use of patents in both Europe and the US. The need to articulate what was unique about a given 'invention', which was sometimes a product but more often a technique, technology or process of making, drove patent applicants (and their increasingly professionalized advisors) to become more focused on language and terminology. Almost exactly contemporary with Sheraton a patent was issued to the English inventor and naval architect Samuel Bentham (1757–1831) in 1793 that appears to give the first description of a plywood or laminated wood board – 'pasteboard' – formed from glued wooden 'shavings' (although these are not explicitly described as being cross-grained; see p. 39).[6]

During the early nineteenth century many skilled furniture makers experimented with methods of using

20 and 21 (above and right)

**Mahogany chair, with detail showing laminated seat frame and leg**
Designed and made in the workshop of Jean-Joseph Chapuis, Brussels, c. 1805

layers of wood glued together in place of solid wood. The motivation for this was to achieve the desired form through simplified construction techniques. One such technique was the bending of either solid wood or thinner veneers, which became popular in many countries including Belgium (figs 20–21), Prussia, Denmark and the US.[7] While economies of production may have been a driving force for this, it was not coincidental that so many uses of laminated and, occasionally, plywood construction, in chairs especially, occurred when the neo-classical taste was so very popular. Interpretations of ancient Greek and Roman furniture required suitably curvilinear construction and furniture makers responded with innovative techniques of making.[8] When, in the mid-nineteenth century, the Rococo style was revived by furniture makers such as John Henry Belter (see below), plywood was used not so much for structural strength but for the cheaper construction of chair frames and their ornate, carved decoration.

**Patenting and pressing wood: the creation of modern plywood (1850–c. 1900)**

A wealth of documentary evidence about plywood is available from the second half of the nineteenth century, particularly in the form of patents, and especially in the US, where patents were much easier to obtain than in European countries.[9] As access to the manufactured product or to other contemporary sources is not always possible to support the understanding of plywood patents, the latter must often be considered on their own. Given that patents provide a crucial way of documenting at least one aspect of the development of plywood, it is necessary to understand the nature and limitations of patents as evidence.

A patent was (and remains) a form of legal protection or monopoly, the chief aim of which was to gain the patentee protection from imitators and remuneration from the invention. The practicality or applicability of an invention was not crucial to the granting of a patent in the US. The form of words in a patent was aimed solely at meeting contemporary standards for achieving recognition of the claim for novelty or patentability, rather than at convincing a reader that the product could work, or even at providing an accurate or full description of what others might consider to be the most significant, useful or appealing aspects of the invention.[10] In addition, the process of patent administration, including the examination and granting of patents, until at least 1870 has been described as a process of 'developing by trial and error', one subject to wildly inconsistent standards and practices.[11] The fact that one patent was granted while another was rejected, or that one claim of infringement was upheld while another was dismissed, cannot be taken as evidence of the importance of the idea patented.

The German émigré cabinetmaker John Henry Belter (1804–63, born Johann Heinrich Belter), owner of a 'furniture factory' in New York City, emerges as an important figure in the early history of plywood patents. Belter's first patent was granted in 1847 for a machine for cutting chair backs, although it is not clear that it was intended solely for plywood. In 1856 Belter was granted the first of three patents covering furniture made from a technique of moulding plywood that he called 'pressed work'. In fact, Belter may well have been making chairs using such a technique since the late 1840s (see note 19); but, regardless of the precise year of its introduction, what is most important about his furniture for the history of plywood is that it was accompanied by patents in which the details of his manufacturing technique are explained in both words and illustrations. Unlike many examples of patented inventions and/or manufacturing processes, a sufficiently large amount of Belter's furniture survives to enable us to draw conclusions as to the utility of his inventions. In addition, a number of contemporary or near-contemporary accounts survive, along with the furniture of his competitors, allowing us some understanding of Belter's place in the market.

22 (right)

**John Henry Belter, patent for 'Bedstead'**
Issued 19 August 1856, US patent no. 15,552

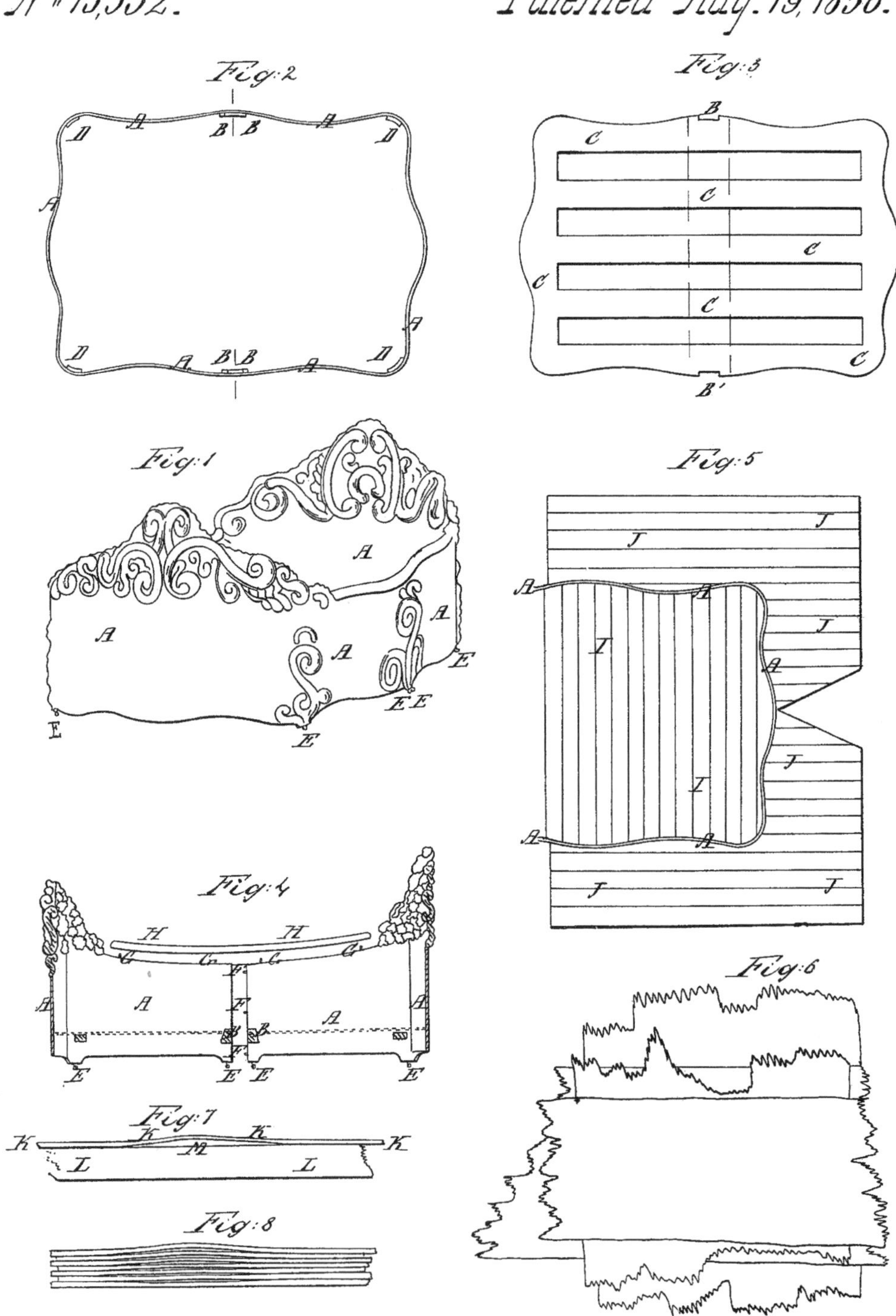

Belter first explained a technique for pressed work in his 1856 patent for a bedstead (figs 22–23).[12] Such work was clearly plywood: '...composed of thin layers of 1⁄16th inch [1.5 mm] veneer glued together. Each alternative layer is placed with the grain standing perpendicularly [vertically], while the others are placed with the grain running in a horizontal direction...The whole are glued together one time under pressure.' These veneers were moulded in either two or four large parts, bent on one plane (following the curvilinear shape of the bed) and joined to form a bed frame with integral foot and headboard.[13]

Completing his general description of his design, Belter wrote that the 'veneers which are presented to the eye...should be of rosewood or other choice wood', while the internal layers could be of oak or black walnut. 'Any odd number of layers may be used, but I prefer nine...'. Belter's patent thereby made explicit what would have been standard practice in any carpentry or cabinetmaking workshop: that finer woods were used for what the customer saw and cheaper woods for the parts that were hidden. Like Sheraton before him, Belter also made clear that in cross-grained (plywood) construction an uneven number of layers was best, although in his moulded construction (as opposed to Sheraton's flat boards) the ability of the moulded wood to withstand the tension and compression inherent in his curving designs was especially important.

Owing to the size and design of the bed, and whether it was made of two or four large sections, the sheets of veneer that formed its moulded, curvilinear structure were large and were pressed into shape in special moulds (Belter called them 'calls') of his own design. These calls would be heated, in order to keep the glue liquid and active while the layers of veneer were being applied. A call was illustrated (in plan) in the patent and represents an important and early depiction of a specialist plywood mould intended for serial production. The size of each moulded plywood section was exceedingly large and this bed may well have been the largest contemporary example of moulded veneers, if not of moulded wood of any kind. By moulding his bed in sections, Belter was able to make a frame that was lighter than one of solid rosewood. The bed frame could also be moulded into a curvilinear shape, without having to carve away expensive solid wood.

Belter explicitly compared his bedstead to 'ordinary veneered bedstead[s]' (those with a single sheet of veneer over a structure made of solid wood, common in the 1850s).[14] Such comparisons to related techniques, processes or products were an essential element of patents, aimed at articulating the novelty of the patent applicant's invention and how it represented an advance (or, in the language of patents, an 'improvement') over previous techniques, processes or designs. The inventions for which Belter was granted his patent seem, in retrospect, of relatively minor significance: the ability to assemble or take the bed apart without the use of tools and the avoidance of internal recesses in which insects might live.[15] Further, using a rhetorical technique common in patents, Belter concludes his patent by stating that he does not claim as his own the technique of plywood construction: 'veneers glued together with the grain of each layer standing at right angles to the next have been long

23 (below)
**Rosewood bed**
Designed and made by John Henry Belter, New York, c. 1856

24 (right)

**John Henry Belter, patent for 'Improvement in the Method of Manufacturing Furniture'**

Issued 23 February 1858, US patent no. 19,405

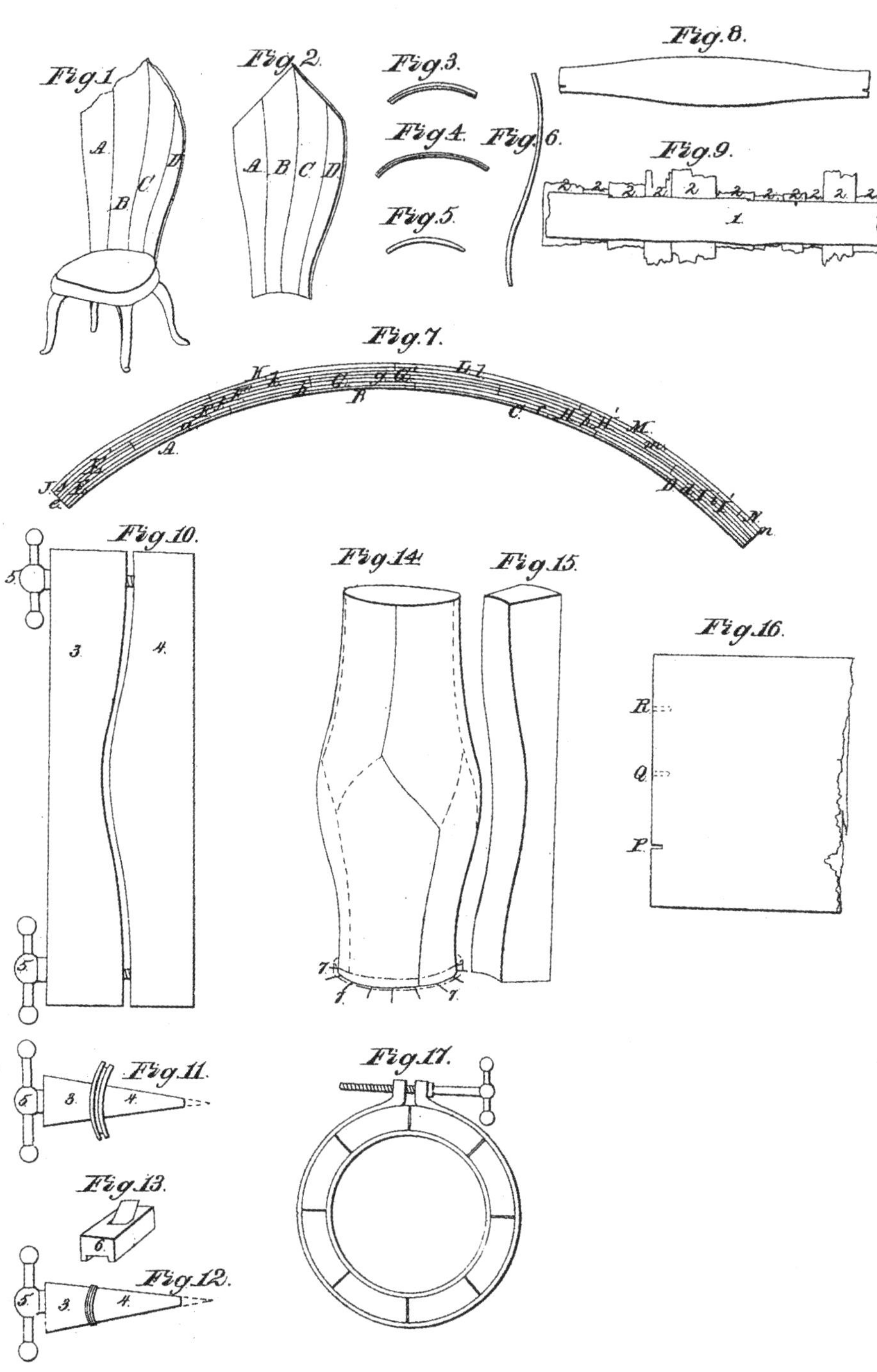

in use for the purpose of combining strength and lightness. This I do not claim nor...the above described method of producing it...'. Belter's denial of the novelty of his method may well have been part of his attempt to focus solely on the aspects of his patent that would, without argument, see it granted. It might also have been related to the background to Belter's next successful patent application, namely, that he might have been previously turned down for a claim of having invented pressed work chair backs.

In 1858 Belter was granted a patent for a very different and much more complicated method of using pressed work to manufacture furniture, chiefly for chair and sofa backs (figs 24–25). As is seen in extant Belter chairs and sofas (figs 26–28), the seats and legs were made of carved solid wood with the back attached as a single moulded piece to the seat frame. The moulded plywood created the form of the seat back; the decoration was achieved by a combination of sawing into the plywood using a special non-mechanized 'machine' patented by Belter in 1847 and hand finishing with chisels and rasps.[16] Raised carvings, made separately, were then attached using dowels and glue. This technique allowed Belter to manufacture furniture carved in fashionable Rococo-style high-relief, but using much less rosewood, and of a much lighter weight, than a solid carved seat back.

The chair backs were not made one by one, like the bed parts, but eight at a time on a tall, cylindrical mould (in this patent called a 'cawl' rather than a call). Three layers were placed around the cawl, each of thirty-two long strips or 'staves' (figs 11–12 in fig. 24) of cross-grained plywood that had already been prepared. The innermost and outermost layers were of two-ply staves, and the inner layer of three-ply staves (figs 7–9 in fig. 24). The staves were set so that they overlapped one another slightly, to increase strength, and glue was applied between the layers. The staves were then clamped against the heated mould for twenty-four hours before the dried plywood was cut, on the mould, into eight chair backs, four above and four below (figs. 10, 12–15, and 17 in fig. 24).

25 (above)

**Patent model for a rosewood chair**

Designed and made by John Henry Belter, New York, 1858, US patent no. 19,405

In Belter's patent drawing the tall, columnar mould was circular in plan so that the chair backs would be emphatically curved from side-to-side, along its circumference. Significantly, the mould bulged out towards its centre (towards the top of each chair back) so that that the resulting chair backs would also have the gentlest possible reverse S-curve, from top to bottom. The surviving patent model (fig. 25) that Belter submitted with his application shows this unusual and compound-curved back. It was this three-dimensional shaping of the chair back that Belter called 'dishing', or 'spherical work'.[17] Belter was granted his patent specifically for the method by which he manufactured 'spherical work' using staves.

Interestingly, while Belter's patent and model demonstrated his new method for 'dishing', it does not appear that this proved to be a successful technique for manufacture.[18] For while many of the curved-back plywood chairs that Belter manufactured survive, all but a few known examples are bent two-dimensionally, from side-to-side, rather than three-dimensionally in compound curves. The reasons why the three-dimensionally moulded chair was not a viable product might have been technical (the moulding technique was too complicated), economic (it proved too expensive to sell) or a combination of both. The patent application, as was often the case, might well have been submitted before the chair had been marketed. Or, as suggested by an almost exactly contemporary journal article (see below), it might possibly have been related to Belter's attempts to patent some aspect of pressed work chair

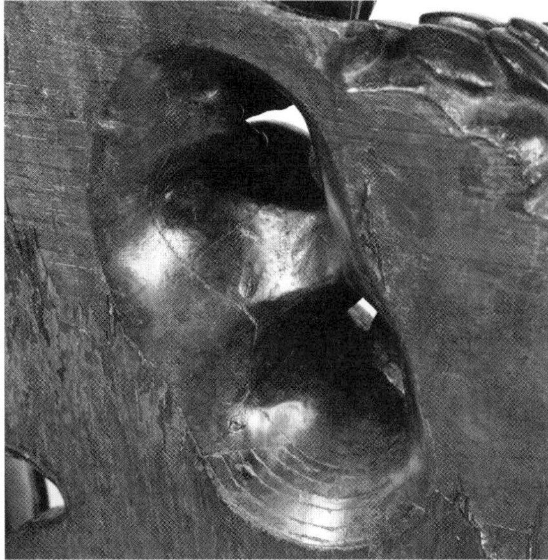

26, 27 and 28
(top, above and right)

**Rosewood sofa, front and back view with detail showing seven-ply construction of back**
Designed and made by John Henry Belter, New York, c. 1856

backs that would give him a measure of legal claim to his moulding technique.

Two months after the 1858 patent was published an article appeared in the British magazine *The Practical Mechanic's Journal*, written by Thomas D. Stetson, who had signed as a witness to Belter's patent, and would subsequently sign another in 1860. The fact that Stetson had a business relationship with Belter requires a critical, even sceptical, reading of his article; nonetheless, the text is sufficiently informative as to demand attention, not least because Stetson is not the only source for certain key statements in the article.[19] The article acknowledges that 'furniture composed entirely of veneers, and known as "pressed work" has been manufactured in [New York City] for several years', a statement that reinforces Belter's disclaiming of the personal invention of pressed work in the patent of the same year. Stetson then makes numerous bold claims that seek to establish why Belter is, in fact, 'entitled to the credit of originating this variety of work': the furniture maker, writes Stetson, first applied for a patent for pressed work in 1847; the application was rejected (no explanation is given for why, although the granting of patents in this era was very much at the discretion of a small number of patent examiners); and, since 1847, other firms had started making pressed work.

Stetson specifically cites a patent of 1851 granted to Mr Cornelius Bogaud of New York City (almost certainly Cornelius Bogard), illustrating drawings of four cross-grained veneers that form a soundboard for a violin (fig. 29), which Stetson suggests relies upon Belter's technique.[20] He compares these to drawings of two layers of Belter's chair backs, apparently bent on only one plane (from side-to-side), which by implication relate to Belter's rejected patent of 1847. According to Stetson, had the patent examiner had access to Belter's application of 1847, Bogaud's [*sic*] patent would not have been granted. 'The manufacture of pressed-work sounding boards has not been carried on, owing to the very limited demand, and there has been no conflict of patents,' Stetson adds. He also informs readers that, in mid-1858, Belter's dished chair backs had not been 'yet introduced to the public, but the machinery is completed, and the work is as perfect as could be desired'. The 'dishing' of his chair backs is unique to Belter, Stetson concludes, adding for the benefit of his British readership that no style of pressed work had then been patented in Great Britain.

While it is entirely possible that Stetson was seeking solely to publicize Belter's work in Britain and, at least in the press, to establish his pre-eminence as the innovator of pressed work, Belter had by 1858 already manufactured a great deal of moulded furniture. The Stetson article is also valuable as he informed readers that Belter's 'most unpretending chairs of this kind, without arms or rockers' cost two or three times as much as 'common chairs equally well upholstered and carved' – hardly a claim to make when seeking a larger market share, despite the assertion that 'the extreme lightness and immense strength of such chairs make them very deservedly popular'.

29 (below)
**Layers of veneers for cross-grained construction of a violin soundboard**
From T.D. Stetson, 'Mechanical Notes from America', *The Practical Mechanic's Journal* (1 April 1858), p. 9

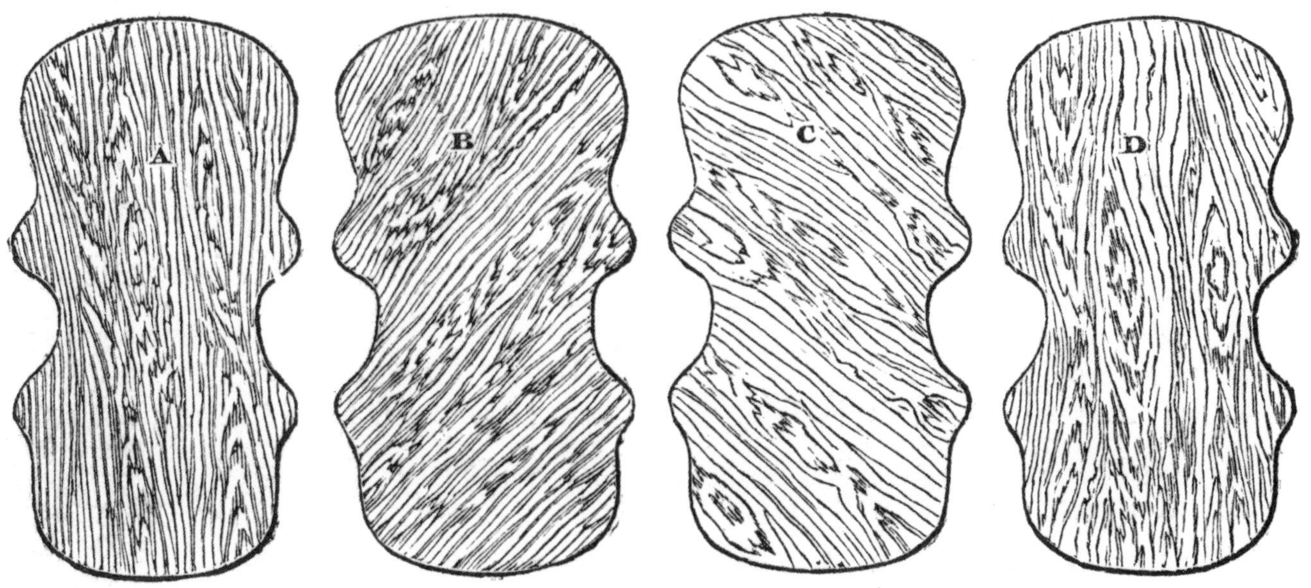

## Patents of the 1860s

The Belter patents highlight the means by which plywood furniture could be moulded, on a large scale, in the mid nineteenth century (and the commercial advantages to be gained from this by optimizing the use of materials, allowing batch production and greatly reducing the labour required for hand carving). The plywood patents of John K. Mayo (died 1880) and of the Gardner family, on the other hand, provide useful examples not only of potential uses of plywood, but of the different ways in which patents were used for commercial purposes and the manner in which they did or did not reflect products brought to market.

In December 1865, nearly a decade after Belter's first pressed work patent, John K. Mayo of Portland, Maine, was granted a patent for plywood itself (fig. 30, patent reissued in 1868, fig. 31), despite Belter's previous use of the material and his assertion (in his 1858 patent) that it was not then new. Mayo clearly had a background in woodworking as his earliest patent was for a circular saw mill. His 1865 patent, 'Proved Material for Roofing, Tubing, Tanks, Wainscoting, Boats, and Other Structures', used the term 'scale' and 'scale-board' to describe 'a thin layer of wood cut from a board or log and forming a veneer'.[21] Indeed the 'claim' of his patent was for 'The application of scale-boards or veneers in layers, the direction of whose grain is crossed or diversified, and which are connected together, forming a material for the construction, lining, or covering of land and marine structures'. The essence of a US patent was 'to distinguish the [invention] from all other things before known' in the form of the 'claim'.[22] The claim was, in legal terms, the key part of the patent and anything else to be protected by the patent must be covered by the claim.

Mayo explained and illustrated that the scales could be used flat or moulded. He did not, as Belter did, illustrate his moulds, but described the process as making use of 'wet and dry heating' to achieve 'pliablity...to readily assume various figures, or be laid upon irregular objects'. Mayo's patent lists an astonishing range of applications for his 'firm material':

> the construction of houses, boats, ships, tanks, floors, pipes, drains, sewers, packing-cases, boxes, barrels, sidewalks, cans, pails, tubs, firkins, measures, cheese-boxes, trunks, valises, dry-docks, canal-locks, mill and factory plumes, masts, spars, outside covering and inside finish of houses, stores, shops, depots, and warehouses, fences, covering of piles, railroad-cars, railroad and suspension bridges, railroad tracks and sleepers, wagons, carriages, and carts, bedsteads, sacking, mattresses, and covering of beds, sofas and sofa-bedsteads, divans, loungers, chairs, and settees. In house-architecture the weather-boarding and inside finish of the house may consist of this material....an effective and elegant substitute for the usual covering of the walls of rooms. For flooring...especially in cases where it is an object to make apartments air-tight, as in ice-houses, fruit-chambers...

While the range of objects listed by Mayo may seem improbably broad and unlikely to have been so widely tested, the listing of possible applications represented an attempt to seek patent protection for the uses based on the proposition that these were covered by the central claim of the patent. Indeed, Mayo sought even to go beyond his list: 'I cannot pretend to anticipate all the various uses to which this scale-board may be applied...I am enabled to make a very strong and light structure of whatever shape it may be, or for whatever

30 (below)

**Illustration from John K. Mayo, patent for 'Material for Roofing, Tubing, Tanks, Wainscoting, Boats and Other Structures'**
Issued 26 December 1865, US patent no. 51,735

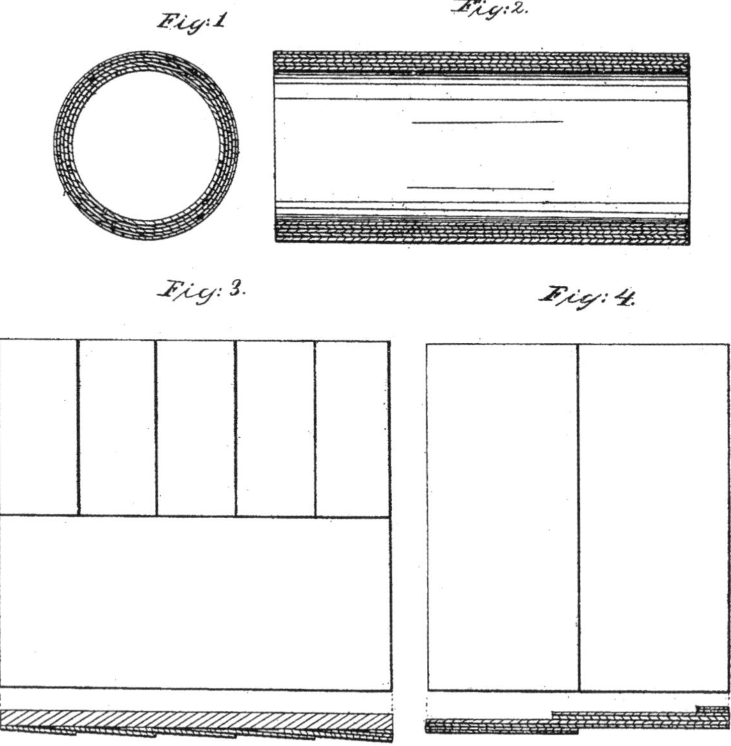

purpose it may be designed.' Although the listing of specific applications was not unusual, two years before Mayo's patent the US Supreme Court seemed to encourage this practice when it ruled that patents were granted not 'for a "principle", or a "mode of operation," or an idea, or any other abstraction'. The scope of what was patentable through the claim was left not to the US Patent Office to determine, said the ruling, but was for the courts to decide as and when disputes arose. It was therefore crucially important to use patent text and illustrations (as Mayo did) to make evident the physical nature of the claim.[23]

Within three years Mayo had applied for and been granted four 'reissues' of his patent, which detailed additional or more specific applications of his scale-boards, in most cases illustrating products that had not been shown in his original patent of 1865 but all repeating its claim, namely the use of scale-boards or veneers in plywood construction. In principle, a patent reissue was made when a patent already granted might be considered to be 'invalid or inoperative'. It was an amendment of a patented invention, and was intended to correct errors in the original patent by allowing revised descriptions and claims to be published. Such reissues were the subject of considerable abuse until about 1860, when new legislation was passed aimed both at preventing patentees from expanding their claims and protection beyond their original invention, and also at ending predatory practices by non-inventors who bought up existing patents and then attempted to change their scope. Especially when they overturned previous claims, patent reissues might well result from an ongoing infringement dispute or lawsuit, at least one of which would later involve Mayo.[24]

Among the applications listed in Mayo's reissues were carriage frames, trunks, materials for constructing bridges, and household furnishings. In virtually all of his patents Mayo claims that the nature of his plywood would afford the layers of veneer 'mutual strength, support, and protection against checking [natural splits along the grain], splitting, swelling or shrinking'. In his patent devoted to bridges and 'other works in civil engineering' (thirty-three are listed towards the end of the patent), plywood is the basis for both round and rectangular enclosed bridges described (and known at the time) as 'tubular'.[25] Mayo claimed his plywood to be superior to iron as a bridge-building material

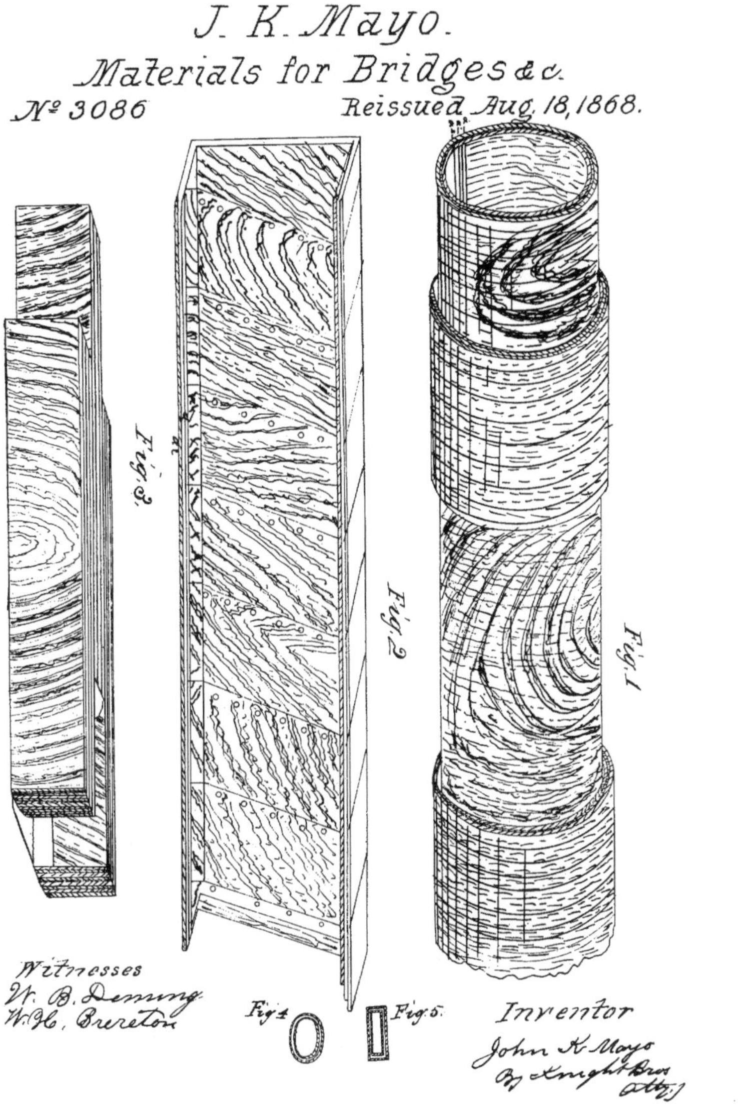

31 (above)
**John K. Mayo, patent for 'Materials for Bridges &c.'**
Reissued 18 August 1868, US patent no. 3,086

as it would not expand when hot, would not corrode, would have greater tensional strength and would be impervious to water. Wood could more easily be floated to pier supports and raised up for attachment, owing to its lighter weight compared to that of iron. For bridges or their parts, construction could be in sections, 'giving greater facility of handling in the construction and... increased strength and stiffness'.

Although it is not known whether Mayo's tubes were ever put into widespread use, his 1865 patent had at least one very dramatic and public application when the largest plywood structure yet built was shown at the American Institute Fair, New York, in 1867 (fig. 32). Mayo's patent for plywood was credited in the construction of a 107-ft (32.6-m) section of an elevated pneumatic passenger railway. Proposed by Alfred E. Beach (1826–96), an inventor, patent agency owner, and co-owner and an editor of *Scientific American* magazine, the railway was supported in a tube that was 6 ft (1.83 m) in diameter and constructed entirely of plywood. The tube, 1½ in. (38 mm) thick, was made of fifteen layers of veneer, each 'laid upon each other transversely and spirally, and joined together by cement. The grain of the woods thus crossed and recrossed gives a structure of remarkable strength and power of resistance to either blow or pressure'.[26] Powerful, engine-driven fans were

32 (right)
**'The Pneumatic Passenger Dispatch Tube in Operation at the Fair of the American Institute, Fourteenth Street, NY'**
From *Frank Leslie's Illustrated Newspaper* (26 October 1867), p. 85

said to create a vacuum within the tube, propelling and then sucking back the twelve-person passenger car from one end to the other to the delight of the more than 75,000 riders said to have 'enjoyed the atmospheric ride'. The car was made from sections of the tube cut in half and rejoined with a roof section cut away, 'forming an open cradle'.[27] An additional, smaller postal dispatch tube was also exhibited, although it is not clear if it was made of plywood.

While Beach wrote about laying iron tubes underground, thereby allowing for pneumatic railways under the rivers surrounding Manhattan, he also suggested to the press that the exhibition tube demonstrated the more economical solution of 'an elevated road....[a] light wooden pneumatic tube resting upon brackets attached to buildings' or raised on columnar supports (fig. 33). 'This plan', a contemporary newspaper suggested, 'possesses the merit of cheapness of execution' compared to underground construction, and was also 'less cumbersome' than contemporary elevated railways. In the event, Beach and his business partners pursued only the underground solution, opening in 1870 a short leg of Beach Pneumatic Transit along Broadway in lower Manhattan. With the economic depression of 1873 investment dried up and the project foundered.

33 (right)

**'The Pneumatic Elevated Railway'**
From Alfred E. Beach, *The Pneumatic Dispatch* (New York 1868), fig. 10

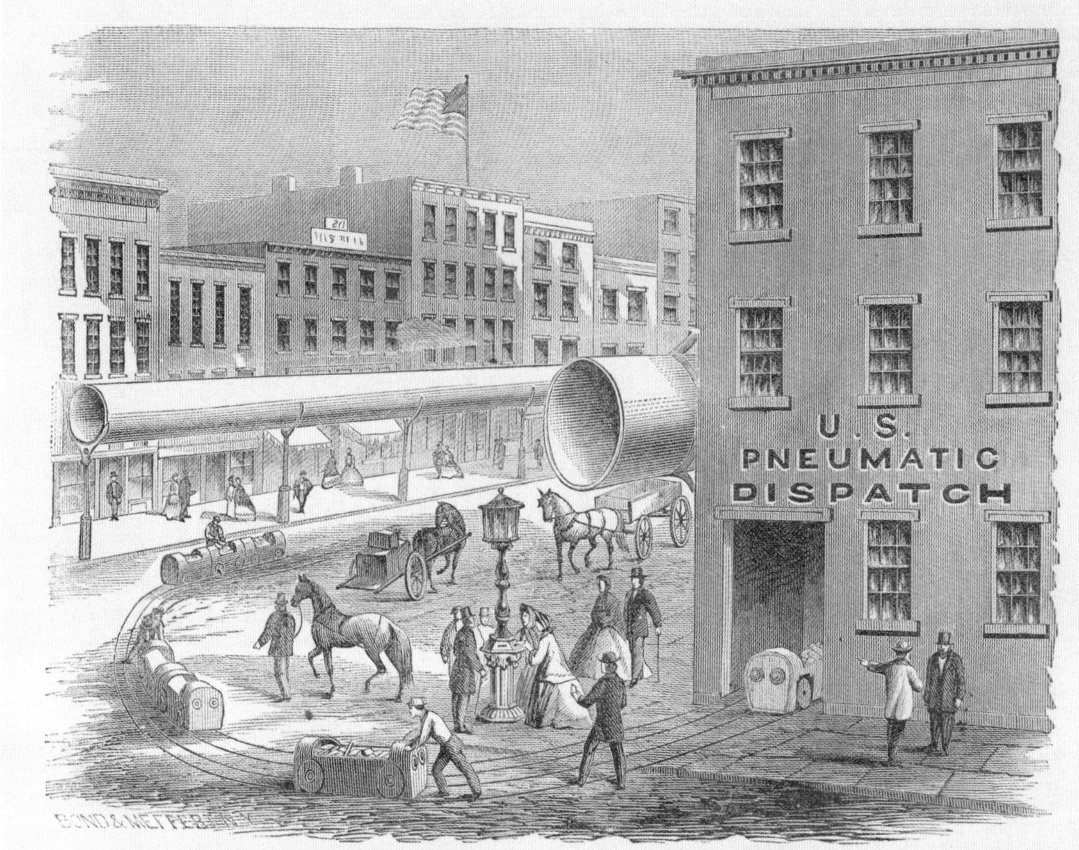


**Patent furniture: Gardner & Company**

Of the nineteenth-century plywood products known to have been sold in considerable quantity, the seating furniture of the American firm Gardner & Company was perhaps the most significant (fig. 34). Their use of plywood seats and backs preceded that of the much more famous Thonet company of Vienna, Austria (figs 52–53). Particularly noteworthy is the surprising extent to which Gardner's products were imitated in Europe and their impact on furniture manufacturing there, which, in the case of the A.M. Luther Company in Reval, Russia (present-day Tallinn, Estonia), led directly to what became a major plywood company (see p. 44). As with Belter, an understanding of Gardner's output is enhanced by the existence of numerous patents, by the survival of many examples of their products and marketing material, and by facts arising in several court cases and reports by a financial rating agency.[28]

The Gardner family firm was in business by 1857, originally as a manufacturer and distributor of frames based in Philadelphia, New York and New Jersey. In the 1870s they turned to the making of furniture including chairs, and on 21 May 1872 George Gardner, one of six brothers running the firm, was granted two patents (figs 35–36), for near identical chair seats.[29] Why such an apparently modest design became so important requires some explanation.

The Gardner patents were both granted for 'Improvement in Chair-Seats'. The first of the patents (no. 127,044) describes 'this invention' as, 'Consist[ing] of layers of veneering, each alternate one of which has its grain running in an opposite direction to that of the intermediate one, in combination with one or more layers of textile or fibrous material...'. The second patent (no. 127,045) was identical to the first but did not mention a textile layer. In both patents Gardner illustrates three layers of veneer, and writes that 'the seat may be perforated for ventilation and ornamentation' (the perforated seats became closely identified with the firm and in fact the Gardner & Company stand at the 1876 Philadelphia Centennial Exhibition was decorated with large cut-out sheets of perforated plywood; fig. 34).[30] Gardner also explains that the utility of his wooden seats is that they are 'cheaper and durable' (no. 127,044), more so in particular than the cane seats then widely used on chairs (no. 127,045).

While it is clear that the two patents were granted to Gardner for 'a new article of manufacture, a chair-seat constructed of' cross-grained veneers and glue

34 (left)

**Gardner & Company stand at the Philadelphia Centennial Exhibition, 1876**

(and textile in the first patent), subsequent reissues of the patents in 1876 and 1880 gradually modified this claim. This suggests both a retreat from the rather bold sole claim of the original patents, and the very flexible nature of patent examination in these decades. The amendments, and the extensive reissuing of the Gardner patents, also reveal something of the highly competitive commercial culture in which Gardner's plywood seats were manufactured.

In 1876 Gardner's reissues of his original patents (nos 7,202 and 7,203) refer to his invention of 'a new and useful Improvement in the Bottom of Seats'. The greater specificity of his claim in these reissues was presumably part of an effort to retain the integrity of the patent. More significant was his application for a reissue in 1879 (granted in 1880 as Reissued Letters Patent 9,094, for the seat without textile), in which he offered a view of 'The state of the art in relation to devices having a similarity to my invention'. Here Gardner listed, for the first time, other past patents relevant to his plywood seat design.[31] Although he must have known about all of these patents and products before filing his first claims in 1872, this is the first time that his patents acknowledge in full the previous history of plywood manufacture.

Gardner listed seven patents related to his own. These included patents for: Belter's bedstead, with its use of cross-grained veneers 'combining strength and lightness' (fig. 22); Belter's chairs made of the same materials 'glued together, and pressed to shape' (fig. 24); plywood boxes (no. 40,509, 1868); a solid wood seat moulded into a concave form (no. 23,225, 1859); a barrel made of cross-grained veneers aimed at dispensing with staves normally employed for barrels, vats, tubes and pipes (no. 110,096, 1870); a perforated sheet-metal seat bottom (no. 20,376, 1858, reissue no. 2,016, 1865; these patent numbers not in Gardner's list); and a chair bottom of perforated gutta-percha (a form of hard rubber; no. 54,863, 1866). Gardner then claims his invention as 'relat[ing] to a new article of manufacture, consisting of a chair-seat', listing its characteristics but going on to state that he does 'not lay any claim to the veneers crossing each other and glued together...even for furniture...[as these] have become public property'. He specifically denies any claim to the other processes or designs noted in the other patents, while pointing out that the perforated sheet metal is too cold for practical use, and is liable to break and to catch clothing; and that perforated gutta-percha is too expensive for common use. His seat, on the other hand, is strong,

35 and 36 (right)

**George Gardner, two patents for 'Improvement in Chair-Seats'**
Issued 21 May 1872, US patent nos 127,044 (right) and 127,045 (far right)

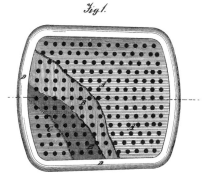

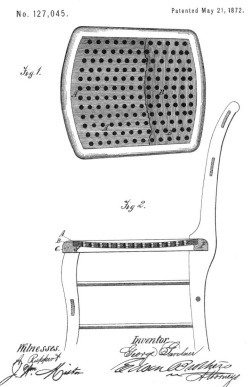

GEORGE GARDNER.
Improvement in Chair-Seats.
No. 127,044. Patented May 21, 1872.

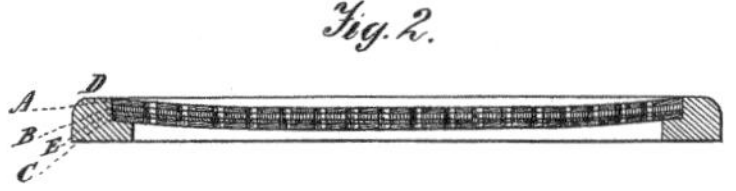

GEORGE GARDNER.
Improvement in Chair-Seats.
No. 127,045. Patented May 21, 1872.

light, comfortable, neither hot in summer nor cold in winter, is handsome, offers 'the required ventilation', can be easily cut and fitted to any chair frame, and is cheaper and more durable than cane seating.

The very different nature of Gardner's patent reissue of 1879 must relate to a series of lawsuits that took place in that year between the Gardner company and the New York veneer products manufacturing firm of Herz & Co.[32] It seems likely that the Gardner company applied for a patent reissue in an attempt to avoid claims made against it for infringing upon John K. Mayo's 1865 patent (fig. 30); in the small world of plywood patentees and product manufacturers, Mayo was Martin Herz's business partner from 1878 until the former's death in 1880. In the face of Mayo's existing patent for plywood, Gardner's increasingly specific descriptions of his invention attempt to claim a product that was clearly, by this point, common enough that it could not be patented. The ultimate outcome of the dispute between Gardner and Herz was that, in 1886, the US Supreme Court ruled that Gardner's patent for chair seats (no. 127,045) could not be reissued. The judgment concludes:

> The fabric being old, the suggestion to construct chair-seats out of it being old, the shaping of it in a former being old, the perforation of a seat for ventilation and ornamentation being old, and the giving of a concave shape to a wooden seat by pressure being old, there cannot ... be anything patentable in the structure.[33]

While the Gardner vs Herz cases highlight the commercial competitiveness around plywood products in the late nineteenth century, and the advantages that could be gained, at this time, by advertising the 'invention' of a new material, it was in fact through the design of their plywood seats that Gardner & Company managed to make the biggest market inroads. In delivering his verdict on the Herz case, the Supreme Court judge stated that the success of the Gardner seats was not to do with patentable materials, but instead with their adaptability for use by unskilled workmen – they could be fitted without great skill to chair frames of many different sizes and forms.

These qualities came to the fore in an entirely different form of single-piece seat and back that was patented by William Gardner in 1873 (fig. 37). Here, the seat and back 'made from some suitable material' allowed 'the seat frame...[to be] dispensed with, which lessens the expense incurred in the manufacture of the chair, and makes it less cumbersome'. Although no material is specified, given the Gardners' experience with plywood and the fact that the only other structurally

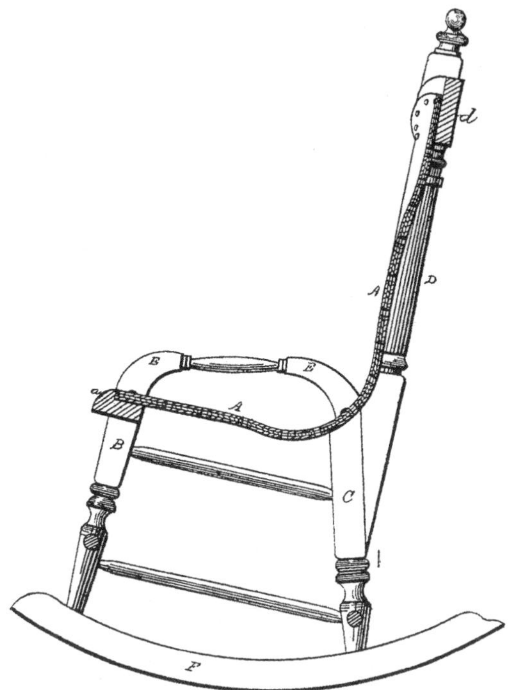


37 (left)
**Illustration from William Gardner, patent for 'Improvement in Chairs'**
Issued 3 June 1873, US patent no. 139,568

38 (below)
**Doll's chair, birch plywood seat with stained beech frame**
Manufactured by Gardner & Company, New York or New Jersey, after 1873

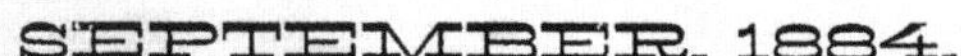

39 (above)

**Gardner & Company catalogue title page, New York, 1884**

40 (right)

**Gardner & Company advertisement**
From *Car Builder's Dictionary* (New York 1879), p. 69

suitable material, sheet metal, was later specifically described as impractical for perforated chair seats, it must have been this patent that signalled Gardner's turn to single-piece, plywood seats and backs (fig. 38). This design, especially, along with George Gardner's 1872 perforated seat, would rapidly become the basis of the success and influence of the Gardner firm. While the use of the single-piece seat and back was both unusual in form and highly practical in its strength and durability, the patent described the other innovative but possibly overlooked aspect of the chair from a manufacturing point of view: the unit was attached only along the front edge of the seat, the middle outside edges, and the top of the back. No complete seat frame need be used, thus making it cheaper to produce as well as lighter ('less cumbersome') than most chairs. The continuous seat/back also gave a particular visual character to the chairs, distinguishing them from most contemporary designs.

Very rapidly, it would appear, the Gardners started to manufacture their new chairs with single-piece seats and back, mounting a large display in 1876 at the Centennial Exhibition in Philadelphia. A photograph of their stand (fig. 34) shows at least thirty-nine chairs and benches, all of them probably different models and all apparently made with single-piece seats and backs. While Gardner advertisements and catalogues have been found only from the 1880s, the Centennial stand makes clear that they were steadily increasing their production and product range during the 1870s.[34] They described their business as 'Manufacturers and Patentees of Three-Ply Veneer Seats, Chairs, Settees, Car and Steamboat Seats' (figs 39–40). They sold their

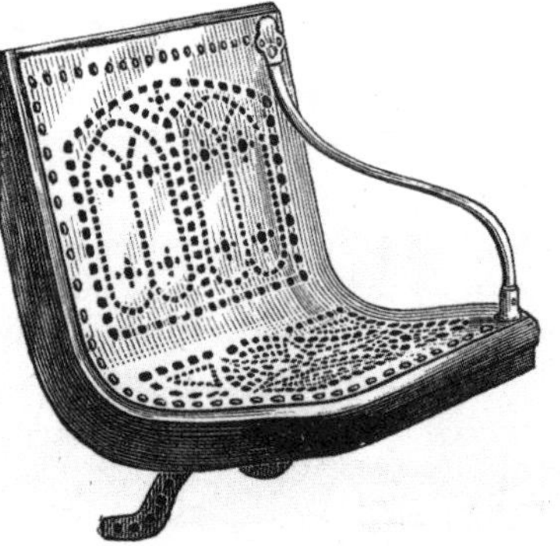

seating for commercial, institutional and domestic uses and were evidently particularly successful supplying it for railway cars, trams and steamboats but also for hotels, railway station waiting rooms, shops and government buildings. Their large catalogue contained approximately 146 examples of seating, all but sixty-four of them (including stools and folding chairs) with continuous seat/backs applied to all manner of supports including rocking frames, high chairs, nursing chairs, settees with symbolic decorative perforations for masonic lodges, churches and steamboats.[35] In addition, they apparently continued to sell veneer seats to be fitted to other makers' chair frames.

The Gardners were not the only designers of continuous plywood seat/backs. In 1874 Isaac Cole, an individual active in the veneer business since 1859 and after his death referred to as 'a pioneer in the veneer trade', designed a chair made entirely of three pieces of plywood (fig. 41). Although it was a somewhat impractical design and clearly less robust than Gardner's chairs, the patent indicates the contemporary interest in finding ways of exploiting plywood and the possibility that it was one of scores of speculative patents designed to protect and possibly make money from an idea with uncertain commercial potential.[36]

The significance of Gardner & Company's furniture is not diminished by the result of their lawsuits against Herz. Until that time, their manufacturing of perforated seats and continuous seat/backs were undoubtedly successful as well as influential on other firms, both those who purchased Gardner seats to apply to their own furniture and those who imitated them. What is still to be understood is whether Gardner had meaningful competition for the manufacture of perforated seats and seat/backs before the mid- to late 1870s. What is clear is that after Gardner & Company lost their first court case in 1879, other competitors, including new ones, founded veneer seat businesses that eventually, owing to their large number, drove Gardner out of business. For about twenty years, until this fierce competition in combination with an economic depression in the US caused the Gardner family to lose control of the firm, they achieved great success.[37]

41 (above)

**Patent model for a moulded plywood chair**
Designed and made by Isaac Cole, New Jersey, 1874, US patent no. 148,350

# 2 Manufacturing Plywood (1807–c. 1910)

## Rotary veneer cutting

The manufacture of plywood products and, eventually, the mass production of plywood boards, was dependent upon a plentiful supply of relatively low-cost veneers. This supply was, in turn, based on the gradual change from cutting veneers by hand to cutting by machine, which led to a meaningful decline in veneer prices from the early nineteenth century (see p. 41). While the finest veneers continued to be cut by hand (fig. 43) until about 1850 in Britain, the mechanization of veneer cutting was the key technological development affecting plywood in all industrialized countries in the nineteenth century.[1]

Veneer-cutting technology in Britain began to change after 1807, when the civil engineer Marc Isambard Brunel (1769–1849) opened a saw mill in Battersea, London, which was 'erected principally for the cutting of veneers' (initially from expensive hardwoods such as rosewood and mahogany) and which included steam-powered veneer cutters. Brunel had patented such a machine the previous year (fig. 44) and would have been familiar with Samuel Bentham's machine for cutting veneers patented in 1791.[2] Bentham's patents did not illustrate his machine as Brunel's did but the descriptions are similar. Both machines were based on a table of adjustable height across which a large blade (widely described in the nineteenth century as a knife) horizontally cut the full width of a rectangular block of wood: a type of machine later referred to as a 'flat cutter'. Both patents described the sliced wood that came off the block as 'shavings'. Bentham wrote of the 'formation of laminated work from shavings...out of no more than three, or even two shavings, I make a new kind of pasteboards' [*sic*]. While Bentham was the first to patent such a device and was, nearly a century later, credited with having set the standard for veneer cutting, Brunel's Battersea saw mill was much visited by, commented upon and imitated by contemporaries.[3] There veneers were cut both parallel to a table and, as an account of 1817 makes clear, with 'circular saws' 18 ft (5.48 m) in diameter, driven by a 16-horsepower steam-engine 'used for the purpose of separating [cutting] veneers, and a more perfect operation was never performed. I beheld planks of mahogany and rosewood sawed into veneers the sixteenth of an inch thick...nine or ten feet long by two broad...'.[4]

In addition to the use of saw cutting and knife (blade) cutting, many rotary veneer cutters were developed in the mid-nineteenth century in which a log was made to rotate against a blade at least as wide as the length of the log. This blade would cut one long continuous sheet of veneer from the log as it rotated. The first rotary cutter to have been patented,

42 (opposite)

**Digging out stores after the plywood cases had been buried in ice during a blizzard**

Ernest Shackleton's first Antarctic Expedition (Nimrod), February 1909

43 (below)

**Method of cutting veneers with a newly developed saw**

From André-Jacob Robou, *L'Art du Menuisier Ébéniste* (Paris 1774), pl. 278

[4] 30 Jan? 1807
Horse power and not a 20 horse as I before misunderstood - Saw parts of the Veneering Machine in a state of preparation. The follow-ing Sketch may serve to explain

F A B D D B A A Floor C C

the principle of the Machine altho it must ~~must~~ by no means be taken for a correct exhibition of the parts and construction being ~~made of it~~ put together from imma-gination after having seen a few detached parts - A.A.A. a Strong cast Iron frame placed on the

44 (above)
**Sketch of Brunel's patent veneer slicing machine (patented in 1806)**
Simon Goodrich, London, 1807

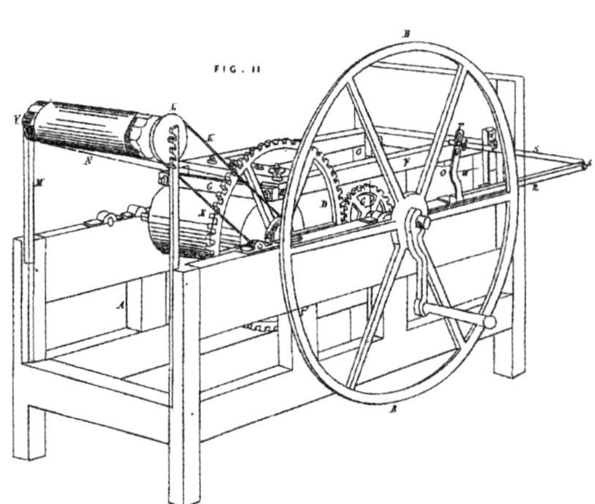


45 (right)
**Illustration from Henry Faveryear, patent for 'Machine for Cutting Veneers, &c.'**
Application filed 25 December 1818, issued 24 June 1819, British patent no. 4324

documented in commercial use, and also widely publicized and imitated was that of the Briton Henry Faveryear. Faveryear was described as both a musical instrument maker and an agent for piano makers who, among other business interests, had a warehouse in St Petersburg by 1803.[5] In 1817, the year before he applied for his British patent, 100-ft (30.5-m) long samples of his rotary peeled birch and mahogany, 'which at first glance seems impossible', were brought to Bavaria from Reval in the Russian Empire. Faveryear's residency in St Petersburg has led to the many subsequent assertions that the rotary peeler (as it also came to be called) was a Russian invention. No other contemporary Russian rotary lathes are documented, although a more complete story awaits further research.[6]

Faveryear's 1819 patent included detailed drawings (fig. 45), which, through a well-established international network of technical and patent journals, became known in Europe and the US (as had Bentham's and Brunel's). In 1822 the Polytechnic Institute in Vienna produced a model of Faveryear's machine uncredited to the inventor, which was subsequently misinterpreted as an Austrian development.[7]

Faveryear's patent for a 'Machine for Cutting Veneers in Wood and other Substances' described and illustrated a device that established the fundamental elements of all nineteenth-century rotary cutting machines, although details of the machine changed over time. These machines, variously known as planers, cutters and only much later as rotary cutters, rotary lathes or rotary peelers, held a de-barked log that was made to revolve and was pressed to a stationary blade. The knives of these machines were often of enormous width, designed to cope with the widest log used by the particular mill. The peeled veneer produced by Faveryear's machine spiralled itself back into a circular form after cutting (as that made by Brunel's table cutter, fig. 44, had done), though later peelers allowed the veneer to be gently rolled out more or less flat after it came off the blade. More than one contemporary described the action of the rotary cutter to be 'as if the veneer were uncoiled like a piece of silk or cloth from a roller'.[8]

By the 1850s 'all veneers' in London were described as being cut by steam-powered machinery, leading to the disappearance of the specialist and well-paid veneer sawyer. These machines were mainly circular saws (fig. 46), but also table cutters (like Bentham's, some with a moving blade, some with a stationary blade), reciprocating saws (with the blade moving backwards and forwards across a stationary block) and, increasingly, rotary cutters (fig. 47). The

1850s saw an increase in the number of patents for rotary cutters in the UK and US (where water-powered mills were more common), suggesting a growing demand for their product, and by the 1860s and into the 1870s rotary cutters were sufficiently widely used in the US for advertisements to appear seeking a 'Veneer machine (new or secondhand), for cutting veneers round the log…'. Numerous American patents for rotary cutters were filed in the 1870s, though reciprocating saws were also common.[9]

### Falling veneer prices

Although veneer-cutting technology was taken up somewhat unevenly in the nineteenth century, in those centres where machines were adopted their use provided much quicker cutting and more (and thinner) veneers per log than was possible by hand cutting. This immediately led to a marked decrease in the price of the veneers. In London by 1811 standard cabinetmakers' price books began listing 25% lower labour costs for providing veneered mahogany and other machine-cut veneers. This was owing to the ease and speed with which thinner, machine-cut veneers of consistent thickness could be applied. The price per foot for veneer sold by sawmills (species unspecified) was bitterly described by a former London veneer sawyer as having dropped by 83% between 1810 and 1850, although he mentioned increased competition as an additional cause.[10]

The result of the fall in prices was seen in the furniture trade, where veneers that had previously been too expensive for cheap furniture could be used for the first time on lower-cost items. Mechanical saws, of course, cut not only veneer but the unseen solid woods that formed the carcasses for the full range of the market – mainly cheaper softwoods known in Britain as 'deals'.[11] By the mid-nineteenth century furniture makers were, most typically, able to sell furniture made of a pine substructure covered with a lesser quality mahogany veneer as 'mahogany furniture' at a cheap price (fig. 73).[12] As a large variety of popular literature demonstrates (see chapter 3) such cheap furniture was responsible for a widespread negative public perception of veneered wood and veneered products, including, later, those made with plywood.

Although all machine-cut veneer was cheaper than hand-cut, there was a hierarchy of quality and price within the veneers produced. Saw-cut was the most expensive as it was also the most wasteful of the raw material and could not be cut as thinly as veneers made by other methods; however, as with much less wasteful blade/knife slicing, saw cutting allowed for the most desirable grain patterns. Rotary cutters produced a more random grain pattern and were very rarely used for the best-quality or most highly figured woods, although like more expensive knife slicing they produced the very thinnest veneers. These veneers were used widely for furniture.

By the 1870s various industries had started to take advantage of the fact that the rotary veneer cutter provided sufficient quantities of cheap veneers for the manufacture of plywood. Plywood started to be used in products made on an increasingly industrial scale. One of the most widespread and significant of these was furniture made for sewing machines.

46 (below)
**'Veneer-Saw'**
From Edward H. Knight, *American Mechanical Dictionary* (Boston 1882), fig. 6950, p. 2702

47 (bottom)
**Traditional veneer cutting methods, still employed in 1942**
From Andrew Dick Wood and Thomas Gray Linn, *Plywoods, Their Development, Manufacture and Application* (Edinburgh and London 1942), fig. 2, p. 13

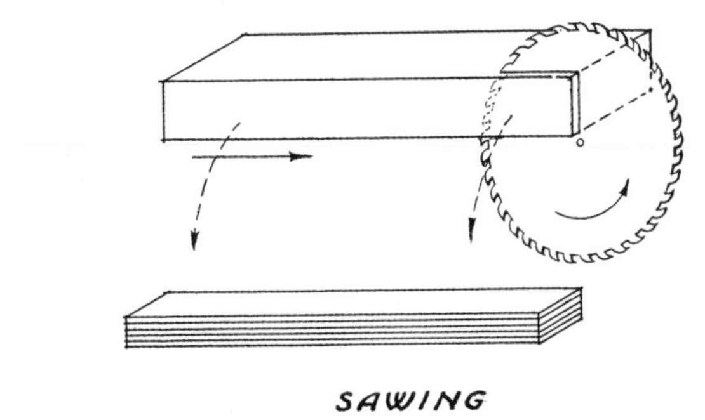


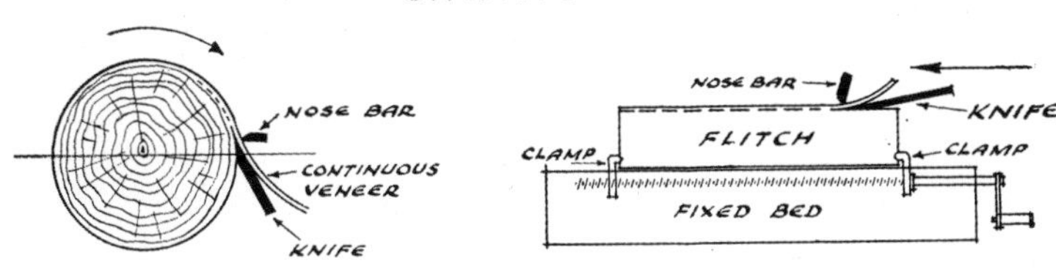

## Sewing machine furniture

Throughout the nineteenth and much of the twentieth centuries, plywood was used as a cheap structural material in a huge amount of sewing machine furniture. This included large, ornamental cabinets, but more often either the wood elements built onto the cast-iron bases of treadle machines or the small single machine cases with handles. While some American sewing machine manufacturers made such furniture themselves as early as the 1850s, much of it was supplied by woodworking firms documented as having used rotary peelers. By 1873 the French Manufacturing Company of Cincinnati, Ohio, was, according to one account, making 78,000 plywood machine cases a year as part of a larger veneer business.[13]

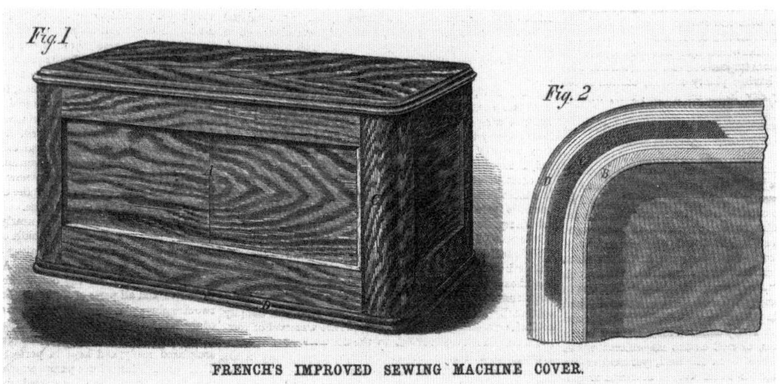


48 (above)
**'French's Improved Sewing Machine Cover'**
From *Scientific American* (21 January 1871), p. 54

E.F. French, a cabinetmaker by trade, was granted at least three patents related to plywood sewing machine covers. His first patent (1870) differed from most box forms of the era in that all its corners were rounded (fig. 48), a feature made possible by clamping and gluing heated, cross-grained veneers to a rounded former. French's patent is clear that the 'advantages' of his invention are that 'a very strong and durable cover is obtained, one not liable to warp, check or crack', but puts even more emphasis on the cost savings of his method: using glued veneers avoided the need to season solid wood for three years (veneers dry much more quickly and are cheaper than solid wood); cheap woods could be used for the inner veneers; and, French wrote, 'the labor of making and building up my improved covers is quite trifling, less than in making the ordinary solid wooden covers'.[14] In other words, dispensing with traditional joints to connect separate boards of solid wood also made the product cheaper. As it had been for Belter (see pp. 21–27), and would be through the later history of plywood, this was one of the chief merits of plywood to manufacturers.

The large sewing machine manufacturer Wheeler and Wilson, of Bridgeport, Connecticut, had been making their own cases in the 1850s. Some time between 1867 and the mid-1870s they built a woodworking mill in Indianapolis, Indiana, which cut veneers and produced plywood tables and panels

49 (right)
**Singer sewing machine mounted on five-drawer table with drop leaf**
From *Catalogue of Singer Sewing Machines for Family Use* (1893), p. 12

for their furniture.[15] It appears that the economies involved in manufacturing from plywood led their even larger competitor, the Singer Sewing Machine Company, to start experimenting with built-up veneer furniture, having in 1868 built a case factory 140 miles (225 km) away from Indianapolis in South Bend, Indiana. Both firms made their own specialist, veneer-related machinery. When, in 1881, Singer built another woodworking facility in Cairo, Illinois, the firm, in addition to using solid wood, moved into the mass production of not only plywood tables (fig. 49) and cabinets but also small, portable cases with moulded tops and handles, which catalogues described as covers (figs 50–51).

The Singer cover made (mainly) of thin plywood was possibly the longest-lived of all plywood designs until the twenty-first century. It was manufactured from 1884 until about 1950, replacing an earlier design made with carved panels.[16] The precise design and size of each cover depended upon that of the machine it enclosed but the basic shape was curved. The base of the case consisted of a piece of solid wood to which the sewing machine was fixed. The handled lid was made of a curved central piece of moulded plywood fitted into grooves on solid side and base pieces. Although the covers were intended originally to have outer surfaces of walnut, cheaper gumwood or nyssa (American black tupelo) was instead chosen as part of Singer's relentless drive for minimum production prices. By 1919 the covers were mainly lesser-quality oak and cheap gumwood.[17]

In the two decades after 1881, as Singer gradually switched to making its furniture mainly of 'built-up' veneers, the company must have been the largest manufacturer of plywood furniture in the world, and by some considerable margin. Yet its product range was limited to cases and a range of table furniture (mainly combined with cast iron) for its sewing machines. Singer made 60,000 machines a year in 1868, when it built its first case factory, and was building over 500,000 in 1880. Its furniture factories were producing 800,000 units by 1882 and close to 3 million units of the plywood cases by about 1900. Until plywood furniture became more commonly produced in the decades after World War II for commercial and institutional use, Singer almost certainly remained the world's largest plywood furniture manufacturer. Singer's adoption of plywood was done entirely for reasons of cost, and ease of mass manufacture – factors that also greatly influenced the material's adoption for other nineteenth-century products.[18]

### Plywood manufacturing in Europe

The profile of the Gardner furniture company (see pp. 32–37) was increased greatly, especially in Europe, by their presence at the Centennial Exhibition in Philadelphia in 1876 (fig. 34). It was at this fair that a number of European manufacturers saw the Gardner stand with its display of moulded plywood seats. Among them was Franz Thonet (1820–98), one of the owners of the Austrian Gebrüder Thonet (Thonet Brothers) bentwood furniture company, who was on the exhibition committee that gave Gardner an award for their 'neat and serviceable perforated wood seating for halls, churches, railway cars, and general use, combining great durability with reasonable price'.[19] Within a year of his Philadelphia visit Thonet lectured an Austrian trade association on the American wood industry, citing especially noteworthy achievements in both knife cutting and rotary peeling veneers. In 1880 Gardner's chairs were exhibited in Vienna by an Austrian importer, by which time buyers were being warned of inferior

50 (below left)
**Singer hand sewing machine with cover**
From *Catalogue of Singer Sewing Machines for Family Use* (1893), p. 20

51 (below)
**Detail of underside corner of Singer sewing machine cover, 1888**
A thin sheet of three-ply, which forms the cover's rounded surface, is jointed into the solid wood base

European imitations. In 1881 a German magazine stated that: wood-veneer bench seats had first been used in Germany on imported, American horse-driven trams; the Viennese Thonet firm were making veneer seats for their bentwood chairs (fig. 52); German sales agents were selling such seats 'on behalf of American companies'; and Gardner were holders of the American patent for such seats.[20] The Thonet company's plywood seats were initially perforated; in 1888 they added a range of plywood seats and backs embossed with decorative patterns (fig. 53).

Another visitor to the US who was evidently impressed with Gardner's furniture was Christian W. Luther (1857–1914), who, before completing his education and joining his family's timber business, the A.M. Luther company, in Reval in the Russian Empire, travelled to England and the US about 1880–81 to learn about the mechanization of the wood industry. Luther's native Baltic region had long been an important centre for growing, processing and exporting Russian timber, although the east coast of Russia was also becoming significant in the late nineteenth century.

Luther's American trip had a profound influence on the future of the A.M. Luther company. While in the US, Luther began a two-decade-long association with a New York woodworking machinery firm. At this time he must also have become familiar with Gardner's plywood seats and their furniture for, after his return to

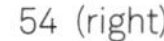

52 (above)
**Armchair with perforated plywood seat and back, introduced by 1881**
From Gebrüder Thonet catalogue (Vienna 1895), p. 23

53 (above right)
**Moulded plywood seats with embossed decoration (one imitating cane), introduced by 1888**
From Gebrüder Thonet catalogue (Vienna 1895), p. 42

54 (right)
**Settee with seat and back made from a single piece of moulded plywood**
Manufactured by A.M. Luther, Reval, Russia (present-day Tallinn, Estonia), 1890–1900

55 (far left)

**Plywood hatboxes, about 1930**
Manufactured in Reval, Russia (present-day Tallinn, Estonia), by (top) Luterma (previously A.M. Luther), from 1895 to the 1930s, and (bottom) in the US by Samson

57 (below left)

**Plywood suitcase, formerly owned by P. Morton Shand**
Manufactured by Luterma (previously A.M. Luther), Reval, Russia (present-day Tallinn, Estonia), 1920s

56 (left)

**Plywood suitcases**
Manufactured by Luterma (previously A.M. Luther), from about 1895. From Luterma catalogue, c. 1920

58 (below)

**Plywood display trays**
Manufactured by Luterma (previously A.M. Luther), sold in the UK by Venesta
From *Venesta Plywood Sundries* catalogue (1936)

Reval in 1882, Luther set out to make three-ply veneer perforated seats. Luther's seats are clearly based on Gardner's, and the start of their production coincided with the company's urgent need to find products suitable for mass production, in order to make their steam-powered machinery financially viable.[21]

Following experiments in 1884, production of the plywood seats began in March 1885 using a rotary cutter developed by the Luther firm. By the year's end 45,000 seats had been made, followed by 135,000 in 1886 and 608,000 in 1887, representing nearly the firm's entire production. About 1888 Luther began making a range of chairs and settees that directly imitated Gardner's designs (fig. 34) by using a continuous moulded seat and back (fig. 54). These were described by Luther as 'American furniture' and, in an illustration, could easily be mistaken for the originals.[22]

This turned out to be only the beginning of Luther's involvement in the manufacturing of plywood products, and it may well be that Luther was the first large-scale European plywood manufacturer. The company began to manufacture a huge range of products including hatboxes (fig. 55), suitcases (figs 56–57) and other domestic objects (fig. 58), for which they had a special factory, as well as a range of barrels, buckets and storage boxes in many sizes. While furniture production – plywood and solid wood – remained the mainstay of the firm's output, flat plywood boards and tea chests came to take up an increasingly significant part of their business from the 1890s.[23]

59 (right)

**John K. Mayo, patent for 'House Decorations, Furniture, Fittings, and the Like'**

Issued 26 December 1865, reissued (no. 3,089) 18 August 1868, US patent no. 51,753

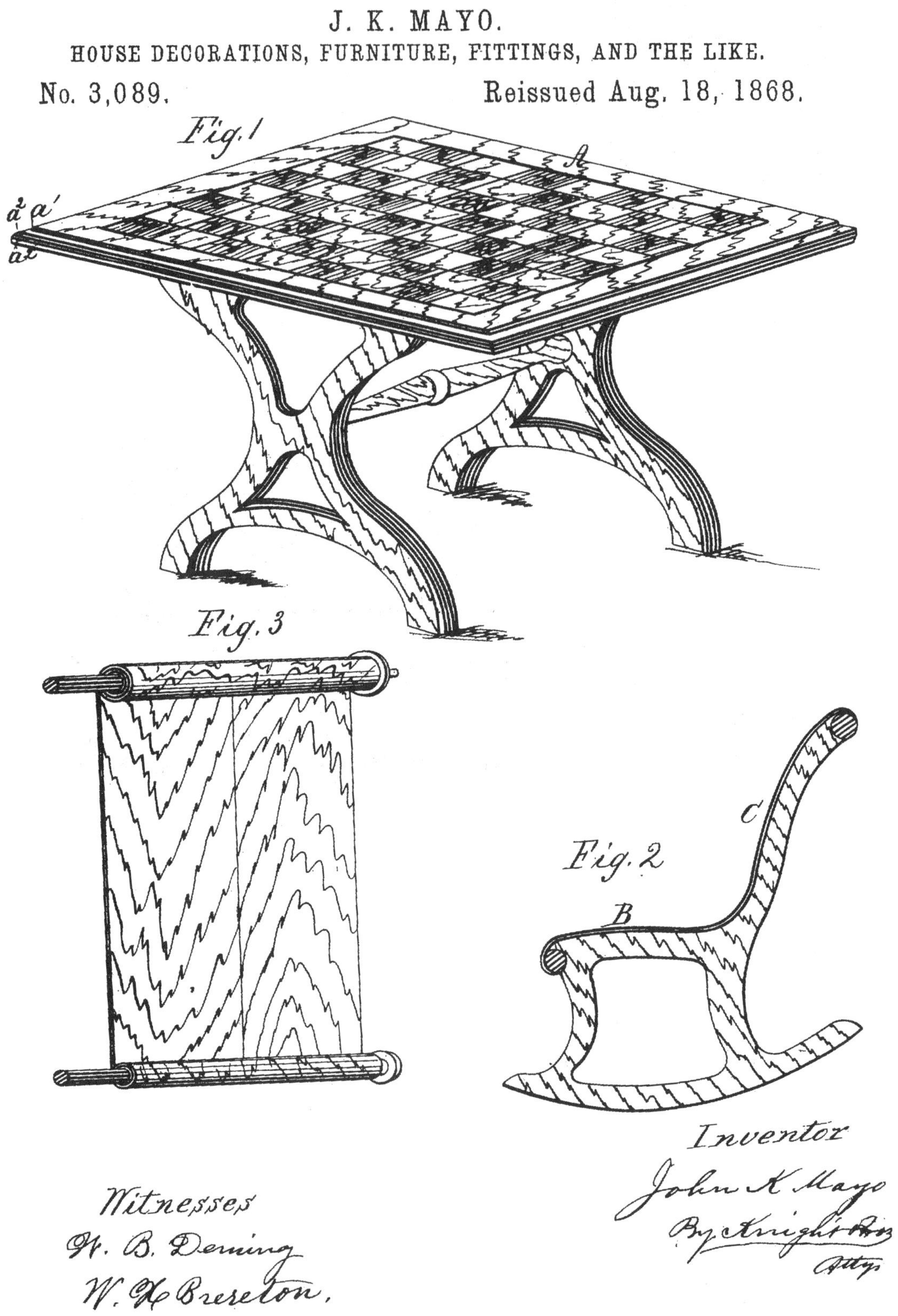

J. K. MAYO.

HOUSE DECORATIONS, FURNITURE, FITTINGS, AND THE LIKE.

No. 3,089. Reissued Aug. 18, 1868.

Fig. 1

Fig. 3

Fig. 2

Witnesses

W. B. Deming

W. H. Brereton.

Inventor

John K Mayo

By Knight Bros

Attys

### The plywood board

Despite the fact that plywood is often associated with the flat board, the history outlined above has shown that many significant advances in nineteenth-century plywood related to moulding. Early references to flat plywood include some of the uses suggested in John K. Mayo's patent of 1865 (fig. 59), which illustrates a table with cut-out plywood supports and a rectangular top, a rocking chair with cut-out plywood sides and a single-piece seat/back unit, and a window shade made of veneers 'as thin as paper'.[24] William Hassalwood Carmont of the Patent Steel Frame Carriage Works in Manchester, England, had received a patent in 1886 for an apparatus to 'cement together' cross-grained veneers, which could be used in moulded form or in the making of 'straight panelling' in horse-drawn carriages. But it was only in 1905 that built-up 'panels' were first advertised as a stock item by businesses in various parts of the world. Before then furniture workshops and factories made their own small, thin plywood boards for use in drawer bottoms and sides, and larger boards for desk tops. Such was the scale of these uses that in 1898 the *New York Sun* newspaper notably reported from the furniture manufacturing centre of Grand Rapids, Michigan, that 'Modern furniture is not solid, but is built up.'[25]

By 1905 the American Veneers and Panels Association of manufacturers had been established, and within a few years the 'veneer panel' and 'three-ply panel' were discussed and advertised widely in the English-speaking world (fig. 60, see also fig. 75 for an early use of the term 'ply wood').[26] While the plywood board clearly evolved from firms making their own panels for specific uses, its appearance on the market led to the creation of specialist plywood manufacturers, many of whom were also in the veneer business. The A.M. Luther company in the Russian Empire played an important role in the European evolution of this industry.

In 1889, following the acquisition of a 'steam-heated hydraulic press', Luther began the manufacture of three-ply boards for commercial sale. It is entirely possible that Luther were the first to produce and sell plywood boards on a large scale, although there were other manufacturers in Russia, including the firm part-owned by the inventor Ogneslav Kostovich (1851–1916). Kostovich began making 'flying machines' from plywood

60 (above)

**E.C. Young, timber merchant, advertising three-ply panels**

From *Cabinet Maker and Complete House Furnisher* (2 February 1907), p. 152

in the 1880s (see pp. 73–74) and manufacturing products made of 'artificial wood', which was clearly described as plywood. By the end of the century he had given the trade name of arboryte to his material, which was, apparently, made from aspen wood and used in a wide variety of applications.[27] Elsewhere in northern Europe a German firm, Blomberger Holzindustrie B. Hausmann, started to manufacture and sell beech plywood in 1893. Some five years later the German firm Kümmel, in Rehfelde, is said to have produced a kind of plywood-covered blockboard that was referred to as cabinetmaker's panels (*Tischlerplatten*); these came to be used extensively in Germany. However, as no other contemporary manufacturers are as yet remotely as well documented as Luther, the latter's history deserves special attention.[28]

Luther worked steadily on improving the glues that held the boards together and in 1896 they patented a new 'waterproof' glue. This was possibly the first to be noticeably better at resisting water than previously available glues, although genuinely waterproof glue would have to await the invention of synthetic glues (see chapter 4). However, the qualities of Luther's new glue were sufficient for it to became a major selling point for Luther's flat and moulded boards, as well as other products such as buckets and barrels, which were later also made by Luther's competitors (fig. 61). From a production point of view it claimed one very notable (potential) characteristic, as described in its British patent: it could be applied to individual veneers and then allowed to dry completely. Later, the veneers could be stacked in a hot press and then moulded. This process entirely separated the application of wet glue from the need to immediately mould the veneers into plywood.[29]

Initially Luther's boards were ribbed, a feature arising from an idea that this would let steam escape more easily when they were pressed. While the ribs were seen as usefully distinguishing Luther's boards from those made by others, once such competing products existed Luther abandoned ribs (in 1902) in favour of smooth surfaces. Another change towards simplification and standardization that Luther made in their first decade of board manufacture was to shift from making three-ply boards with a thicker veneer core (as had been the case in American manufacture) to making 4.5-mm (⁵⁄₆₄-in.) boards from three veneers of identical thickness. About 1900 Luther settled on standard board sizes of 482 × 482 mm (19 × 19 in.) and 482 × 610 mm (19 × 24 in.), while also producing boards in custom sizes for tram companies and railway carriage manufacturers who required moulded seating (fig. 62) and both moulded and flat boards for cladding and structural elements. This marked the beginning of a sustained process of maximizing efficiency through the manufacture of standard sizes, useful for manufacturers and clients. Within a few years, the board size increased.[30]

At the turn of the century Luther were manufacturing 8.7 million sq ft (approx. 800,000 sq m) of plywood boards per year, which was the basis of their prosperity until about 1910. Their most successful board product at this time, and the basis on which they adopted their standard board sizes, was their move into the manufacture of plywood tea chests. This would lead to the creation of a major plywood sales and distribution firm in England (in which Luther were a partner) and, owing to demand, the founding of the first plywood factory in Finland, which was devoted almost entirely to the production of tea chest boards.[31]

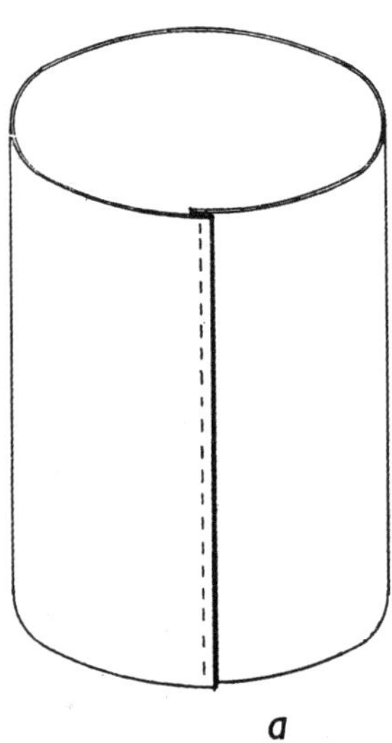


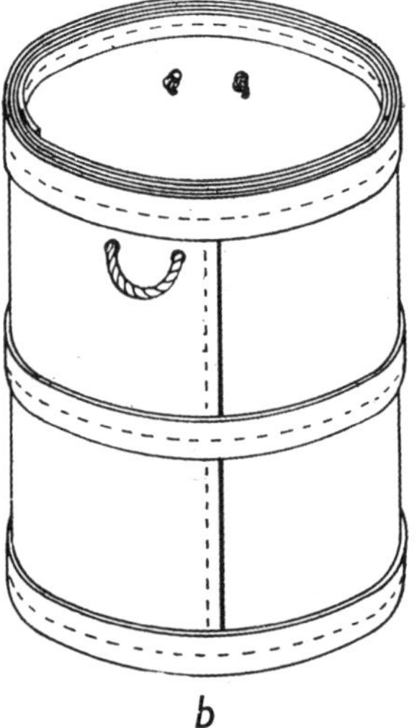


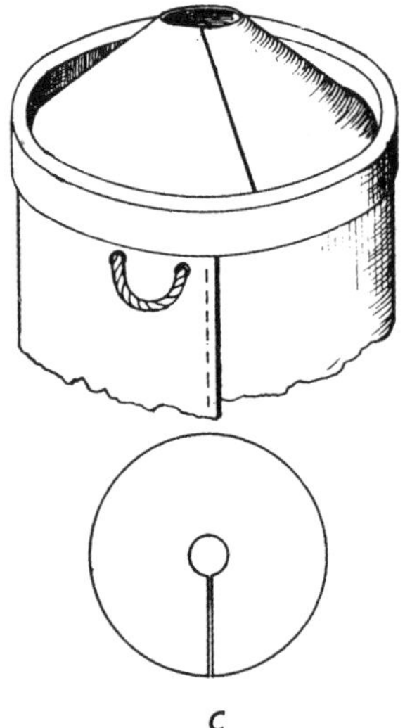


61 (right)
**Construction of plywood potato barrels**
From Andrew Dick Wood and Thomas Gray Linn, *Plywoods, Their Development, Manufacture and Application* (Edinburgh and London 1942), fig. 172, p. 416

62 (opposite)
**Moulded plywood benches for railway carriages and trams, introduced about 1890**
From Luterma (previously A.M. Luther) catalogue, c. 1926

№ 659.

*Profile. Profil № 423.*

**Seating.**
**Siège et dossier combinés.**
**Sitz und Lehne zusammenhängend.**

№ 670.

*Profile. Profil № 423.*

**Seating.**
**Siège et dossier combinés.**
**Sitz und Lehne zusammenhängend.**

№ 682.

*Profile. Profil № 423.*

**Seating.**
**Siège et dossier combinés.**
**Sitz und Lehne zusammenhängend.**

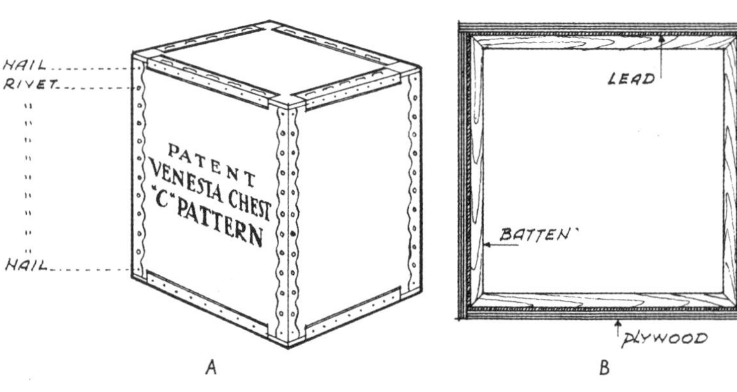

63 (top)

**Diagram showing tea chest construction**
From Andrew Dick Wood and Thomas Gray Linn, *Plywoods, Their Development, Manufacture and Application* (Edinburgh and London 1942), fig. 170, p. 413

64 (above)

**Dock workers moving tea chests inside a Cutler Street warehouse, London, 1949**

**Tea chests**

Little is reliably known about crates used for shipping tea during the nineteenth century, although they were probably first made of solid wood.[32] By 1895 E.H. Archer, a London businessman said to have invested in tea plantations and who was then working for tea packaging specialists, adapted an existing, patented chest made of 'thin metal sheets' and made it collapsible to enable economical reuse.[33] However, it was said that 'the blenders and grocers' receiving these types of crates were dismayed that, unlike wooden crates, they were useless as firewood. Having been either presented with 'the latest American novelty', a piece of three-ply wood, or, in a more romantic version of the story, having discovered a wet but intact piece of plywood marked 'Luther' on a beach, Archer wondered if it could be made resistant to the damp Indian, tea-growing climate. After discovering Luther's waterproof adhesive patent in London, he went to Reval in the Russian Empire to buy Luther plywood boards and discussed the possibility of manufacturing tea chests in Britain. In 1896 Archer formed the Patent Veneer and Metal Case Co. Ltd, while, in December of that year, Christian W. Luther applied for a patent to make rectangular boxes from cross-grained 'plys or veneers'. In 1897 Archer formed the Venesta Syndicate Ltd (from 1898 Venesta Ltd) to make tea chests with Luther boards and glue and to sell them in Britain and in British colonies (fig. 63). Venesta's business later extended to other parts of Europe, while Luther sold products in Russia. The name Venesta was an acronym either of the words veneer and chest, or veneer and Estonia, and Christian W. Luther was both an investor and a director of Venesta Ltd.[34]

The Venesta product seemed to be the answer to all that was required in a tea chest. The wood used for tea chests (fig. 64) must ideally be as inert as possible, without sap that could corrode the metal lining in which the tea was packed; it should be seasoned, so as not to warp when hot tea leaves were packed in it, and free of odour. The plywood should not delaminate. The box should be as light as possible and, as it would require return shipment when empty, knock down for flat packing.[35] Venesta first produced the lead linings for the chests in 1900 in Limehouse, London, and then, from 1905, near Calcutta (now Kolkata), where they switched to aluminium. The chests were made using Luther's standard board sizes (see above), and the boards were joined together at the corners using internal solid wood battens and external metal strips that were hammered into the boards.

The Venesta tea chests were instantly successful: by 1901, 60,000 were shipped to Britain each month and demand exceeded supply. Luther's close connection with Venesta, hence with the thriving British tea industry (assured by colonial rule of the Indian subcontinent), was one foundation of the company's dominant position in the European plywood business. Equally important was that its business (including the export of Luther/Venesta boards to other European countries) carried on during the recession of 1900–03 and into the early years of the Russian Revolution (from 1917). Until the Revolution, Russia was the largest exporter of plywood in the world, Britain the largest importer and the US the largest producer.[36]

In order to prevent anticipated foreign competition for the tea chest business in Russia (a large consumer of tea), Christian W. Luther managed to convince the Russian authorities to impose an import duty on tea chests.[37] However, other firms in Britain entered the tea chest market, some setting up manufacturing plants in England, and others attempting to manufacture boxes for their own tea businesses, while some officials and businessmen tried to set up local manufacturing in colonies including India, Ceylon (Sri Lanka) and the Dutch East Indies (Indonesia). This local manufacture was often not successful and only the onset of World War II allowed, for example, an Indian manufactory to gain some traction, owing to disruption of trade in Europe.[38]

At the same time that Venesta's tea chest business expanded so too did they begin the importation and sale of the Luther boards used for tea chests but trademarked as Venesta boards. These boards did not meet the standards of other Luther plywood boards: as their appearance did not matter, they were not required to be knot- and crack-free on any one side. This did not seem to affect their popularity as the Venesta board rapidly became a synonym for plywood in Britain and France.[39] The boards and the boxes that Venesta sold (not only tea chests) gained special notoriety from their use on two well-publicized Antarctic expeditions. Ernest Shackleton's Nimrod expedition (1907–09) took some 2,500 Venesta boxes to the Antarctic (fig. 65), where they withstood difficult conditions including exposure to salt water and burial in ice, and were reused in many ways: as furniture and fittings within living quarters, 'for the making of the hundred and one odds and ends...in such an expedition as this', and also as covers and binding for the fewer than 100 copies of *Aurora Australis* (fig. 66), 'the first book ever written, printed, illustrated and bound in the Antarctic'. Shackleton's memoirs, with his descriptions of Venesta boxes, were quoted in advertisements for trunks 'made on the... principles' of Venesta boards (fig. 67) throughout

65 (below)

**Digging out stores after the plywood cases had been buried in ice during a blizzard**

Ernest Shackleton's first Antarctic Expedition (Nimrod), February 1909

66 (below)

**Ernest Shackleton (ed.), *Aurora Australis* (Antarctica 1908)**
Bound in Venesta plywood boards

67 (bottom)

**Advertisement for the 'Composite' Cabin Trunk**
From *The Times* (15 July 1911), p. 10

1911–13. For Captain Robert Falcon Scott's ill-fated Terra Nova expedition of 1910–12 (fig. 68), Venesta crates were reused to make the covers of the *South Polar Times* (a newspaper produced by the men of the expedition) and (with sealskin) to make boots.[40] As Venesta tea chests and other crates became more widely known by the general public through their everyday use in Britain and in tea-producing and tea-processing countries, so too did plywood as an exposed material become more common in the early twentieth century.

68 (above)

**Captain Robert Falcon Scott in his winter quarters hut with bookshelves made of plywood packing cases**
Ross Island, Antarctica, 1911

# 3 The Veneer Problem (1850s–1930s)

> At present, the successful practitioners of the art of veneering are rampant. The average modern Englishman...is becoming superficial and unreal in everything. In mind and body he is veneered.[1]

Plywood was, from its beginnings until as late as the 1930s, synonymous with veneers in the English-speaking world. Not only was it made from veneers and itself a veneered wood product, but it was also described as veneer, veneers, veneer work or built-up veneers. Once the word 'ply-wood' or 'ply wood' was introduced (by 1906), and even when the term 'plywood' came into widespread, though not universal, trade use in the 1920s, there were still those who used veneer as a synonym for plywood. This linguistic curiosity would be of only slight interest were it not for the fact that during the nineteenth century the word 'veneer' was used very widely in a pejorative, metaphorical way. It came to represent all that was cheap and false, a meaning no doubt associated with the proliferation of cheap veneers, and of cheap veneered furniture, throughout the nineteenth century (see p. 41).

The 'anti-veneer' sentiment ran deep in nineteenth-century popular culture and it is not possible to understand the lowly status of veneer and plywood in the eyes of the public without a clear explanation of its origins. So widespread was this negative view that it led those retailing wood products to avoid the words veneer or plywood; and gave rise to lawsuits for mis-selling (in Britain), to great consternation and debate within the wood business, and to government regulatory hearings (in the US). It cast a shadow over the public perception of plywood that has lasted, especially in terms of domestic use, until the present day. Appropriately enough for a veneered material, this story has long remained hidden.

THE VENEERING DINNER.

69 (opposite)
**Rubbing Department, Berkey & Gay Furniture Company factory**
Grand Rapids, Michigan, c. 1928

70 (left)
**'The Veneering Dinner'**
Illustration by Sol Eytinge, Jr, from Charles Dickens, *Our Mutual Friend* (London, Boston and New York 1870 edition), pl. 2

## Veneers and Veneerings

In his last major novel, *Our Mutual Friend* (1865), Charles Dickens introduced into popular culture two of his more unappealing characters, Mr and Mrs Veneering (fig. 70):

> Mr and Mrs Veneering were bran-new people in a bran-new house in a bran-new quarter of London. Everything about the Veneerings was spick and span new. All their furniture was new, all their friends were new, all their servants were new, their plate was new, their carriage was new, their harness was new, their horses were new, their pictures were new, they themselves were new...
>
> For, in the Veneering establishment, from the hall-chairs with the new coat of arms, to the grand pianoforte with the new action, and upstairs again to the new fire-escape, all things were in a state of high varnish and polish. And what was observable in the furniture, was observable in the Veneerings – the surface smelt a little too much of the workshop and was a trifle sticky.[2]

Ever sensitive to physical materials, Dickens introduces the Veneerings' deficiencies of character through a rich description of the contemporary interior. The focus is on their extreme, even monstrous, superficiality, their love of ostentation and the fact that they are nouveau riche. For the history of plywood it is Dickens's choice of name, associated with the Veneerings' character, that is meaningful. As the story develops we learn that the Veneerings' money comes from the manufacture of 'drugs' of dubious efficacy and that, beneath their shiny exterior, there is no inner substance; the Veneerings rely on others to guide them through society, obtain them friends, purchase their goods, and tell them what to think and what to say. Dickens mocks the Veneerings without mercy and ended up searing their elevation of showy triviality and deep-seated materialism onto the Victorian imagination. Indeed, more than thirty years after the novel was published, an early and popular history of furniture gave the novel just such credit: 'veneers, thus used and abused, came to be a term of contempt, implying sham or superficial ornament. Dickens... introduced the "Veneer" family [*sic*], thus stamping the term more strongly on the popular imagination.'[3]

71 (below)
**'Dam'me, you couldn't treat me with less respect if I was veneered'**
Illustration by Phiz (Hablot K. Browne) from Charles Dickens, *The Posthumous Papers of the Pickwick Club* (London 1874), p. 89

Although Dickens's use of the term is particularly rich, by the time *Our Mutual Friend* was published the notion of veneer as a term to denote a sham surface (intentionally hiding something beneath) was already well established.[4] Eighteenth-century examples of the word veneer used in everyday language seem to have been rare in the English-speaking world – unsurprising at a time when wood veneers were expensive and more associated with top-end, often foreign cabinetmaking – but an Irish novel of 1757, *Bradstreet's Lives*, contained the fleeting appearance of a sympathetic French character called Mr Veneer. In France itself, the word veneer (*placage*) used pejoratively arises in non-fiction.[5]

Dickens's first, very popular novel, *The Pickwick Papers* (1836), had used veneer in a negative sense when referring to veneered as opposed to solid wood in furniture.[6] Here, a character tells a story about one Tom Smart, a travelling salesman who, after falling asleep drunk, imagines that an 'old chair' has assumed the form of an 'ugly old gentleman' (fig. 71). Smart addresses the man as 'old nut-cracker face!', which causes him to take offence and say: 'Come, come Tom... that's not the way to address solid Spanish mahogany. Dam'me, you couldn't treat me with less respect if I was veneered.' In 1836, a year before the Victorian era started with that Queen's coronation, the word veneer was already being used as a term implying disrespect, low status, and the very opposite of something solid and of high quality.

Nineteenth-century references to veneer in popular literature – both fiction and non-fiction – vary from literal mentions of veneered wood or wood products (mainly of their poor quality), to the more pervasive and more powerful metaphorical use of veneer or veneering. To have served as an easily understood metaphor, the word veneer must have been deeply embedded in the popular culture and language of Victorian Britain. This is reflected by its use in novels, magazines and daily newspapers. Indeed, by the 1850s, a series of six hard-hitting and well-publicized essays by George Henry Francis accused the British of living in an 'Age of Veneer': 'John Bull is veneered *in toto*, in all aspects of life, society, the arts and sciences' but also in the physical reality of daily life: 'He lives in a stuccoed house – or fragile structure of rotten timber and porous brick, faced with the real stuff; he sits on veneered chairs, in veneered garments; and he eats off veneered mahogany, with electrotyped plate.'[7]

Written as the Great Exhibition of the Works of Industry of All Nations was in preparation in London in 1850, Francis chose a metaphor firmly grounded in the Victorian world of material goods (fig. 72). In many nineteenth-century uses of the term veneer, it is these physical (and often domestic) associations that are key. A heavy undertone of class anxiety accompanies the image of veneered goods. In a manner similar to Dickens's description of the Veneerings, the author of the 'Age of Veneer' articles suggests a correlation between a proliferation of cheaply veneered or 'false' consumable products and unstable class distinctions: the British 'housewife...Mistress Bull', laudably sought to 'adorn...with every beauty' the 'Temple' that is her home. But 'Those who could not buy carved mahogany in the solid were content to put a pious fraud on themselves, and accept in lieu a bulk of deal or pine, with a thin layer of richer wood spread over it.' This, says the author, has led to state of affairs in which those 'who never bought before' now buy sham goods, 'and those who little bought now buy the more'.[8]

Educational, as well as political, philanthropic, artistic and even statistical veneering, as Francis expounds throughout his series, are all 'very showy on the outside, but very deceptive, very taking and varnishy...very liable to peel off, exposing the coarse and crude material beneath'.[9] Veneering thus not only threatens the foundations of polite society, but also the social order:

> ...the successful practitioners of the art of veneering are rampant....You cannot suddenly convert a boor into a gentleman; you cannot, by merely telling a people that they are changed, transform them from coarseness of taste, and an almost exclusive admiration of the merely physical, into *virtuosi*, men of science, adepts of literature, and patrons of, and participators in, the arts. You cannot by the magic of mere hope or assertion, disseminate among the middle and lower classes the tastes, habits and means of enjoyment, and hitherto exclusively possessed by an aristocracy.[10]

The 'Age of Veneer' essays offer the most robust and comprehensive metaphorical and negative use of the term veneer to date; in fact, they remained the most all-encompassing example of the nineteenth century,

72 (above)

**Interior view of the Crystal Palace, London**
John Absolon, from *Recollections of the Great Exhibition* (London 1851), pl. 3

even though the influence of Dickens's *Our Mutual Friend* more than a decade later was more profound – it was certainly more widely read. In 'The Age of Veneer' the author covered virtually all of the themes around the word veneer that would be reprised time and again throughout the nineteenth and early twentieth centuries, in fiction and non-fiction, in highbrow and popular literature, and in the serious and the satirical.

The overarching metaphor for veneer in the nineteenth century was that of superficiality. This was generally used with a negative inflection, indicating lack of depth, conviction or sincerity, if not falseness, dishonesty and a sham. For example, The Hon. Arlington Veneer was the name chosen for the false and insincere 'Elegant Friend' in the 1855 London stage production *The Man of Many Friends*. The metaphor of veneer was almost always a characteristic or attribute generally lying thinly on the surface of an individual, who was mainly attempting to conform to societal norms and usually hiding a baser or less appropriate sentiment, motivation or character. Alfred, Lord Tennyson's poem *The Princess* (1847) described a college master 'as a rogue in grain / Veneered with sanctimonious theory'. One character in the Anglo-American playwright William Bayle Bernard's *The Evil Genius* (1856) described another as possessing 'a mere veneer of good taste on a surface of wormwood'. A newspaper article (1865) referred to getting 'under the smooth veneer of conventional manners' and another (1884) to 'the veneer of good manners', while a playwright used the term 'her veneer of candour' (1876).[11] An article in an American children's magazine described politeness in individuals metaphorically by comparing a chair of solid wood to veneered furniture:

> There are persons of genuine refinement [but]....Others are coarse timber, poor sticks perhaps, veneered with a thin, a very thin covering of fine manners. This veneer...is sometimes so artistically laid on that the sham mahogany passes for the real...but it is sure at last to peel off and betray the shabby interior.[12]

The revelation of coarseness beneath indicated the possibility that an individual did not, in fact, belong to the class within which they lived their daily life, while a lack of coarseness indicated order in the world. An earnest magazine article on 'Company Manners' (1868) stated that 'a thorough gentleman or a high-bred lady is one who has no veneer of company manners, but whose whole nature is so penetrated with the self-respect of courtesy, that nothing coarser can be shown under any provocation'. The serialized novel *Veronica* (1869) by Frances Eleanor Trollope explained that 'Sir John Gale's studied good breeding partook less of the nature of polish – which beautifies and displays the natural grain of the wood – than of veneer...though not unskilfully applied, occasionally cracked, revealing glimpses of a rather coarse and ugly material beneath it' (1869).[13]

A common veneer metaphor in relation to manners – one used often in print and on the Victorian stage, and which especially remains with us in the present day – was someone trying to deceive others with 'a veneer of politeness' (1876). This was often a 'thin veneer of politeness', which could self-evidently be seen through. But such a veneer could, in positive terms, take into account the complexities of human interaction and the need for civility, as exemplified by the character of Mr Allen in the novel *What Can She Do?* (1873) by the once-popular American writer Edward Payson Roe: 'He always maintained a show of gallantry and deference; which, though but a thin veneer, was certainly better than open disregard and brutal neglect.'[14]

While probably most nineteenth-century examples of the veneer metaphor refer to behaviour in polite society, the single phrase most commonly encountered in publications of the period is a 'veneer of civilization' or, frequently, 'of Western civilization'. This was more the case for the later decades of the nineteenth century and it is not surprising that during the heyday of the British Empire this racist metaphor should have been so common. Thus, during wars between Māori and the British over sovereignty and land ownership in New Zealand, Māori Christian converts were described in 1865 as having only 'the thin veneer of civilization'; while the Turks, at the time of the Russo-Ottoman War (1877–78) in particular, were savaged and condescended to in newspaper articles for applying 'a thin and worthless veneer of Parisian culture' (1877) and for wearing a 'fez, black coat, European clothes, and thin veneer of French polish' (1879). Reports of 'progress' in China in 1881 were said to be instead, 'all the old China he knew, with a little veneer'. Egypt had 'a tawdry veneer of Western civilization' (1883) and a 'veneer of civilization [that was]...thin and fragile' (1896), while Indian judges 'acquire little more than a sort of veneer' in attempts to adopt British law (1883).[15] Suggesting the need to control what lies beneath, not only in the British working classes but across the globe, the image of the veneer is generally very thin indeed.

73 (right)

**'Garret-Master; or Cheap Furniture Maker'. Note the sign reading 'cheap' visible on top of the chest of drawers**
From Henry Mayhew, *London Labour and the London Poor*, vol. 3 (London 1861), after p. 96

GARRET-MASTER; OR CHEAP FURNITURE MAKER.

[*From a Sketch.*]

## The 1887 UK Trade Descriptions Act

Given the fact that the veneer metaphor comes into prominence at the exact same moment as (and must have been prompted by) a huge increase in the manufacture of cheap veneered furniture (see p. 41 and fig. 73), it is perhaps unsurprising that it was within the furniture trades, rather than other wood product sectors, that controversies regarding veneer had the most visible impact. One notable outcome of public suspicion about veneers was the filing of lawsuits in British courts between 1903 and 1928. These alleged that furniture purchased on the basis that it had the name of a single wood (typically, walnut or mahogany, most frequently sold as 'solid' walnut or mahogany; fig. 74) had, in fact, been made using only veneer of that wood, sometimes in the form of plywood (it is often very difficult to ascertain whether the complaints related to the use of a single veneer or to plywood, highlighting the high degree of elision that existed between these terms). The legal context for this was the Trade Descriptions Act of 1887, which stipulated that sellers must not apply 'false trade descriptions to goods'. The trade description pertained, among other points, to 'any statement, direct or indirect…as to the material of which any goods are composed'. Penalties for violations of the Act were, in theory, severe: 'imprisonment, with or without hard labour' for up to two years and/or a fine.[16]

A range of legal cases were brought by consumers suing retailers, house furnishers or furniture makers; by retailers suing suppliers; and a smaller number by retailers or manufacturers seeking payment being withheld by clients complaining of false descriptions of goods. Not all cases concerned veneers or plywood, but early cases centred on what

74 (below)
**'A House Furnisher's Shop as it May Be in the Future'**
From *Furniture Record* (20 October 1905), p. 495

was meant by 'solid' wood drew the veneer problem straight into the disputes. For example, the judgment of Salford County Court in northwest England in 1903 that a shopkeeper had fraudulently described a pair of bedroom stands and two chairs as solid walnut when secondary (solid) woods were also used did not state that any veneer was used. The trade's response was to say that the term 'solid' was intended to indicate that the pieces were 'not veneered' – although this did not necessarily mean they were made from only one wood – and that such a definition was essential to a successful business.[17]

When a buyer sued a furniture dealer the following year in Liverpool, the 'solid walnut' suite turned out to be walnut veneer over cheap American whitewood. The buyer lost the case on technical issues, the judge adding that although the description of the wood was not accurate, it was 'trade accurate'.[18] Such a judgment in favour of the trade view was to become very rare in subsequent years, yet the trade continued to put forward a wide range of explanations for why, in defiance of common sense, an elastic use of terminology should be acceptable.[19] One furnishing company declared in Shoreditch County Court in London that their 'solid walnut' wardrobe was merely 'what was called a "solid walnut", being made mainly of "stained white wood" except for round the mirror'.[20] At no point did these arguments serve to enhance the reputation of veneers or built-up veneers, which were frequently cited as the (less good) substitutes for solid wood.

Although World War I saw few lawsuits they resumed by 1920 at the latest, with one held in Newcastle in August 1922 attracting an especially large amount of comment and activity within the trade.[21] The case itself was straightforward. A retailer/manufacturer sold a bedroom suite of their own design as 'solid mahogany' and was sued by the buyer. According to the vendor, the suite was made from Honduras mahogany with decorative veneers of the same wood. The judge ruled that as the suite was not made entirely of solid mahogany, the buyer had been deceived and he ruled in favour of the plaintiff.

While the details of the Newcastle case were similar to past lawsuits, and the trade press claimed not to be surprised by the court's ruling, the decision became a flashpoint within the industry for a number of reasons. Above all, the case coincided with fervent expectations of an improving economy after the war and the catastrophic depression of 1920–21; the furniture trade therefore worried especially about unfavourable publicity that would affect confidence in its products at such a moment. The more widespread heating up of the debate on the solid wood issue was fuelled by simmering trade indignation at consistent court rulings against sellers. Finally, there was increasing agreement from many within the trade for a pressing need for terminology that would avoid future court cases and ensure greater transparency in discussions of the veneer problem. It was these discussions of terminology that became increasingly important in the manufacture and sale of plywood and its products, in both the UK and the US.[22]

75–78 (right)

**Early British advertisements for plywood, including the first known use of the term 'ply wood' in 1906**
Dated, left to right: December 1906, January 1907, February 1908, March 1911

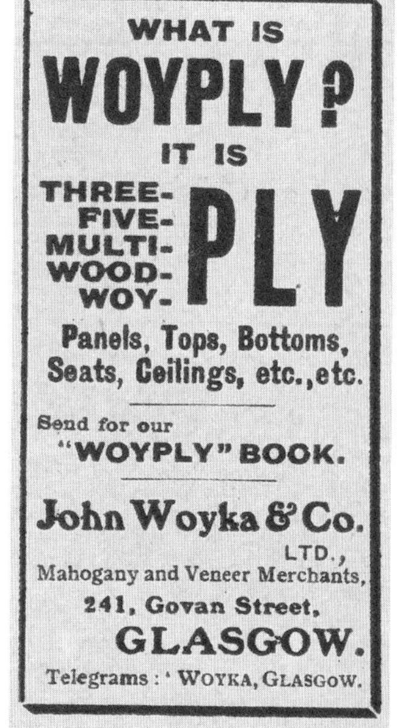

### 'There is no sham in plywood'

Within the American timber trade the argument in favour of plywood (still called built-up work or panels) was framed in several ways. None of them was immune to the hyperbole and ambiguity characteristic of any trade press then, as now, arising from the fundamental basis of such publications as promotion. First, it was pointed out that plywood was, perhaps unexpectedly for its critics, already widely used by the end of the nineteenth century in manufacturing commercial furniture and need not be the source of disquiet: 'Modern furniture is not solid, but is built up...from five to seven distinct layers of wood, each layer running crosswise in grain to its neighbour.' Second, it was suggested that veneered furniture (explicitly identified as made of ply construction) was not cheap but 'the finest and most expensive furniture made today...far more beautiful than solid wood' and 'arranged cross-grained'.[23] Indeed, it was frequently argued that products – panels, boxes or furniture, for example – could be more rather than less expensive when made of built-up work rather than solid wood.[24] Alongside these assurances about cost and quality, product manufacturers were also often conversely assured that the lower price of plywood relative to that of solid wood would lower the cost of their goods.[25] Finally, the most convincing and consistent argument made in favour of plywood was that, unlike solid wood, it did not shrink (or by no more than 1%), split, swell or check (naturally separate along the grain), and that it was, in recommended applications, undeniably stronger than solid wood.[26]

Another tactic aimed at improving the status of built-up work was to find a new, more market-friendly term for it that avoided any mention of veneer. From the 1890s until the late 1920s those in the wood trades and especially furniture firms debated the need for a terminology that would improve the image of veneers and built-up work and, with a slightly different intention, distinguish built-up work from veneer used solely as a thin, decorative layer on a solid substructure. A word both independent of veneer, and one which would make built-up veneers sound like a new product, was sought.

A 1907 letter to the American trade magazine *Veneers* suggested a competition to find a new name 'for the wooden stock or material we all know and use, which is built-up, crosswise bound, of multiply, rotary-cut sheets of wood'.[27] Precisely such a name had been used the previous year in Britain by a timber merchant, one of many agents selling mainly woods from the Baltic countries, advertising 'ply wood' in oak, birch or alder (figs 75–78).[28] The term was undoubtedly trade shorthand for both 'three-ply veneer' (a term that appeared in print as early as 1887 in the US) and 'three-ply wood', a parallel term to the contemporary and mainly American 'three-ply stock'.[29] In the UK, the term '3-ply' appears only later, possibly not until the earliest part of the twentieth century. Timber merchants did not sell to the general public and their motivation for using a new term probably had little to do with a belief that the product was tainted by association with veneer. Instead, it is likely to have reflected a desire to distinguish built-up work as a

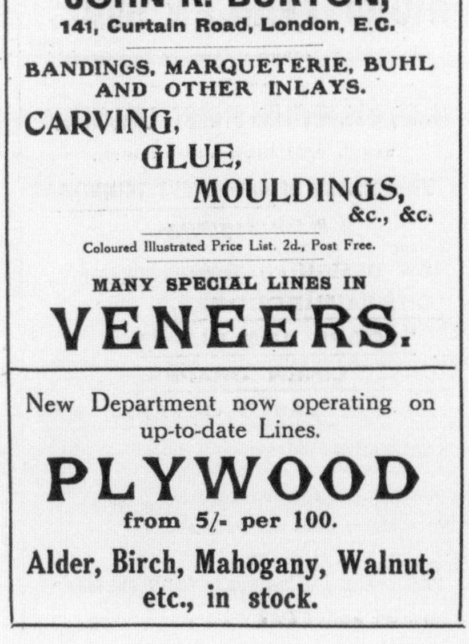

WORRY
PERPLEXITY
TROUBLE
NEW GRADING RULES
OTHER HARDWOOD CONSUMERS
WAGON
COFFIN MANUFACTURERS
FURNITURE
HARDWOOD MANUFACTURERS ASS'N
CASE GOODS MANUFACTURERS
HARDWOOD RECORD CARTOONIST

product separate from veneer, precisely at a moment when cabinetmakers or small factories started to give up making their own plywood, as it became increasingly available in both made-to-order and stock panel sizes from manufacturers and importers.[30] At the same time timber companies started to adopt grading standards in order to increase confidence in both their manufacturer clients and, in turn, the end users of those products (fig. 79).

Interestingly, the German woodworking trade was also changing its terminology at about the same time. In 1906 a trade union magazine for woodworkers described a method of cross-graining veneers as new, without assigning a name to it; in 1907 it referred to making large panels by a method of blocking (verb: *absperren*; noun: *das Absperren*) or stabilizing the natural movement in the veneers through cross-lamination; in 1909 it employed the word *das Sperrholz* (a compound noun of 'blocked' and 'wood') as a term for plywood as a finished product; and by 1911 it had a separate column under the title *Sperrholz*. More general adoption in Germany followed in the 1920s only, although the term 'strong wood' (*Starkholz*) was also used. The Swedes then used the more precise term 'crossed veneers' (*Kryssfaner*) for plywood.[31]

Adoption of the term 'plywood' was gradual but steady in the English-speaking world, and noticeably faster in Britain than in the US. In 1915 an American commentator noted: 'what we call built-up panels are universally called plywood or multiplywood in Europe...'[32] The previously most popular term, '3-ply', disappeared from advertisements and articles in British trade magazines by about 1918, precisely at the time when plywood saw expanded use in wartime aircraft construction. Indeed, during the later years of the war, timber firms (both importers and manufacturers of plywood) had aimed their advertising directly at the aircraft industry, although this stopped abruptly after the Armistice of 1918.[33]

While British furniture firms spent the early 1920s still debating terminology in terms of plywood's comparison to solid wood, and very slowly moved towards urging the trade to abandon the term 'solid' entirely, American debates focused more on the ongoing problem of the word 'veneer'. Echoing pre-war views, and at a time when the term 'plywood' was already widely, though not universally, used, a trade journalist wrote that 'if veneered products are ever to gain popularity it will have to be under another name, and for that reason I would sentence 'Mr Veneered' to be shot at sunrise and buried without benefit of clergy'. Another wrote that while 'The public can be educated to an appreciation of plywood or some such name for panel stock...it would be entirely hopeless to attempt to popularize the word "veneer"'.[34] During the early 1920s, then, American advocates pressed the case for the word plywood, positively promoting 'Pride in Plywood' and reminding their colleagues: 'There is no sham in plywood.'[35]

The US and British timber trades were comfortable discussing the arguments around veneers and plywood, addressing the prejudice against them head-on. The commercial furniture trade press, however (read only by the trade itself, not by consumers), scrupulously avoided both terms, as if somehow even stating them in print could lead a tradesperson to accidentally mention them to a consumer, thereby jeopardizing a sale. This attitude would persist well into the 1930s.

### The US Federal Trade Commission hearings

Much as the 'solid versus veneer' court cases had caused problems for and damaged the reputation of the British furniture and wood industries, so too did the same American industries face a period of public excoriation arising from standard but deceptive practices by certain furniture firms. In September 1924 the Federal Trade Commission (FTC), the US government agency charged with ensuring that

79 (opposite)
**Cartoon concerning timber grading rules**
From *Hardwood Record* (25 February 1910), p. 22

business did not engage in unfair competition or deceptive practice, held hearings with representatives of the furniture, timber and advertising industries in an effort to find 'suitable trade terms to use in describing furniture to the consumer'.[36] The trade initially expressed enthusiasm for rules that would enable the FTC to prosecute those charged with misrepresentation, not least because it supported the FTC's then-current efforts to stop companies falsely advertising 'factory to you' furniture when such firms were not, in fact, manufacturers.[37] In a spirit of industry-led regulation, terminology first adopted by national furniture bodies became part of the 'rules' arising from an FTC 'trade practice conference' with the retail furniture trade held in New York City in November and again in December 1925.

The rules agreed with the retail trade (but not manufacturers or wholesalers) were seemingly straightforward and covered virtually all of the issues raised in the controversies of the early twentieth century. Clarity and accuracy in description were sought so that at every step of the supply and retail chain – from manufacturer to consumer and including invoicing and advertising – the same exact terminology would be used for any product. The use of plywood was covered in the 'interpretation of rules' that explained that if veneer was of the same type as the solid wood used on other exposed parts, it could be called solely by the name of that wood; if it was applied to a different wood (almost always the case with plywood), it must be described as veneered. Among an additional nine points of consequential interpretation was one stating that 'a wood popularly regarded as of higher value shall not be named under Rule II if an insubstantial amount' was used.[38]

Although the announcement of the rules was signed by twenty-three leading New York retailers (including many well-known department stores), in the form of a request that they receive approval for their descriptions from the FTC, manufacturers' organizations detected the heavy hand of inexpert government bureaucrats and reacted with hostility.

80 (below)

**Berkey & Gay Furniture Company catalogue page, c. 1928**

81 (above)
**Rubbing Department, Berkey & Gay Furniture Company factory, Grand Rapids, Michigan, c. 1928**
Plywood sides and backs are being abraded with wet sandpaper before polishing

Throughout 1926 trade bodies and trade journals railed against the FTC, specifically attacking the requirement that there be an obligation to designate veneered construction. A petition filed by the Furniture Manufacturers' Association of Grand Rapids, Michigan, stated that any obligation 'to specially designate veneered construction is unnecessary, harmful to the industry, and unfair to the public, because there is an unjustified prejudice against furniture of veneered construction'.[39] The latter term was clearly used at the time to indicate plywood.[40]

In June 1926, following attempts by furniture manufacturers to get the FTC to reconsider the rules, the regulator published the names of 722 firms that, following a letter from the FTC, had signed up to the new rules, as well as those of seventy-five who had not.[41] A month later, after additional firms had signed up and others had shown that they did not sell to retailers, twenty-seven firms were charged with violating Section 5 of the Federal Trade Commission Act (1914), which prohibited unfair methods of competition.

The complaint stated that the twenty-seven firms, all from the 'furniture city' of Grand Rapids, manufactured furniture that was identified as being made of 'walnut and gumwood' or 'mahogany and gumwood'. 'Practically all of the pieces of furniture' were veneered (in fact, made using plywood for flat surfaces) and this fact was not disclosed in catalogues (fig. 80), advertisements or invoices. This mislabelling resulted in retail dealers committing 'a deception or fraud upon the public', given that 'numerous persons have been induced by such means to purchase veneered furniture manufactured and sold by respondent[s] in the belief that the exposed portions of such furniture was [*sic*] made of solid mahogany or solid walnut' (fig. 81). Finally, as competitors of these firms clearly labelled their similar furniture as 'veneered' and named the woods

82 (opposite)
**'Is Veneer Better Than Solid? If So, Why?',**
*Furniture Record* cover, April 1926

of 'the core of such furniture', the firms' alleged violation of the 1914 Act 'causes trade to be diverted to respondent[s] from such competitors'.[42]

For the next four years those firms that refused to follow the new rules tussled with the FTC in briefs, hearings and, finally, the US Court of Appeals, where the FTC was sued by the original group of companies charged.[43] During this time the arguments on both sides remained the same. The FTC held that despite the fact that 'all of the respondents utilize so-called plywood in the manufacture of their furniture, which they veneer with an exterior ply of walnut or mahogany...the core consists of [woods]...less expensive' that were never identified to the customer.[44] Manufacturers argued that although:

> efforts are now being put forth by the cabinet wood producers, by the manufacturers of veneers and plywood, by the trade journal [*sic*], and by many other agencies to educate the public to the value of veneered construction...we feel that the time is coming when its value will be generally known...we submit, however, that that time has not yet come and that the industry should not be required to bear the burden of that education at the cost not only financially but its artistic progress, which would be inevitable if the designation veneered be insisted upon.[45]

On the matter of accurately describing their furniture, the Grand Rapids manufacturers initially replied that they did so correctly by naming the woods of the exposed surfaces, as was standard industry practice. Later in the legal process they changed tack, asserting that they 'do not build their furniture of a wood of inferior value, with a veneering of superior wood'. They argued that the FTC was wrong to suggest that the purpose of 'a veneer covering' of fine wood was 'to cheapen production and palm off on the consumer an *inferior product*'; that 'ply-wood or veneer panels are the only practical construction for flat surfaces'; and that it was a matter of record that 'plywood construction costs twice as much as solid construction'. Highlighting the extent to which plywood was used in US furniture manufacture by the late 1920s, lawyers for the manufacturers argued that they could not possibly have misled furniture dealers, who 'were thoroughly conversant with ply-wood construction' as it was used in 'substantially all of the case goods sold by them'.[46]

Finally, in June 1930, the US Court of Appeals ruled against the FTC, finding that there was no intention to deceive on the part of the manufacturers. The judge, somewhat surprisingly, also agreed against the FTC that 'the record affirmatively discloses, without dispute, that all furniture of the better quality has its flat surfaces constructed of ply wood, or laminated and veneered woods, and that only the cheaper and poorer grades of less valuable material are construction of solid woods'. The judge contributed to the contemporary view of plywood by writing that 'The record discloses, without dispute, that the finest of modern furniture, having exposed flat surfaces...are constructed of laminated wood, with the grains of the various layers running in different directions...The practice is substantially universal.'[47]

# FURNITURE RECORD

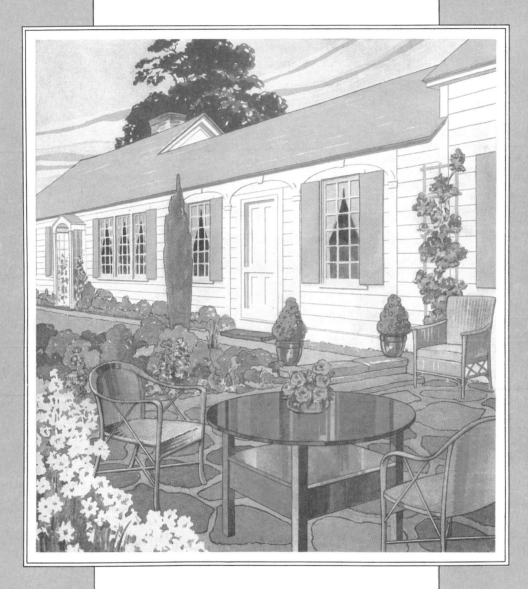

## Is Veneer Better Than Solid? If So, Why?

A Most Comprehensive Discussion in Word and Picture on How Plywoods are Made

PERIODICAL PUBLISHING CO.

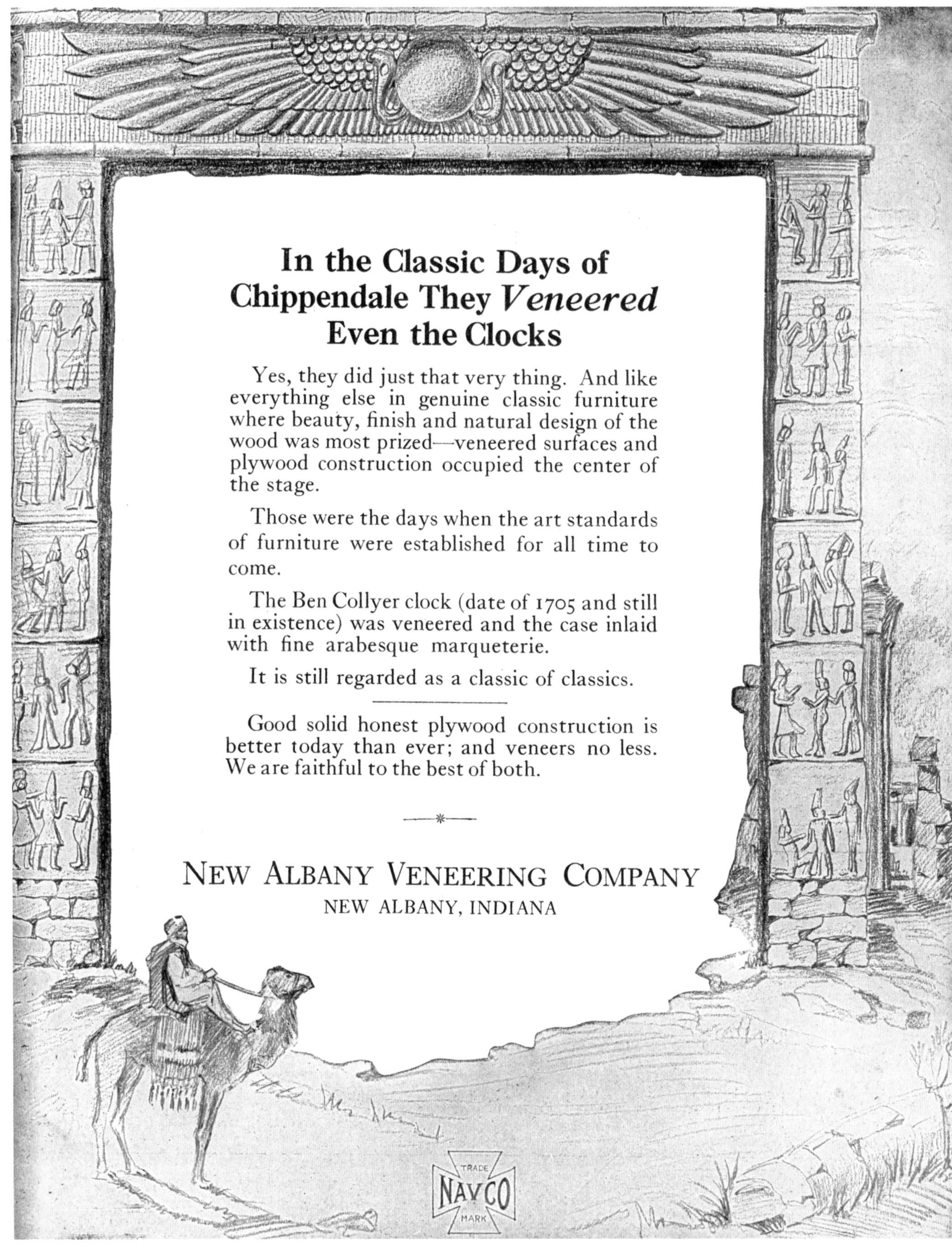
In the Classic Days of Chippendale They *Veneered* Even the Clocks
Yes, they did just that very thing. And like everything else in genuine classic furniture where beauty, finish and natural design of the wood was most prized—veneered surfaces and plywood construction occupied the center of the stage.
Those were the days when the art standards of furniture were established for all time to come.
The Ben Collyer clock (date of 1705 and still in existence) was veneered and the case inlaid with fine arabesque marqueterie.
It is still regarded as a classic of classics.
Good solid honest plywood construction is better today than ever; and veneers no less. We are faithful to the best of both.
NEW ALBANY VENEERING COMPANY
NEW ALBANY, INDIANA
TRADE
NAVCO
MARK

## The fight for a reputation

Well before the conclusion of the FTC case in the US, and concurrent with the 'solid versus veneer' debate in Britain, the international effort to educate the trade as to the qualities and benefits of plywood had begun (fig. 82). This had heretofore consisted mainly of advice on how to follow best practice in making and using plywood. But in the mid-1920s a concerted effort began to improve the status of plywood by invoking an (allegedly) venerable history of veneers and plywood stretching back to the ancient world. This included citing famous historical figures associated with key examples of furniture that was said to be plywood, but was in fact only veneered (fig. 83). Those two terms – veneer and plywood – were, as they had been in the nineteenth century, used synonymously, sometimes with no distinction between them. For example, a long article entitled 'Plywood Makes Better Furniture and Here's Why', published in the American trade magazine *Furniture Record* in 1926, began by invoking the long history of veneered furniture and associating it with the French queen Marie Antoinette and Napoleon, Emperor of France, among others.[48] It even addressed head-on the common meanings of 'superfluity or unreality' and everyday usages such as 'a veneer of respectability'. But 'Plywood', its author Thomas Perry wrote, 'is a newer and better term to apply to the use of veneer in furniture'. In fact, Perry used arguments and vocabulary identical to those raised against advocates of solid furniture and against the FTC. In Britain, plywood was described as 'a new material in furniture construction', thus arguing not only for its basis in history but also for its modernity.[49]

In 1927 the first substantial book on plywood was published in New York, with a British edition the following year and a German one in 1930.[50] Written by two industry professionals, E. Vernon Knight and Meinrad Wulpi, promotional and educational in nature, and aimed squarely at woodworking professionals, the first 100 (of 350) pages were, remarkably, devoted to the history of veneering and plywood (fig. 15) and filled with illustrations of historical furniture; however, relatively few of these examples were clearly identified by the authors as being of plywood construction. In 1928 *Good Furniture* magazine published 'The Romance of Cabinet Woods. Antiquity of Veneering', which began with mention of Pliny and the etymology of the word veneer. After this point, most general literature on plywood invoked this same history.

By this time there was one area of manufacture where the reputation of plywood was not in doubt and where important technical advances had been made: the manufacture of aeroplanes. Although this use was covered extensively in aeroplane trade journals, mentioned extensively in Knight and Wulpi's 1927 book, and occasionally referred to in wood trade publications, this significant of use of plywood was not the subject of much attention in popular literature until during and after World War II.

83 (opposite)
**New Albany Veneering Company advertisement**
From *Hardwood Record* (25 October 1925), p. 41

# 4 'Plywood Flies and Fights' (1911–1945)[1]

Efforts by the wood industry to argue or publicize its way to public acceptance of plywood represented a long, even arduous, struggle in the first decades of the twentieth century. At the same time plywood gradually earned a reputation for exceptional strength, durability and reliability, not through a product with which most people came into contact but, instead, through its use in aeroplanes. While plywood was employed for many aeroplane parts, this chapter focuses primarily on the material's use in monocoque fuselages, one of the most radical and successful innovations in twentieth-century aircraft design.

Until the mid-1930s most aeroplanes were made primarily of wood. Some notable and well-publicized experiments with plywood in aircraft construction were undertaken before the start of World War I in 1914, but it was war-related use that led to increased knowledge of and interest in the material. As war began, the pressing need to increase production, to make aeroplanes faster to build and to fly, to maximize the use of wood and, above all, to create planes that were lighter and stronger drove the first sustained and science-based research into the properties and performance of plywood. This research went hand in hand with work to create a standard, efficient form for aircraft design. Plywood was centrally important in early twentieth-century attempts to create a discrete, streamlined and self-supporting structure for mass-producible planes.

### Plywood before World War I

In 1884 Captain Ogneslav Kostovich, a Serbian engineer resident in St Petersburg, began constructing an airship made mostly from plywood (fig. 85). The airship was built around a central shaft, from which struts and cross-braces held in place a hydrogen-filled silk membrane, with a gondola at its base. Plywood was used for structural parts including the shaft, the gondola, the tunnel for the main drive shaft, the propeller and the steering wheels.[2]

A magazine article of 1882 described the airship's proposed construction from, in part, 'a special material invented by Mr Kostovich, comprising silk and wood', which was 'distinguished by its particular density...

84 (opposite)
**Workman carrying a complete Deperdussin monocoque fuselage**
Deperdussin factory, Paris, c. 1912

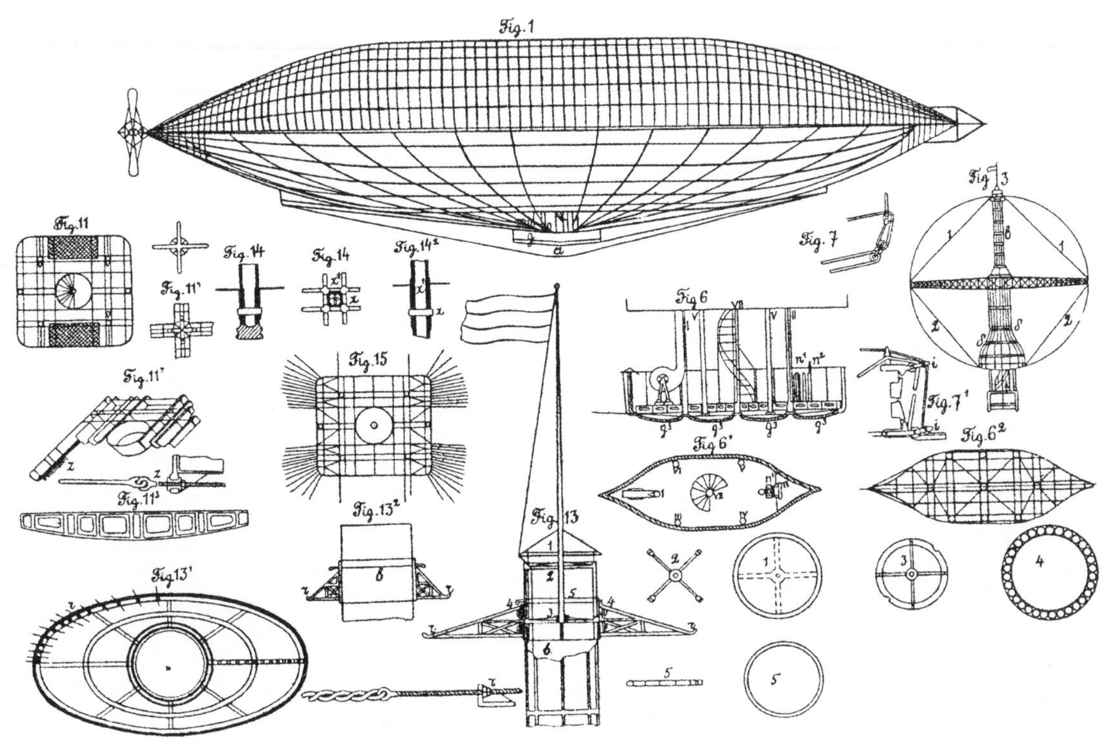


85 (left)
**Designs for plywood-framed airship**
Ogneslav Kostovich, St Petersburg, 1884

elasticity and lightness'. Kostovich is said to have developed the machines and technology to produce this type of plywood (which he called 'arboryte') as none then existed in Russia. He also manufactured a glue later described as not dissolving 'in hot or cold water' and made from a secret recipe.[3]

In 1884 Kostovich applied for a Russian patent (said to have been granted in 1887) for the production of hollow timber vessels with a drawing of 'an airship's gondola, which could also serve as a boat in water'.[4] Precisely such a drawing (fig. 86) was included in Kostovich's British patent (no. 5942), which he applied for in the same year (granted in January 1885) and which described the use of plywood for the 'construction of aerial machines, furniture and carriages'. Echoing George Gardner's original seat patent of 1872 (fig. 35), Kostovich stated that when extreme tightness between layers was required – as in the case of tubes – 'layers of silk, calico or the like' could be placed between the veneers. Like John K. Mayo's patent of 1865 (fig. 30), Kostovich's advocated in particular the use of plywood for round forms including 'conduit pipes, hoops, columns, [and] masts'.[5]

Despite support from shareholders and, eventually, the Russian War Ministry, Kostovich ran out of money and had to abandon his project in 1890. By this stage he had already completed construction of many parts of the airship.[6] Although never flown, Kostovich's airship is the earliest known example of plywood being used in the construction of aircraft. The requirement that airships be as light and strong as possible meant that it continued to play a part in their design, most notably in the plywood skeletons used for dirigibles built by the German company Schütte-Lanz in the 1910s.[7]

### Plywood-clad aeroplanes

In the period from 1909 to 1919 plywood was increasingly introduced into European aircraft design.[8] Its initial use was as a cladding to the most common fuselage construction of the period, described at the time as box (or lattice) girder or truss construction (fig. 87). The box girder design was derived from bridge building and consisted of a series of longitudinal and vertical solid wood girders forming the external frame of the aircraft. Normally the box girder structure required extensive wire bracing within the fuselage and to support the wings, in both cases adding strength and stiffness to the structure. Such early aeroplanes were generally covered with canvas or linen (sometimes rubberized) to minimize weight and to reduce drag. In 1909 the design by Léon Levavasseur (1863–1922) for the French Antoinette monoplane (fig. 88), although of box girder construction, differed from typical versions in that most of the front section of the aeroplane, nearly half of the fuselage length, was covered with cedar-veneered plywood.[9] The function of the cladding was to add strength to the structure and improve on the functioning of the canvas covering. Unusually, the fuselage was

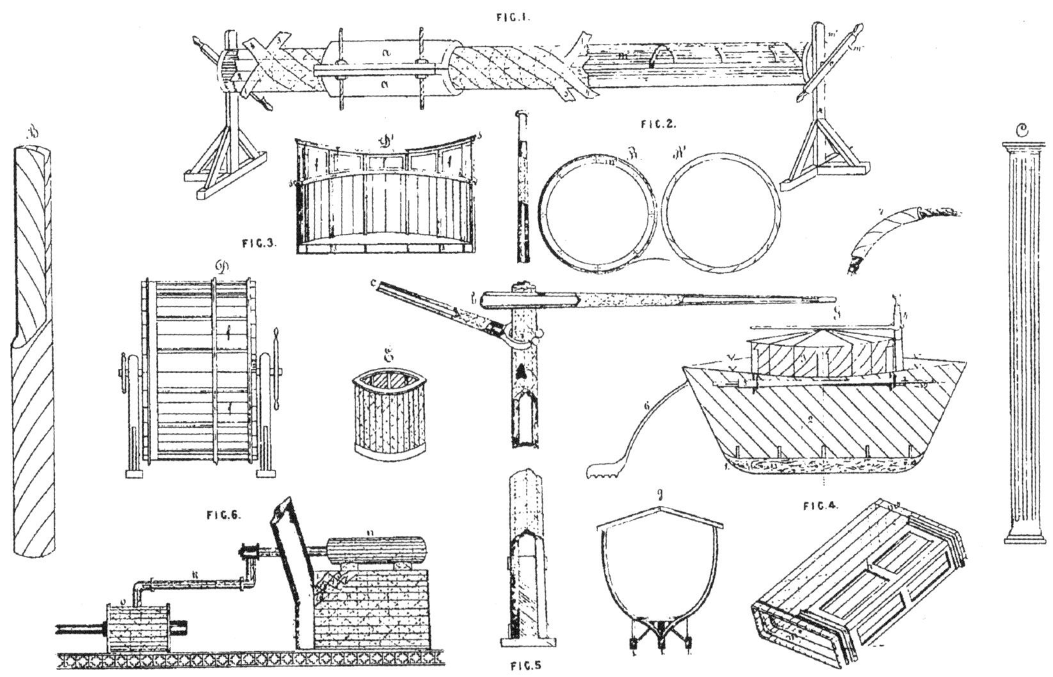


86 (right)
**Illustration from Ognеslav Kostovits [Kostovich], patent for 'Improvements in the Manufacture of Various Articles of Wood'**
Application filed 4 April 1884, issued 2 January 1885, British patent no. 5942

87 (left)

**The American aviator Harriet Quimby standing in front of a truss-constructed Blériot XI type monoplane, 1911**

88 (below)

**'Fighting the Storm'**
I.E. Delaspre, chromolithograph of Hubert Latham's Antoinette at Blackpool, Lancashire, 1909

89 (above)
**Airco DH-4 biplanes in flight over France during World War I, 1914–18**

V-shaped in elevation, like the bow of a boat, suggesting the many close connections that existed in this period between aeroplane and boat design.[10]

Other early aeroplane designers to experiment with part or full plywood cladding include the Russian financier Steglau whose biplane, flown in the 1912 Russian Military Aviation Competition, was described in the contemporary British press as having been 'entirely constructed of wood, even to the plane surfaces'.[11] Plywood cladding was also used in early planes designed by the Russian engineer Igor Sikorsky (1889–1972), first in his S-6A (tested in March 1912), a biplane whose aft-fuselage was clad in 4 mm (5⁄32 in.) plywood.[12] Sikorsky went on to design the Russian Grand (1913), the world's first four-engined, multi-passenger plane. The Grand's very large, 72-ft (22-m) long fuselage was built in two parts, constructed of four main ash longerons supported by transverse and vertical members of pine. The structure was diagonally braced, then clad in 4 mm plywood.[13]

### Plywood research during World War I: plywood and glue

Plywood-clad box girder structures were used extensively during World War I. The British de Havilland DH-4 bomber biplane (fig. 86) was particularly important owing to its adoption in 1917 by the American military, for whom 3,400 were built in the US as the Airco DH-4.[14] Of traditional box girder and biplane construction, each American version of the plane required 143 mainly three-ply panels, some 500 sq ft (46.5 sq m) in 20 sizes.[15] More than half the length of the DH-4 (from the front of the fuselage as far back as the gunner's cockpit) was clad in plywood, meaning that wire bracing could be dispensed with. The rearmost of the five bays of the rear fuselage was also covered in three-ply, while internal plywood formers helped retain the fuselage shape along its axis, and machine-gun and control supports were made of thicker 13- and 26-ply.[16] Research undertaken in the US in 1917–18 led to the introduction of plywood for these parts, and also for the wing ribs. This was a modification from the plane's original manufacture in Britain.

It was the use of plywood in American planes (particularly the DH-4) that led to much of the early scientific research into the material. Government-sponsored research on plywood was first undertaken in the US and with a sense of urgency in June 1917, owing to demands that the US War Department produce 22,000 aeroplanes within 13 months. The research was undertaken by engineers and scientists at the Forest Products Laboratory (FPL) in Madison, Wisconsin (founded in 1909), part of the US Forest Service. The FPL collaborated with manufacturers to develop technologies and products, and (when not a matter of national security) freely disseminated all of its findings to the public. In addition to a range of research into solid woods used in aircraft, FPL staff were charged with finding formulas for waterproof glues that would work in demanding and constantly changing atmospheric conditions, and with comprehensively testing 'the mechanical and physical properties of plywood', then described as 'an unexplored field'.[17]

Up until 1917 most plywood in the US was made with animal glue (made with gelatin from animal hides, hooves and bones) or starch glue (a vegetable base of cassava, sometimes mixed with corn or potato). While such glues sufficed for the then largest plywood uses such as panels or doors, neither type was water-resistant, let alone waterproof. European and American companies had attempted to use glues based on blood albumin (or serum albumin, a component of animal blood) or casein (milk protein) as a water-resistant product and some, like Luther (see p. 48) or the Haskell Manufacturing Company (Ludington and Grand Rapids, Michigan) had some success. Haskell marketed their 'veneer' or 'v'neer' canoe (fig. 90), made with blood albumin glue, as a revolutionary, waterproof product of extraordinary strength. However, private companies closely guarded their formulas for such water-resistant glues, meaning that the FPL did not pursue cooperation over their development. The FPL was experimenting in 1917 with casein glue for use in joining solid wood propeller laminates, as it had potential for greater resistance to moisture but was then made by only one firm in the US.[18]

The need for waterproof glue for plywood became more pressing in late 1917, when additional government funding was allocated to speed up work on the US construction of the de Havilland (Airco) DH-4 bombers (fig. 89). During 1917 and 1918 the FPL, having canvassed industry practice and tested glues from relevant firms, instituted inspection standards, established that insufficient supplies of blood albumin required the use of more than one type of glue, and, finally, in April 1918, developed water-resistant casein and blood albumin glue formulas, which they supplied to manufacturers. Plywoods made from these glues survived twenty-four-hour boiling tests and ten days' immersion in room-temperature water. The FPL then provided advice on the making, mixing and applying of glues, and – as they would for their other plywood

90 (below)
**Haskell Manufacturing Company, advertisement for veneer canoe**
From *Popular Science* (November 1922), p. 533

# Frail Canoe Supports Heavy Weight

**The weight of seven men added to the ton load of heavy sand failed to buckle this canoe built of thin layers of veneer**

TO DEMONSTRATE the strength of a new style canoe built of veneer, it was subjected recently to a weight of 3420 pounds. The sag was only three-quarters inch. By making the veneer in long sheets, the canoes are molded without joints below the waterline, except at the ends.

91 (below)

**Method of testing the strength of thin plywood by dropping a cast-iron ball from different heights**
US Forest Products Laboratory, Madison, Wisconsin, c. 1919

92 (right)

**Method of testing the strength of plywood through 'column bending'**
US Forest Products Laboratory, Madison, Wisconsin, c. 1920

93 (below right)

**Electric dough mixer used for mixing glue**
US Forest Products Laboratory, Madison, Wisconsin, c. 1944

research – shared their results through publication, trained government inspectors, answered enquiries from the trade, and sent 'trouble men' to assist with problems at plywood panel factories. The result of the work on glue was described by the FPL after the war as 'practically…developing…a new industry [and]… removing scarcity of plywood as a controlling factor in aircraft production' owing to lack of sufficient suitable glue.[19] Glue would from this time become the key area of technological development that would enable significant improvements to plywood (fig. 93).

Gaining an understanding of the material properties of plywood paralleled the work on glues, and the FPL were almost certainly the first organization to adopt standardized methods of testing wood.[20] The types of tests undertaken on plywood concentrated on the following areas: bending (fig. 92), tension, splitting, warping, shrinkage, and measuring stiffness and strength (modulus of elasticity; fig. 91). Most of these tests involved a huge number of experiments varying the species of veneers used (up to thirty-four) when analysing the thickness of plies, the number of plies, the angles at which the plies were glued, the effect of using different woods for core and faces, and the methods of joining ply panels and of cutting veneers.

New ways of making aeroplane parts from plywood were developed based on the results of these tests, among them the radical redesign of wing ribs, in a much lighter form, and of wing beams. Both parts were made from plywood for the first time (fig. 94). The wing beam designs, and also new designs using plywood for engine bearers or bulkheads, were immediately used in the building of the DH-4 (fig. 89).[21] The FPL's research established that plywood had a superior strength-to-weight ratio, a measure of the efficiency of a material in terms of how much weight it can carry in relation to its own. This was crucially important in aircraft, which aim to be as light and as strong as possible.

Information on the FPL's wartime experiments was published after the end of the war in 1918. The free availability of their reports, and the publication of these within government reports and trade journals, meant that from 1920 onwards the FPL's research informed design and manufacturing not only in the US but also around the world. The wood and furniture trades welcomed the success of plywood's military use, hoping that 'the seal of Government approval placed on built-up stock for airplane construction will probably be the last indorsement [*sic*] required to forever lay the bugaboo associated with veneers'.[22]

94 (below)

**Prototypes for the DH-4 wing rib**
US Forest Products Laboratory, Madison, Wisconsin, 1918

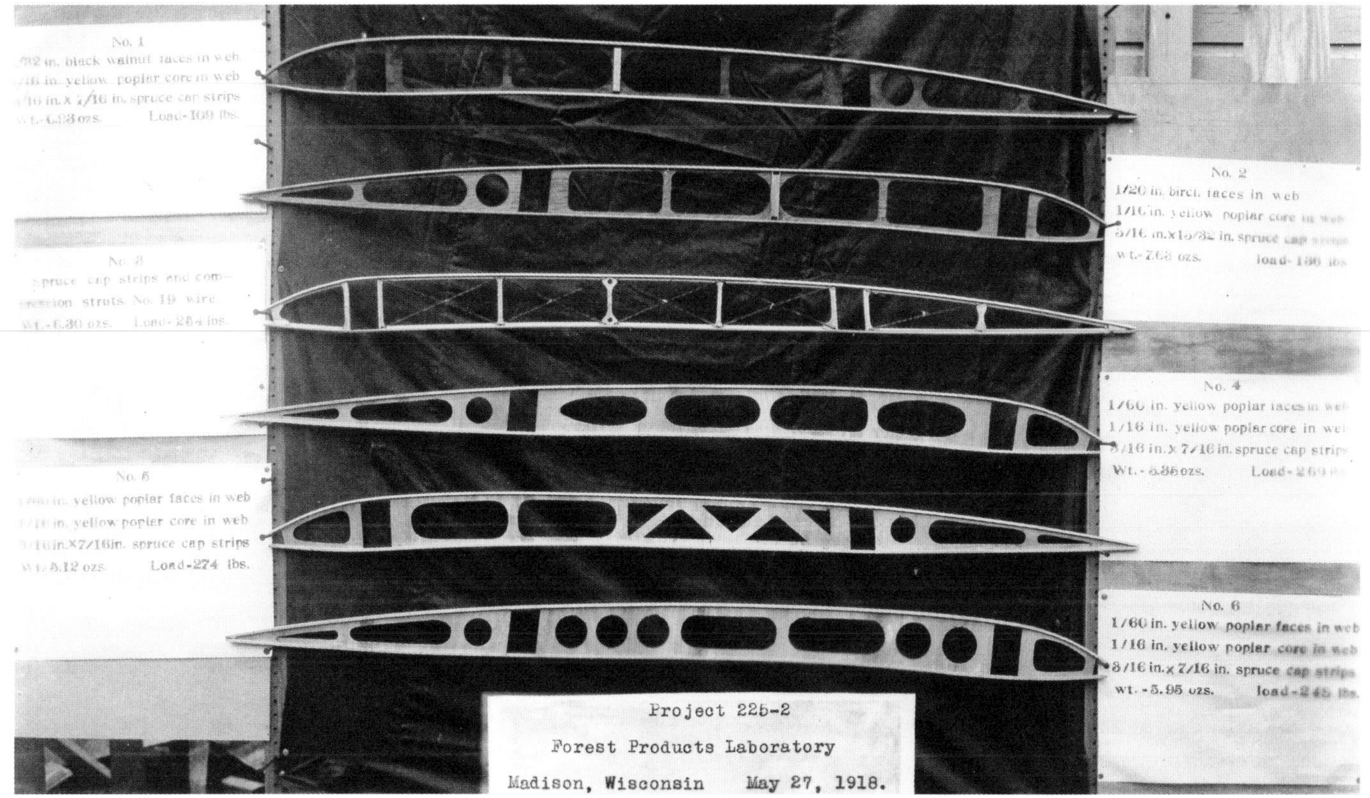

## Plywood monocoques

Alongside this history of scientific testing and standardization, experiments were being made throughout the early twentieth century with new types of fuselage design. In many ways it was plywood that enabled the most radical change in this field in 1911: a new type of fuselage that dispensed entirely with box girder construction. This streamlined design quickly became the most sought-after form for modern aeroplane construction.

A patent application was filed in April 1911 (granted in August 1911) by the French businessman Armand Deperdussin (c. 1866–1924) for the fabrication of fuselages for aeroplanes, boats and other craft (fig. 95).[23] The patent describes the forming of a fully enclosed body, built using a plywood technique of layering thin strips of poplar (*tulipier*) veneer over a two-part mould. Three layers of wood were built up, each running diagonally across the mould and with the grain in the opposite direction to that of the layer below. These narrow strips of veneer attached along both sides of the mould to longerons, long timber struts that ran the length of the body and held the two moulded halves together in the finished plane. Once the two parts of the plane had been moulded and joined, the whole was covered in a varnished textile in order to strengthen the body.[24] This type of plywood construction, with each layer made of narrow strips, worked on a similar principle to the ideas that both Mayo (fig. 30) and Kostovich (fig. 85) had for the construction of plywood tubes. Known as a monocoque ('single shell'), from its French origins, the design for this new type of fuselage was attributed to Deperdussin's head engineer, Louis Béchereau. It was revolutionary, mainly because its moulded construction in a streamlined shape enabled flight at then unheard-of speeds.

The moulded plywood shell was strong enough to be self-supporting, meaning that the plane did not need any internal structure or cross-bracing. This type of construction would later be called 'stressed skin', as the structural stresses were distributed throughout the entire surface of the shell rather than carried by beams and additional structural members. The moulded plywood shell held the plane's fuselage in constant, equal tension – unlike truss and box girder fuselages, which had to be regularly readjusted to ensure that tensions between the structural members remained well-balanced. The monocoque design made Deperdussin's plane very streamlined and light – the completed fuselage weighed only 22 kg (48½ lbs) (fig. 96) and the shell was only 4 mm (5⁄32 in.) thick. The monocoque's 'torpedo type' body reduced air resistance by 60 to 85%, enabling it to set a world speed record of 200 km (about 124 miles) per hour in 1913.[25]

Deperdussin were by no means the only or the first firm to experiment with monocoque construction.[26] Almost exactly contemporary with Béchereau's plane, the Swiss aviator Eugène Ruchonnet designed and, in late 1911, flew another plywood monocoque, dubbed the 'cigare' (fig. 97). Ruchonnet had applied to patent a technique for moulding a monocoque fuselage around a trellis-like structure in June 1911. The plane, which had a much longer fuselage than Deperdussin's, was never developed due to Ruchonnet's death in a plane crash in January 1912.[27]

95 (below)

**Illustration from Armand Deperdussin, patent for a 'Method of Manufacturing Fuselages for Airplanes, Boats and other Craft'**
Application filed 12 April 1911, issued 30 August 1911, French patent no. 428412

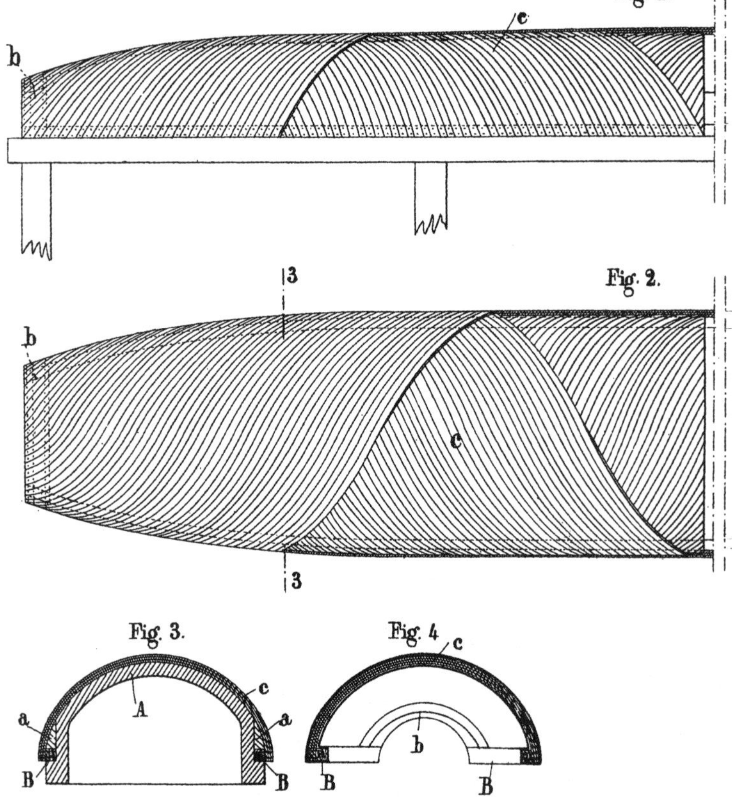

*Aérodrome de la VIDAMÉE, entre CHANTILLY et SENLIS*
Monoplan Ruchonnet - Le « Cigare » (Moteur Verdet 60 HP)

Prévost, photo. Chantilly (Oise)    Reproduction interdite

96 (above)

**Workman carrying a complete Deperdussin monocoque fuselage weighing only 22 kg**
Deperdussin factory, Paris, c. 1912

97 (left)

**Eugène Ruchonnet sitting in his monocoque plane, the 'cigare'**
France, 1911

Despite Ruchonnet's attempt at a closed, single-shell fuselage, the Deperdussin was by far the most successful early example of this type of design. Béchereau's plane took the aviation world by storm in 1912, when Deperdussin monocoques won the world's speed air racing competition (the Gordon Bennett Trophy); they then did so again in 1913 (fig. 98). The planes were lauded everywhere for their remarkable construction and speed and were the stars of the Paris Air Shows (Salons d'Aviation). As the French newspaper *Le Journal* reported in its article about the 1912 show: 'Everyone has arrived at the 1912 Salon with the idea of "doing a Deperdussin", that is to say designing a monocoque plane, of strong construction and made of the best quality materials.'[28] An aircraft magazine wrote, 'A perfect fuselage...is the Deperdussin monocoque, whose construction we see as great progress....We have here a fuselage of only 4 mm thick and which weighs only 22 kg. It has nonetheless a perfect rigidity and offers great resistance to all localised shocks, protecting the aviator very effectively in the case of a crash.'[29] An American journalist reflected international interest: '...why shouldn't we construct a racer along "Dep" lines, if a racer is going to be constructed? The "monocoque" is the last word in high speed construction and all racers will be along the same lines.'[30] And the speed and compactness of the Deperdussin were also quickly seen by a British journalist as a useful starting point for a new breed of military aircraft: 'The *monocoque* is supreme.'[31]

### 'True' and semi-monocoques

Although there were practical reasons why traditional truss or box girder aeroplane design continued to hold sway (in particular, the speed of its construction), the competitive success and publicity of the Deperdussin in the decade after 1912 made it a touchstone in the design of monocoque aircraft. The case for and against monocoques involved a question of terminology that bears explanation, as it is so central to the use of plywood in aircraft.

The Deperdussin type of construction was, soon after its introduction, described as a 'true monocoque', indicating that it was made without (or with very few) internal reinforcements. A different method of building up the fuselage from flat pieces of plywood over a

98 (below)
**Deperdussin monocoque flown by Maurice Prévost winning the Gordon Bennett Trophy**
Reims, France, 1913

combination of longerons, ribs, formers and bulkheads to form a single, streamlined unit was described as a semi-monocoque or built-up construction. In a semi-monocoque aeroplane the weight was distributed not only over the body of the fuselage but also through the internal supports. There was and remains a wide overlap of usage between the two terms and a strict definition would, in fact, describe virtually all plywood monocoques as semi-monocoques (the Deperdussin, for example, is actually moulded around two longerons).[32]

Despite this consistent need for internal support, descriptions of aircraft design from the 1910s to the 1940s insist on a distinction between the 'true' and the semi-monocoque. This fetish to classify highlights the importance placed in this period on the development of a purely moulded form. As in the field of prefabricated housing, where the aim of much early twentieth-century theory was the creation of a template that could be rolled in its thousands off the assembly line (see chapter 5), attempts to design a mass-producible 'true' monocoque were very closely linked to the question of materials. Plywood occupied a central but tenuous position in this discussion, as it offered at the time the most successful means of building strong fuselages, but was also time-consuming to mould and often seen as an insufficiently standardized or modern material.[33] Much of the work on plywood monocoques, from the 1910s onwards, aimed to standardize both the means of production, and the material itself. This was done firstly through the development of new techniques for moulding monocoque and semi-monocoque fuselages (both during and after World War I). The image of an entirely self-supporting plane then reappeared with particular force in the late 1930s, when the advent of synthetic adhesives promised a new type of entirely modern plywood.

### New moulding techniques

There was a frenzy of activity involving plywood monocoques both immediately before and during World War I.[34] While military authorities in various countries were enticed by the speed of monocoque aircraft and dreamed of future possibilities, there were fears that true monocoques could not be adapted to large-scale production during wartime owing to the amount of time required both to lay strips of wood over a mould and for the glued assembly to dry completely (seven days was cited for one American example). Built-up, semi-monocoque construction was faster, and most of the early aircraft (both experimental and manufactured models) used substantial internal frameworks aimed at combining competitive manufacturing times with lightweight, streamlined forms. The US Army – working with the Haskelite plywood company (previously the Haskell Manufacturing Company, see p. 77 and n. 18), two furniture manufacturers, and the FPL's plywood research – built a series of experimental plywood semi-monocoque fuselages during the war (figs 99–100).[35] Different techniques were attempted, including the application of a fully moulded plywood skin versus the

99 and 100 (below)

**Monocoque fuselages developed for the US Army by the Haskelite Corporation (above) and J.C. Widman Co. (below) in collaboration with the US Forest Products Laboratory**

From *Bulletin of the Engineering Department, Aeroplane Engineering Division* (October 1918), pp. 6 and 11

101 (below)

**Albatros D.Va brought down by Australian airmen**
France, 17 December 1917

102 (opposite)

**Loughead S-1 on the cover of *The Ace* magazine, May 1920**

use of small moulded pieces to build up a cladding, and although this project was abandoned owing to the Armistice, the US Army (and, later, the US Navy) felt positive about the possibilities of semi-monocoque construction.[36]

Despite this American experimentation, Germany was the only country to successfully produce semi-monocoque planes in large numbers during World War I. The Berlin-based Albatros Werke began life building the plywood-clad French Antoinette aeroplane and between 1916 and 1917 made a series of semi-monocoque reconnaissance and fighter biplanes. These included the flat-sided but curved-top 'C' class, clad entirely in plywood and with transverse bulkheads (including engine bearers) and formers in plywood that allowed for dispensing with struts and cross-members in the fuselage.[37] Of more obviously streamlined, monocoque form was the engineer Robert Thelen's successful series of 'D' class fighters, in particular the 1917 Albatros D.V (and the slightly modified D.Va, the final iterations of the plane and the only models in the series with fully rounded fuselages; fig. 101). Each side of the D.V's fuselage was formed as a single plywood skin using a very different technique from that found in the Deperdussin monocoque. The skin was made up of rectangular panels of plywood that were scarf-jointed, then moulded into shape as a continuous curved piece. Once moulded, the two long skins were attached with screws, nails and glue to the plane's formers and longerons.[38] The formation of a moulded skin from panels had clear advantages in terms of speed of assembly over the Deperdussin technique, and one American commentator who unfavourably compared the British and French use of plywood to that of 'better German aeroplanes' was clearly referring to the Albatros.[39] The best-known and most fruitful work on monocoques in the interwar years came from the designs of the Loughead (later Lockheed) brothers, working in southern California from 1919.[40] There they designed a very small, pared-down, sporting biplane, dubbed the S-1 (fig. 102), which they thought would be suitable for a post-war market of recreational flyers. For this model they created an innovative method for making a strong monocoque shell at considerable

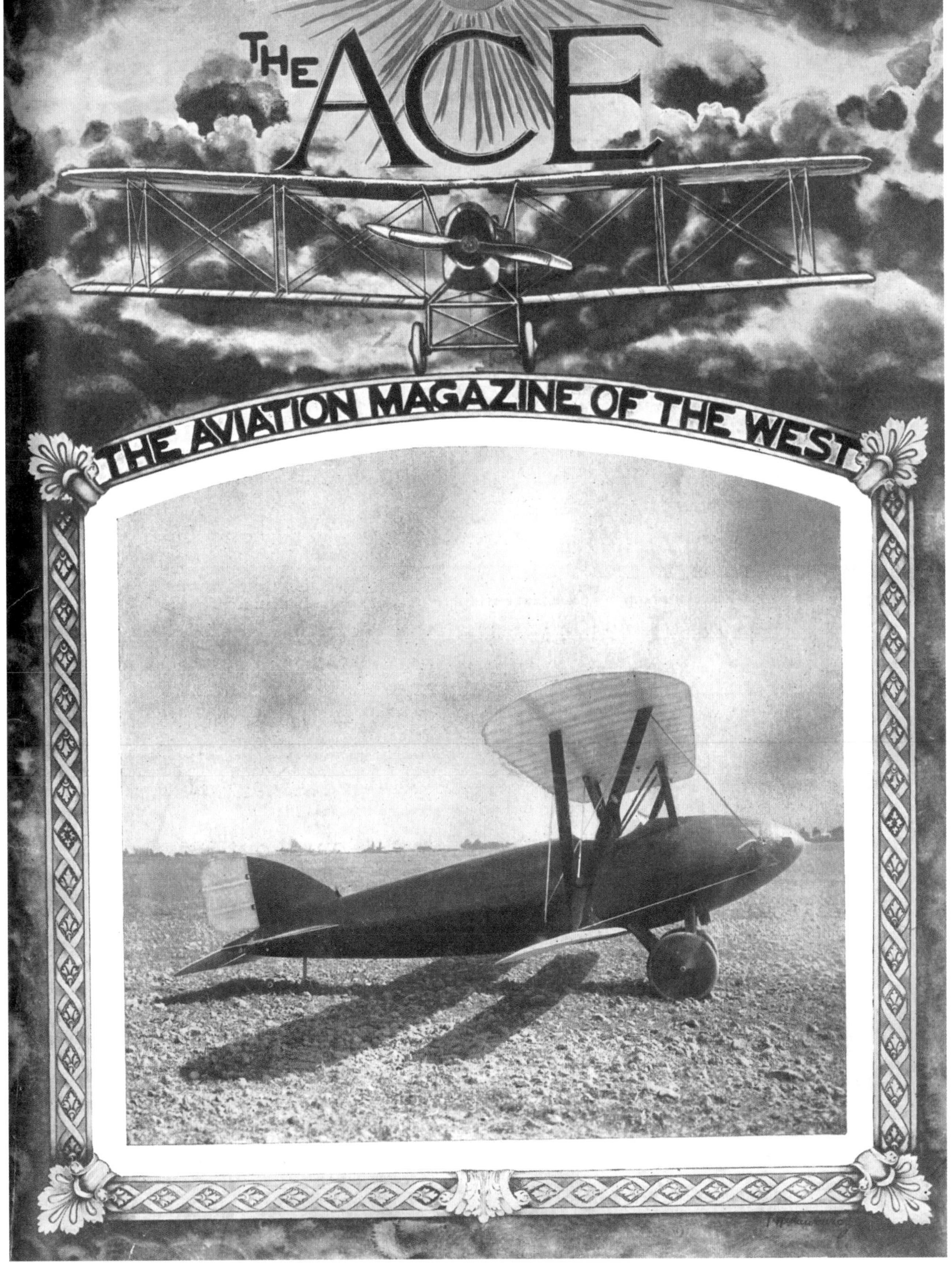
THE ACE
THE AVIATION MAGAZINE OF THE WEST

speed that they would apply to numerous of their later aeroplanes.

At the time the Lougheads first began designing monocoque fuselages, an Albatros D.Va (given by the French government after the war) was on display at the De Young Museum in San Francisco.[41] One of the chief Loughead engineers is said to have studied an Albatros plane, and while documentation of this has not been found, the contemporary display of the D.Va in California supports this suggestion. The Albatros's public exhibition highlights the means by which information about plane design was transferred both during and immediately after World War I: the aeronautical press was at that time full of articles describing the construction of captured enemy planes, and a number of different German aircraft were sent for study and display in Allied countries. The quick dissemination of technical information that this allowed could clearly be very fruitful. Whether or not any member of the Loughead team had studied an Albatros, the Loughead S-1 very cleverly combined aspects of both Albatros and Deperdussin moulded construction.[42]

In 1919 Malcolm Loughead (1887–1958) applied for a patent for 'Manufacturing Curved Forms of Plywood...particularly applicable to the manufacture of airplane bodies...' (fig. 103).[43] The patent described and illustrated part of an innovative, two-stage process for making a monocoque in two parts. The first stage made use of a convex wooden form onto which each of the three layers of veneer that would form half of the fuselage was individually laid as a series of strips and 'temporarily fastened', but without the layers being bonded to one another. In the patent the top and bottom layers were composed of diagonally laid strips and the middle layer was made from longitudinally laid strips running the entire length of the fuselage (said to have been 21 ft [6.4 m]). Each of these shaped layers was removed from the form and stored until required for final assembly. The three thin layers were then joined in a substantial concave mould (neither described nor illustrated in the patent). Both casein glue and 'binding cloth' were added between layers and uniform pressure of 20 lbs (9 kg) per square inch applied until the glue was set.[44]

Photographs of the S-1 production process were not published at the time the prototype was first flown in 1920 (hardly unusual as the designers would have wanted to protect key features of the process), and it was not until nine years later that important details of the construction were fully revealed. This was largely because the patent was not granted until 1922, by which time the Loughead company had gone out of business.[45] A new firm named the Lockheed Aircraft Company was formed in 1926 as a partnership between Allan Loughead (1889–1969) and his former collaborator the engineer Jack Northrop (1895–1981). At this time they returned to the S-1 monoplane design and, by 1927, had modified it as the Vega, a larger and faster aeroplane aimed at a wider market.

In 1928 Lockheed's chief engineer, Gerard Vultee, published a detailed, extensively illustrated description of the Vega's construction. Disseminated widely, this description filled many of the gaps in the Lougheads' original patent.[46] In Vultee's account, each fuselage half-shell was made from sliced (rather than rotary-cut) spruce veneer, with the external and inner layers running longitudinally along the fuselage length and the middle layer around its width. This was the opposite of the arrangement of layers described in the S-1 patent – the use of two longitudinal layers was probably intended to speed up the production process as forming perpendicular layers was more time-consuming.[47] The long pieces were taped together on the form, then folded and set aside while the middle layer (glued together) was removed from the mould.

103 (below)

**Illustration from Malcolm Loughead, patent for a 'Process of Manufacturing Curved Forms of Plywood or Fibrous Compositions'**
Application filed 12 August 1919, issued 8 August 1922, US patent no. 1,425,113

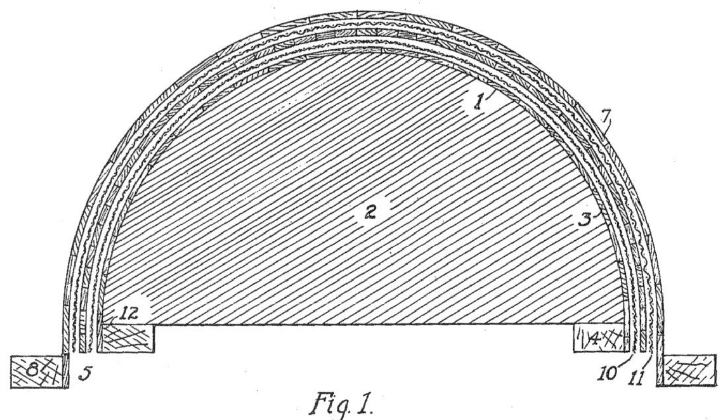


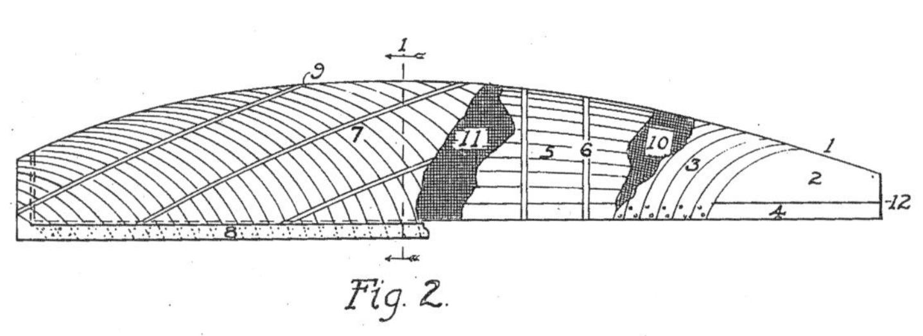

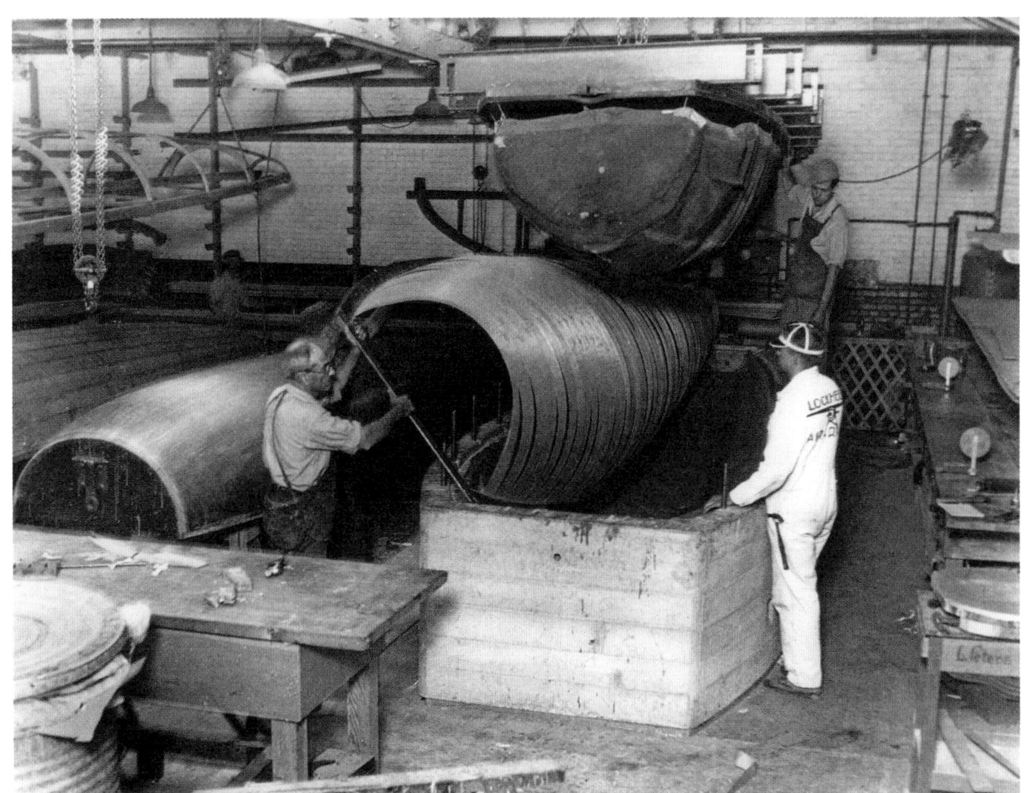

104 (left)

**Moulding the fuselage of the Lockheed Vega: middle layer of veneer being inserted into concrete mould with rubber bag visible above**
Lockheed factory, Burbank, California, c. 1927

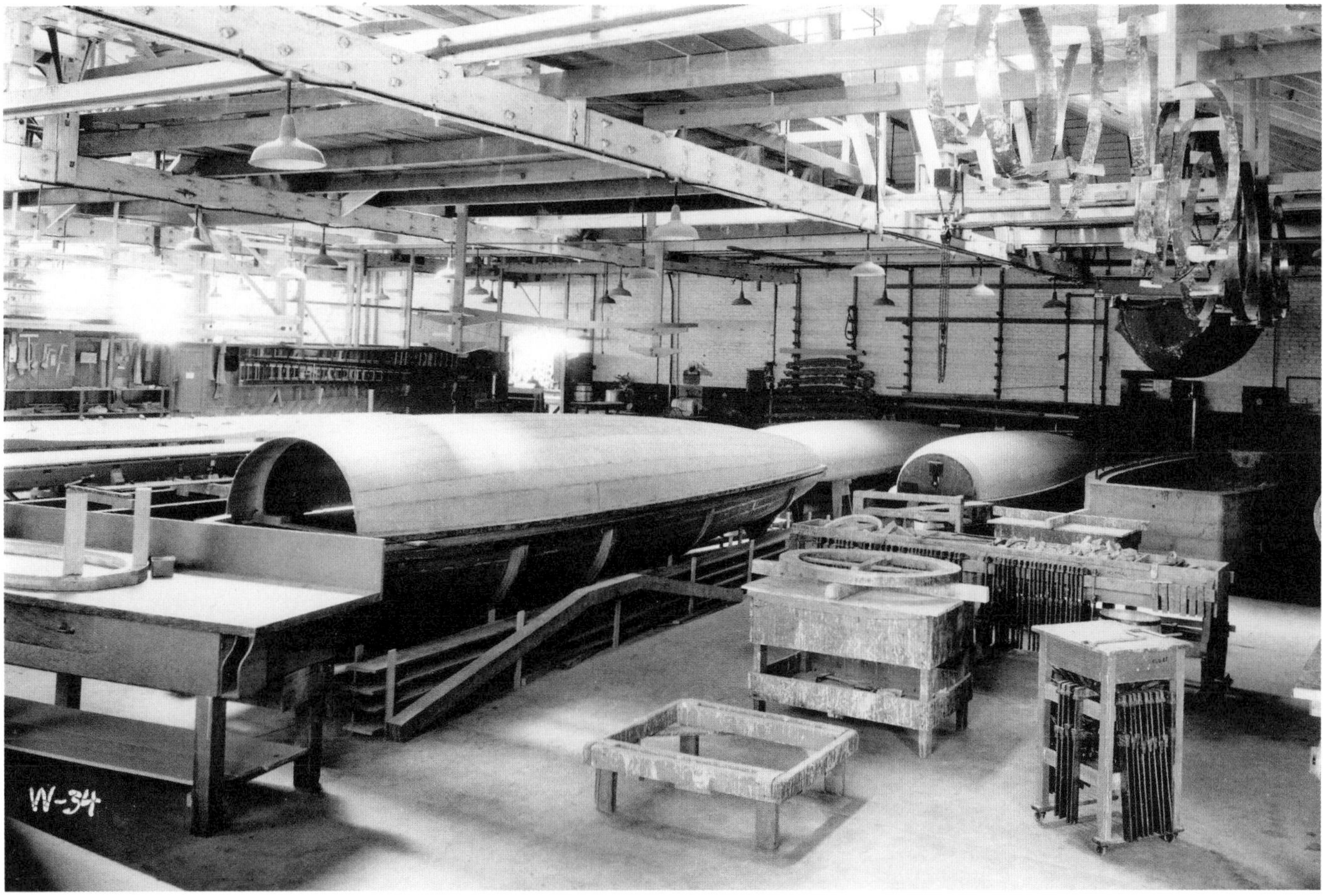

105 (below)

**Lockheed Vega fuselage halves awaiting assembly, with concrete mould and rubber bag visible at back right**
Lockheed factory, Burbank, California, c. 1927

106 (right)

**Half of a Lockheed Vega fuselage. The plywood skin is about to be attached to its supporting frame of longerons and elliptical rings**
Lockheed factory, Burbank, California, c. 1927

107 (below right)

**Vega fuselages in various stages of assembly, some with windows and openings cut**
Lockheed factory, Burbank, California, c. 1927

The concave mould for the next stage was made of reinforced concrete in the shape of one half of the fuselage (fig. 104). It weighed 10–30 tons, depending upon the size of the fuselage. The veneer layers, cloth and glue were inserted into the mould layer by layer. A large rubber airbag was attached to the inside of a wooden lid, and was lowered into the mould. Pressure of 15–20 lbs (6.8–9 kg) per square inch (depending on the fuselage being moulded) was applied, exerting 150 tons of pressure evenly over the pieces of veneer. This part of the procedure, which glued the fuselage together, took only twenty minutes.[48] Once the two fuselage halves were moulded (fig. 105), they were fixed with nails and glue to a framework (figs 106–107) made of twelve or more elliptical rings and four horizontal longerons. Openings for the windows, doors and cockpit were then cut and reinforced (fig. 108), and the exterior of the Vega was painted or lacquered.

The Vega featured a fully enclosed engine cowling, wheels covered with fairings, an enclosed cockpit, a single rather than double wing without external supports, no external control wires, and no fabric covering on the fuselage or wing. All of this greatly improved the aerodynamics of the plane and Lockheed claimed that the Vega offered 'considerably less than half the air resistance of [an] ordinary steel-tubing fuselage'. The Vega was famously flown by Amelia Earhart (fig. 109) in record-breaking flights across the Atlantic and also from the west to the east coasts of the US (both in 1932), as well as by numerous other aviators setting speed records (fig. 110). In addition to speed, the larger Vega fuselage offered passenger or cargo space unobstructed by the cross-bracing required in increasingly common metal-fuselage aircraft of the period. Lockheed made a number of Vega models, as well as two other aircraft using an identical fuselage design, some made in the

108 (below)

**Fully assembled Lockheed Vega, with cut-out windows visible, before painting or lacquering**
Lockheed factory, Burbank, California, c. 1927

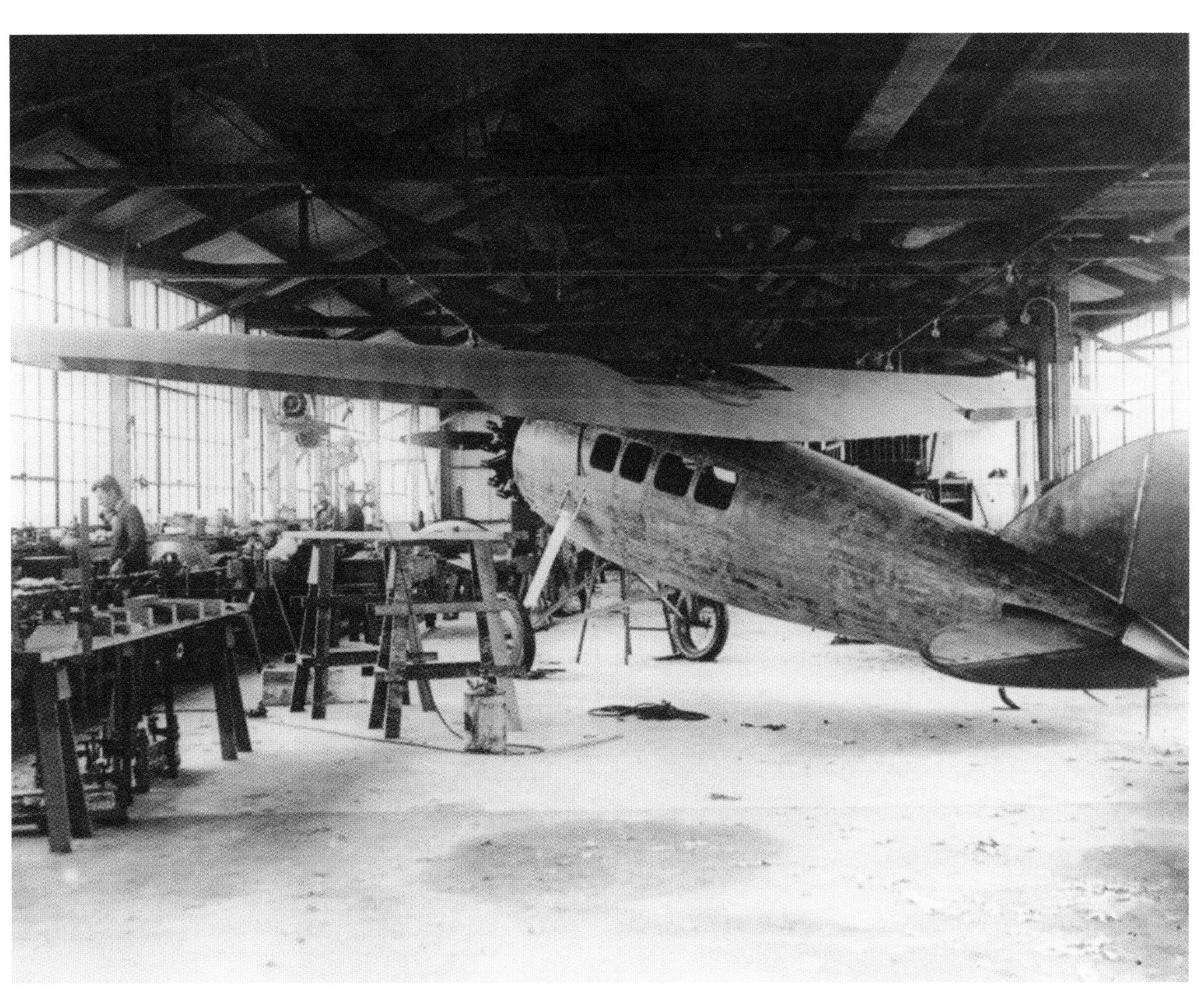

same moulds as the Vega: the Sirius (1929), initially made for the American aviator Charles Lindbergh, and the Altair (1930).[49]

While the S-1 never found a market, its streamlined form and manufacturing technique provided the basis for a design that was eventually transformed into the commercially successful Vega. It is almost certainly the case that both the concrete mould, and the means of applying pressure that later came to be called bag moulding, were initially used for the S-1. The Loughead's bag moulding technique was almost certainly derived from processes first invented in the nineteenth century for the rubber tyre industry, and also used in veneer presses of that period.[50] The adaptation of these processes to aircraft manufacture represented a bold innovation, one that become widely used (mainly on an experimental basis) but not until the mid-1930s, after the technique had been publicized by the Lockheed firm. The ability to apply pressure evenly was (and remains) crucial to moulding forms that would not delaminate in poor weather conditions and at different air pressures. Although the Loughead process was a two-stage one, it greatly reduced the overall time required to make the Deperdussin-style monocoques, while allowing for larger fuselages and greater strength.

Despite the success of these plywood monocoque aircraft, the Lockheed models coincided with the demise of wooden aircraft in mainstream manufacturing. Manufacturers, not only in the US but also in Britain and Germany, influenced by their important military clients, viewed wood as an old-fashioned material incompatible with their view of mass-produced aircraft of the future. Instead, they embraced metal construction as a sign of progress.[51] Until the eve of World War II, when metal shortages became a cause for deep concern, wooden aircraft, wrote one British commentator, had passed 'through a period of almost total eclipse'. During the mid-1930s two areas of work would be developed further for wartime plywood aircraft production, as well as for post-war plywood products: the use of synthetic glues and advances in bag moulding.

109 (opposite)

**The American aviator Amelia Earhart standing beside her Lockheed Vega**
Probably Hickham Field, Hawai'i, 1935

110 (above)

**Lockheed Vega Model 5 'Century of Progress'**
In flight over New York City, 1933

## Plastic planes

The introduction of synthetic adhesives during the mid-1930s represented the most significant innovation in plywood manufacture to date. Above all, these were genuinely waterproof and resistant to fungi (including mould), bacteria and insects. This made them invaluable for moulding strong, resistant fuselages. The idea of creating a synthetic glue by combining phenols (carbolic acid, extracted from coal tar in the form of colourless crystals) and formaldehyde (a compound found widely in the natural world) in a process of condensation (also called polymerization) was proposed by the Belgian-born American chemist Leo Baekeland in the first of his American patents (1909). This method led him famously to create Bakelite plastic. In 1919 a chemist working for the Westinghouse Electric Company patented a process for making plywood using dried sheets of paper or fabric impregnated with phenolic adhesive that would be activated by heating.[52] But it was not until 1929 that paper impregnated with synthetic glue found its way to market when a German firm, Goldschmidt AG, introduced its Tego film. By 1933 Tego film was exported in large quantities to leading plywood manufacturers in Estonia, Finland, the UK and elsewhere, while an American licensing agreement was signed in 1934. It was, initially, apparently more popular abroad than in Germany.[53] It became one of the most widely advertised glue products in the 1930s and during wartime, and the use of glue film was quickly imitated by other companies (fig. 111). Its advantage rested in the ease with which the film could be applied between layers of veneer. Tego film was activated during the moulding process only by the use of heat; liquid glue, by contrast, had to be brushed on and kept warm for a period of time in order that it did not dry prematurely.

An alternative urea-formaldehyde resin (liquid) adhesive – synthetic urea is a crystalline

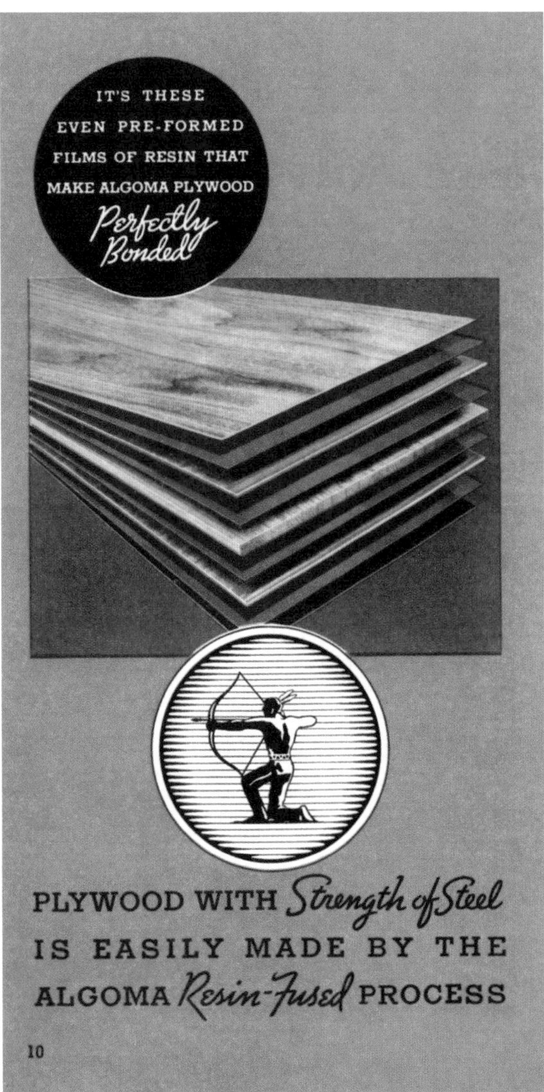
IT'S THESE
EVEN PRE-FORMED
FILMS OF RESIN THAT
MAKE ALGOMA PLYWOOD
Perfectly Bonded
PLYWOOD WITH Strength of Steel
IS EASILY MADE BY THE
ALGOMA Resin-Fused PROCESS
10

111 (below)
**Glue film illustrated in advertisement for Algoma Resin-Fused Plywood**
From *Algoma Resin-Fused Plywood*, Algoma Plywood & Veneer Company brochure, Algoma, Wisconsin, 1936

BETTER INDUSTRIAL PRODUCTS

• The search for plywood panels with strength and minimum weight ends today with this modern plywood. For all fabricating uses Harbord SUPER Plywood does a better job at less cost. The panels shrink less, and warp less, and make saws and cutting tools last longer. The low moisture content makes them far more workable, far more practical. For special purposes or for use in certain climates, the moisture content can be varied to any degree wanted. For makers of outdoor furniture, Harbord SUPER Plywood presents ideal durability and moisture resistance:

| | |
|---|---|
| Store and Office Fixtures | Portable Houses |
| Booth Panelling | Desks |
| Mirror Backs | Elevator Shaft Lining |
| Bulletin Boards | Machinery Shelters |
| Outdoor Furniture | Screens |
| Book Cases | Lockers |
| Kitchen Cabinets | Freight Cars |
| School Equipment | Baggage Cars |
| Radio Cabinets | Refrigerator Cars |
| Luggage Carriers | Mail Cars |
| Refrigerators | Outdoor Signs |
| Drawer Bottoms | Doors |
| Cabinet Lining | Ship & Boat Building |
| Curved Frames | Trucks and Buses |
| Chair Backs and Seats | Factory Floors |
| Trunk Sides | Factory Roofs |
| Core Stock | Temporary Store Fronts |
| Battery Separators | Electrotype Blocks |
| Bee Keepers Equipment | |

3
GENERA

[ 10 ]

112 (below right)
**Page from booklet promoting Harbord Super Plywood**
Harbor Plywood Corporation, Hoquiam, Washington State, 1935

chemical product – was developed for use in plywood manufacture by the German company I.G. Farben in 1929 under the Kaurit brand name. In the late 1930s the British chemist Norman A. de Bruyne worked to develop a material called Aerolite in which fibres (in the form of 'cords', later fabric or paper) impregnated with Bakelite could be used in fuselage moulding. Prior to the initial sale of Tego film in the US (late 1935), the Harbor Plywood Corporation in Washington State introduced Super Plywood panels – 'hot pressed' of Douglas fir plywood using dry resin glue (fig. 112). These panels were very heavily marketed by the company, both for aircraft and for building construction (see chapter 5). In an advertising stunt typical of the period, the Harbor company promoted their product's waterproofness with the 'Spruce Girls' – women photographed wearing specially made veneer swimming costumes on Washington beaches (fig. 113).[54]

Although they were used mainly experimentally and for war-related manufacture of boats and aircraft until 1945, the availability of synthetic adhesives in the general marketplace would eventually transform the strength and structural reliability of plywood. They played an important role in finally securing plywood's reputation as a modern, dependable material that could be used for its own qualities, rather than as an inferior substitute for wood. Starting in the late 1930s, the term 'plastic plywood' was widely used by both the specialist and the popular press to suggest that newly developed synthetic resin glues, when combined with veneer in new moulding processes, created a form of plywood with entirely different properties than earlier types – even a new material. It was the use of these moulding processes that allowed for the dream of a mass-produced 'true' monocoque plane to be revived, and that led the press to declare (expectantly) that 'The Plywood Plane is Here'.[55]

113 (below)
**'Spruce Girls' in spruce veneer swimming costumes**
Probably near Hoquiam, Washington State, 1929

114 (below)

**Illustrations of different methods of bag moulding plywood**
From Bruce Heebink, 'Bag-molding of Plywood', US Forest Products Laboratory report R1431, May 1943

The Lougheads had employed a bag exerting pressure against a concave mould without requiring heat, and had used casein glue. About 1935–36 American furniture manufacturers adopted a technique of vacuum-bag moulding veneers onto curved forms: veneer was tacked or taped onto the piece requiring veneering with glue applied to the curved form, the piece was then inserted into a large rubber bag, the bag was sealed, and a compressor created a vacuum removing all the air from the bag and causing it to press evenly against the surfaces of the piece.[56] Traditional furniture glues were used.

From the late 1930s this method was adapted in a number of new moulding techniques with the names Duramold, Vidal and Aeromold, among others. All variations upon one another and using synthetic glues and heat or steam, these processes were developed in the US in connection with moulding aircraft parts.[57] They all required a single-piece mould onto or into which veneers and synthetic adhesive (film, liquid or mixed from powder) were placed and, as in the S-1 and Vega, within or around which a rubber bag was placed (fig. 114). In the most common techniques, these parts were all put into a large metal tank (or autoclave; fig. 115)

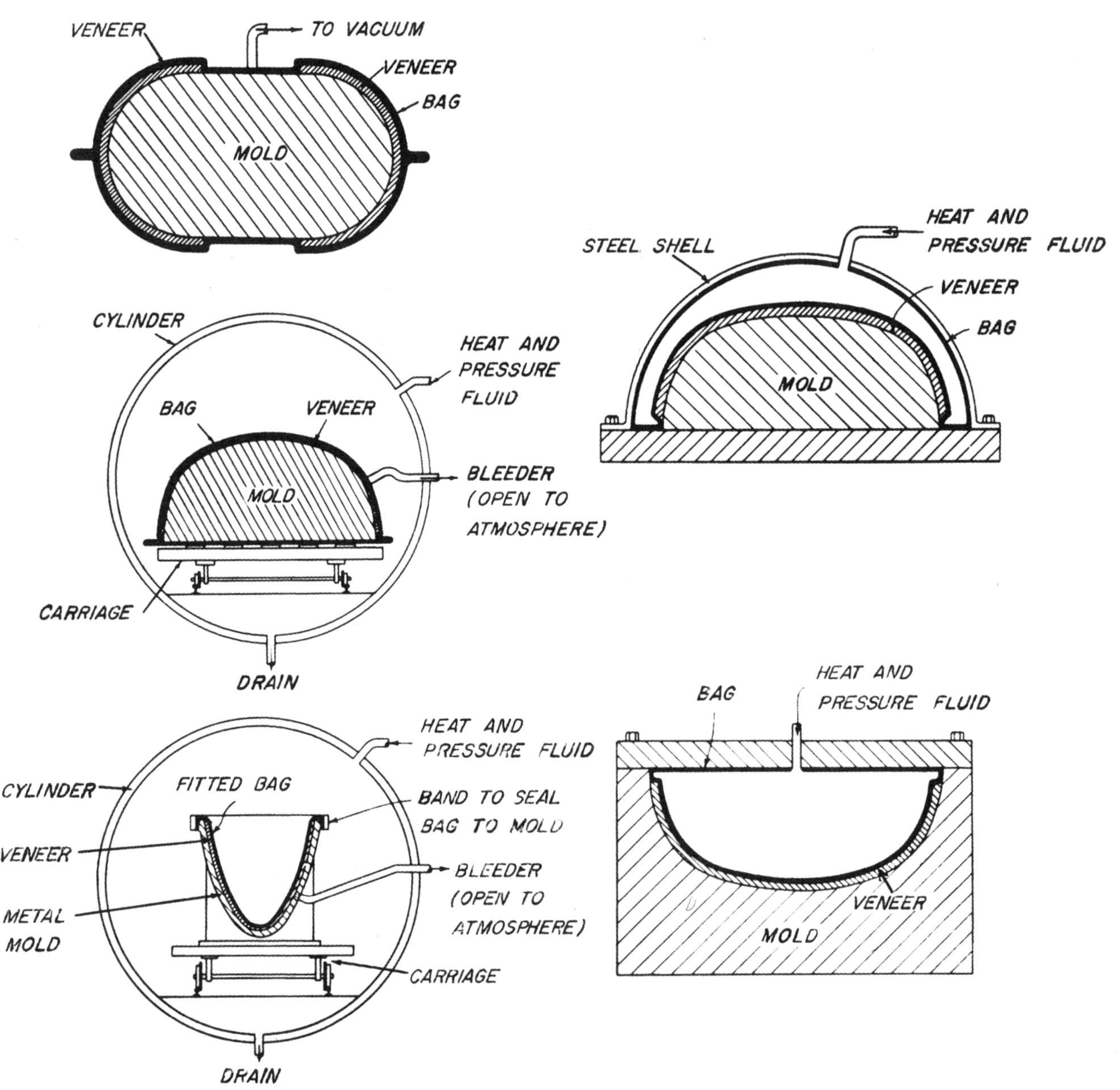

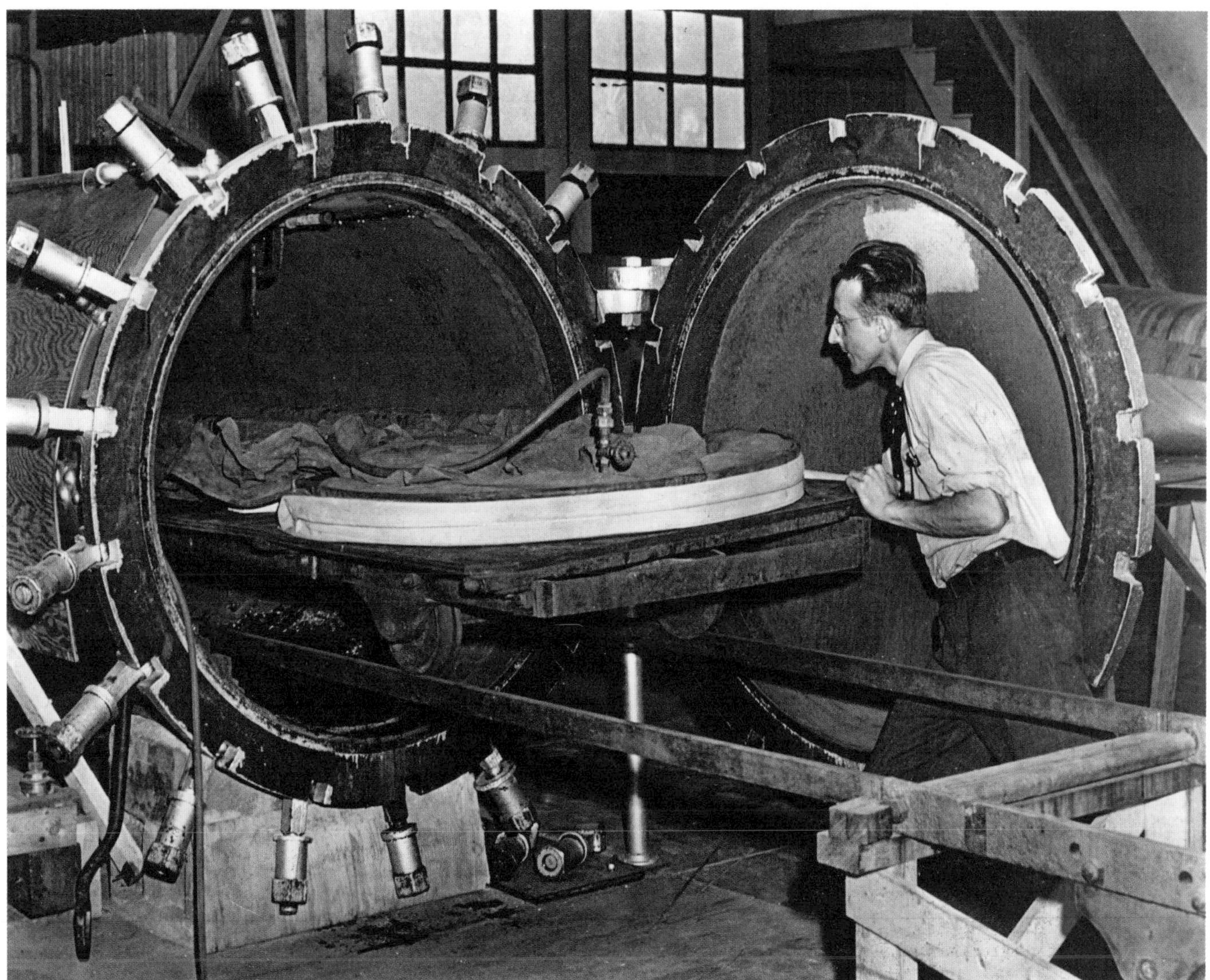

115 (above)

**Autoclave (bag moulding tank), Resinous Products Company, Philadelphia, c. 1940**

The object to be moulded is sealed in the uninflated bag and locked in the tank

within which considerable pressure and heat were applied; owing to this, the part was formed relatively quickly. All of these processes required equipment more expensive than that used in cold-pressing and were best suited to the large-scale manufacture of forms requiring compound curves, for which other methods of moulding were not easily available.

These new techniques received a huge amount of press, particularly in the US, where they were seen to provide the potential for moulding a streamlined fuselage. Articles tended to emphasize the technical sophistication of the moulding processes, with the implication that this method was advanced enough to offer a reliable means of mass-producing highly standardized planes. The 'plastic' qualities of the resulting aircraft were also celebrated – the planes were described as smooth, strong forms that could ostensibly be moulded into any shape, finally allowing for the quick production of a true monocoque form.[58]

From the early 1940s the FPL devoted considerable effort to studying these new moulding techniques on behalf of the US Army.[59] Although plywood was a hugely important material in the construction of World War II aircraft (fig. 116), the promise of an assembly line producing thousands of 'plastic' planes was never realized. The US military used new moulding techniques most successfully in a number of trainer planes made during the war – such as the Morrow Victory Trainer (fig. 117), a semi-monocoque with an applied Duramold-moulded plywood skin. Aside from these experimental trainer planes, the most ambitious and extravagant demonstration of a Duramold process was in the American businessman and aviator Howard Hughes's

116 (right)

**'Wood Flies to War'**
US Government poster, 1943

117 (below)

**Workers holding plywood skin of a Morrow Victory Trainer**
San Bernardino, California, 1941

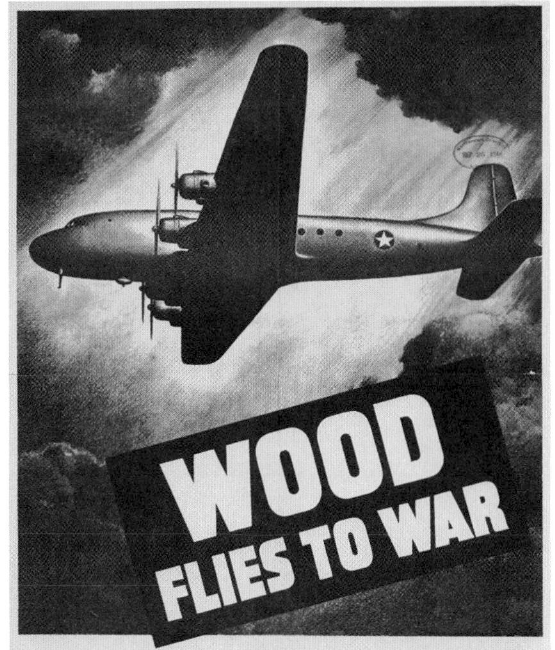


Hughes Hercules – both the largest wooden aircraft ever built and the biggest and most public aviation failure of World War II (figs 118–119). Facetiously dubbed the 'Spruce Goose' by the American press, the aircraft was made mainly of birch and balsawood with additional spruce – the same combination as used in the British Mosquito (see below). Started by the industrialist Henry Kaiser (originator of the successful 'Liberty' cargo and troop transport ship and, before that, builder of the Hoover Dam on the Colorado River) in collaboration with Hughes, the plane was intended as an alternative means of transporting war materiel across oceans, owing to the danger of enemy attacks on shipping. It was to be the largest, heaviest and most powerful plane ever built, a seaplane intended to be capable of carrying one 60-ton tank or three lighter tanks, or 350 hospital patients on stretchers with doctors, nurses and a surgery. Commissioned in November 1942 by a government desperate for a cargo plane made from non-essential materials, it was to be delivered in an unachievable thirteen months. Only one version of the plane was ever completed, and it flew only once, in November 1947.[60]

118 and 119
(left and below)

**Hughes Hercules ('Spruce Goose') fuselage under construction, exterior (above) and interior (below)**

The outside of the plane was finished in aluminium paint, visible at the tail end in the photo of the exterior. Los Angeles, c. 1945

120 (above)

**De Havilland Albatross (DH-91) in flight, c. 1938**

121 (right)

**De Havilland Mosquito Mk XVI bomber in flight, c. 1943**

## The Mosquito

The availability of synthetic glues and new (and still experimental) moulding processes provided one half of the argument in favour of plywood planes. The other was the superior speed and lower cost of manufacture of wooden over metal aircraft. The argument was made – ultimately unsuccessfully in the US but successfully in Britain – that the ability to source metal and, specifically, aluminium for manufacture would be limited in wartime; that the thousands of rivets required for a single metal aircraft were time-consuming to attach and created aerodynamic drag that was avoided in plywood monocoque construction; that metal aeroplanes took years to develop and build owing to the time required to design and build tools and dies, whereas moulds for wood could be made much more quickly and cheaply; that expensive, highly skilled labour was required for metal aircraft, whereas woodworkers were cheaper; and that wooden aircraft were quicker and easier to repair.[61]

Neither the outbreak of war in Europe in 1939 nor America's entry into the war in 1941 convinced the US Army that wood was of sufficient utility for combat aircraft (although it was extensively used for trainers and gliders). Even when attempts at manufacturing were made, the lack of any recent experience in the mass production of wooden aircraft within the industry stymied positive efforts.[62] Ironically, the British Mosquito (DH-98), shrouded in secrecy until 1943 and the most unusual design of any wartime aeroplane, did not make use of any of the newest moulding technologies and was in fact based on construction principles first used in the de Havilland Albatross mail plane (DH-91) in 1937 (fig. 120). Although the Mosquito was eventually made using synthetic glue, this was initially applied with a brush in the old-fashioned way.

The Mosquito bomber – also built as a fighter and as a high-altitude reconnaissance plane – was the most remarkable and successful plywood aeroplane ever built (fig. 121). It flew higher and faster than any other bomber of World War II until a jet engine-powered German plane, the Arado Ar 234, was introduced for limited use in the last year of war. The Mosquito's designer, Geoffrey de Havilland (1882–1965), was an engineer, pilot and founder (in 1920) of the de Havilland Aircraft Company and, above all, a tireless advocate of wooden aeroplanes for civilian and military use (in the face of frequent opposition from the British Air Ministry). While hyperbole is a staple of writing on the history of wartime aircraft, it is not an exaggeration to state that the fact that the Mosquito was eventually ordered by the British government, and delivered so quickly, was a tribute to the unique expertise and utter tenacity of de Havilland's team. They argued the case for what appeared to most as a counter-intuitive or illogical proposal: a smaller rather than larger bomber, one made of wood that would fly faster than fighters and do so without the need for (and weight of) defensive armament.[63]

The Mosquito consisted of a plywood monocoque fuselage (fig. 122) built in two halves (41 ft 2 in./12.55 m in overall length) and (unusually) a single-piece, stressed-skin wing (54 ft 2 in./16.51 m span). Although plywood fuselage development in the US especially was focused on the use of various newer bag or (as it became called) fluid-pressure moulding techniques, the Mosquito was made with speed of production utmost in mind. For the fuselage, a more conventional

122 (below)

**Detail showing three-layer construction of Mosquito fuselage, 1943**

From Wilfred E. Goff, 'The De Havilland Mosquito: Part I', *Aircraft Production* (June 1943), p. 267

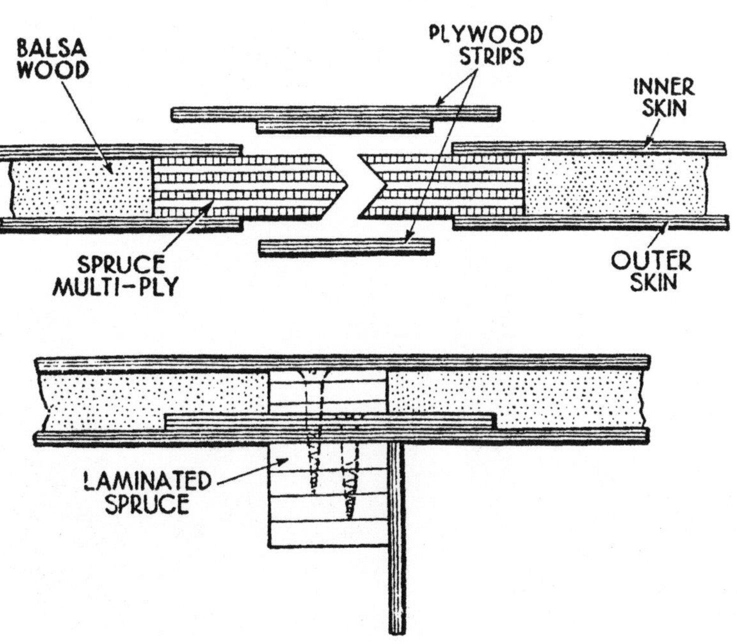

123 (above)

**Metal bands are strapped on to mould each layer of the Mosquito fuselage**
Rolls of veneer are visible leaning against the wall at left of photo.
De Havilland factory, St Albans, Hertfordshire, c. 1943

124 (right)

**Mosquito half-fuselage lifted off mould**
Harris Lebus furniture factory, London, c. 1943

125 (left)

**Balsawood pieces being fitted to middle layer of Mosquito fuselage**
De Havilland factory, St Albans, Hertfordshire, c. 1943

126 (below)

**Installing equipment inside Mosquito before joining two fuselage halves**
Harris Lebus furniture factory, London, c. 1943

127 (above)
**Construction of a Mosquito wing, with vertical plywood ribs**
Harris Lebus furniture factory, London, c. 1943

but still high-pressure, cold (rather than hot) moulding technique was used. This involved laying birch veneer sheets onto a single-piece, concave, concrete and mahogany former; steel bands were then strapped (fig. 123) along the entire surface and tightened to mould the shape of each of the three layers and then, finally, that of each entire half-fuselage (fig. 124). The veneers were laid diagonally in the Mosquito but, unusually, only where the greatest stresses occurred (especially at the tail end). They were laid straight where diagonal support was not essential in order to save wood – one of many time- and cost-saving aspects of the design. Space for spruce longerons or stringers (which ran the length of the fuselage) and for seven thin bulkheads to reinforce the monocoque structure was allowed for in the mould.

A particular de Havilland innovation, first employed in 1937 in the DH-91 (fig. 120), was the use of a ⅜ in. (9.5 mm) balsawood filler layer applied in strips between the outer and inner plywood fuselage layers (each of these three-veneer fuselage layers was about 3 mm [⅛ in.] thick; fig. 125). The balsa, too light to serve any structural function, separated and stabilized the plies evenly, allowing them to function as a stressed skin resistant to buckling under compression.[64] The fuselage overall was about 16 mm (⅝ in.) thick. The vertically oriented fuselage halves were fitted out with 60% of their internal equipment (fig. 126) before being joined together. This design feature, which aimed at allowing maximum access for fitting out the planes before the fuselage was enclosed, was widely commented upon at the time. Longerons were then attached before the two halves were joined at top and bottom with special plywood-reinforced joints.

The wing (fig. 127), which to contemporary eyes tapered dramatically to its trailing edge, was constructed of a combination of birch plywood and laminated spruce (for the very long box spars); birch plywood was used for the outer skins (fig. 128), the upper skin a double one filled not with balsa but with solid lengths of spruce. Such were the compression loads on the top of the wing that they would have

128 (above)
**Application of plywood skin to upper surface of Mosquito wing**
De Havilland factory, St Albans, Hertfordshire, c. 1943

buckled without the extra support. Although the earliest Mosquito production made use of casein glue, by 1942 a variety of synthetic glues were employed for different parts of the aeroplane, including a recently produced British phenol formaldehyde adhesive, marketed under the names of Aerolite and Beetle.[65]

Among the most noteworthy aspects of manufacturing a wooden aircraft in large quantity were: the necessity of sourcing raw materials from other countries during wartime; the extent to which the manufacturing was contracted to so many firms in Britain, but also abroad; and the fact that Mosquitoes were also manufactured in their entirety in both Canada and Australia from 1943 to 1945. Large quantities of balsawood from Ecuador, birch veneers and Sitka spruce from Canada, and birch veneers and plywood from Midwestern America were among the essential materials required. At least 23 furniture, woodworking and coach building firms, among a total of 223 British subcontractors, provided the right mix of specialist but cheaper (relative to metalworking) labour required to build the major parts of the Mosquito. Underutilized furniture factories (figs 124, 126 and 127) were thus drawn into the project, making the case for smooth skill transfer arising from the use of wood manufacture. Such workers were also perfectly suited to repair damaged Mosquitoes.[66]

The Mosquito was publicized around the world starting in 1943. Its operational effectiveness, its speed arising from a combination of powerful Rolls-Royce Merlin engines, its aerodynamic design, its light weight (relative to that of metal) and, above all, its manufacture from (ply)wood, garnered the material special attention during and after the war. Despite the commercial and ideological antipathy of the aircraft industry itself to reconsidering the manufacture of wooden aircraft after the war, the Mosquito especially (but also a range of gliders and trainer aircraft) unquestionably contributed to raising the status of plywood among designers and manufacturers in other fields, as well as among the popular press and general public after the end of the war.

# 5 Building the Modern World (1920s–1940s)

The use of visible plywood in interior and exterior architecture was, like its use in aircraft, important for convincing the public that it could be a reliable, useful and even attractive material. Its architectural use was (especially in the US) highly publicized from the late 1930s onwards, when largely government-supported housing schemes associated it closely with the idea of efficient factory prefabrication. Plywood's presence in world's fairs of the 1930s contributed to raising its profile meaningfully both within the architectural profession and for a wider public.

Plywood is today a staple of the building industry and of architectural and, especially, interior design, particularly in countries with a tradition of building in wood. These uses were, however, highly unusual in the early twentieth century, the subject of much experimentation during the 1930s, and became common only in the late 1940s and 1950s. The attraction of plywood as a building material was its cheapness, its uniformity (once consistent standards of manufacture and reliability could be guaranteed) and the fact that it was factory-produced in modular sizes. Its large size relative to that of timber, and its board form, meant that it could be used to cover large surfaces with less labour (in time and level of specialism required) than standard lath and plaster wall construction.

Plywood could also be used structurally, making it particularly attractive as a material for demountable, factory-produced housing schemes or exhibition buildings. It was one of a raft of new, 'modern' building materials introduced and experimented with from the 1920s, but especially in the 1930s and 1940s. Within this history it occupies a unique position, as it was both a modern and a conventional material: 'high-tech', standardized and industrial; but with strong links to more traditional timber construction. Although plywood was much tested by by architects, particularly in schemes for the design of an affordable modern house, its success often came through more market-friendly, conventional designs. Its ability to be turned to mass-produced, mobile, panel-constructed housing was frequently posited in the 1930s and 1940s as the model for a new kind of twentieth-century domesticity.

129 (opposite)
**Finnish Pavilion, New York World's Fair**
Designed by Alvar and Aino Aalto, detail of interior perspective, 1939

130 (below)
**Concrete formwork by Harbor Plywood Corporation**
From *The Timberman* (November 1929), p. 210

## Formwork for concrete

The most significant, but also most hidden, use of plywood in the worlds of building and architecture has been, since the late 1920s, in the process of casting concrete (fig. 130). Before that time, liquid concrete was mainly poured and set in moulds called formwork, usually made entirely of solid wood boards.[1] Plywood began to replace solid timber for the lining of formwork (also called shuttering or, in Britain, form lining) by at least 1929 – an inauspicious year to introduce a new product, owing to the Wall Street stock market crash – when the US Harbor Plywood Corporation (in Washington State) began marketing a lower-quality plywood that could be ordered in large or small panel sizes for concrete forming. The plywood was initially made using water-resistant glue and treated with oil so it would not stick to the dried concrete and could be reused (six to twelve times, said the manufacturers). The use of plywood meant larger, flatter and smoother surfaces to mould concrete against. These were easier to handle than form lining made of many pieces of solid wood, and also reduced the number and appearance of joints between parts (fig. 131). Plywood greatly reduced labour costs, both because of a huge reduction in the amount of finishing needed to smooth joint seams after moulding; and because it reduced the need for the most skilled and expensive labour required in the process of making and using concrete, the specialist formwork carpenter or joiner. The lower grade of plywood and easy availability from suppliers also made it cheaper than solid wood.[2]

By 1939 specialist plywood types were marketed for concrete forming under trade names such as Plyform, and metal-covered plywood was introduced too for this use. The shortage of solid timber relative to plywood during World War II led to increased use of plywood for concrete forming and even slowed the recent experimentation with steel shuttering. In Britain the builders Bovis created a plywood panel shuttering system that was used to build the so-called Mulberry artificial harbours, which were towed to northern France as part of the Allied invasion on D-Day (6 June 1944). At the same time shaped plywood panels were used in combination with flat panels to pour concrete beams and floors. Plywood panels bonded with synthetic resin glue came into use in the mid-1930s. These panels, which became cheaper after the war, could be used for both sheathing and form lining. As they could be reused they also increased the longevity of plywood formwork. Plastic- and metal-covered plywood panels offering especially smooth finishes were increasingly marketed after the war specifically for formwork, having previously been sold for interior uses (for example Plymax or Plymetl, see p. 110). Although the use of metal (aluminium) forms became common in the post-war era, plywood, claimed the building industry, was by 1955 'the standard material' for concrete forming. It remained the most commonly used material throughout the twentieth century, even from the 1950s to the 1970s, when Brutalist architects demanded rougher concrete surfaces. It remains in widespread use at the time of writing in most parts of the world and the APA – Engineered Wood Association claims their specialist Plyform boards can be reused twenty to fifty times.[3]

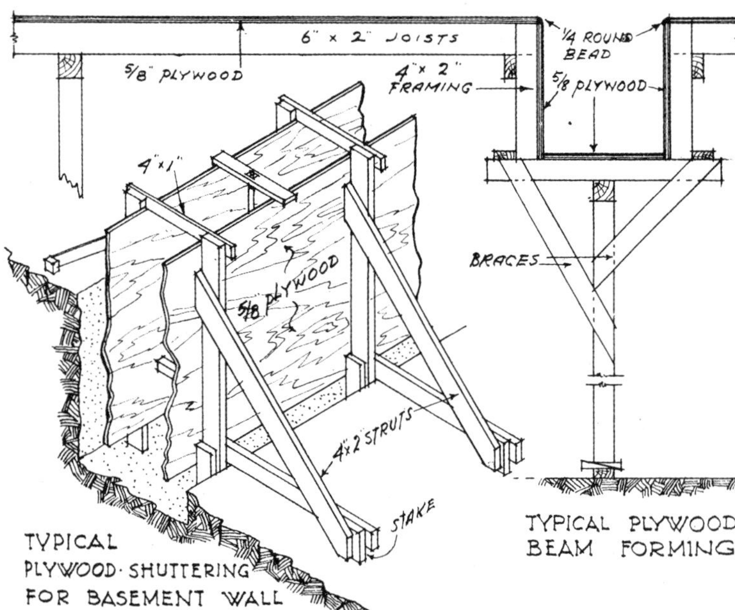


131 (below)
**Use of plywood for reinforced concrete shuttering**
From Andrew Dick Wood and Thomas Gray Linn, *Plywoods, Their Development, Manufacture and Application* (Edinburgh and London 1942), fig. 178, p. 424

## Plywood in the interior

At the same time that plywood was starting to be used to mould smooth concrete surfaces, it was also increasingly adopted as a decorative material for interiors. One of the most common uses of plywood in the early twentieth century was for doors, with plywood introduced both to avoid the shrinking typical in doors made of joined solid timber and to reduce the selling cost. These were first made about 1900 in two forms, neither completely of plywood. The first appeared to be a standard, solid wood, recessed-panel door, but with uprights and cross-pieces made of plywood covering a core made up of narrow solid battens joined or glued together. This combination of materials, used as panels, would by the late 1920s come to be called laminated board, laminboard or, if made with wider pieces of solid wood, blockboard, battenboard or lumber-core (fig. 4). One version of it had already been named cabinetmaker's board (*Tischlerplatten*) by about 1900 in Germany.[4]

The more successful plywood door in terms of market appeal was the flush door (fig. 132). These were made without recessed panels or raised mouldings, although about 1900 sometimes with incised or inlaid decoration, and of the same combination of materials as the panelled doors. Real savings in terms of labour costs were possible in this door type as there were fewer, longer (door-height) battens to join and the plywood could be applied to each side of the door as a single full-length panel. Although flush doors found some favour after the turn of the century, when a lingering taste for the Arts and Crafts style was still popular, they seemed to have found a wider market

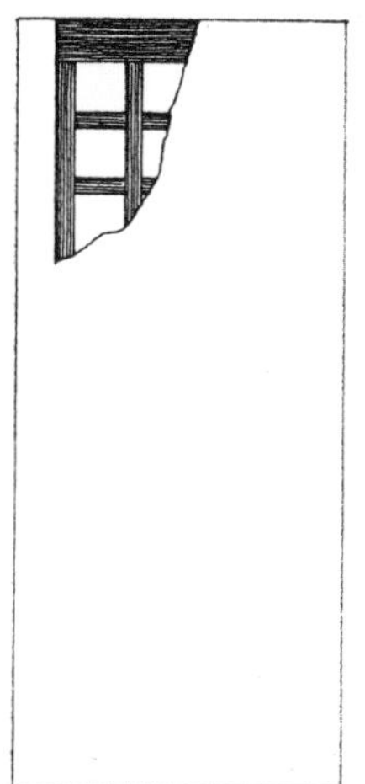

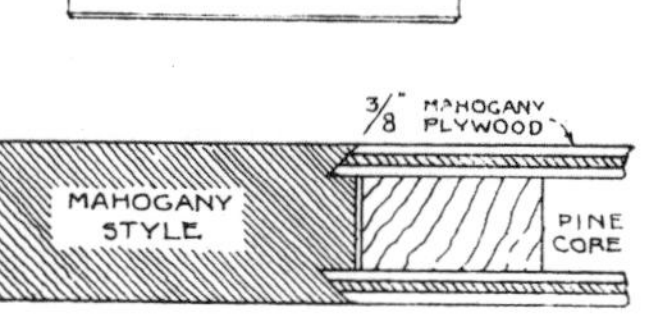


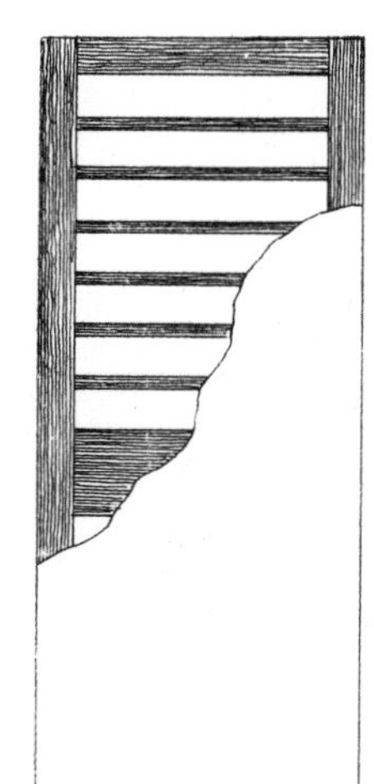

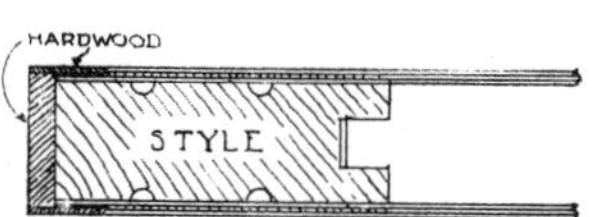


132 (left)
**Flush door construction**
From Shirley B. Wainwright, *Modern Plywood* (London 1927), pl. 26

133 (above)
***Art-Ply for Modern Interiors***
Cover of Vancouver Plywood & Veneer Company brochure, Canada, 1938

only in the late 1920s and especially into the 1930s.[5] This was partly owing to their lower cost compared to that of traditional door construction (certainly in higher-end uses, with more expensive materials). Such flat surfaces also fitted into the fashionable *moderne* style of interior design that had originated in Paris and had influenced, to varying degrees, all manner of contemporary interiors and furnishings in Europe and the US (fig. 133).

It was, however, in wall panelling that plywood found its most significant place in 1930s interiors (fig. 134), from offices to ocean liners, and government buildings to shops, but also in more expensive private homes (fig. 135).[6] Here, prefabricated plywood boards veneered with a variety of highly decorative, grained and/or figured woods offered panelled interiors that could be installed more easily and at a lower price than those available using traditional woodworking methods. Avoidance of shrinking wood, and the possibility of unusually large or wide panels that reduced the number of joints between pieces (compared to traditional panelling) and offered ease of installation were key selling points for the intended specifiers, interior designers and architects. Plywood was marketed both as a cheaper alternative to traditional wood panelling and as a replacement for labour-intensive plaster walls. Plywood panelling could be attached (by glue, screws or nails) to a batten

134 (right)
**Venesta advertisement for plywood panelling, 1939**

135 (opposite)
**Plywood-panelled entrance hall, Eltham Palace, London**
Designed by Rolf Engströmer, 1933–36

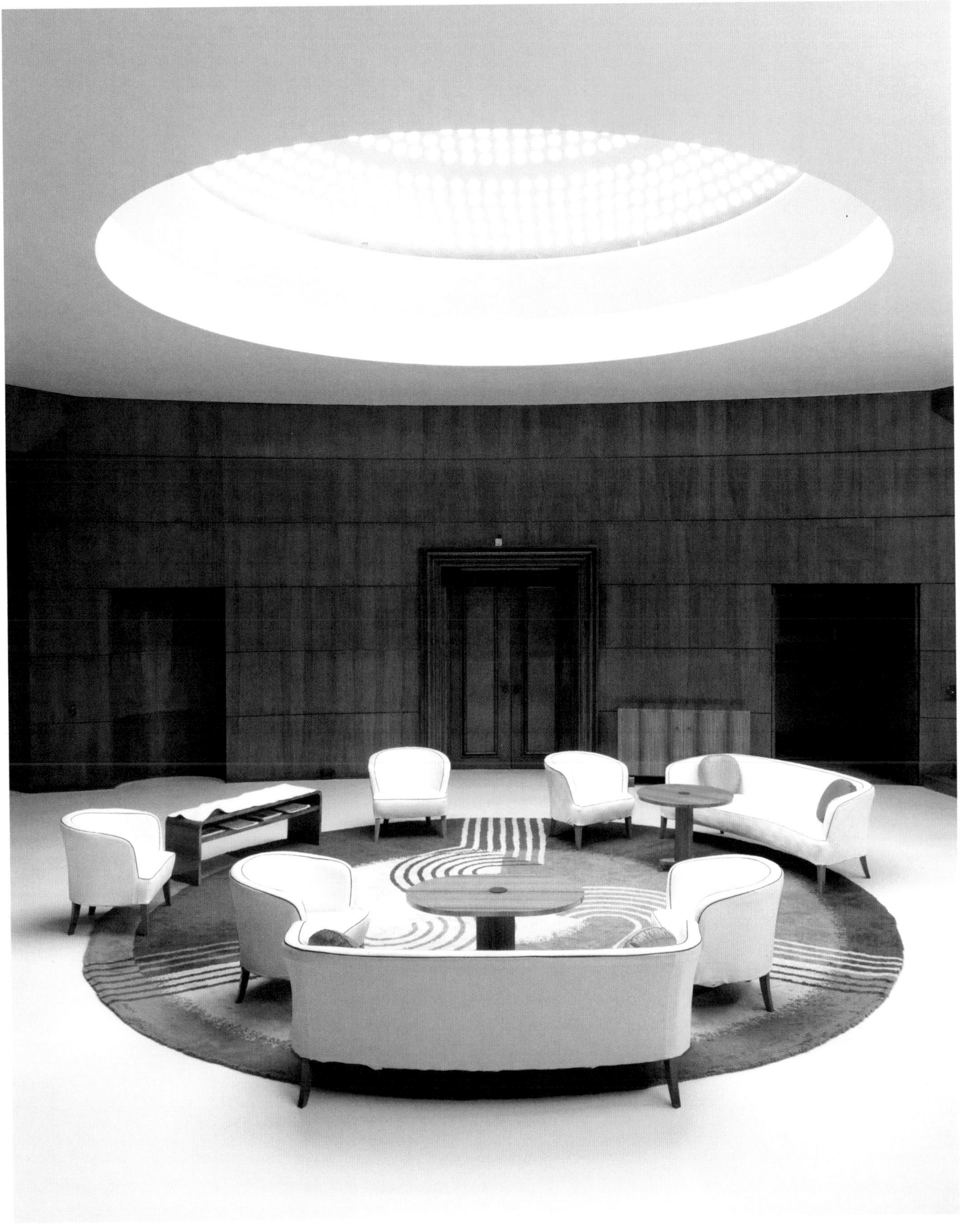

or frame structure (fig. 136), to (ply)wood sheathing, or directly onto plaster, and such methods were the subject of well-publicized research for strength and rigidity at the Forest Products Laboratory (FPL). Joins between panels were normally covered by stiles, rails, mouldings (occasionally metal) or wood mastic.

In addition to offering ease of installation, plywood panels were also straightforward for designers because of their standard sizes. These were first introduced in about 1900 (see p. 48) and by the 1920s and 1930s had increased significantly in dimensions and in the range of different sizes available. Standardized board sizes were often used by architects as the basis for a room or building's dimensions, as in the office that Frank Lloyd Wright (1867–1959) designed for Edgar J. Kaufmann (1885–1955) for his Pittsburgh department store. Made entirely of swamp cypress plywood (both panelling and furniture), Wright used the dimensions of a standard plywood board size – 4 × 8 ft (1.22 × 2.44 m) – to lay out the room. The office is made as a three-dimensional module of 4 × 4 × 4 ft, the height of a single sheet forming the room's height (8 ft) while the ceiling and floor are clad with 4 × 4 ft squares. The plywood panelling was also used decoratively by Wright, most spectacularly in the abstract mural surrounding Kaufmann's desk, which Wright described as a 'marquetry plywood wall' (fig. 137).[7]

Various manufacturers created or marketed many specific products for wall panelling (figs 138–139). Among these were: Venesta's Plymax (late 1920s); Haskelite's Phemaloid (by 1932), Plymetl (by 1933), Duraply (before 1936) and less conventional products such as a thin, paper-backed plywood suitable for curved walls; US Plywood's Flexwood (by 1936); and Oceana and Ribply, both French products offering curved surfaces (both 1936). American plywood companies promoted such products at national and international expositions starting in 1933, and plywood panelling laid the foundations for the widespread use of the material in the residential interior after 1945, especially in the US.[8]

136 (above)
**Illustration showing installation of plywood panelling**
From *Art-Ply for Modern Interiors*, Vancouver Plywood & Veneer Company brochure, Canada, 1938

137 (opposite)
**Office for Edgar J. Kaufmann, Pittsburgh, Pennsylvania**
Designed by Frank Lloyd Wright, 1935–37. Walls, ceiling, floor and furniture of swamp cypress plywood

138 (above)

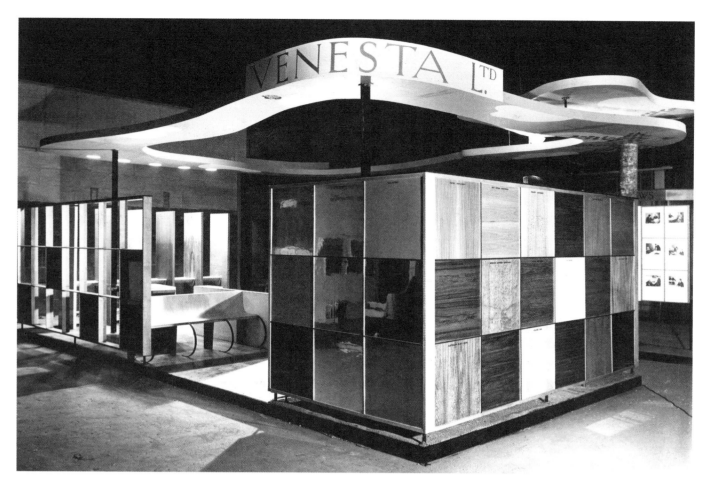

**Venesta display stand, showing different finishes for plywood panelling and moulded plywood bench seat**
Designed by Skinner and Tecton, London Building Exhibition, 1934

139 (right)

**Venesta brochure advertising branded plywood boards**
London, 1930s

**Exhibition buildings**

While panelling was an important example of the commercial introduction of plywood into the interior, much of its most prominent early marketing as an architectural material came from its structural use in temporary exhibition buildings. World's fairs in the US in the 1930s provided a showcase for plywood as a modern material, precisely at a moment when it was being improved (in particular for exterior use), and starting to be aggressively marketed by American manufacturers and trade associations. Fairs, along with demonstration houses, were picked up by the industry as important vehicles for plywood promotion.

Buildings at the 1933–34 Chicago Century of Progress World's Fair were specifically intended to demonstrate new materials, construction techniques and an American architecture optimistically aspiring to move on from the Depression. Plywood was used for the centrepiece of the fair, the Hall of Science (fig. 140), designed by the classically trained architect Paul Cret (1876–1945). The entire building was clad with standard 4 × 8 ft (1.22 × 2.44 m) five-ply panels, the boards and supporting battens (attached to a steel frame) forming geometric patterns on the building's extensive exterior surfaces. The Hall of Science included the quintessentially American form of a skyscraper in one corner, also plywood-clad. Plywood on the back of the building's U-shaped court was perforated with a geometric pattern (fig. 141).

140 (above)

**Poster for the Chicago Century of Progress World's Fair showing the Hall of Science**
Designed by Weimer Pursell, 1933

141 (left)

**Hall of Science, Chicago Century of Progress World's Fair, 1933.**
Designed by Paul Cret. Geometric perforations in plywood cladding visible to right of tower

Plywood was initially used in Chicago as the cheapest board material available. After the first three fair buildings had been built using plywood, cheaper alternatives became available from manufacturers keen to publicize their new products, and other buildings made use of a variety of new manufactured boards, such as gypsum board, Masonite Presdwood and Sheetrock. The use of all of these boards was intended to demonstrate one of many examples of the progress of humanity through scientific technology.

By the time the American world's fairs planned for 1939 were being organized, the plywood business in the US had undergone a transformation. Partly this was in response to dramatic declines in sales as the effects of the Depression continued (except for a moment of stability in 1936–37), but also to the development of increasingly water-resistant and even waterproof plywood. These new plywoods were used as a building material from the mid-1930s, offering the opportunity for new markets.

The most unrestrained celebration of plywood in any twentieth-century world's fair was undoubtedly the San Francisco Golden Gate Exposition of 1939–40 (opened in February 1939). While organizers had pledged themselves to the use of plaster in its buildings, 57 were built, or clad, almost entirely in plywood (fig. 142), making use of more than 8 million sq ft (approx. 743,200 sq m) of the material. The fourteen plywood buildings (of seventeen in total) of the California State Group were especially praised by the architectural critic Frederick Gutheim: 'a whole quarter...lightly built up in plywood...more attractive, gayer, more suitable, more modern, more economical and more imaginative than the "official" architecture of the Fair', which he described as 'a triumph of mediocrity'. The California State Group structure most lauded by critics was the US Government (or Federal) Building (figs 143–145) by the local architect Timothy L. Pflueger (1892–1946). One of the largest and most prominent buildings at the fair – occupying a 7-acre (2.8-ha) footprint with a frontage of 675 ft (approx. 207 m) – it was located on one of the main fair axes. The building was split in half by a towering colonnade of 48 solid redwood columns (one for each of the then US states), each 106 ft (32.3 m) tall, fixed to roof trusses with 3-in. (76-mm) thick, 29-ply, resin-bonded plywood panels (gusset plates), each 6 ft (1.83 m) long. Flanking this along the façade were two porticos entirely covered in plywood onto which colourful murals had been painted (described by an art critic and admirer of the building as 'screaming, chaotic').[9] The exterior walls and roofs of the building were clad in hundreds of Douglas fir plywood panels, varnished only and hence putting on show the much-publicized prefabricated manufacture of the material. The 'cheap' price of the Federal building received a lot of attention. It was said to have been constructed at $6.90 per square foot, 'a tenth of the price' of any previous Federal exposition building.[10]

142 (below)
***Plywood goes to the Fair***
Douglas Fir Plywood Association brochure, publicizing use of plywood at the Golden Gate Exposition, San Francisco, 1939. Marks for recently introduced grading standards at bottom of page

THOUSANDS DAILY MARVEL AT DOUGLAS FIR PLYWOOD'S VERSATILITY AS IT GOES TO THE FAIR . . . AND SETS THE PACE!

LOOK FOR THESE DOUGLAS FIR PLYWOOD GRADE MARKS

Printed in U.S.A.—Form 39-70

143 (above)

**Federal Building, Golden Gate Exposition, San Francisco**
Designed by Timothy L. Pflueger, 1939

144 (left)

**Design for promotional material for the Golden Gate Exposition, San Francisco, showing the Federal Building**
Designed by Ken Sawyer, 1939

145 (above)
**Federal Building under construction, Golden Gate Exposition, San Francisco, 1939**
Designed by Timothy L. Pflueger

Gutheim favourably contrasted the Golden Gate Exposition with the New York World's Fair (1939), which he pilloried as architecturally representing 'the holy façade of finance capitalism'. In fact, the high profile of plywood in San Francisco was due in large part to the efforts of the Douglas Fir Plywood Association (DFPA), a trade body representing firms in the important and neighbouring timber-growing and -producing states of Oregon and Washington. Although many types of plywood were used in the US, Douglas fir (or Oregon pine) gained the largest share of the American market (including exports) from an early stage.[11] For the San Francisco fair, plywood could thus be presented as an important part of the regional economy.

Starting in 1936, the DFPA had started a technical and engineering department to undertake a programme of research and testing (taking advantage of previous research by the FPL) on behalf of its members. In 1938, under a new and especially energetic director (W.F. Difford), it actively pursued new or improved strategies for increasing the market for plywood. It had been responsible in 1932–33 for successfully promulgating voluntary, industry-wide standards (not only for Association members) for Douglas fir plywood that were then issued annually by the US Bureau of Standards as national 'commercial standards' (fig. 146). These were (literally) signed up to by national associations of wood producers, architects, timber dealers, purchasing agents, and manufacturers of other products, as well as wood product manufacturers. Such publicly declared standards served the interests of producers as well. In 1938 the DFPA successfully lobbied to update the standards to include new classes of moisture-resistant plywood ('suitable for construction where subjected to occasional deposits of moisture by condensation...or leakage') and exterior Douglas fir plywood ('the ultimate in moisture resistance...for permanent exterior use').

These specially made and individually branded products represented the best opportunity for increased plywood sales in the coming years. The testing regimes used to ensure the quality of the products – of the sort followed by leading manufacturers and the FPL for many years, and which included subjecting plywood to extremes of temperature and moisture – were published as part of the standards document, allowing customers to have greater confidence in the products. The publication of new standards, combined with a new system of inspection by DFPA inspectors, as well as a new DFPA system to mark every standard size piece of plywood from Association manufacturers according to type and use, addressed end users' most pressing concern about plywood: namely, the stability (or instability) of the glue that held panels together.

The promotion of exterior plywood relied on its specification by builders, architects and interior designers and it was those specifiers who were targeted in trade journal advertising campaigns starting in the late 1930s, including by means of solicited (and presumably paid) endorsements by prominent figures (fig. 147). The provision of Douglas fir plywood for the world's fairs – especially San Francisco – and the accompanying publicity originating, in part, from the trade association itself, were part of the wider promotion of the material.[12] By 1942, when the joint government–industry standards for plywood were revised again, the 'moisture-resistant type' of plywoods, including exterior boards, were described as 'the majority of production', a dramatic change from 1936 when the type was not even mentioned in that year's published commercial standards.

146 (below left)

**Douglas Fir Plywood Association advertisement for Dri-Bilt housing system, using recently graded DFPA products, 1939**

147 (below)

**Douglas Fir Plywood Association advertisement, with endorsement from the American architect William Wurster, 1938**

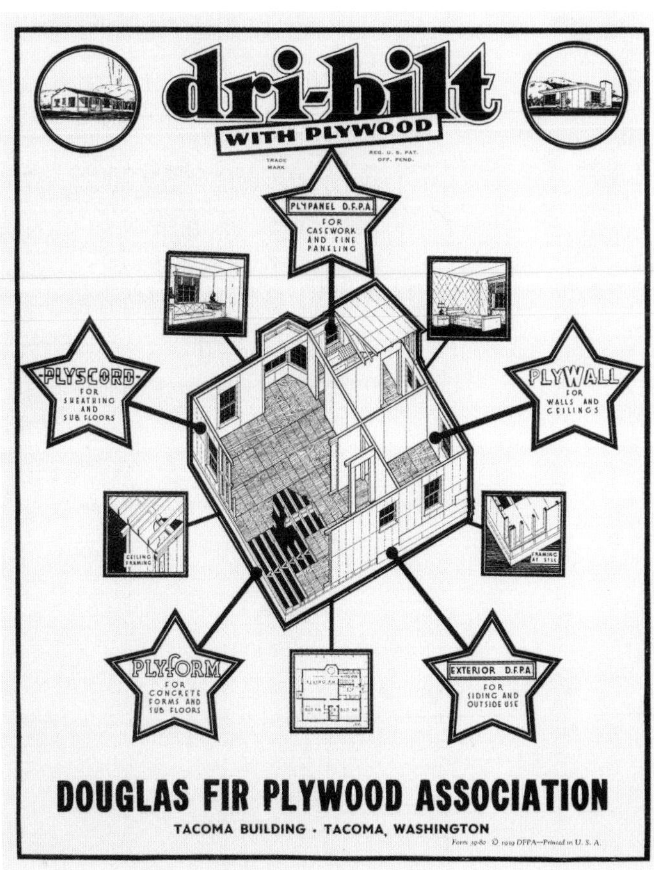


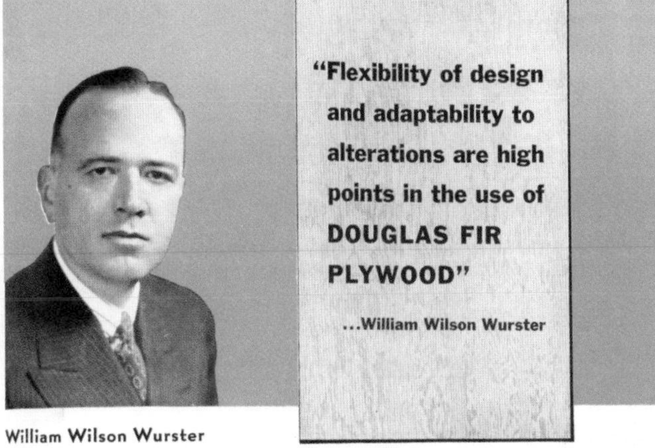


**William Wilson Wurster**

*Direct, honest solutions—free from affectation—have won national recognition for the work of William Wilson Wurster. Featuring his work in its May, 1936, edition, Architectural Forum said, "His houses not only have a remarkable range of expression but, by virtue of their adaptability to special conditions, possess a strong local character which can today be found in the work of few men."*

*Mr. Wurster was born in Stockton, California, and studied architecture at the University of California. He has traveled in Hawaii, the Philippines and the Orient, and has lived in Europe and New York. His first work in America was in the San Francisco office of John Reid. In 1926 Mr. Wurster opened his own office in San Francisco. One reason for the wide acceptance of his work is that he never feels he must put over a given expression.*

DOUGLAS FIR PLYWOOD is one material that places few limitations on the architect. It is practical for both exterior and interior use. And it combines the unusual strength of cross-grained lamination—light weight—low cost—and the labor saving advantages of large panels.

Specify Douglas Fir Plywood for wall and roof sheathing and sub-floors in home construction. You'll add extra strength and rigidity to the structure—substantially reduce labor costs. For interior finishing Douglas Fir Plywood is adaptable to practically any use—wall paneling, cabinet work, built-ins, ceiling and walls of playrooms, etc.

Douglas Fir Plywood Concrete Form panels allow the architect freedom of expression in designing mass structures. They give a smooth finish with minimum joints, sharply reduce rubbing and finishing costs—and can be reused repeatedly.

Stock panels of Douglas Fir Plywood (3, 5 and 7 ply) are manufactured in various thicknesses, as large as 4 x 8 feet, and even larger on special order. Standard grades include Wallboard, Sheathing, Standard Panel and Concrete Form. Special grades can be obtained for any building and industrial need, including hot-pressed, resin-bonded plywood for permanent exterior exposures.

Sweet's Catalog contains complete data on Douglas Fir Plywood. Our well-equipped Technical Division offers cooperation to architects, engineers and others in adapting Douglas Fir Plywood to special problems, and recommending the proper types and grades to produce utmost serviceability and economy. Address DOUGLAS FIR PLYWOOD ASSOCIATION, Tacoma Building, Tacoma, Washington.

Flexibility of design possible with Douglas Fir Plywood adds charm to the walls and ceiling of a bedroom in this Wurster-designed home at Carmel, Calif.

DOUGLAS FIR PLYWOOD

*Real Lumber*

MADE LARGER, LIGHTER SPLIT-PROOF STRONGER

148 (right)

**Douglas Fir Plywood Association promotional brochure, detailing construction of 'House of Plywood'**
New York World's Fair, 1939

DEMONSTRATION HOME No. 2

NEW YORK WORLD'S FAIR 1939

UTILITY RM 7'-0" x 7'-9" HEAT
TRAY
SINK
KITCHEN
RANGE
CLOS.
COUNTER CASES
DINETTE
CUPBD.
PLYWOOD HOUSE
BOOK SHELVES
PORCH SCREENED
LIVING ROOM
DESK
COATS
DRESSER
CLOSET
LINEN
CLOS.
CLOS.
TERRACE
BED ROOM
BATH
BED ROOM
DRESS. T.

No. 2

THE HOUSE OF PLYWOOD

*Sponsored by*

Douglas Fir Plywood Association

Crane Company
General Electric Company
Johns-Manville
S. C. Johnson & Son, Inc.
National Adequate Wiring Bureau
National Better Light-Better Sight Bureau
New York Telephone Company
Orange Screen Company
Truscon Steel Company

**Furnishings by Modernage**

*Architect:* A. Lawrence Kocher, 4 Park End Place, Forest Hills, N. Y.

The DFPA also sponsored 'The House of Plywood' at the 1939 New York World's Fair (figs 148–149). This fair set out to address social concerns such as the ongoing effects of the Depression, the alienation of the individual within industrial society and the importance of democratic principles as a bulwark against fascism. In a combination that would become increasingly familiar in the post-war period, much of it was also devoted to a celebration of the consumer culture that was portrayed as just around the corner. One part of this was the Town of Tomorrow, consisting of fifteen demonstration houses making use of a range of building technologies. Designed by the New York architect Lawrence Kocher (1885–1969), the Plywood House featured the full range of Douglas fir plywood products deployed in what to contemporaries was the most up-to-date *moderne* style: waterproof exterior plywood (Exterior DFPA) on top of an intermediary layer of strengthening Plyscord sheathing, a roof of those same materials, interior walls of slightly pigmented Plywall ('Douglas Fir Plywood Wallboard'), Plypanel interior cabinet work, a kitchen and a bathroom finished in (experimental) 'enamelled fabric' over plywood, subfloors of water-resistant Plyscord, and a concrete foundation poured into Plyform forms.

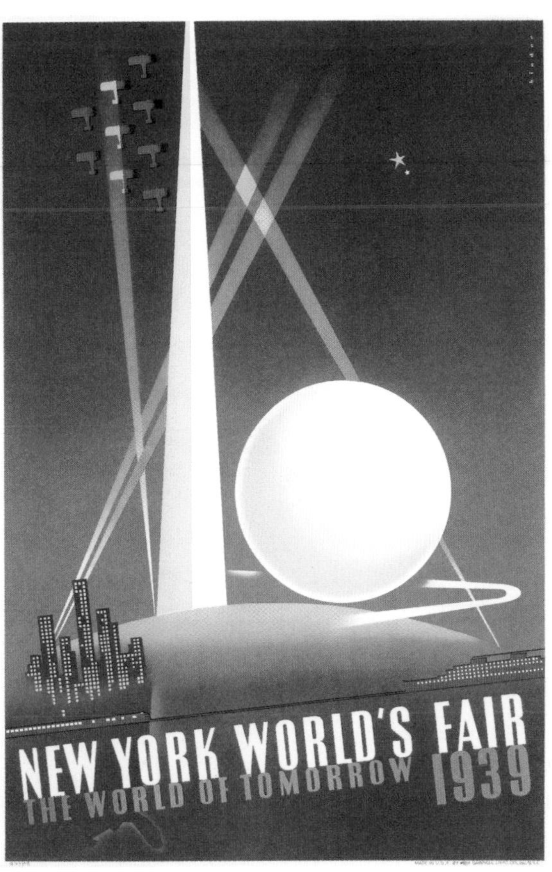


149 (above)

**Douglas Fir Plywood Association display of the Dri-Bilt construction system in 'House of Plywood'**
New York World's Fair, 1939

150 (left)

**Poster for the New York World's Fair, showing the Trylon and Perisphere**
Designed by Joseph Binder, 1939

The structural system for the Plywood House was the Dri-Bilt prefabrication method that had been developed and patented by the DFPA (figs 146 and 149), although its details were actively shared with the public. It was, in fact, a conventional wood frame system to which was attached (using nails) the full range of plywood products manufactured by members of the DFPA. The name Dri-Bilt was part of a wider effort to market plywood (and other board materials) as an alternative to traditional lath and plaster construction. It did not represent the more ambitious structural use of plywood combined with bonding processes seen elsewhere (see pp. 130–31).[13]

Alongside industry promotion by the DFPA, plywood had two other significant appearances at the 1939 New York World's Fair. Plywood received an unexpected showcase in October and November 1939, when large slabs of plaster (60 ft [5.57 m] square) dropped from a great height from one of the architectural symbols of the fair, the towering structure known as the Trylon (fig. 150). The Trylon's 700-ft (213.4-m) high surfaces were entirely reclad in plywood panels for the second season of the fair in 1940 (figs 151–152), and a number of articles were published in both the *New York Times* and the engineering press, documenting this improved (and now waterproof) cladding.[14]

151 (opposite)
**Steel structure of the Trylon and Perisphere, before initial cladding**
New York World's Fair, 1938–39

152 (left)
**Construction workers nailing plywood cladding to the Trylon**
New York World's Fair, 1940

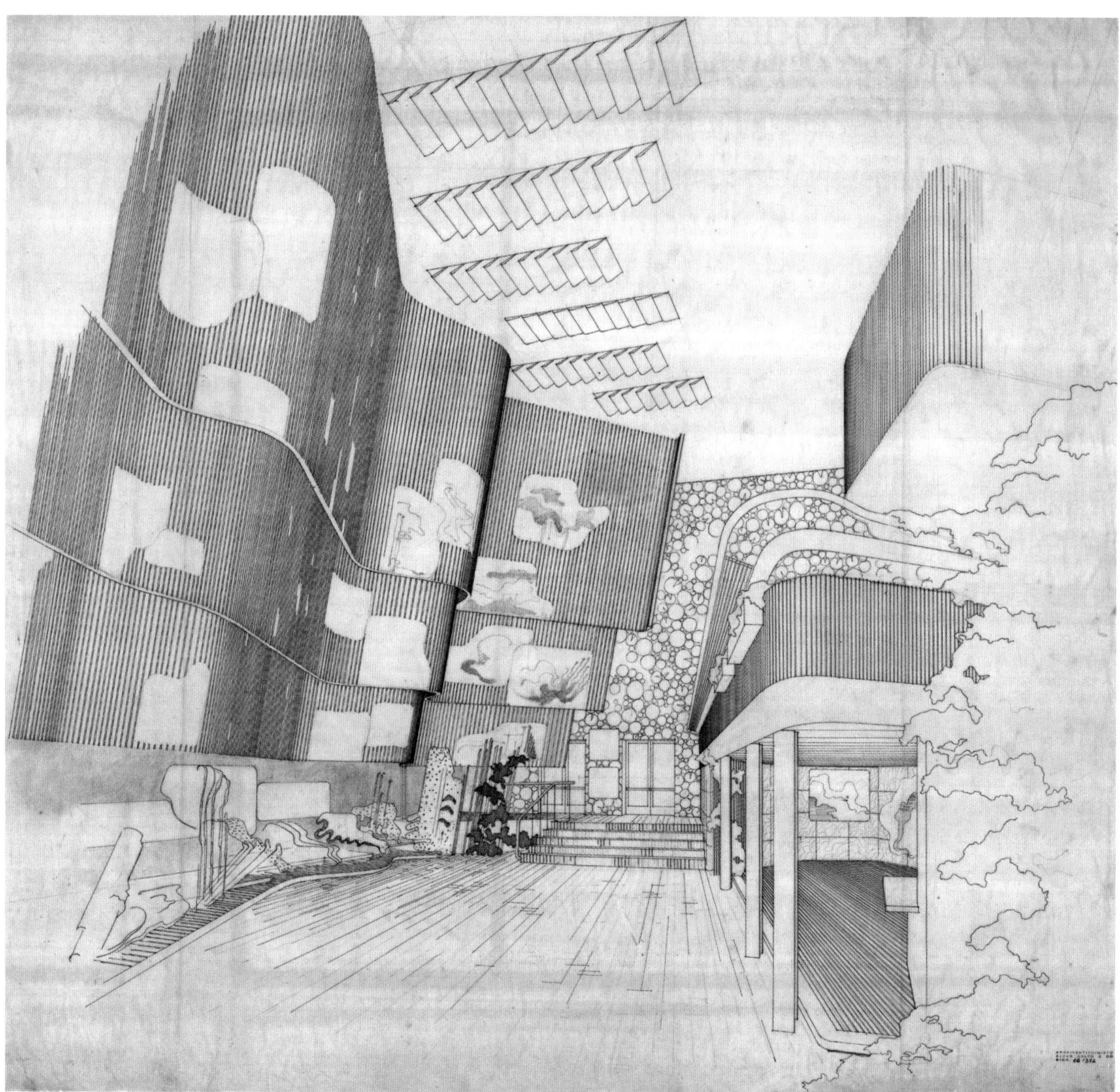

153 (above)

**Finnish Pavilion,**
**New York World's Fair**
Designed by Alvar Aalto and Aino Aalto, interior perspective, 1939

In great contrast to this practical application as a durable, easy to erect, streamlined surface material, the most dramatic and unexpected use of plywood at the New York fair was provided by the Finnish architects Alvar Aalto (1898–1976) and Aino Aalto (1894–1949) for the Finnish Pavilion (figs 153–154). Within an anonymous, rectangular exhibition building, the Aaltos created an interior dominated by a 40-m long, 16-m high undulating plywood wall that curved along two sides of the building and inclined into it. The wall was built in three tiers, with each level projecting out beyond that below it. Each tier was attached to a steel frame and wooden structure onto which were fixed large birch plywood panels. The panels were covered with a series of irregularly spaced vertical battens of different native Finnish woods. These animated the wall surface and (helpfully) covered the joints between plywood panels. Large blown-up photographs decorated the wall, while a recess under the lowest tier was used to display a range of wooden and non-wooden Finnish products including a large display of Aalto's own plywood and laminated wood furniture. This 'symphony in wood', as Alvar Aalto called it, proclaimed the forest as the basis of Finland's 'industrial progress'. Its dynamic form – said to have been based on the 'curtain aurora' of the Northern Lights – provided an exceptional example of the use of plywood as a sculptural material, much as did the forms of Aalto's furniture (see chapter 6).[15]

Although the Finnish Pavilion was in many ways completely at odds with the prevailing American exposition use of plywood as cladding, the resurfacing of the Trylon and the curved walls of the Aalto pavilion both served to highlight plywood's great flexibility as a structural surface material. The Aalto pavilion in many

154 (left)

**Construction of the Finnish Pavilion at the New York World's Fair, 1939**

Joins between the plywood panels that make up the pavilion's curved walls are visible ways heralded the post-war era, when plywood became a highly visible material in mass-produced design (see chapter 6). On the Trylon, which was the key symbol of both the New York World's Fair and of the streamlined modern world that it heralded, plywood entered the scene almost accidentally and for purely practical reasons. Taken together, the 1939 New York and San Francisco fairs suggest the extent to which plywood had, by the late 1930s, emerged as a modern building material. Although the promise of the Aalto designs would not come to widespread fruition until after 1945, a crossover between architectural interest in plywood, and its use in large-scale, quick building projects, would come to the fore in plywood's most significant architectural form of the 1930s and 1940s – the prefabricated house.

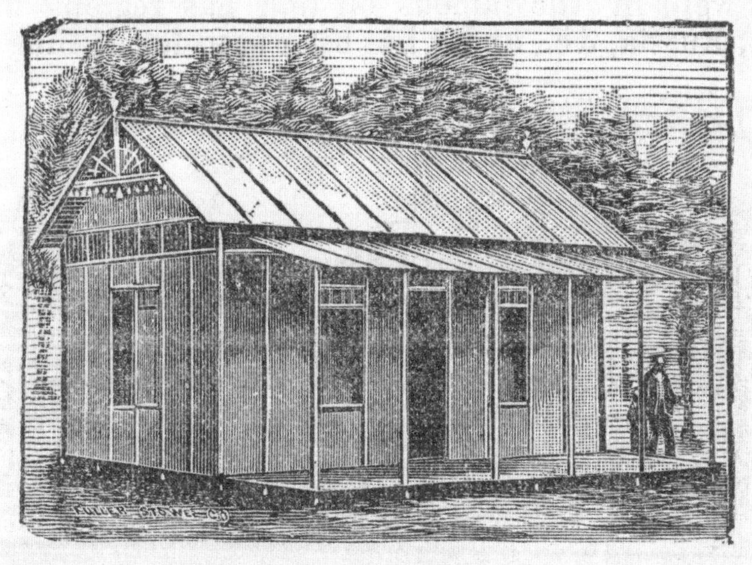


155 (above)
**'Grand Rapids Portable House'**
From *The Australasian Ironmonger* (1 May 1890), p. 131

156 (right)
**Red Cross laboratory packed for transport by lorry (above) and erected for use (below)**
From *Automobilia* (15 November 1919), p. 44

### Prefabricated building

Plywood played an important role in early twentieth-century experiments for factory-produced, prefabricated housing, an effort that attracted a great deal of work from architects, builders and the wood trade. Although the aspiration to have house parts roll off an assembly line and be erected on-site was especially potent in the 1920s and 1930s, its origins are to be found in the nineteenth century. By 1890 at the latest, the Grand Rapids (Michigan) Portable House Company began manufacture of small structures 'made of 3-ply veneer' for hunters' cabins, clubhouses and 'photograph galleries' (fig. 155), but also 'larger and more substantial cottages for summer resorts, and in warmer climates for dwelling houses the year round'. The designs followed a number of American panelled (though not plywood) house systems documented as having been sold from 1861 onwards and, like these, the Grand Rapids buildings were made of solid timber frames onto which were fitted modular panels that could contain windows or doors. The frame and panels were put together with pins and bolts – the lack of nails or screws enabled simple erection and taking down 'without mutilation in two hours'. The Grand Rapids firm is documented as having exported as far as Australia (kit housing being particularly useful to the colonial enterprise) and, by 1891, it had fifteen employees and sales of a very considerable $60,000 per year.[16]

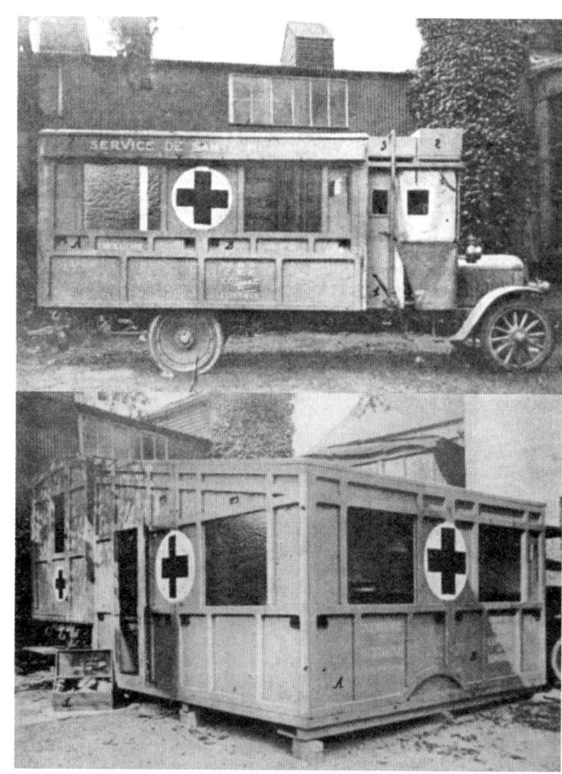

This kind of structure was also built in several European countries. In 1912 prefabricated plywood houses suitable even for the Greenland winter were designed by the Danish explorer Johan Peter Koch and built by the Danish Army for scientific expeditions. The houses were bolted together and contained an air-space between two plywood panel layers, presumably so that the frame could stiffen the structure and in the hope that this would provide an additional barrier to the cold. Each panel was sufficiently small that there was no danger of warping (as had evidently happened on a similar expedition in 1906–07) and in order that two panels could be carried by one Icelandic pony.[17] The portability and demountability of plywood were also the key factor in its choice for 'miniature' laboratories built for the British Army in Egypt and the American Red Cross in France (fig. 156). In these cases double-walled plywood panels insulated with cork were used by 1919.[18] All of these were essentially kit structures, requiring a minimum number of tools for assembly.

Reflecting upon the practice of the decade up to 1941, a leading chronicler of contemporary plywood pointed out that building elements – doors, windows, frames and casings, built-in cabinets, etc. – had long been prefabricated in woodworking shops or factories. The (then) recent push for prefabrication, he wrote, could more aptly be described as an effort to make larger building elements in the factory.[19] In countries with a tradition of building dwellings in wood, an acute need for housing drove efforts towards the building of fully prefabricated plywood housing of all kinds, for example in Germany during the hyperinflation of the 1920s, the US in the decade after the stock market crash of 1929, Finland during World War II, and Japan after the war.

In 1921 in Dresden, Germany, the Deutsche Werkstätten (German Workshops), a well-established manufacturer of furniture and furnishings, began prefabricating *Plattenhäuser* (panel houses). Designed by leading architects, many were made using plywood panels, mainly in the interiors (fig. 157). The firm offered catalogues of various models, most representing traditionally orientated, occasionally rustic designs, although Bruno Paul's was resolutely modernist (fig. 158). Finland's manufacture of unusual plywood

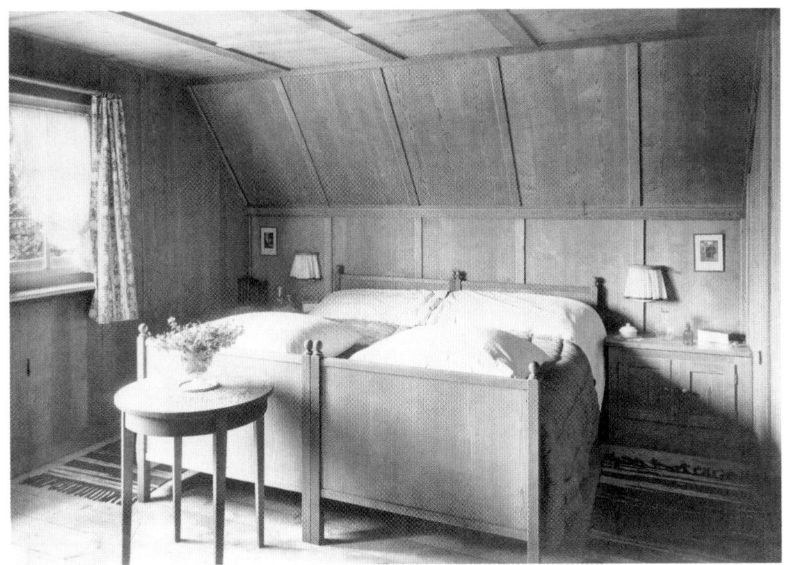

157 (top)

**Bedroom of *Plattenhaus* H 196 for Deutsche Werkstätten**
Designed by Prof. Adalbert Niemeyer, c. 1925

158 (above)

***Plattenhaus* H 1018 for Deutsche Werkstätten**
Designed by Bruno Paul, c. 1925

FINNISCHE
SPERRHOLZZELTE
PUUTALO OY.
HELSINKI - FINNLAND

tents (fig. 159) for the Nazis and then the Italian Army during World War II kept its plywood industry afloat, not least through the supply of synthetic Kaurit glue; food rationing had caused the near-complete disappearance of albumin and casein glues.[20]

From the 1930s plywood was first experimented with on a national scale in the US for the cheap, factory production of prefabricated standard housing, as is discussed below. As with early plywood prefabs in nineteenth-century colonies, the emphasis of these 1930s and 1940s designs, often intended to house a mobile population, was on quick fabrication and demountability. Alongside other industrial board materials (such as gypsum or asbestos), plywood provided an ideal material for this kind of construction, as it lent itself easily to lightweight panel systems that could be factory-built and assembled on site. In contrast to these other board types, plywood could be marketed as both a high-tech industrial product (often through reference to its use in aircraft construction) and an improved version of a familiar building material – wood.

**The Forest Products Laboratory prefabrication research**

The interest in prefabricated construction in the US was spurred by a variety of factors arising from the catastrophic and ongoing effects of the Great Depression throughout the 1930s. By 1933 unemployment was at its highest rate ever (24.9%) and household incomes were at 1918–19 levels. House building had been declining since 1925.[21] There was, during these years, an acute housing shortage and, in particular, a need for housing at the lowest possible cost. An often mentioned aim was to produce a house costing less than $5,000. During Franklin D. Roosevelt's first term as President (1933–37) the Federal government passed a National Housing Act (1933) creating, among other things, a Federal Housing Administration (FHA) and a Federal Home Loan Bank System that created the modern American system of home loans, then especially targeted at the worst-off. FDR's New Deal also created (in 1933) the Tennessee Valley Authority (TVA) to encourage economic development – including the building of housing –

159 (opposite)
***Finnische Sperrholzzelte* ('Finnish Plywood Tents')**
Cover of Puutalo Oy catalogue, c. 1941–44

160 (below)
**Plywood samples exposed to the elements on test fence**
US Forest Products Laboratory, Madison, Wisconsin, 1930s

161 (above)

**US Forest Products Laboratory, first plywood model house**

On view at the Madison Home Show, Wisconsin, 1935

in seven Southern states particularly badly affected by the Depression. This national mobilization to create housing provided the context for all the other attempts at prefabrication before the outbreak of World War II.[22]

The US Forest Products Laboratory (FPL) described its purpose as developing 'methods to reduce wastes [*sic*] and lower costs in logging and in the manufacture and use of forest products...and to develop new and useful products from wood...'. By the 1930s its funding for aircraft research had disappeared, wood consumption in America had been falling since 1906, and the Depression was decimating the largest single area of contemporary wood use: building and construction. New or newly improved materials, especially metals in aeroplane and car manufacture, indicated a 'prevailing tendency toward substitution' of wood, wrote the Director of the FPL, C.P. Winslow, in 1932. His strategy for wood products was to focus on lowering consumer costs, to increase customer satisfaction through improvements in properties and qualities, to develop new or modified products, and to promote popular acceptance and use of the products. All of these, he argued, required a widening and deepening of technical knowledge. In particular, he cited the need to improve the design of wooden structures so as to achieve factory mass production. This required research into timber mechanics, physics, and wood technology and chemistry, which the FPL was uniquely qualified to undertake (fig. 160). One specific outcome of this ongoing research was a new unit system for low-cost plywood panel house construction, a project that would contribute to solving the nation's housing crisis, which fitted well within government policy, but would also usefully raise the FPL's national profile.[23]

Research on unit house construction began in 1932, and the first 'all-wood' – never referred to as plywood – model house was erected at the FPL in early 1935. It was shown to the public for the first time at the local Home Show (in Madison, Wisconsin), from 27 to 31 March 1935 (fig. 161). Although the FPL was careful to describe the house as a demonstration of a unit panel construction system rather than as a finished design for the market, 12,000 visitors queued to see the fully furnished house and marvelled at the fact that the parts were made in a factory and then erected on site by seven men in twenty-one hours. The small, single-storey house (21 × 29 ft/6.4 × 8.84 m), with living room, two bedrooms, kitchen, bath and utility room, and a flat roof that doubled as a sun terrace, indicated the aim of producing an affordable, modern-style house. Because of the size of the standard panel, prefabrication was best suited to such smaller houses.[24]

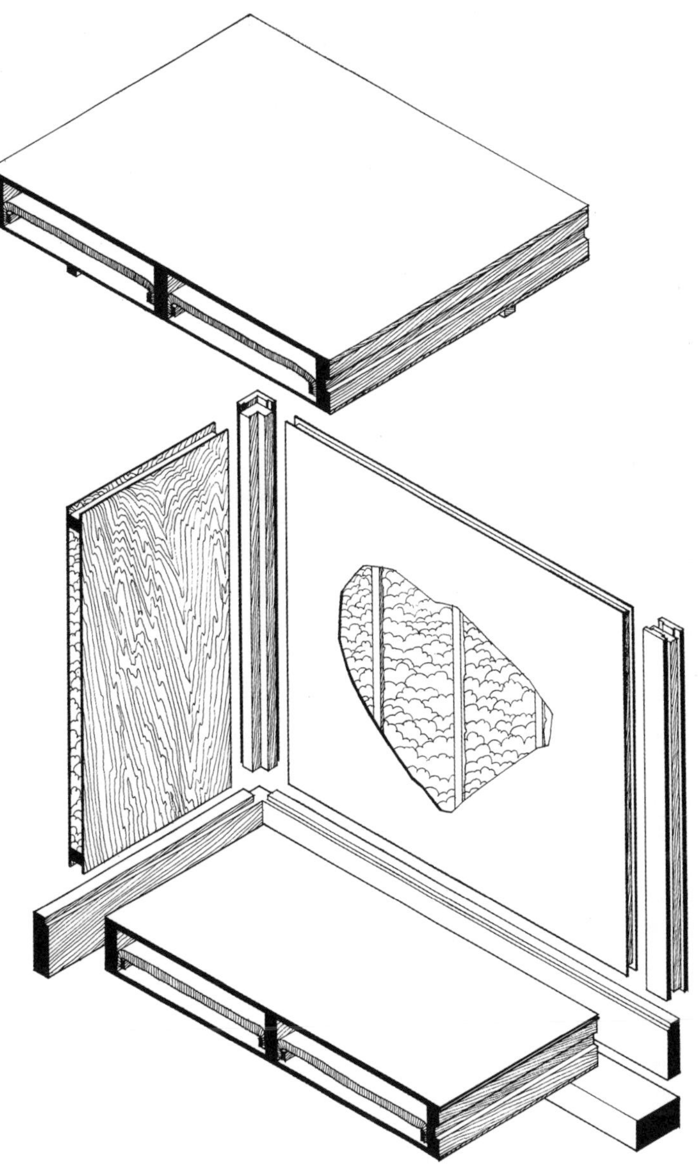

162 (above)

**US Forest Products Laboratory all-wood house system, standard panel assembly, 1935**

163 (above)
**Single-storey US Forest Products Laboratory model house under construction in the grounds of the FPL, Madison, Wisconsin, 1937**
Designed by Holabird & Root

The FPL unit house was based on a system of wall and ceiling or floor panels (fig. 162). The wall panels consisted of two standard, factory-made, 4 × 8 ft (1.22 × 2.44 m), 3-ply panels glued (the type of glue was not specified) to 1⅜-in. (35-mm) wide internal solid wood cross-pieces, between which was 'loose insulation'.[25] The ceiling or floor panels were 4 ft (1.22 m) wide × 8–14 ft (2.44–4.27 m) in length with a more substantial, double-layered internal structure, also filled with insulation. The FPL referred to these units as 'virtually a box girder', the reference to aircraft construction suggesting their special structural role. An essential feature of the system was that the plywood panels were not nailed to their internal structure (as in traditional construction) but were glued together. This produced a continuous and rigid joint that the FPL claimed was impossible to achieve by nailing; it also ensured superior insulation.[26]

The units were attached to one another on site using glue and long, narrow interlocking pieces made of ply facing with a solid wood internal structure. Rather than a self-supporting frame of structural joists (or beams) to which were attached non-structural wall studs, as in a traditional wooden house, the plywood in the FPL system – in both walls and floors – carried most (three-quarters) of the weight of the house. As in the case of the rounded semi-monocoque aircraft structures, or the box girder wing ribs in a Mosquito wing, the properties of plywood were the basis of a novel structural system that the FPL originally

164 (above)

**Single- and double-storey US Forest Products Laboratory model houses, erected in the grounds of the FPL, Madison, Wisconsin, 1938**
Designed by Holabird & Root

referred to as a stressed skin (evoking aircraft design), although they later changed this to 'stressed panel' construction.[27]

The first FPL house was widely publicized in both the professional and the popular press, not least because it was a publicly funded initiative that shared full details of its manufacture and materials. Re-erected in the grounds of the FPL after the Madison show, it was joined there in 1937 by a single-storey (fig. 163) and, in 1938, a two-storey house (both designed by Holabird & Root of Chicago; fig. 164). Lessons learned from the first house resulted in modifications to the later ones. These included the use of synthetic resin adhesive so that parts could be bonded together on hot presses, more fire-resistant and effective 'mineral' insulation, and moisture barriers (asphalt-impregnated and coated paper) within the walls.[28]

The FPL seemed to be aware that the flat roofs of the its demonstration houses would not be welcomed by all who saw them and they anticipated the comments of the US First Lady, Eleanor Roosevelt, who visited the FPL in November 1937: 'This particular house had a flat roof, but they could put on a different type roof, and they are going to experiment with two story houses.' This lean towards a more conventional (less modern) house design was fairly prophetic of the style in which commercial plywood prefabrication developed and, in fact, the FPL had already experimented with pitched-roof construction in 1936 (figs 165–172).[29]

165–172

**Stages in erecting two-storey demonstration house with pitched roof**
US Forest Products Laboratory display at Madison Home Show, Wisconsin, 1936

## The impact of the FPL schemes

The FPL demonstration houses were, within a decade, the most widely known prefabricated houses in America and by 1942 were described as having 'had an enormous effect on the further development of prefabrication in wood'. As the FPL was a part of a government department and not a commercial enterprise, the free dissemination of their research through publications and journal articles encouraged extensive coverage in books on prefabrication, in a range of professional magazines, and also in the popular press in the US and abroad.[30]

In the private housebuilding sector, a firm that would go on to become one of the more successful prefabricators, Gunnison Magic Homes (founded in 1935 and later renamed Gunnison Housing Corp.) made use of the FPL system with certain small modifications (fig. 173).[31] As the company was forming it had relied on Thomas Perry, an engineer and a plywood and adhesive expert, to help develop a suitable design in plywood. Perry was almost certainly the link with developments at the FPL as he would have known their work well, often writing about it (see bibliography). Manufacturing was on a conveyor belt system, with full assembly kits then distributed to local dealers for construction on site. Gunnison plywood homes, built from 1936, were modest, pitched-roof designs that were aimed at semi- and low-skilled workers. At least 2,800 were built before the war effort restricted the marketplace. Such houses aimed to look like typical American single-storey family houses, although their intended buyers, like most American consumers, often feared that the walls were too thin or – as consumer polls of 1944 and 1945 demonstrated – that prefabricated houses lacked sufficient strength and permanence.[32] The use of the name 'Magic Homes' is suggestive of the ways in which Gunnison attempted to override these negative perceptions. Much of the production of plywood prefabs at that time (both governmental and commercial) traded on images of this type, often by focusing on the miraculous speed with which these 'magic', modern houses could be constructed.

## Demountable housing

In 1942 Thomas Perry observed that while the public recognized that standardization in houses was as valuable as that in cars or appliances, they preferred individuality in their own homes. He identified architects as encouraging this latter tendency. The industrial origins, low cost and flat, undecorated surfaces of plywood appealed to modernist architects in particular in a way that the material rarely did to those orientated towards traditional house construction, materials or regional house styles. The use of plywood in prefabricated housing is an

173 (right)
**Gunnison Homes advertising brochure, 1950**

174 (above)
**Evans Plywood Company office building, Lebanon, Oregon**
Designed by Richard Neutra, 1940

interesting site of crossover between the work of modernist architects and state building initiatives of the 1930s.

The Los Angeles architect Richard Neutra (1892–1970), a leading exponent of European modernism, used plywood in a number of his projects, as both an exterior and an interior material. Neutra designed an office building in Lebanon, Oregon, for the Evans Plywood Company (later manufacturers of early Eames designs, see chapter 6) in 1940 (fig. 174). Mirroring the contemporary work being done by the DFPA through vehicles such as world's fairs, Neutra's building was intended to demonstrate the versatility of Evans's plywood as an architectural material. The building used plywood cladding on its exterior (highlighting the material's adaptability through the smooth curve of a long first-floor balcony), plywood panelling on the interior and plywood floors.[33]

The Evans building followed on from an earlier investigation by Neutra into plywood as a material for prefabrication. In 1936 he designed a plywood demonstration house as one of six architect-designed houses shown at the Los Angeles Exhibition of Architectural Building Materials (figs 175–177). Like many American architects urgently in need of clients, Neutra had been designing houses costing under $5,000, which therefore qualified for FHA-backed mortgages (although it is unlikely this house would have met such a budget), and was also a keen experimenter with materials and industrialized building systems.

Although, like most low-cost houses, his demonstration house allowed for a single bedroom only, its spaciousness was revealed in a large living room and separate recreation room opening onto exterior patio spaces, a separate dining room (unusual in low-cost houses) and a second floor (equally unusual). The use of plywood, though extensive, was restricted to interior and exterior cladding employed in a module of 40-in. (1-m) panels of 'superwaterproof plywood' manufactured by the Harbor Plywood Corporation (see p. 93). The use of waterproof plywood was the most-mentioned detail of the construction in the press. The 'prefabricated boards' were attached to a timber frame ('standardized unit type chassis'), the joints of which were clad in aluminium, exposed regularly between panels. This framing system was another element in the building that Neutra was experimenting with more generally at the time. Neutra's model for the house had left the surface of the exterior plywood exposed, although when actually built it was painted white. Much of the interior plywood was left as light-coloured mahogany.[34]

Neutra's house was designed (like so many contemporary prefabs) to be movable. As he wrote of the design:

> The house in order to be used as a vacation place in several localities as the years go by, or to be sold to a subsequent owner who wishes to transport and re-erect it at a new site, was to be 'transport proof,' of elastic integral construction....The transportability of the house reduced the threat of a frozen asset, and so better finishes and more comfortable installations than usual in such a small house become justified.[35]

175 and 176
(above and right)

**Super-Plywood Model House, Los Angeles**
Designed by Richard Neutra, 1936

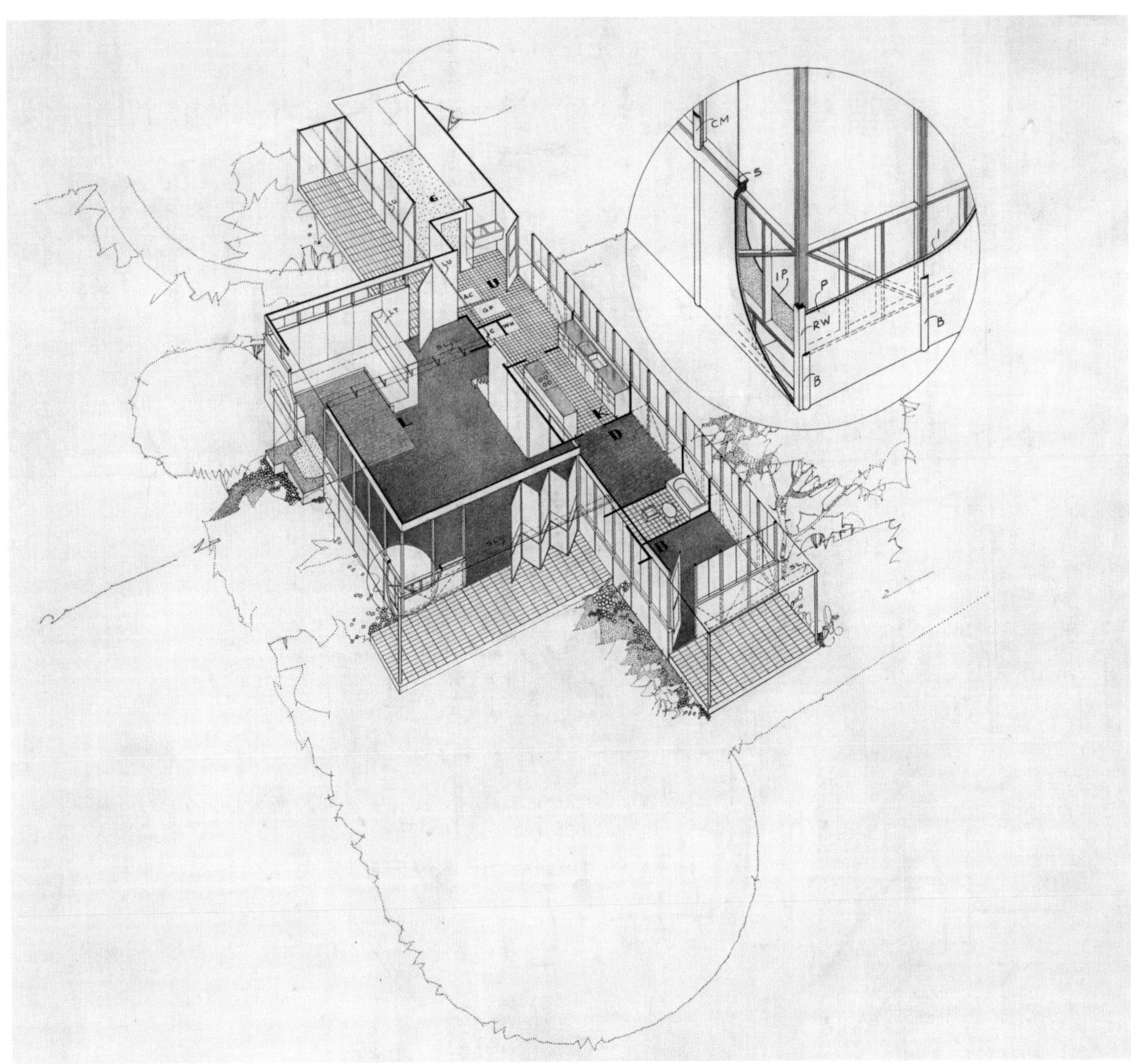


Neutra's plywood house was, in fact, unusual, in that it was documented as having been almost immediately taken down and re-erected: it was raffled after the exhibition, won by a local architect and moved 15 miles (24 km) to a new site.[36] Despite the fact that most prefabs did not, unlike Neutra's, end up being moved, plans for houses that could be moved with their owners recurred throughout the 1930s and 1940s. While closely linked to economic and wartime imperatives (see below), the image of a house without a permanent location became a broader ideal for modern construction. As a 1942 *Popular Mechanics* article stated: 'In the future, the typical American family may rent the ground, instead of the house – a custom for generations in certain cities, like Baltimore – and on moving day a truck picks up the home along with the furniture.'[37]

177 (above)

**Drawing detailing construction of Super-Plywood Model House**

Richard Neutra, 1936

## Defence worker housing

The early years of prefabrication were fraught with difficulty, not only because all new (or newly applied) building materials and production techniques require much problem-solving, but mainly owing to the fact that the biggest challenges for prefabricated housing were not material-related but bound up with financing, land use (zoning or planning) regulations and local politics, as well as its challenge to the traditional building trades. Once the main arena started to shift to US government-backed and then wartime schemes, these problems receded.[38]

Throughout the 1930s, alongside developing a strategy for building low-cost family homes, the US government started to invest heavily in temporary housing for mobile populations. This included major prefabrication by the Tennessee Valley Authority (TVA), which developed a design for factory-built houses that could be shipped to the sites of large infrastructure projects, such as dam building. These houses were intended to be demountable – they were moved onto their site in two fully formed halves, which were then joined together on a concrete foundation. Once a project finished, the houses could theoretically be broken back into halves and mounted back onto trucks for shipping to the next location. While some TVA prefabricated houses used insulation and gypsum board cladding on a timber frame, they also developed plywood-clad demountable houses, as well as a plywood stressed-skin design for their mobile trailer homes. Both of these types were manufactured for defence workers during the war (fig. 178).[39]

The TVA designs were one of many late 1930s plans for government-commissioned housing for defence workers. This housing was built for people who had to move in very large numbers to be near existing factories, mainly in California and elsewhere on the West coast and in Southern states. To prepare for the possible later need to move such workers to new production sites, and the certain need for post-war housing in other locations away from the factories, it was decided by the government that this housing must be capable of re-erection elsewhere. One of the most notable wartime projects, and not only owing to its use of plywood, was the housing designed by the San Francisco architect William Wurster (1895–1973) for Carquinez Heights in Vallejo, California, on San Francisco Bay, home of the largest US naval shipyard.

The first phase of the Vallejo project in 1941 (figs 179–181) involved the building of one-, two- and three-bedroom houses: 690 prefabricated plywood houses and 992 houses of Homasote (cellulose fibre-based) insulating board, both types using stressed-skin panel systems that eliminated the need for a structural frame. Although Wurster was hired after the Federal Works Agency had selected the site and appointed the manufacturers and contractors (normal government procedure at the time, as was the very small budget of $2,845 per house), he made numerous changes to the original plans. These included the siting and stepping of the individual houses to take advantage of views and to cut down on wind exposure, ensuring minimal cutting into the landscape by raising each small house along the slope of the hill (this also aided demountability, as it meant that each house sat on a raised foundation), flattening the roofs, and moving all windows to the long sides of each house.

The plywood system followed that of the FPL closely although the contractor, Plywood Structures of Los Angeles, was said to have perfected the FPL system and developed 'line production manufacture' to reduce costs and speed production. The standard 4 × 8 ft (1.22 × 2.44 m) panels were faced with ⅜ in. (9.5 mm) Douglas fir on the exterior (the same wood type used throughout) and ¼ in. (6.4 mm) three-ply on the interior, and were glued to ¼ × 2½ in. (6.4 × 64 mm) solid uprights spaced 16 in. (406 mm) apart. Casein glue – described as 'waterproof' – was applied with a glue gun specially developed for the project by the glue supplier (I.F. Laucks Inc.), and wood and glue were 'pressure glued' on giant heated presses. The panel units, into which were fitted electrical outlet boxes and conduit, were prefabricated in Reno, Nevada, by W.S. Watkins & Sons and shipped 200 miles (322 km) to a staging area near the construction site, where final preparations for assembly were made. The houses were assembled on site, plumbing and electricity installed, and the plywood surfaces then varnished. Speed of manufacture and erection was essential to all such projects: in this first phase at Vallejo

178 (below)

**Demountable plywood defence worker houses built by Tennessee Valley Authority, c. 1940**

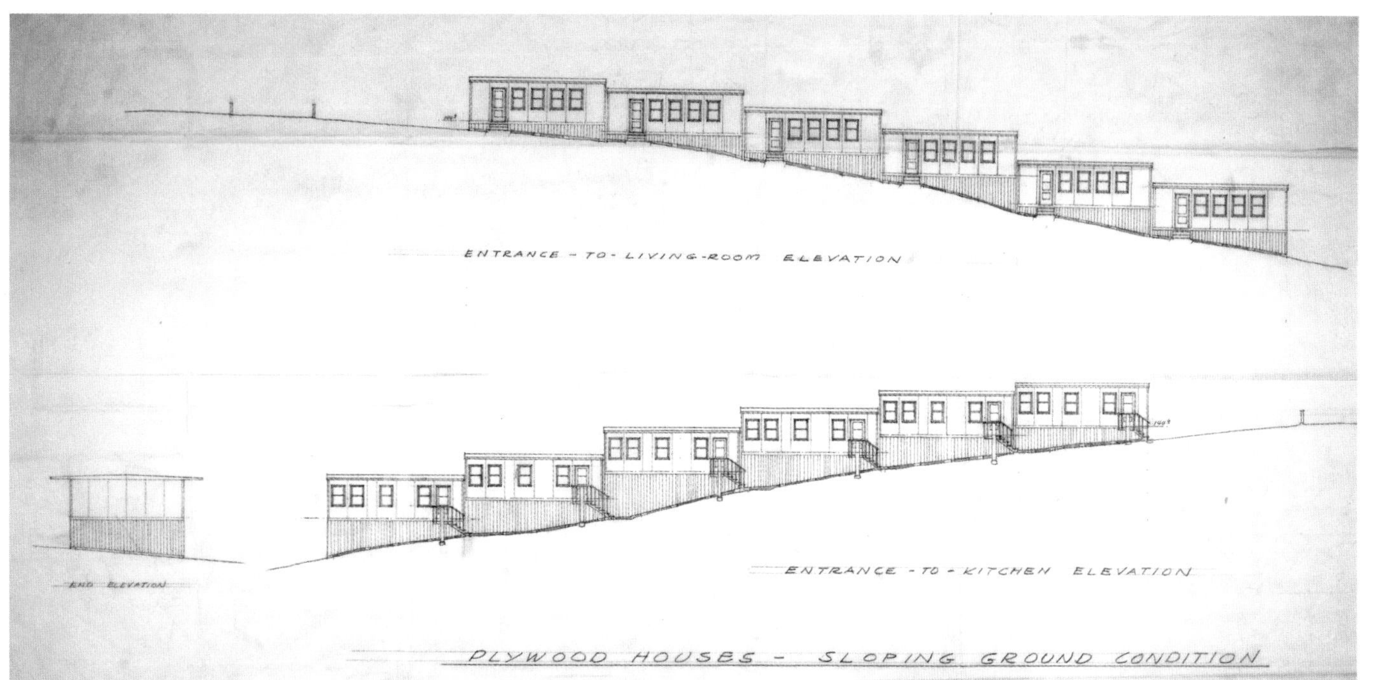

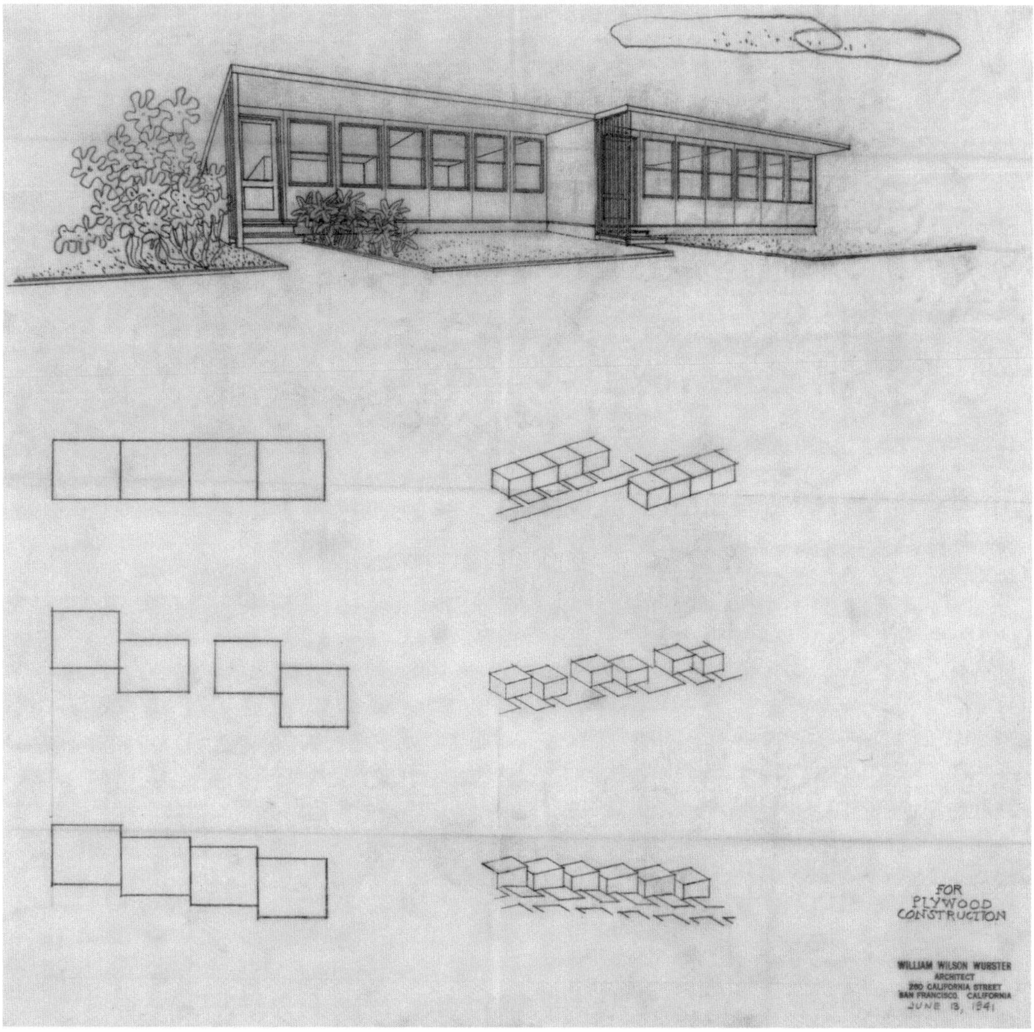

179 (above)

**Elevation of plywood houses at Carquinez Heights, Vallejo, California**
William Wurster, July 1941

180 (left)

**Variations for siting of plywood houses at Carquinez Heights, Vallejo, California**
William Wurster, July 1941

an average of 23 houses were erected every day. In 1942 an additional 1,000 single-storey plywood houses were commissioned from Wurster and built by Plywood Structures using the same prefabricated system as that of the first phase, which led one building magazine to dub Vallejo 'Plywood City'.[40]

Although Wurster's plans at Vallejo remained the most significant wartime building project using plywood, the material was adopted by a number of other modern designers and architects interested in new types of construction. The work of both the Chicago architect Bertrand Goldberg (1913–97) and the industrial designer Donald Deskey (1894–1989) is particularly significant here, in part because of its scale and ambition, but also because they reflect the ways in which plywood started to be marketed, in the late 1940s, as a material for post-war life.

Plywood was used extensively in plans for prefabricated defence housing by Bertrand Goldberg. Goldberg's first experimentation with prefabrication was in 1937, when he built a single plywood-panelled house as part of a research project run by Indiana's Purdue University. The project was intended to test new materials and methods for building low-cost houses.[41] Goldberg went on to form, with three colleagues, a company called the Standard Houses Corporation.[42] Planning to produce houses using factory-built plywood stressed-skin panels (made to the FPL system), Standard Houses published a plan book in 1937 in which they proposed ten designs for low-cost homes, each priced from $4,000 to $7,000.[43]

Standard Houses rented a factory (where the plywood wall panels and house fittings were made) and built their first five houses on land at Melrose Park, on the outskirts of Chicago. The houses were insured by the FHA and their construction was sponsored by companies (such as US Plywood) that agreed to supply materials on credit.[44] They were of a simple, relatively traditional design, each one storey with two bedrooms and a gable roof (fig. 182). A publicity document released by Standard Houses at the time of their building emphasizes the specific advantages of

181 (below)
**Construction of plywood houses at Carquinez Heights, Vallejo, California, 1941**

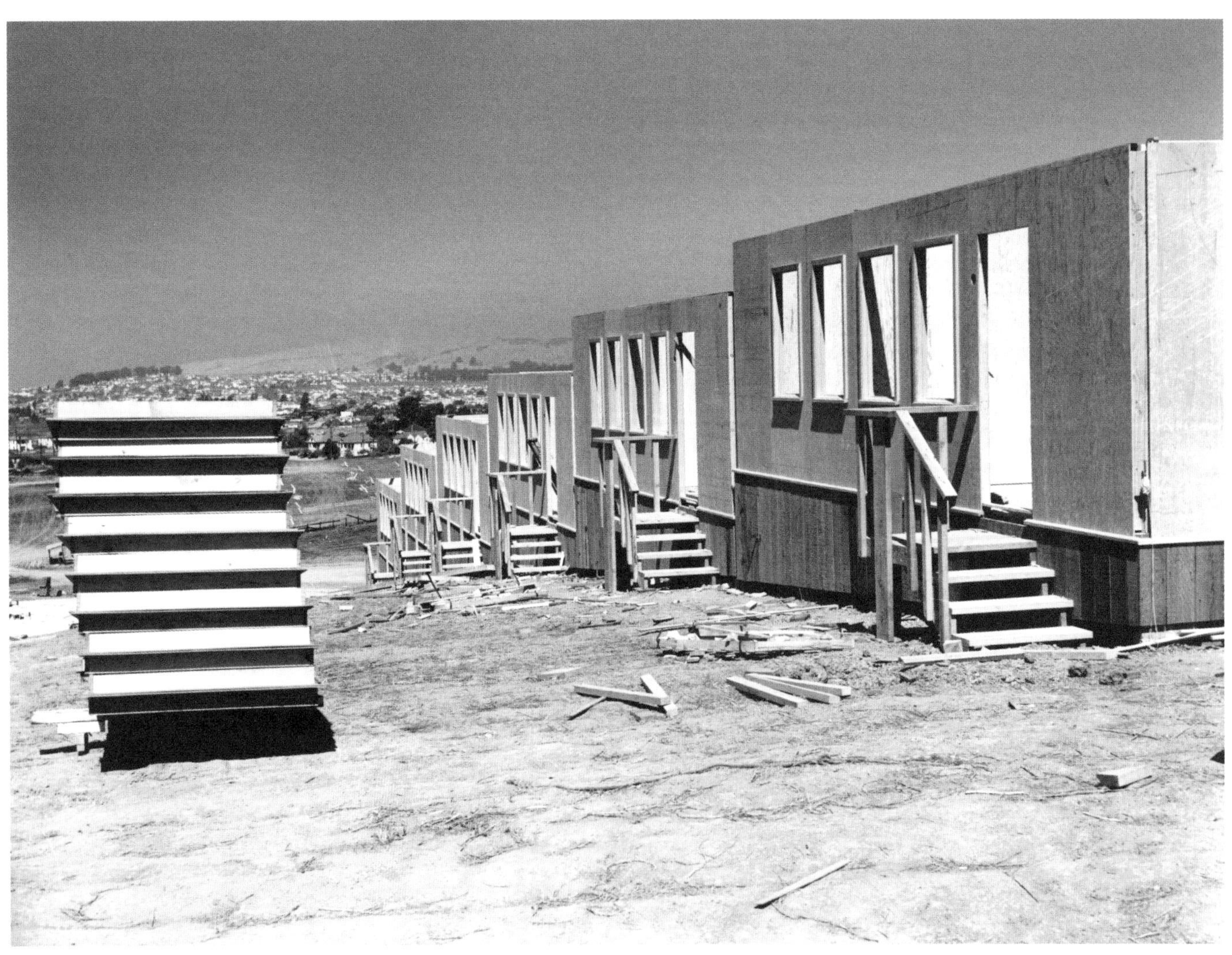

plywood as a material for prefabrication. Describing it as strong, quick to erect on site 'with a sledge hammer and a wrench', available in large standard sizes and durable, the press release finishes: 'Altho [*sic*] the wood itself is a "natural" material, certainly wood never grew with the potentialities that its fabrication with the machine has suddenly given it.'[45]

Standard Houses intended to extend the initial group of five Melrose Park houses into a large neighbourhood of prefabricated housing. While these plans were never realized, the company was shortly afterwards given contracts for two defence housing projects, the first at Indian Head, Maryland (1939–40; fig. 183), and a second, larger group of prefabricated houses at Suitland, Maryland (1941–42).[46] Both the Indian Head and Suitland houses were factory-produced, with Goldberg claiming at Suitland that he was able to produce all parts for up to ten houses per day.[47] As much as possible the defence housing was shipped from the factory as a series of finished parts, including assembled kitchens and bathrooms (fig. 184). These were built into houses that were assembled from panels on site. A series of storyboards made by Goldberg during the war, to document the process by which Standard Houses were built, emphasizes the scale of production (1 acre [0.4 ha] of plant, 500 union employees) as well as the streamlining and technical sophistication of the materials and process used. Plywood was the main construction material, but Goldberg describes a process of 'Plastic Assembly' by which he claims that 25,000 sq ft (2,323 sq m) of urea

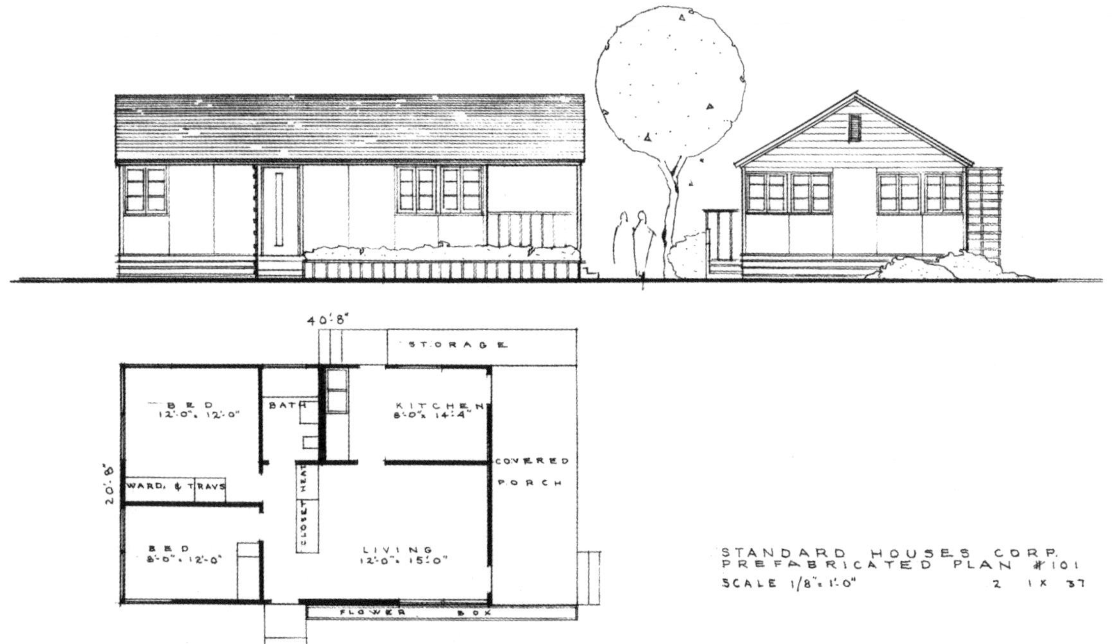


182 (left)

**Plan and elevation for Standard Houses**
Bertrand Goldberg, 1939

183 (above)

**Construction of Standard Houses at Indian Head, Maryland, c. 1941**

resin bonded plywood panels could be constructed each day.[48]

After 1945 Goldberg's work on prefabricated plywood structures led to his design of a stressed-skin plywood railway freight wagon, developed by the Pressed Steel Car Company as the Unicel freight car (fig. 185). The plywood design was intended to circumvent post-war steel shortages, and marketing of the Unicel emphasized plywood's advantages over metal.[49] Goldberg patented the Unicel's design in 1953. The most important aspect of its design was his extension of a stressed-skin panel (as used in the prefabricated houses) to a fully enclosed monocoque plywood structure.[50] As the Pressed Steel Car Company wrote about the project:

> The balloon, the airplane, the automobile body, all of the weapons of modern warfare, are more or less the direct outgrowth of engineering which creates and utilizes the shape of a structure to control the effect of the stress to which it will be subjected in use....the new Pressed Steel Car utilizes the entire car structure to absorb the shocks and stresses and to cushion them. The skins of the car help to push and pull the trains.[51]

The Unicel cars received much publicity, but, despite this and their technical and material advantages, were blocked by the steel lobby and never went into major production. Alongside the Unicel, Goldberg developed the design further for housing, suggesting using the basic plywood form of the wagons to make Unishelters – entirely factory-produced, easily transportable houses (fig. 186). A 1952 *Wall Street Journal* article states: 'A portable dwelling that can be loaded onto a flat-bed trailer...transported to another site, and placed on a new foundation in less than two hours... was unveiled here yesterday.'[52] Although the Unishelter never went into scale production, it represents the culmination of much of Goldberg's experimentation with plywood as a material for factory manufacture of demountable structures. Goldberg's work also suggests the ways in which wartime projects fed into plywood's mass mobilization for design in the years after 1945. This was even further realized in the work of the American industrial designer Donald Deskey.

### 'Why discuss a Sportshack when we're at war?'

Much as pre-war and wartime housing schemes had been designed with post-war use at least notionally in mind, so too did some designers actively produce prefabricated plywood projects during the war solely for anticipated post-war use. One example of this was Donald Deskey's prefabricated Sportshack, a demountable weekend or beach house, or ski or hunting lodge advertised as a 'symbol of a coming

184 (below)
**Factory construction of fitted bathrooms for Standard Houses, Chicago, c. 1943**

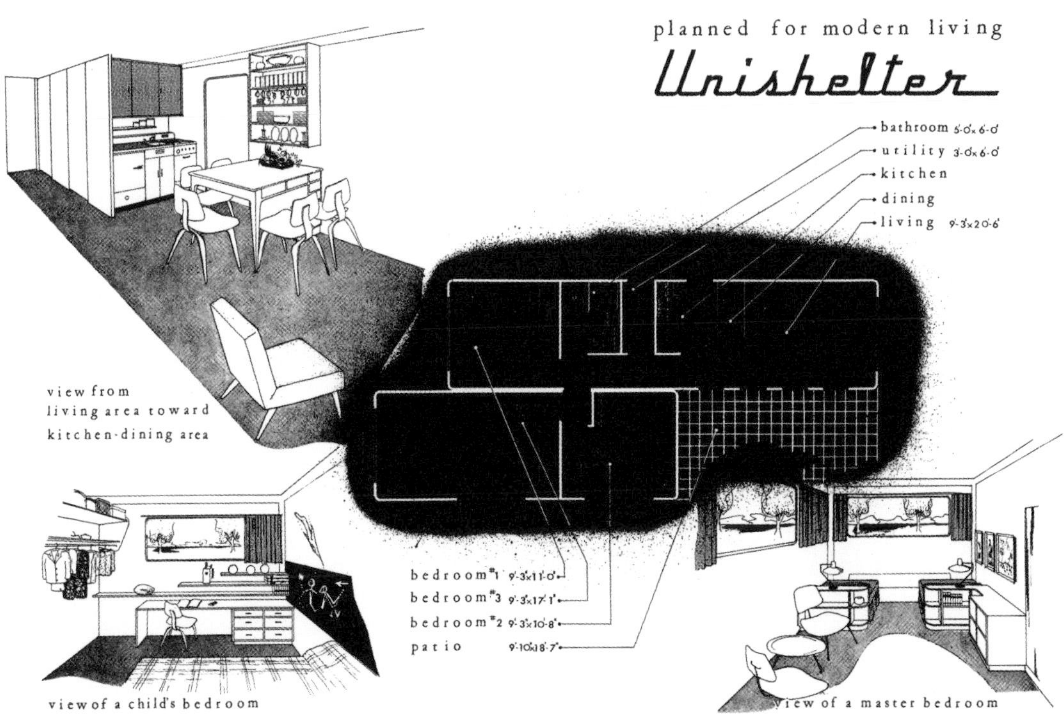


185 (above)

**Cutaway perspective, Unicel freight car**
Bertrand Goldberg, c. 1949–50

186 (left)

**Advertisement for Unishelter prefabricated housing, c. 1953**

187 (right)
**Presentation drawing, Sportshack,**
Donald Deskey, 1940

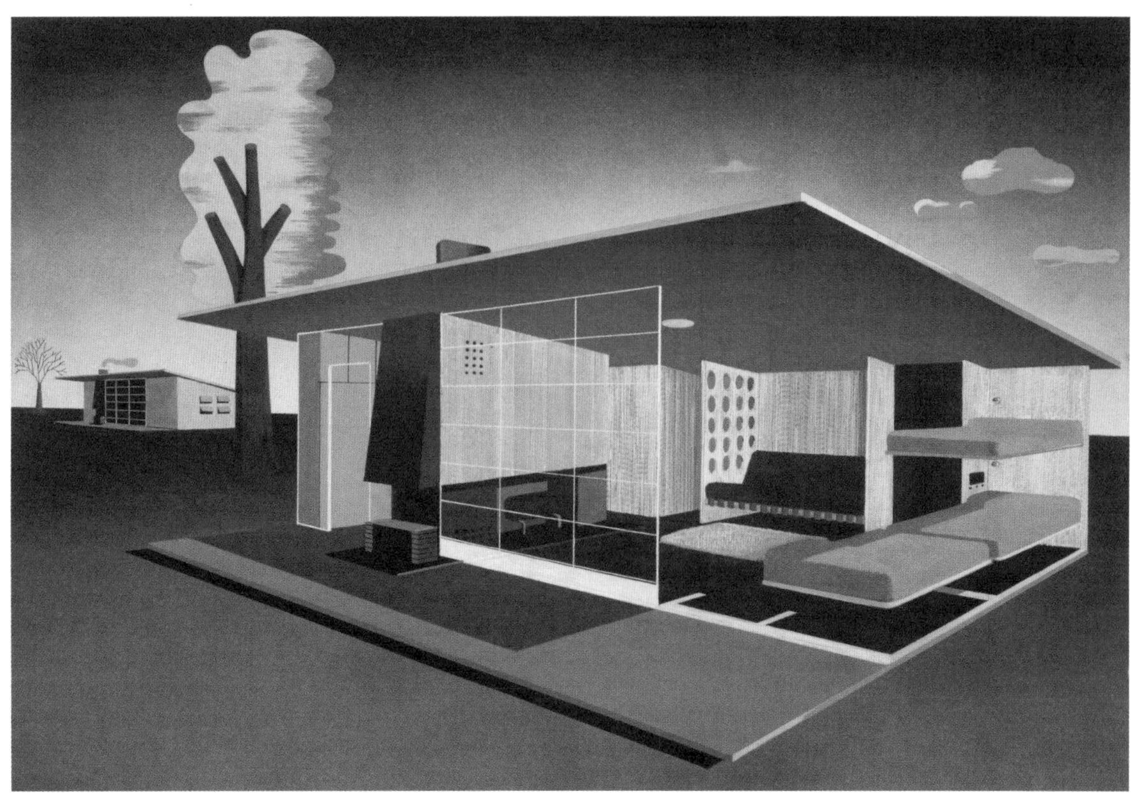

industrial upswing' that would follow victory in the war (figs 187–188). Deskey not only designed this structure and set up a company to sell it, but also, in cooperation with the manufacturer US Plywood Corporation, patented the type of plywood, Weldtex, that made up its three-dimensionally textured exterior and interior walls. Weldtex was a Douglas fir plywood, the surfaces of which were cut into or gouged along the grain with a serrated blade in parallel striations described as irregular, uneven and random, but still creating a pleasing pattern. The purpose of the striations was, alternately, structural – intended to relieve the stresses that caused 'shrinking, cracking, checking, and swelling' – and aesthetic or emotional – with the 'nostalgic charm of the weathered wood in an old log cabin', yet 'modern as today's airplane' owing to its bonding from synthetic resin (branded as Durez). Weldtex surfaces were advertised as improving with age. The striations usefully hid the imperfections of (in this case) cheap Douglas fir as well as the joins between panels.[53]

A version of the Sportshack was displayed in an exhibition of 'Contemporary Industrial Art' at the Metropolitan Museum of Art in New York in 1940 and an entire, full-scale Sportshack was displayed at the New York World's Fair in the same year. While both versions were still on public view, Deskey launched the company Week-end Cabins to sell the shacks but, by the following year, wartime restrictions on plywood (its use strictly limited to authorized defence purposes only) made it impossible to continue the venture.[54] However, after the war Weldtex turned into a very successful product for US Plywood and for Deskey, who had, in 1940, assigned his patent to that company in exchange for royalties. A series of lawsuits between US Plywood and Georgia-Pacific, a competitor that brazenly began manufacture of Weldtex in 1955 using the same trade name, revealed considerable sales of the material during the years 1956–65. US Plywood had marketed Weldtex as part of its Weldwood line of resin-bonded plywood products, advertised as 'Plastics and Wood – Welded for Good'. Weldwood had been widely advertised during the later 1930s especially (although it had been introduced about 1933) as an exterior plywood made in Douglas fir and in hardwoods, and, from 1940, as 'Vidal-process Weldwood', a reference to the process developed by Eugene Vidal for moulding and resin bonding plywood aircraft (see p. 94). Not only did Deskey use Weldtex for his first post-war prefab project (the Shelter Home, where he referred to Weldtex as 'the lowest cost enclosure material available') but also the material was used widely by home builders, as well as by those renovating their homes, as an alternative to 'messy' plaster walls. Sold originally in 4 × 8 ft (1.22 × 2.44 m) panels, Weldtex became available in a wider range of sizes for individual DIY home renovations. Weldtex was successful and desirable enough as a material for interiors that a range of property advertisements from commercial and individual sellers in the post-war era highlighted rooms panelled with it.

Deskey's Sportshack represented a post-war aspiration for plywood grounded in wartime building and research programmes. The latter had led to the creation of over 100 prefabricated homebuilding organizations by 1941, up from 30 before the war. By 1945 over 1.5 million housing units had been built (mainly government-financed), of which 200,000 were plywood. By 1950 20–25 firms within the private sector were building stressed-panel plywood houses of the FPL type, and, although they represented only one-quarter of the housebuilding industry, they manufactured between one-third and one-half of all prefabricated homes and were said to be the 'strongest companies' in the business. Plywood was entering the domestic arena in a meaningful way in peacetime and would be safe for the next thirty years from the reputational problems that it had suffered in previous decades.[55]

WITH BUSINESS AND INDUSTRY engaged up to the hilt in winning the war for America . . . it may seem irrelevant, at first glance, for Durez to focus attention on a Sportshack.

Yet just as surely as victory will be ours . . . the Sportshack is symbol of a coming industrial upswing! But let Donald Deskey, who designed this modern log cabin, give you a clue to its importance . . .

*"The Sportshack has sleeping accommodations for six. Completely insulated, it is equally suitable for beach house or ski cabin, hunting lodge or weekend house. Compact, it is pre-fabricated and demountable. Durez resin-bonded plywood makes possible such new construction features. For both exterior and interior walls are built with 'Weldtex.' This sturdy, striated plywood is as modern as today's airplane in appearance, yet has the nostalgic charm of the weathered wood in an old log cabin."*

"Weldtex" is only one of the many plywoods which owe much of their development to Durez research in phenolic resins. Naturally, along with Durez plastics, these plywoods are finding their way into war material.

But their emergency uses point unerringly to a brilliant future. Post-war production of Durez-bonded plywood pleasure boats at moderate prices is foreshadowed by the use of such plywoods right now in the navy's new mosquito boat fleets. The day will come when army barracks give way to vast economical housing projects. Sooner than you think, the aviation industry will become one of plywood's best customers. The possibilities are almost endless.

Perhaps Durez-bonded plywoods can help *you* serve your country today. Why not consult with Durez research engineers and chemists? Certainly you will also want to know what Durez plastics and resins can do for your business, once the victory's won. A request on your letterhead will bring *Durez Plastics News* to your desk, monthly—keep you abreast of the continuous progress in "tomorrow's" materials.

FOR DEFENSE BUY UNITED STATES SAVINGS BONDS AND STAMPS

DUREZ... plastics that fit the job

DUREZ PLASTICS & CHEMICALS, INC. DUREZ 1024 WALCK ROAD, N. TONAWANDA, N. Y.

188 (left)

**'Why discuss a Sportshack when we're at war?'**

Durez Plastics advertisement from *Fortune* (April 1942), p. 139

# *The* PRACTICAL HOUSEHOLDER

NOVEMBER
1960

1'3

Build this
Unit for
HI-FI Music, Radio and TV

*Also Inside*
Heating the Whole House
Wrought Iron Gates
Laying a Garage Drive

EXTRA INSIDE

*16-Page Guide*
TOOLS AND THEIR USES

*Plus*

*Exclusive Offer!*
7-in-1 TOOL *at Privilege Price*

# 6 Plywood Shows its Face (1930s–1980s)

## The domestication of plywood

The post-war use of plywood built on developments of the 1930s, especially improvements in glue and moulding technology exploited during the war. Owing largely to the strength of the US economy (in contrast to the precarious economies of post-war Europe) the widespread sale of improved plywoods developed particularly in the US in the years immediately after 1945.[1] Plywood was marketed there as one of a number of 'new' materials offering the promise of a more prosperous and up-to-date post-war life. It was extensively promoted to both industry and the individual consumer on the basis of its success as a wartime material (fig. 190).

189 (opposite)
**Plywood project on the cover of *The Practical Householder* DIY magazine, November 1960**

190 (left)
**George E. Ream Company advertisement, 'Plywood for War... Later for Peace'**
From *Arts and Architecture* (February 1944), p. 5

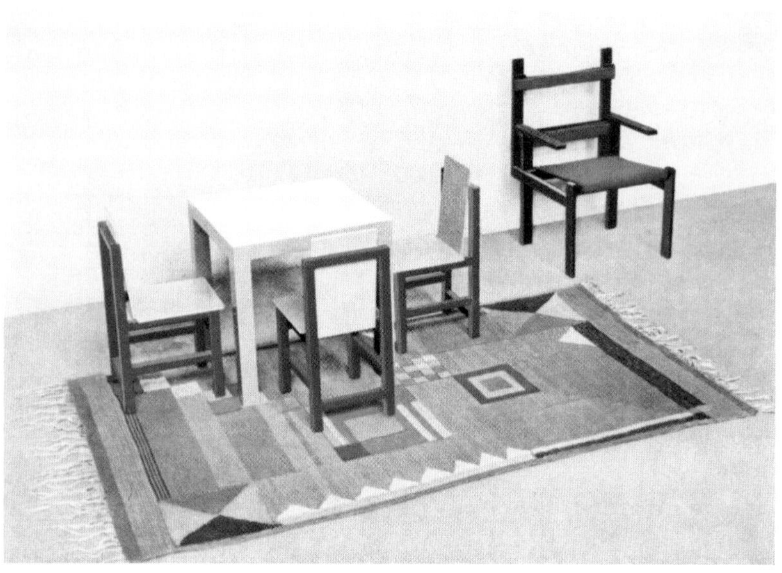

191 (above)
**Chairs and table for children's bedroom, designed by Marcel Breuer, 1924**
From Walter Gropius, *Neue Arbeiten der Bauhauswerkstätten* (Munich 1925), after p. 32

192 (above right)
**Chair, Douglas fir plywood with solid pine**
Designed by Rudolph M. Schindler, California, c. 1946, and following on from his 1930s plywood designs

Although plywood was used inventively by modernist designers in the 1920s and 1930s, it was not until after World War II that it started to become a commonplace material of domestic life. From the wartime collaborations and post-war furniture of the American designers Charles and Ray Eames, to the building of 1980s DIY skateboarding ramps, plywood emerged in the post-war period as a visible material for everyday design. The movement of plywood from war to peace embodied at once marketing rhetoric, adaptation of design types, and transfer of technical skill. Across this period plywood's standardized production and unique material properties enabled its use (often amateur and experimental) on a much larger scale than ever before.

### Pre-war modernist plywood

Before 1945 most plywood used in furniture was hidden. Its main use was in sheet form, as a substitute for wood in drawers, the tops and backs of wardrobes, and the sides, backs and sometimes tops of cabinets, chests of drawers and desks (figs 80–81). Plywood's highly visible move into post-war interiors, in large part owing to the influence of the furniture of Charles and Ray Eames, owed a great debt to the relatively small and decidedly niche production of modernist furniture of the 1920s and 1930s.

Modernist architects and designers used plywood not as a substitute, but for its unique qualities. Ranging from those with a foot in tradition to those firmly within the avant-garde, such designers utilized and displayed plywood among other useful and available 'industrial' materials well suited to mass production and powerful as symbols of the new machine age. In interwar furniture plywood might be used as a simple board material (figs 191–192) or exploited for its unique ability to be moulded (figs 193–194).

It was in 1930–32 in Finland, however, that the architect Alvar Aalto established what can only be called an authoritative design vocabulary for such furniture when he created moulded, single-piece plywood seats and backs for chairs. Within a short time these became exceptionally popular and influential in modernist circles in Europe and America. Aalto worked his way from tentative experiments based on 1920s German cantilevered chairs – placing plywood seats/backs on tubular steel or laminated wood cantilevered bases – to more original and elaborately moulded and curved, single-piece plywood seats/backs joined to either continuous or cantilevered laminated wood supporting elements (figs 195–196). The chair in fig. 195 was first made for the Paimio Tuberculosis Sanitorium in 1932 by a small, established furniture factory in Turku (fig. 197), owned by Otto Korhonen, with whom Aalto collaborated closely. The following year they began manufacturing the furniture for general sale.[2]

193 (left)

**Plywood and tubular steel chair**

Designed by Gerrit Rietveld, 1927, manufactured by Metz & Co., c. 1931, The Netherlands

194 (below)

**Wardrobe, designed by Bruno Paul, manufactured by Deutsche Werkstätten, 1925**

From Ernest Zimmerman, 'Das Plattenhaus der Deutschen Werkstätten', *Innendekoration* (November 1925) p. 407

195 (above)

**Paimio armchair, birch plywood and laminated birch**
Designed by Alvar Aalto, 1930, manufactured by Huonekalu-ja Rakennustyötehdas Oy Ab (Korhonen factory), Turku, Finland

196 (right)

**Cantilever armchair, designed by Alvar Aalto**
Page from *Das neue Holzmöbel Aalto*, catalogue for Wohnbedarf department store, Zurich, 1934

**204** modell aalto

**sessel**

| höhe | 37 cm | breite | 47 cm |
|---|---|---|---|
| tiefe | 47 cm | | |

federnder sperrholzsessel. wird auch mit weicher auflage geliefert.

wohnbedarf typ

Among the earliest clients for this furniture was the Fortnum and Mason department store in London, where an exhibition, '"Wood Only", The Exhibition of Finnish Furniture', was organized in 1933 by the architectural journalist and modernist enthusiast P. Morton Shand (fig. 57) 'under the auspices of' the British magazine *The Architectural Review*. This exhibition was pivotal in creating the first meaningful market for Aalto furniture outside of Finland and for its impact on designers and manufacturers in Britain.

One London designer who saw the exhibition was Gerald Summers (1899–1967), then a very part-time furniture designer and maker (alongside his managerial job at Marconi's Wireless Telegraph Co. Ltd). He had begun experimenting with 'aeroplane' plywood purchased from the Venesta company (see pp. 50–52) in early 1933 and, in the same year, came to know and learn more about plywood from Jack Pritchard (1899–1992), who worked in promotion and advertising for Venesta. In 1929 Pritchard, an ardent modernist, had also founded the Isokon company with the architect Wells Coates (1895–1958) and others. This was devoted to the building and making of up-to-date architecture and furnishings. Pritchard designed various pieces of plywood furniture between 1929 and 1933, as did Coates. Isokon also sold an extraordinarily lightweight stool (1.1 kg/2.42 lbs) made by the Estonian company Luther (see p. 44), the designer of which went unmentioned but was probably someone connected with its manufacturer (fig. 198).[3] In 1935, owing to developments within Isokon and spurred by the arrival in Britain of the former Bauhaus director Walter Gropius (1883–1969), Pritchard founded an offshoot, the very small Isokon Furniture Company, with Gropius as its Controller of Design. In the same year they were joined by the former Bauhaus student and teacher Marcel Breuer (1902–81), who, at Gropius's suggestion, translated into plywood an aluminium reclining chair designed in two sizes some years earlier and then also provided numerous other plywood furniture designs for Isokon (figs 199–201). Comparison of the furniture of Aalto, Summers and Breuer – all sold in London during the mid-1930s – provides an insight into ways of designing and making plywood furniture. It also demonstrates Aalto's key role and influence as what can justifiably be called a 'form-giver' to mid-twentieth-century plywood furniture.

197 (below)
**Bending laminated frames for Aalto chairs**
Korhonen factory, Turku, Finland, c. 1932

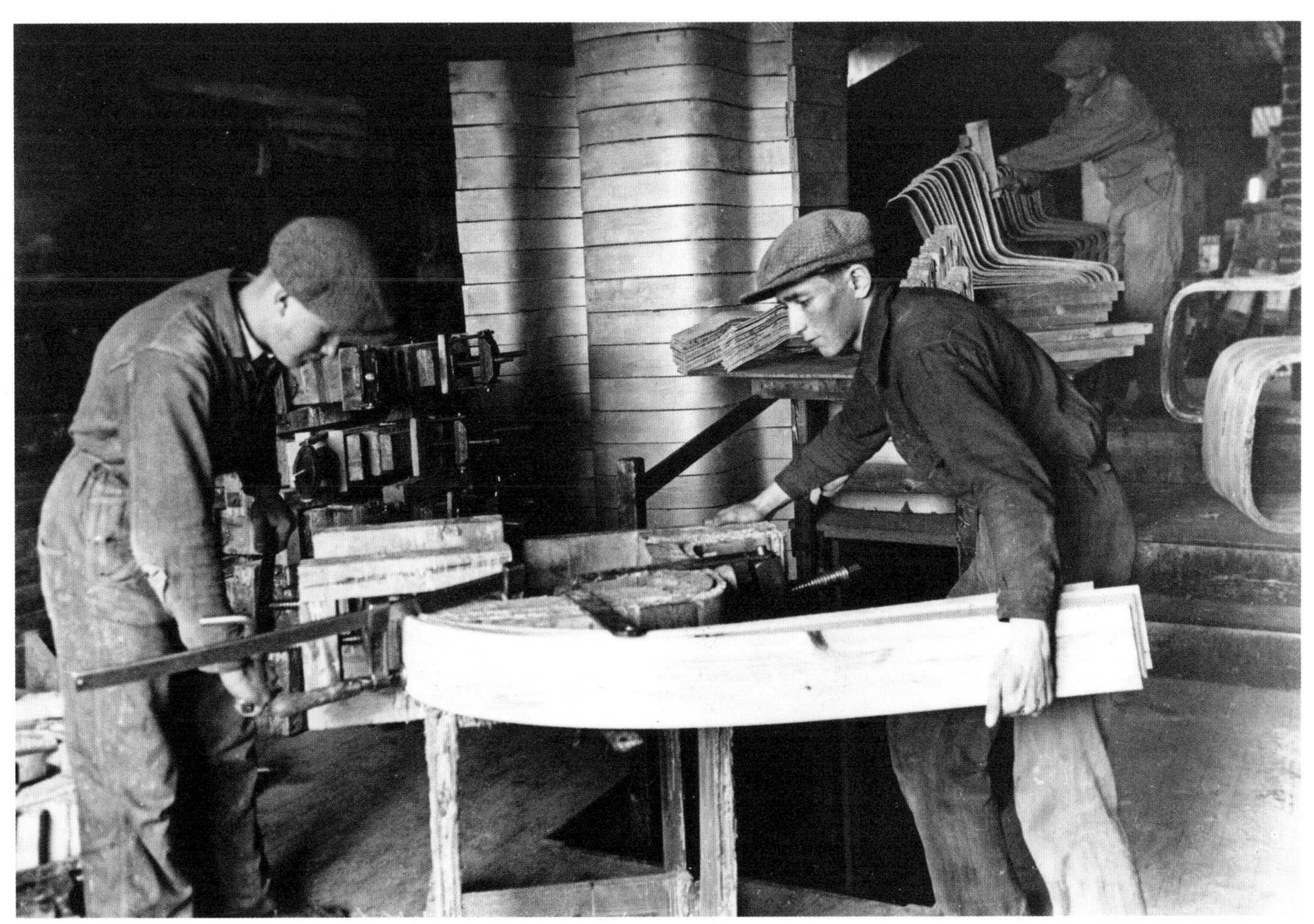

Aalto's Paimio armchair (fig. 195) was made of an undulating plywood seat of Finnish birch moulded into a meticulously drawn and unprecedented curvilinear shape. The narrow arms, equally unusual in shape, acted also as the base and frame of the chair and were joined to the seat by cross-rails of solid birch. The narrow frames were made of laminated wood rather than plywood – as this material was more resistant to the concentrated stress caused by the small area over which the weight was transferred from seat to frame. In contrast, the strength of cross-graining was required to prevent the wide plywood seat from splitting.[4] As with all moulded plywood furniture, these chairs were made by gluing together layers of veneer in a mould – the material becoming 'plywood' after the moulding process was complete.

The contemporary description of this chair as a 'hammock type' suggests an intentional differentiation between supporting arms and supported seat, a typically modernist idea and one followed in Breuer's Short Chair of 1936 (fig. 201). Although a very direct translation into wood of an earlier metal design, the precise forms and appearance of Breuer's suspended seat and supporting framework were undeniably influenced by Aalto's furniture. Breuer's thin plywood seat is supported by laminated arms and base of similar thickness to Aalto's, giving the same sense of a seat floating inside a moulded frame.[5] Breuer and Aalto knew each other's work well; years earlier, Aalto had furnished his flat with Breuer's metal furniture and designed furniture that drew on Breuer's work.

Summers, on the other hand, did not know Aalto's work until he visited the Fortnum and Mason exhibition. This led him to change tack to design an armchair that was uncompromising in terms of both conventions of seating and of contemporary chair construction (fig. 202). Summers took the idea of making a plywood chair to its logical conclusion by dispensing with the structural differentiation between seat, legs and arms. Instead, the chair was designed as a single form and manufactured in a single process from a single stack of veneers (unlike those by Aalto and, later, Breuer, whose chairs were moulded in separate parts). Summers devised a method of manufacture by which seven layers of Venesta aeroplane plywood veneer were cut to size, then cuts made within the sheets to form what would become the rear legs and arms during moulding. Glue was applied to each sheet and the sheets were then placed into the lower (cavity) part of a large convex/concave mould. The space between the two legs was cut out after moulding and before finishing.[6]

198 (below)
**Birch plywood stool**
Manufactured by Luterma (previously A.M. Luther), Reval, Russia (present-day Tallinn, Estonia), 1930–35

199 and 200
(above and left)

**Prototype dining table, with detail showing leg constructed from three layers of birch plywood**
Designed by Marcel Breuer, manufactured by Isokon Furniture Company, London, 1936

201 (above)

**Short Chair, birch plywood and laminated birch with zebrano veneer**
Designed by Marcel Breuer, manufactured by Isokon Furniture Company, London, 1936

While the Summers chair represented rigorous constructional logic, and perhaps an idealized form for a plywood chair, the final product was very heavy. Ten layers of veneers were needed to support the sitter, as all the stress had to be carried by the single moulded plywood sheet. The Aalto system of separate supporting structure and thin plywood seat resulted in a chair that was much lighter.

In the context of modernist furniture, sales of Aalto's designs were successful, especially in Britain, where 40–50% of their total production may have been sold during the 1930s. Fortnum and Mason ordered 772 pieces in 1933 alone, far more than either Isokon or Makers of Simple Furniture, Summers's company, would ever sell. Pritchard claimed that by the outbreak of World War II in 1939 Isokon was just beginning to break even. Makers of Simple Furniture had some modest financial success but, like Isokon, was forced to end production after the outbreak of war, whereas Aalto's furniture was sporadically manufactured during the war and more consistently afterwards.[7]

202 (below)
**Birch plywood armchair**
Designed by Gerald Summers, 1934, manufactured by Makers of Simple Furniture, London

## Eames plywood

While Aalto, Summers and Breuer produced laminated wood and/or plywood chairs, bent and moulded in a single plane, Charles Eames (1907–78) focused on moulding plywood in more than one plane for furniture. Eames worked initially in collaboration with the Finnish-American architect Eero Saarinen (1910–61), then with his wife, Ray Kaiser Eames (1912–88), and finally within the Eames' own design office and in conjunction with external manufacturers. This work, undertaken between 1941 and 1956, was informed by a deep knowledge of and admiration for the work of both Aalto and Breuer, although it went further than they had done. It must also be considered in the context of the research, experiments and innovations in plywood moulding and glue technology introduced during the 1930s (see chapters 4 and 5 in relation to aircraft design and architecture).[8]

The first stage of this work, which won first prize at the 'Organic Design in Home Furnishings' competition at New York's Museum of Modern Art (MoMA), comprised Saarinen and Charles Eames's ambitious, three-dimensionally moulded plywood chair and armchair. The complex seat of the armchair, which they referred to as a 'wood shell' (fig. 203), was an attempt to form a fully supportive shape for the sitter that would provide a very lightweight upholstered chair carried on thin legs (20 lbs/9.07 kg compared to 45 lbs/20.4 kg for a traditional upholstered armchair). The cut-out where the seat meets the back was necessary to allow the plywood to achieve the rounded, three-dimensional form desired and intended to avoid either splitting or overlapping of veneers (fig. 204). This was not achieved by the end of the competition and ultimately could only be resolved in a plastic version.[9]

To manufacture the shells, the designers were paired with the very experienced Haskelite Corporation (figs 90 and 99), one of nine manufacturers that had agreed to help bring to market the competition winners. The organizers hoped this would herald an era of furniture rolling off assembly lines like cars – an aspiration also articulated with reference to prefabricated houses in the 1930s, as well as aircraft production during the war (see pp. 92–93 and 138–42). The jury described the Saarinen–Eames design as the 'one outstanding new development in furniture design in the entries', and the catalogue placed their furniture in a line of development that followed Aalto's 'new structural idea' of bent plywood seating, 'in effect a completely new material since it has very different

203 (right)

**Prototype seat for Conversation chair, May 1941**

Designed by Eero Saarinen and Charles Eames for the 1940 MoMA 'Industrial Design' competition, subsequently referred to by the 1941 exhibition title 'Organic Design in Home Furnishings'

properties from wood'. MoMA presented the Saarinen–Eames chairs as representing a next stage in the development of this 'new material', which matched an 'intelligent structural idea with a brilliant aesthetic expression' – very much the language of a museum rather than industry.[10] When it came to making the chairs, the Haskelite company was challenged by the need to achieve such a complex-curved shape in a size much smaller than that of the aircraft work that formed its usual production. Only a small number of the chairs were completed and offered for sale before the US entry into the war in the same year (1941).[11]

Before the end of the MoMA project (June 1941) Charles Eames and Ray Kaiser married and moved to Los Angeles, where, during the war years, they continued the attempt to mould plywood furniture suitable for mass production. They built their own very small bag moulding device, initially in their flat. This clearly drew on Charles's experience of working with Haskelite (including visits to its headquarters in Grand Rapids, Michigan), on his direct experience of working in factories and on building sites, and on the fact that the technology was widely used by a number of Los Angeles-based aircraft companies, including Lockheed, in Burbank, California (see pp. 84–91). While the Eames'

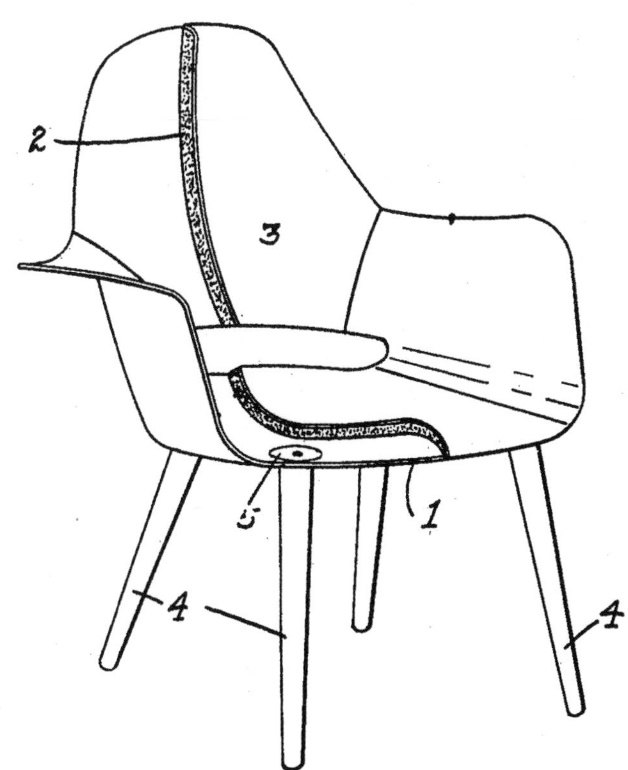


Feb. 26, 1946. C. EAMES 2,395,468

METHOD OF MAKING LAMINATED ARTICLES

Filed May 28, 1942 5 Sheets-Sheet 2

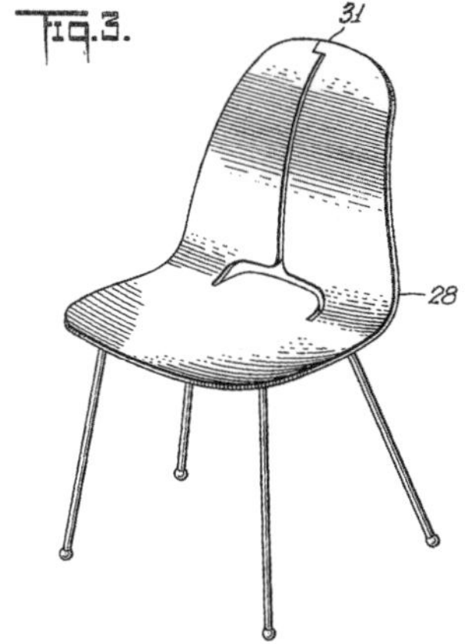


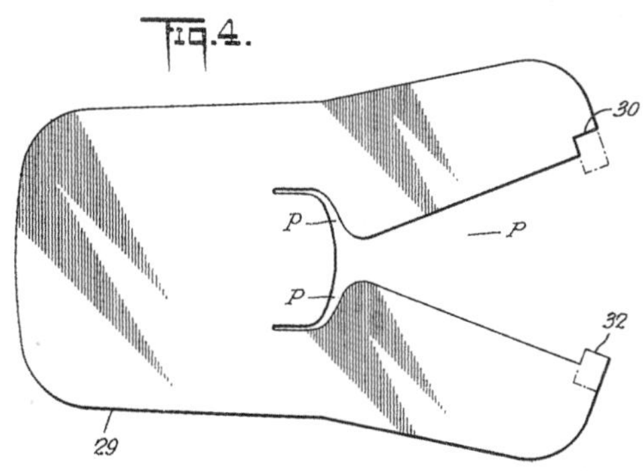


INVENTOR
Charles Eames
BY Blair, Curtis & Hayward
ATTORNEYS

204 (left)
**Illustration from F.T. Parrish, patent for 'Attaching Device for Chair Legs and the Like'**
Application filed 9 January 1942, issued 29 February 1944, US patent no. 2,343,077

205 (above)
**Charles Eames, patent for 'Method of Making Laminated Articles'**
Application filed 28 May 1942, issued 26 February 1946, US patent no. 2,395,468

206 (above)

**Installation shot, 'Design For Use' exhibition, MoMA, New York, 1944**
Plywood sculpture by Ray Eames visible on left

mould was more primitive than any commercial process (it employed a bicycle pump for pressurization), the principles were identical. The first result was a single-piece, three-dimensionally moulded seat and back (fig. 205), similar to the MoMA armless chair but with a slit in the back to allow for simpler moulding. Although wartime restrictions prevented the commercial development of the chair the couple worked on similar seat designs for military aircraft. This demonstrated their ongoing commitment to moulded plywood products, as did the remarkable free-form sculptures made by Ray (fig. 206). Her training as a fine artist made her an ideal collaborator with Charles, who was very much the practical, hands-on designer and maker.[12] The sculptures were tours-de-force of innovative bending of thin plywood, bravura demonstrations of the ways in which plywood was being reimagined as a mouldable material. At the same time they demonstrated the aesthetic sophistication, rooted in biomorphic art of the 1930s, that Ray brought to Eames furniture.

The first moulded plywood object to which the Eameses were able to devote themselves full time (Charles had, until then, worked in the scenery department of MGM Studios), and which they were able to see through to genuine mass production, was an unlikely commission for the US Navy: a plywood leg splint for injured sailors (fig. 207). The moulding of plywood into the correct shape to support a human leg, turning to enclose the foot at one end but curved in the opposite direction at the other, and the requirement that it be lightweight and stackable and allow for a means of tying the splint to the leg, made it a very complex design project. Each of the veneer layers (fig. 208), some with added areas of reinforcement, was slightly different in shape and in the cuts into and through it that facilitated the moulding.[13]

The design and method of manufacture of the splint, initially on a small scale (in 1942–43) and then in quantities of up to 150,000 (1943–45), enabled the most important period of sustained work on plywood

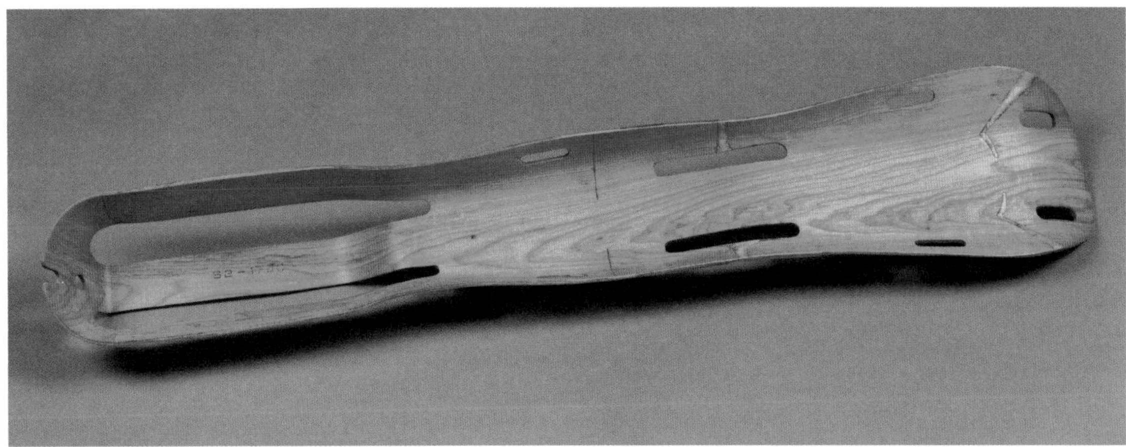

207 (above)
**Birch plywood leg splint**
Designed by Charles and Ray Eames, 1941–42, manufactured by Evans Products Company, California

208 (right)
**Veneer layers, each differently cut, before gluing and moulding into a leg splint**
Evans Products Company, California, 1943

209 (opposite)

**DCM chair, birch plywood and tubular steel**

Designed by Charles and Ray Eames, 1945, manufactured by Evans Products Company, California, c. 1947

in the Eames' careers to date. The taking over of their production by a major wood products manufacturer (fig. 174) in 1943 resulted in their considerable investment in tooling and provision of a larger splint factory.

The expansion of the Eameses' small practice into, first, a small factory and then to a larger one enabled them to take on contracts for plywood aircraft parts for different companies, although they were not pioneers in this production, a fact made clear when the sculpture and splints were exhibited in the wider context of wartime plywood moulding in 1944 (fig. 206). But the experience gained over these few years, from their designs and art, and their venture into manufacturing (including the constraints of military contracts), meant that the Eameses' knowledge of plywood moulding had expanded very fast. Although such work had begun (with Saarinen) on single-shell forms, by 1945 they had dismantled that form in favour of entirely separate seats and backs connected with either wood or metal frame elements (fig. 209).[14] These seats and backs were moulded in three dimensions but the abandonment of the shell form greatly simplified the technical challenges related to moulding.

Although the resulting chair, sold as the DCM (dining chair metal), was a return to the modernist distinction between supporting and supported elements, it demonstrated a radically different approach to that of Aalto and Breuer. The contrast between materials was sharp, potentially jarring, yet the impression of the whole was harmonious and integrated. The DCM was a remarkable design, not least owing to the relationship between the very thin, almost spindly, metal frame and the biomorphic wooden seat and back, each of which seemed to float off the frame. This was achieved by joining wood and metal to rubber mounts using screws and glue. But instead of the modernist imagery of machine production alone, the Eameses' chair was a zoomorphic form, suggestive of a creature with four legs, a pelvis and a head. This impression led the contemporary but more traditional furniture designer Edward Wormley to poke fun at the chair's silhouette as having led within just a few years to 'a mass of mosquitoes posing as tables, chairs and carts'.[15]

Wormley's jibe also suggests the extraordinary impact that this particular chair had on its contemporaries. The British designer Robin Day (1923–2000) said that 'every designer I knew had a picture of the Eames chair [meaning the DCM] pinned to their drawing board'. Within a decade, in virtually every European country, in the US and in Japan, plywood had started to be used both in direct imitation of the Eames chair and, influenced by the Eames' furniture, as well as that of the 1930s, as the material for the most up-to-date design (figs 210–217). It is not hyperbole to claim that the DCM became the most influential and imitated chair of the mid-twentieth century and that it contributed immeasurably to the domestication of plywood; not only did Eames-influenced furniture appear in high-style or design-conscious interiors, but it was also instrumental in plywood becoming a staple of mass-market commercial and institutional furniture.[16]

210 (above)

**SE 42 chair, beech-faced plywood**
Designed by Egon Eiermann, 1949, manufactured by Wilde + Spieth, Esslingen, Germany, from 1950

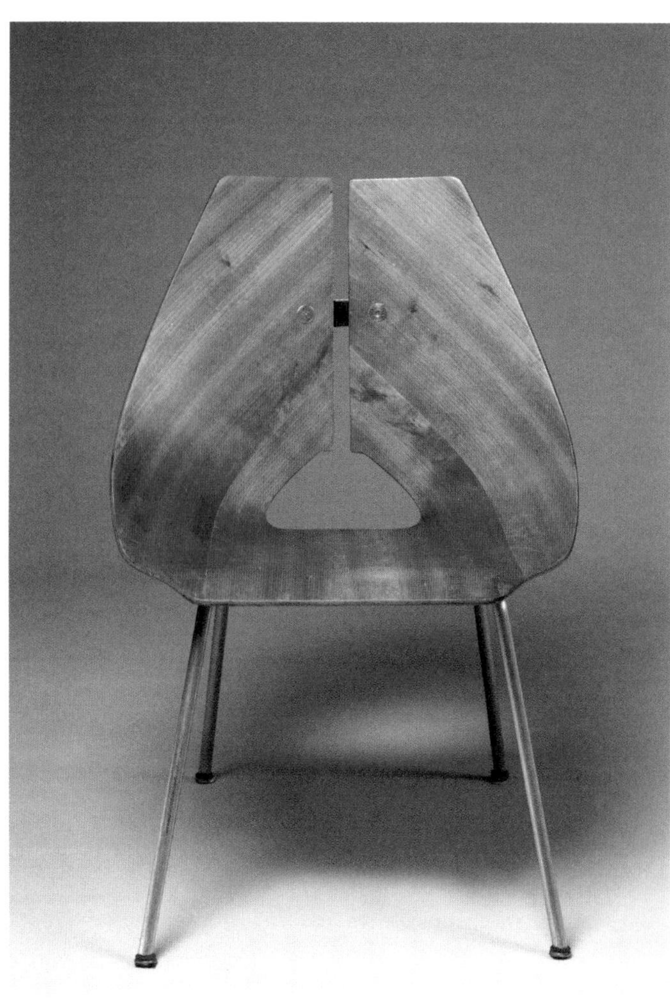

211 (above)

**Walnut-faced plywood and tubular steel chair**
Designed by Ray Komai, 1949, manufactured by J.G. Furniture Co., Brooklyn, New York, from 1950

212 (above)

**Q Stak chair, cherry-faced plywood and tubular steel**
Designed by Robin Day, 1953, manufactured by Hille Ltd, London, 1950s

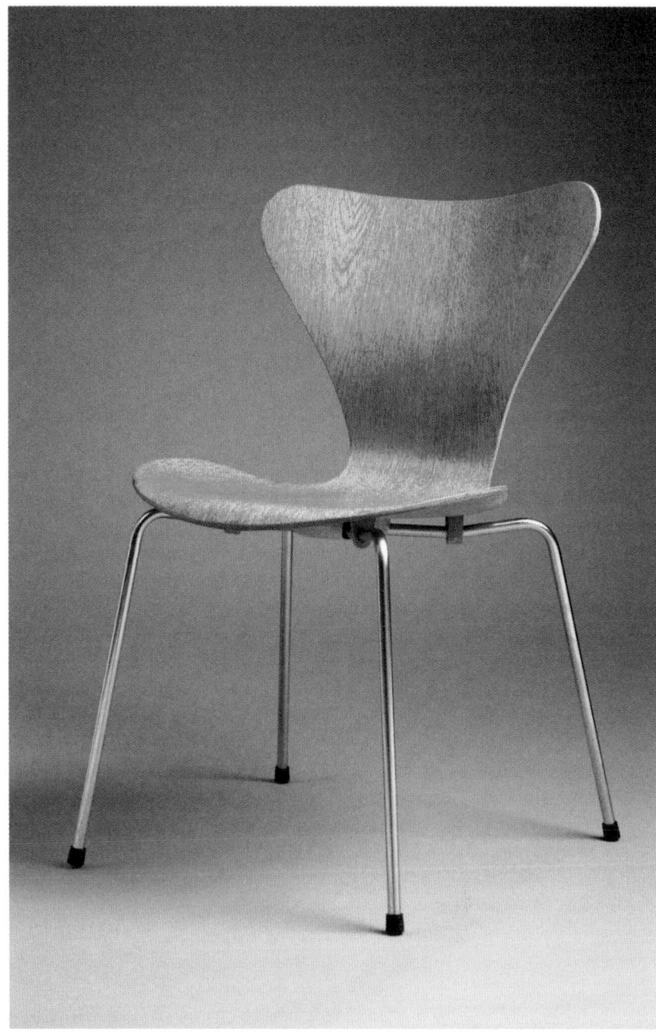

213 (above)

**Model 3107 chair, oak-faced plywood and tubular steel**
Designed by Arne Jacobsen, 1955, manufactured by Fritz Hansen, Denmark. This example manufactured c. 1967 for St Catherine's College, Oxford

214 (above)

**P31 chair, rosewood-faced plywood and tubular steel**
Designed by Osvaldo Borsani, 1957, manufactured by Tecno, Italy, early 1960s. Brass fitting on chair back an early 1960s addition to the design

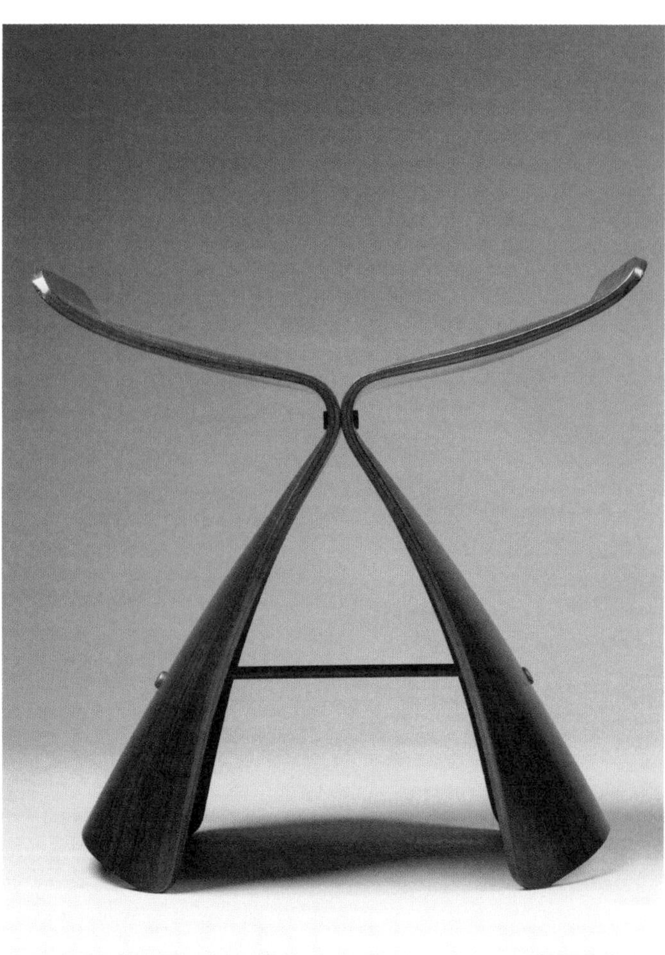

215 (above)

**Butterfly Stool, rosewood-faced plywood with metal fittings**
Designed by Sori Yanagi, 1954, manufactured by Tendo Mokko, Japan, late 1950s

216 (above)

**Plywood chair for Kenzō Tange's Sumi Memorial Hall, Ichinomiya, Japan**
Manufactured by Tendo Mokko, Japan, c. 1955

217 (above)

**Teak-faced plywood chair**
Designed by Grete Jalk, manufactured by Poul Jeppesen, Denmark, 1963

## Plywood at sea and on the road

> Whether the war is going to make plastic plywood the steel of the 1950's...no one can say in 1942. Wars, however, have an ambivalent nature. At the moment they are snuffing out life and progress at one point, their camp follower – invention – seems to leave the battlefronts well seeded for the future life as well as industry.[17]

In addition to the very direct impact that their work had on the contemporary interior, Charles and Ray Eames are useful as a case study because their progression from the Navy to the department store describes in broad terms the arc that shaped much post-war adoption of plywood as a material. Both during and after World War II plywood was one of a number of 'new' materials celebrated for offering the promise of a wealthier, more comfortable, more technologically sophisticated domestic life. Although, in fact, much of the plywood manufactured in the early 1950s was still being supplied to US forces engaged in the Korean War (1950–53), this classic 'swords into ploughshares' narrative extended from the increasing visibility of plywood as a domestic material, to a highly publicized transfer of technical knowledge and skill from wartime to post-war industry.[18]

In the years immediately after 1945 the transfer of knowledge was frequently state-sponsored, including through a series of lengthy reports on German industry that were published by British and American government agencies. These reports, based on information gathered by technical advisors sent in to inspect German factories at the immediate end of the war, were explicitly intended to allow for the adoption of German techniques by manufacturers of the Allied nations.[19] In the US the Committee on Military Affairs also published a report on domestic wartime technology across different industries – this included general sections on plywood ('a material for which extensive peacetime demand may be expected'),

218 (below)
**Fairmile patrol boat**
Egypt, 1942

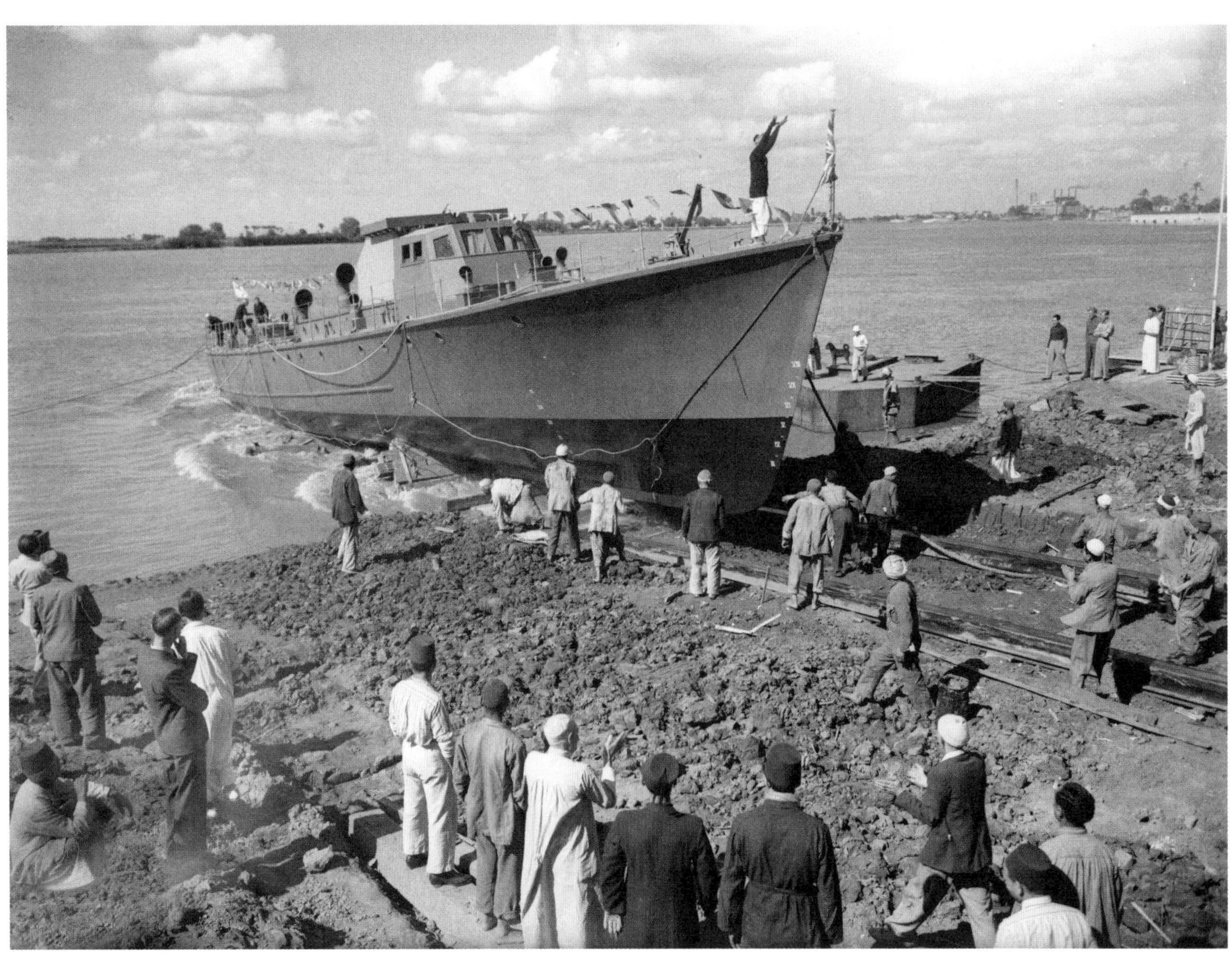

as well as extensive listings detailing specific uses of plywood during the war.[20] In the years after 1945 the transfer of technical skill had an impact on plywood's use in a number of areas, both in real terms with the adoption of new types of design and technique, and, more metaphorically, in the stories that were told about plywood as a new and sophisticated material of the future.

Although it seemed, during the war, as if aircraft would offer a home for recent developments in moulding and glue technology, it was in fact in boat design that plywood had possibly its most publicized post-war impact. Much of this was the result of both plywood boats becoming better known in the popular press and of plywood being promoted extensively in marketing material produced both during and immediately after the war. Plywood was used widely for boatbuilding during the war, in part because it was not subject to materials restrictions as tight as those placed on metals such as steel or aluminium. One of the most successful schemes for plywood parts in wartime boats was the British Fairmile – a centralized programme for building naval patrol boats (fig. 218). The large, transverse framing elements of these relatively large craft were made using 'bakelite-bonded plywood' (fig. 219).[21]

Fairmile boats were built on a prefabrication system that was similar in many (but not all) ways to the assembly line architectural systems of the 1930s (see chapter 5). In an effort to produce far more boats than specialist yacht-building yards could deliver, the British car manufacturer Noel Macklin came up with a decentralized mass production scheme that allocated the manufacturing of the boat's wooden parts to a range of factories (furniture, car and piano) that would deliver finished parts to boatyards. The frames were cut from plywood scarf-jointed together into units at a coachbuilding firm. As with the Mosquito aeroplane (see p. 103), less skilled labour could be used for the assembly of parts already made by specialist workers and production was much quicker.[22] Fairmile boats were also made closer to warzones across the British Empire, including in India, Egypt (figs 218–219), Tanganyika

219 (below)
**Fairmile patrol boat under construction**
Plywood frames being attached to keel, Egypt, 1942

(present-day Tanzania), Hong Kong, Australia, New Zealand and the (then) Union of South Africa.

While the Fairmile system was a very successful example of plywood parts being used in naval construction, by far the most famous use of plywood during World War II was in American PT (patrol torpedo) boats. These small craft, which were used extensively in both the Pacific and the Mediterranean, came to take on almost mythical significance in the American press during and after the war. Although they did not in fact use very much plywood in their construction (only in decks, in internal fittings, and as an inner and outer skin to the bulkheads on some models), the boats were widely described (either mockingly or heroically) as part of a 'plywood navy'.[23]

The Italian *carabinieri* police mocked the American 'plywood navy', while the Germans were said to ridicule the Fairmile coastal patrol boats as 'the plywood walls of England' (a British journalist retorted that 'in the channel to-day are [*sic*] Britain's "plywood navy" and they still have hearts of oak').[24] Wartime coverage of plywood's use in a range of military boats, including D-Day landing craft and storm boats for river crossings, led to stories in the popular press with titles such as 'Plywood PT Boats Are Making History' and 'Their Shields Were Plywood', and descriptions of the 'production miracle' that turned 'stacks of plywood' into 669 boats a month. These, along with advertisements for plywoods and synthetic glues that illustrated military aircraft and boats, not only suggested the remarkable strength of the material but also ascribed near-heroic qualities to 'frail plywood craft' that let 'loose their torpedoes against battleships, cruisers and destroyers alike'. Such articles and advertisements presciently pointed to synthetic resin-bonded plywood as the material for the boat of the future.[25]

Once the war and restrictions on materials ended, the use of plywood in boatbuilding in the US became 'commonplace'.[26] Post-war commercial boatbuilders were able to take advantage of synthetic resins and moulding processes developed or improved during the war, and small craft were increasingly made with plywood hulls. By 1949 the Michigan Wagemaker company were advertising a range of 'Wolverine Molded Plywood Boats', selling these as the latest in modern technology:

> laminated out of 4 to 7 plys of clear veneer… bonded together with a phenolic resin water proof glue under heat and tremendous pressure. This improved construction method produces the lightest possible hull, highly resistant to dry rot, and unsurpassed for strength and durability. The adaptability of molded plywood to compound curves and contours permits greatly improved design – hitherto impossible – affording greater speed, sea-worthiness and manoeuverability.[27]

Alongside its use in these small leisure craft, plywood was also picked up for the construction of more expensive boats. Best known among these were the elegant speedboats of the Riva company of northern Italy. In 1950 Carlo Riva (1922–2017) took over his father's boatyard at Sarnico, on the edge of Lake Iseo. Riva began experimenting with plywood as a cladding for hull frames, largely in order to speed up and standardize the existing method of construction, in which the boats were covered with double or triple layers of solid cedarwood planks. Riva collaborated with Remo Lodi, head of the aircraft section of the INCISA plywood company, where he had worked on aeronautical plywood during the war. Starting in 1949 the two experimented with plywood for hull bottoms and, later, hull sides and transoms on a number of Riva boats.[28] In 1957 Riva and Lodi became partners in Marine Plywood SNC, a company set up to supply Riva's plywood needs, as well as that of other potential customers (notably the American Chris-Craft firm). Using their own plywood glued with phenolic resin – which they originally dubbed 'armoured laminated wood' as the Italian word for plywood, *legno compensato*, had connotations of cheapness – from 1958 they began bag moulding 'preformed' mahogany three-ply hull sections (two on the bottom, two on the top), each the entire length of the boat (figs 220–222).[29] By the mid-1960s the use of plywood is said to have increased annual production of Riva boats from 10 (in 1949) to 270.[30]

The best-known Riva boat to be made using plywood was the Aquarama (figs 222–223), a model famously owned by the actress Sophia Loren. Many European film stars were photographed or filmed in Riva boats throughout the 1950s and 1960s, as they became synonymous with the post-war glamour of *la dolce vita*. Both English and Italian sales catalogues emphasized the technical sophistication of the hull construction. One English-language catalogue stated: 'Bottom and keel in nine armored plankings, strengthened by special adhesive compounds resistant to the sun, salt-water and boiling-water, will make wood practically indestructible.'[31] In many ways this description rounds off neatly the narrative of wartime technology for peace – new glues and moulding techniques transferred, via the wartime experience of Remo Lodi, to a better life on the sunny shores of 1950s Italy.

220 (below)

**Construction of Tritone boats, Riva boatyard, Sarnico, Italy, 1950s**

The bottom of the hull is clad in plywood (this process can be seen on the left)

221 (above)

**Two moulded sides of a Riva boat hull, ready to be attached to framework**
Stacks of veneer and veneer press are visible. Riva boatyard warehouse, Sarnico, Italy, 1950s

222 (above)

**Mahogany plywood being removed from mould**
This will form a side of an Aquarama boat. Riva boatyard, Sarnico, Italy, 1970s

223 (left)

**Aquarama**
Manufactured by Riva from 1962

224 (right)
**Frank Costin sitting in Marcos plywood car chassis**
Great Britain, 1960

225 (below)
**Marcos Gullwing, raced by John Hine and Dick Prior**
Le Mans, France, 1962

226–231 (opposite)
**Plywood projects on British and American DIY magazine covers, 1946–60**

Wartime expertise also played a direct role in the manufacture of a series of sports cars originally designed by the former de Havilland aeronautical engineer Frank Costin (1920–95), who became famous for his work in car aerodynamics and his steadfast belief in the superiority of plywood chassis construction. With his business partner Jem Marsh (1930–2015), Costin formed Marcos Engineering in 1959. Using plywood chassis (fig. 224), the company built first the successful Gullwing racer (fig. 225) followed by a series of GT (road) sports cars between 1964 and 1971. In Marcos cars the chassis was built from flat and rounded pieces of 3, 4 and 6 mm 'waterproof and boilproof' marine plywood, joined by small, solid battens of spruce (the preferred wood in twentieth-century aircraft), all glued with aircraft-grade synthetic adhesive. The glass-fibre-reinforced plastic bodies were bonded to the chassis wherever there was contact.[32] Like a Riva boat, the Marcos car was made in limited quantity in small batches for aficionados with deep pockets. Both the cars and the boats demonstrated how far the image of plywood had changed, but also, at least in certain markets, the acceptance of plywood as a high-performance material on the basis of its war use.[33]

### Do-it-yourself (DIY) projects

One of the most significant areas of plywood's use in the post-war period was as a material for DIY enthusiasts (figs 226–231). Although seemingly far removed from the glamour and technical aspiration of the Riva hull or the Marcos chassis, it was arguably in DIY that the two most prominent strands of plywood's post-war use (design and technology) most successfully came together. At the most basic level, DIY was responsible for introducing plywood on a significant scale to the domestic interior. Immediately after the war the DIY industry also very successfully incorporated broader images of wartime technologies being adapted for new kinds of post-war leisure.

While plywood had already been introduced in the 1930s for uses including boatbuilding in the US or home modernization in Britain (especially the covering up of unwanted fireplaces or stair banisters), there was a veritable explosion of DIY in the 1950s and 1960s in both countries. DIY projects reached the public through reports and eventually specialist columns in newspapers and general interest magazines; through magazines and books aimed at an audience interested in making and fixing (such as *Popular Mechanics* in the US); and through new, specialist magazines aimed exclusively at the DIY market (for example *Practical Householder* in the UK from 1955).[34] The BBC had broadcast radio shows by 'DIY expert' W.F. Matthews

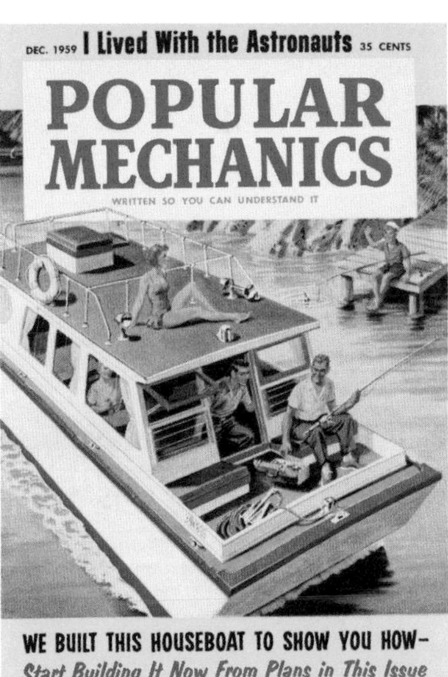

during the 1930s and, in 1947, moved him to television, where he was succeeded in 1956 by the immensely popular Barry Bucknell. Finally, public exhibitions such as Britain's long-standing *Daily Mail* Ideal Home Show or new, annual DIY shows in the Britain and US in the late 1940s and 1950s drew huge numbers of consumers.[35]

Through its promotion in these magazines and shows, plywood seeped deeper into popular culture, both in the presentation of DIY projects using plywood and in continued reports of its use in industry. DIY magazines shared the most recent industrial and technical innovations, including articles on new synthetic adhesives, methods of setting these using an electric current, and new types of moulding.[36] Although plastics had a greater reputation as a material of the future, and the term plastic-plywood continued to be used as a way of trading on this, plywood was much more suitable than plastic for working at home: more projects could be undertaken using it; and it was easier to shape, did not require complicated tools, was more forgiving of amateur workmanship and was more easily integrated into post-war leisure culture. It was described in 1955 as one of 'the do-it-yourself movement's four "P's" – plywood, power tools, paints and plastics'.[37] Home improvement – from flooring to panelling, seating to storage – became the dominant use of plywood in the post-war period (fig. 232).

232 (right)
**Marking out chair frames to be cut from a single plywood board**
From Mark West, 'California Cut-Out Chairs Cut the Cost of Comfort', *Popular Science* (March 1951), p. 213

233 (opposite)
**Cover, *The Mirror Class Dinghy*, advertising brochure**
Great Britain, c. 1963

Post-war DIY was tightly bound up with ideas about leisure – seen to offer a profitable way to spend leisure time, but also often the means to build leisure equipment cheaply. By looking at the history of three specific kinds of DIY, all aimed at new (or newly democratized) leisure activities, it is possible to map connections between DIY and the longer history of plywood in post-war design. In all three of these case studies – a commercial boat kit-set, a design for a new type of surfboard and early designs for skateboarding ramps – plywood allowed for experimental new forms, built with relatively low-level equipment, and accessible to a very broad (global) group of makers. These three histories demonstrate both plywood's great ubiquity in the post-war era and the creativity that this could foster.

DIY boats, based on the publication or purchase of plans or of kits including prefabricated parts, used plywood extensively in the 1950s and 1960s. Although by no means the first, the British Mirror dinghy, made mainly of marine plywood, was by far the most successful and influential kit-set boat of the post-war era in any material (figs 233–234). The dinghy's prototype was designed by the DIY television presenter Barry Bucknell in 1962. Bucknell's idea was picked up by the *Daily Mirror* newspaper, who brought the boat designer Jack Holt (1919–95) in to develop the design. The Mirror dinghy was sold as a complete kit of parts for home assembly. Manufactured by Bell Woodworking, the kit cost £63 11s. when first sold in 1963.[38] The boat was intended to be affordable – not only was it significantly cheaper than other kits on the market, but also repayment schemes set up by the *Mirror* meant that the cost of the kit could be paid off in twelve monthly instalments. The dinghy's advertising material (which included a booklet of instructions for those who had never sailed before) made it clear that it was aimed at a very wide market of beginner sailors: 'Until recently...only the wealthy have been able to get the health and happiness that a good boat brings. We at the *Daily Mirror* thought that thousands more could and would take to the water if a really low-priced boat were available.' It was consistently marketed for its extreme ease of assembly: 'In kit form, we wanted something simple enough for a teenager to assemble with perfectly commonplace tools.'[39]

The Mirror Class Dinghy©
Reg. Des. No. 909370.

The Mirror dinghy differed from other boat kits on the market in that it used a construction method advertised as 'Stitch and Glue'. Essentially this involved drilling holes into marked positions along the edges of the pre-cut three-ply panels that made up the hull. These pieces were then joined using short loops of copper wire threaded through the holes. The insides of the joints were covered with resin and glass-fibre tape, and once the resin had dried the copper wire ties were removed.[40] The use of 'sewn' plywood allowed for the very easy construction of a strong boat, by amateurs with little or no experience of woodworking. A set of building instructions reissued in 2004 states: 'DON'T try to build to a thousandth of an inch – it is not necessary. Try, by all means, to achieve accurate work but don't get worried if there is a tiny gap between the seams (the resin will fill it) or if a piece of wood doesn't quite fit (trim it off slightly).'[41]

The Mirror dinghy had huge commercial success. Its design was picked up internationally, with Mirror Dinghy Associations formed in countries such as Canada and Australia. The strength and simplicity of the boat's plywood construction (as well as the global availability of standard-graded sheets of ply) meant that local designers could modify the boat's original form in order to fit better with local conditions.[42] It remains on sale today.

While the proliferation of plywood sailing dinghies had its origins in a strongly commercial model of DIY, plywood was also key (for many of the same reasons) to more experimental types of making found in surfing and skateboarding. Both of these activities underwent huge change over the course of the twentieth century. In both cases this was in part due to adaptations made possible by the use of new materials. Plywood offers a good starting point from which to consider the cultures of making, skill and experimentation that developed around both surfing and skateboarding.

Surfing has a very long and significant history in Polynesia and designs for surfboards have always travelled and been adapted across the Pacific. This continued in the early twentieth century as, from the late 1930s onwards, changes in surfing style and technology led to a search for lighter, more waterproof board designs. Plywood was recommended for wave riding from as early as 1928, when an article in *Popular Science* magazine described how to make a very simple 'belly board' (essentially just a cut-out sheet) from plywood: 'desirable because of its lightness and the fact that it is not likely to split or warp'. Boards such as this (which must initially have been largely disposable, given the then lack of waterproof glues) continued to be made throughout the 1930s. At the same time plywood started to be adapted into more sophisticated designs. The most significant of these was the development of hollow wooden surfboards in the early 1930s.[43]

234 (below)
**Back cover, *The Mirror Class Dinghy*, advertising brochure**
Great Britain, c. 1963

She weighs less than most wives! At 98 lbs ready for rigging the Mirror is a *true* car-top dinghy. Two people—or one extra strong man—can push the boat up onto *any* car. The smallest kind will do. You can sail at a different place every weekend when the getting there is so easy. Our special roof rack makes it extra easy. It fits most cars and the boat slides smoothly over its tubular steel cross-pieces. But really any roof rack will do so long as the boat rides on it upside down. That way she cuts the air smoothly. Your top speed may be a little lower, but otherwise your car behaves quite normally.

colour photographs by Eileen Ramsay

IMPROVED
Hollow Surfboard
FOR ALL-AROUND SPORT

235 (above)

**Surfers riding hollow plywood surfboards designed by Tom Blake**
From Tom Blake, 'Improved Hollow Surfboard for All-Around Sport', *Popular Science* (June 1939), p. 174

The shift to hollow boards, which involved the construction of a wooden framework clad in thin sheets of wood, was a revolution in surfing technology as it made the boards far lighter and more waterproof (fig. 235). The Californian surfer Tom Blake (1902-1994) is usually credited with making the first hollow boards and patented a design for one in 1931. Although Blake's boards initially called for the use of solid mahogany as cladding, from at least 1937 (as waterproof plywoods became increasingly commercially available) plywood was offered as an alternative both on Blake's commercially produced boards and in his very widely distributed plans for DIY board design.[44] Plywood-clad boards quickly became standard and hollow board construction spread to other surfing centres, for example Australia. Even after surfers had started to move towards plastics such as fibreglass in the late 1950s, amateur boards continued to make use of plywood as a cheap standard material, easy for home construction. In 1965 Percy Blandford published designs for a hollow plywood surfboard (with spruce framework) in the British *Boy's Own* magazine. Costing only £4 to make, this board was considerably cheaper than commercially available fibreglass boards.[45]

While the use of plywood in surfing was in many ways an intermediary step to that of other lighter and more waterproof materials, its impact on the related history of skateboarding was much more significant and long-lasting. Plywood has been the most common material for skateboard decks since boards were first made in the 1950s. Early boards were simple cut-out sheets of flat ply, although changes in skateboarding style prompted adaptations to this design – most significantly in the early 1990s, when boards started to be moulded with pronounced kicktails at both front and back. The use of plywood for decks meant that DIY boards were relatively easy to make – either by cutting from a sheet of ply or by moulding individual sheets of veneer.[46]

Plywood is used for deck construction because it is strong, light and mouldable. Its importance to skateboarding extends beyond this, however, as it also has a significant history as a material for ramp building – in the 1980s and 1990s plywood ramps were central to a DIY revolution in the way (and places) that people skated. From the late 1970s skateboarders without access to permanent curved structures (usually either purpose-made skateparks or empty concrete swimming pools) started to build large ramps so that they could continue to skate in the freestyle, vertical way that increasingly defined the sport. These ramps were built as a wooden framework, almost always clad in a curved plywood surface. With the closure of large numbers of skateparks in the early 1980s, free-standing ramps became increasingly important.[47]

In 1977 *Skateboarder* featured a ramp built by Tom Stewart outside his California house (fig. 236), the article emphasizing the new flexibility that plywood ramps could give: 'Ramps can be built to match the hottest wave, or park, yet poured...and with considerable savings.' Stewart went on to sell (very successfully) plans for making ramps, via his company Rampage. Other plans were available for free, and in the early 1980s *Thrasher* magazine published

236 (below)
**Skateboarding ramp designed by Tom Stewart for Rampage**
California, 1977

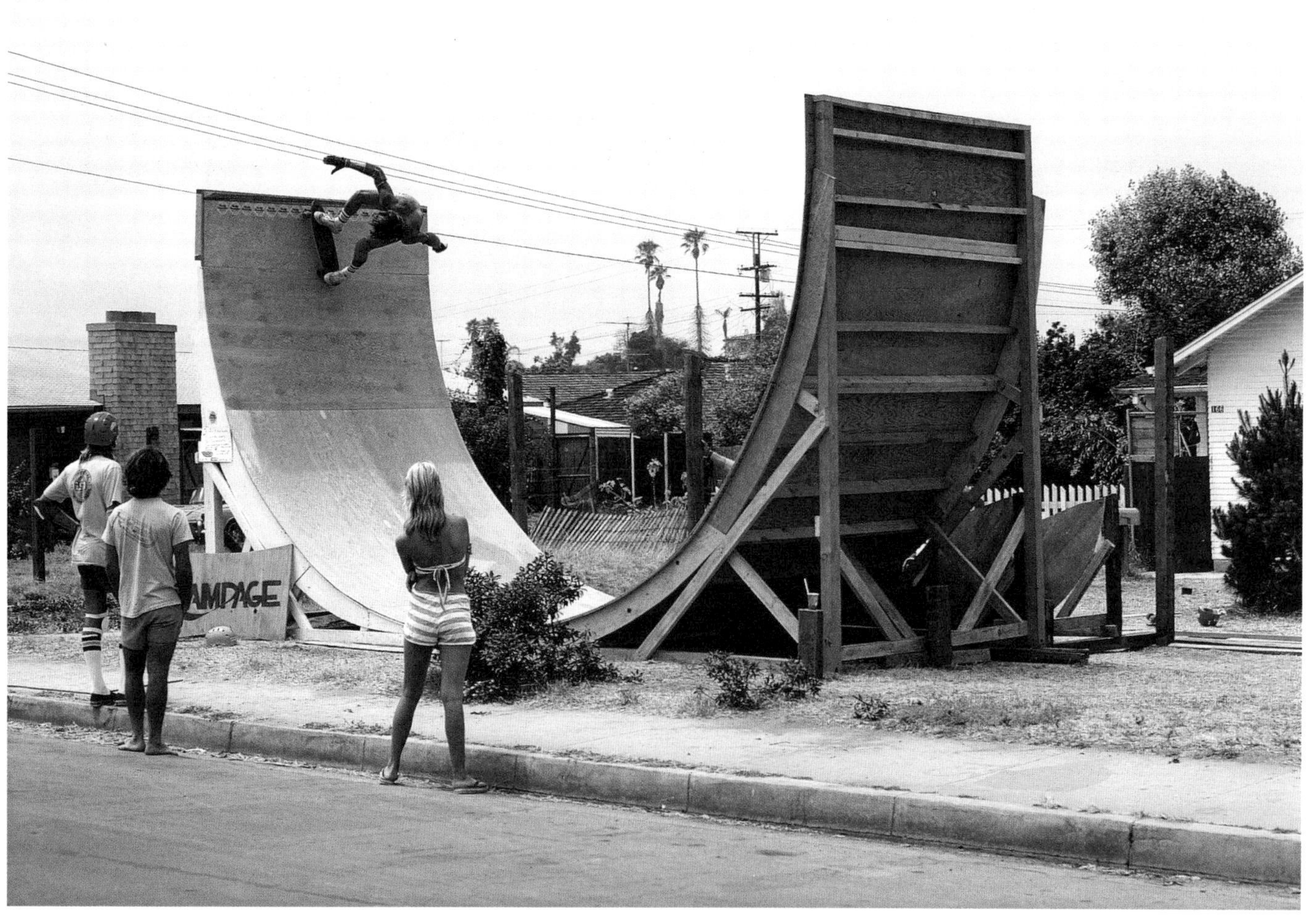

both detailed plans for building your own ramp and numerous profiles of ramps built across the US and internationally. Particularly noticeable in these articles is the adaptable, creative approach to design and construction. Suggestions are given for the best method for curving plywood sheets over a wooden framework, while articles and letters to the magazine offer tips for sealing and painting your ramp, how best to repair damaged areas, and how to orientate the plywood boards for best strength and speed. Plywood is described as a relatively expensive material, so the investment in a ramp was considerable, but *Thrasher* suggested trying local timber yards for offcuts.[48]

The skateboarding magazines reveal a vibrant international culture of making, with tips shared and examples of new ramp design showcased. Plywood is key not only because it is readily available, and offers a smooth, curved surface that can be formed without complicated tools, but also because it can be easily taken down and replaced. Lots of letters mention the removal of a plywood skin for the winter, or a replacement skin put on to repair damage. Whole ramps can be dismantled and moved to new locations, if neighbours or the city authorities start to complain. Most importantly, if building a whole ramp is too expensive, or there is no location in which to put it up, a single plywood board can be a transportable prop for skating in the city: 'A piece of ¾" thick plywood is all you need and you're in business. Whenever you get the urge to skate a bank just drag that old piece of plywood out and "set it up"' (fig. 237).[49]

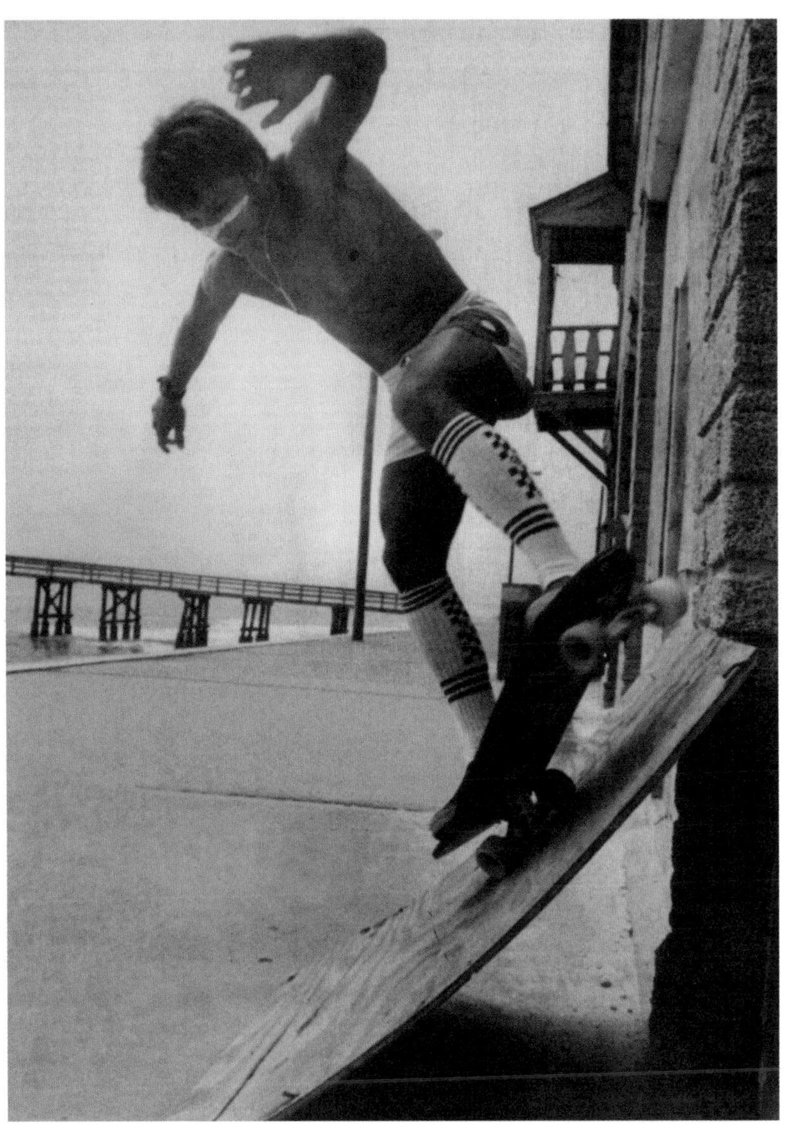

237 (above)

**Mike Folmer skating a makeshift ramp, Florida**
From *Thrasher* (April 1983), p. 37

DIY plywood was clearly woven into a wider narrative about post-war leisure and prosperity, one that was fairly deeply implicated in the politics of the period. Improving your home in the post-war US has been described as part of a 'virtuous consumerism' that expressed confidence in family life and a (wished for, if not genuine) sense of security in a Cold War world.[50] DIY could be a patriotic act, something that was almost achingly directly demonstrated in 1962 by US Defense Department plans for the building of simple plywood DIY nuclear fallout shelters (figs 238–239).[51]

In contrast to the plywood box shelter, *Thrasher* magazine's ad hoc skateboarding ramps make it clear that plywood could also be used as a DIY material in unauthorized forms of design. Much of its history in the twentieth and twenty-first centuries has been as a salvageable sheet material, not used for government-sanctioned suburban fallout but instead

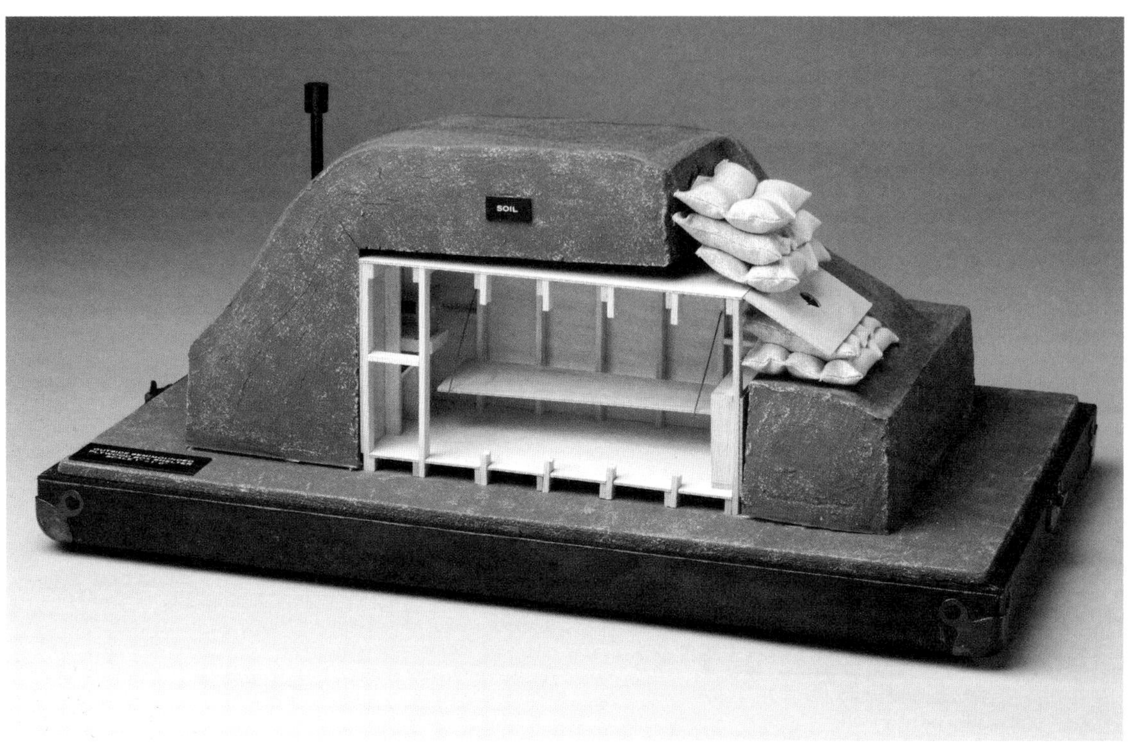


238 (right)
**Model for a plywood box shelter**
Designed by the US Department of Defense, made by Art Designers Inc., Virginia, c. 1962

239 (below)
**Plywood box shelter**
Illustration from 'Family Shelter Designs', booklet issued by the US Department of Defense, 1962

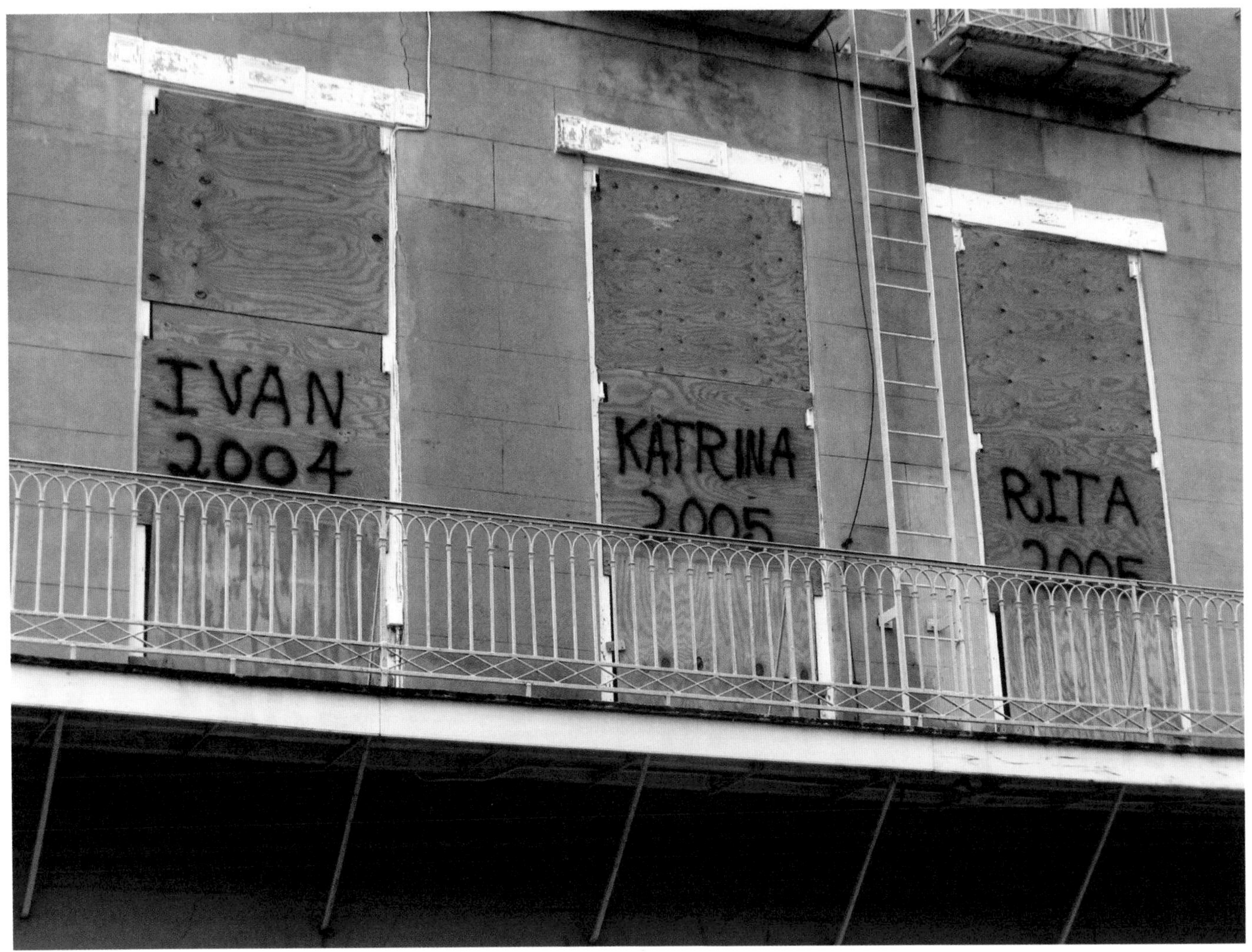


240 (above)
**Plywood boards used as hurricane protection**
New Orleans, 2008

ideal as hoarding for a broken window (fig. 240), or as the wall for a temporary house. Plywood's history in the twentieth century thus walked a fine line between mass production and experimentation, specialist use and disposability. These questions are explored in more detail, in relation to contemporary design, in the next chapter.

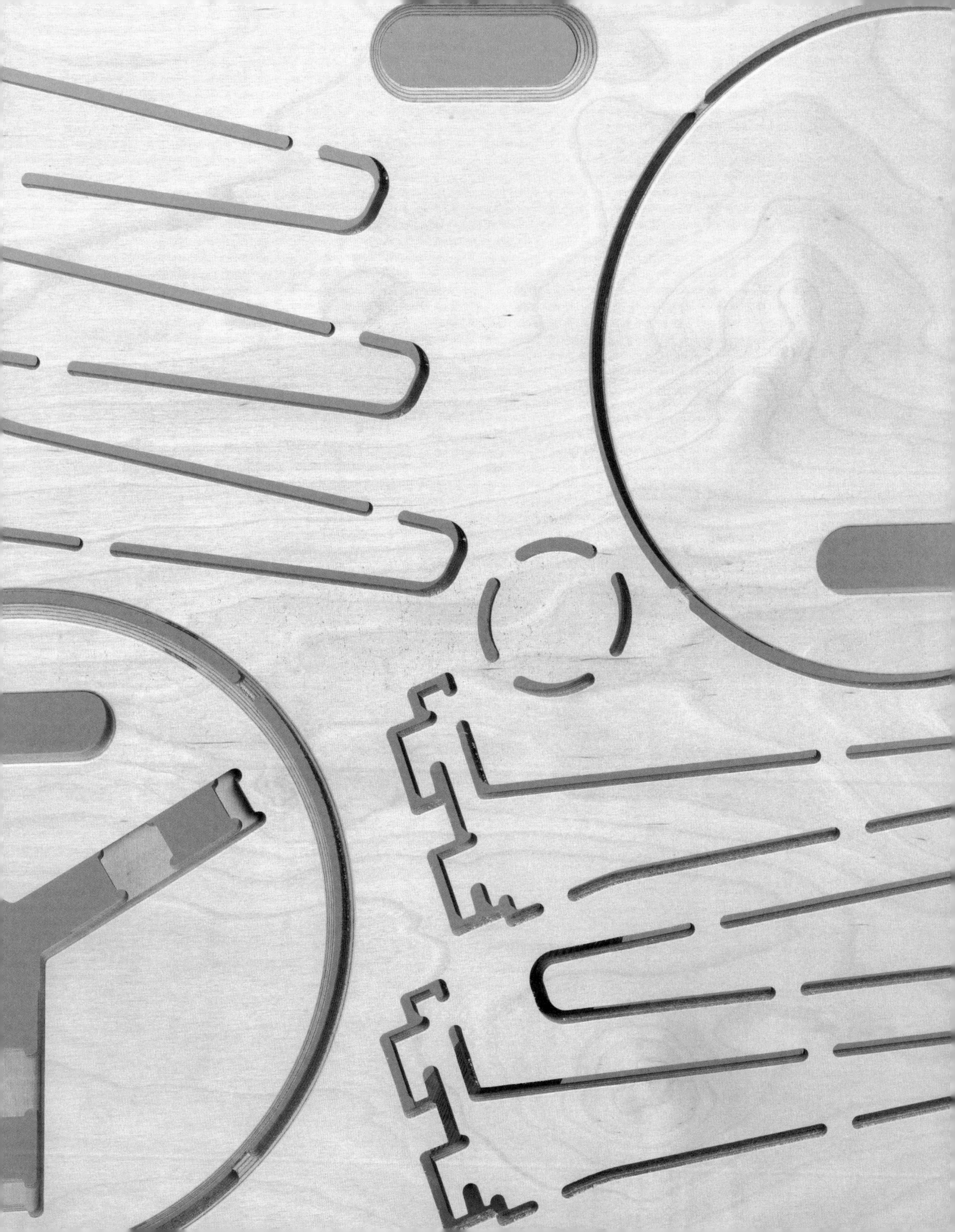

# 7 The Fall and Rise of Plywood (1960s–today)

Plywood's image and reputation, the way in which it was perceived by the public and by industry, shifted decisively during the 1970s. Within industry plywood was gradually supplanted by cheaper composite boards; the public sphere, on the other hand, focused on the accusations that plywood and other board products were poisoning home and workplace environments. These concerns over human health coincided with growing ecological disaster, as plywood manufacture in the post-war boom contributed to unprecedented levels of global deforestation. This chapter concentrates on these shifts in attitude, and on the actual global impact of plywood manufacture over the past seventy years. It also looks at the ways in which uses of plywood, and systems of its design and manufacture, have been transformed in the digital age, leading to a renewed popularity of the material. Although many designers continue to work with plywood, the story of the material since the 1960s is not primarily one of products or of individual designs. Instead, this chapter offers a history of the fall and rise of a material.

**Substituting plywood**

Plywood's success in the 1950s and 1960s as a material for DIY, housebuilding (in the US especially) and industrial uses coincided with a concerted effort to find cheaper substitutes (fig. 242), as well as a desire to make use of the substantial and virtually cost-free waste products of sawmills, plywood mills and furniture factories.[1] Particle boards (many referred to as chipboard), made from various forms of wood residue mixed with synthetic glue, were industrially produced mainly in Germany, then Switzerland, from the 1940s and in the US from the 1950s (fig. 243). Mainly used for decorative panelling, furniture and floor underlay, these boards were cheaper than plywood. Despite this benefit, these products only seriously threatened plywood's place in the market after 1975, when, despite its poor resistance to moisture, medium-density fibreboard (MDF, a non-structural particle board) came to supplant plywood as the prime wood-based panel, especially in furniture. This trend continued in the late 1970s, when supplies of timber for plywood declined in the US, and companies, research institutes

241 (opposite)
**Detail of Edie Stool (unassembled), birch plywood**
Designed by David and Joni Steiner for Opendesk, London, 2013

242 (below)
**Types of composite woods (top to bottom):**
Oriented strand board (OSB), chipboard, medium-density fibreboard (MDF) and hardboard

WOOD RESIDUE JUST BURNED AS "WASTE"
WOOD RESIDUE MANUFACTURED INTO USEFUL COMPOSITION BOARD


243 (above)
**'Composition board' (a 1950s synonym for particle board) manufactured from waste wood**
From Pacific Power & Light Company, *Wood Composition Boards* (Oregon 1955), p. 12

and universities focused on developing structural particle boards. Once industry standards were set for such products (about 1978) and accepted in building regulations, plywood's use in structural applications – a major part of the softwood plywood market – declined precipitously as a percentage of market share. From about 1986 a newer version of structural particle board, oriented strand board (OSB), replaced plywood and other competing structural materials for building use, gaining a majority of the international market in building panels, which it retains today.[2]

Although used in large quantities, panel materials such as MDF were generally unseen – either structural, or laminated with a top layer of veneer or plastic. Plywood retained its place as the optimum material for moulding, and for many specialist uses where moisture resistance, superior strength and the appearance of wood were desired.[3]

### Plywood's dirty secret

One of the legacies of plywood's development during the 1930s and World War II, especially in terms of the widespread availability of synthetic resin adhesives, was the creation of what one historian has called the post-war 'petrochemical house' – the gradual replacement of sawn timber and organic glues with plywood and synthetic adhesives in American houses and, to a lesser extent, in northern European countries. Urea-formaldehyde (UF) based adhesives were used both in post-war construction plywoods and in particle boards as they entered the market. UF glue, invented and first used in Germany in the 1930s, was much cheaper than other synthetic adhesives and did not require heating during laminating. Despite technical and economic advantages, UF glue had a number of negative environmental impacts, most notably in the emission of formaldehyde gases.[4]

The adverse effects on humans of the off-gassing of formaldehyde from UF glue in interiors were first suspected in the very early 1960s.[5] Within a decade its impact on workers making such products was also receiving attention. But it was the introduction of urea-formaldehyde foam insulation (UFFI) in the early 1970s that led to the first government action to regulate that material in Germany (1977) and the US (1979), and to a total ban in Canada (1980).[6] Mobile homes in America and, to a lesser extent, prefabricated homes in Germany were especially toxic environments as they were relatively draught-free and lacked the ventilation essential for dispersing gases, especially when new. Homeowners exposed to high levels of off-gassing experienced stinging eyes and respiratory problems, coughing, skin rashes and a range of other symptoms. Following denials from manufacturers that formaldehyde resins could be the source of the problem, and accusations that 'the public [were being used] as a test laboratory', American homeowners began suing the manufacturers of board products at the end of the 1970s. By 1982 these lawsuits were the subject of much attention in the press. Formaldehyde emissions were the subject of congressional hearings and, in the same year, the US Consumer Product Safety Commission banned the use of UFFIs.[7]

The wider cultural context for these events was an increasing concern with the effect of chemicals and manufacturing processes on the environment, with the decade following the 1962 publication of Rachel Carson's *Silent Spring* (German and French editions followed in 1963) seeing the founding of: environmental advocacy groups (Friends of the Earth in the US in 1969, and Greenpeace in Canada in 1971); the US Environmental Protection Agency in 1970; the first Earth Day, also in 1970 (fig. 244); the first political parties based on an environmental agenda (in Australia and New Zealand in 1972, and later in Britain and Germany); and the United Nations (UN) 'Conference on the Human Environment' in Stockholm in 1972. In the design world Victor Papanek's book *Design for the Real World: Human Ecology and Social Change* (1971) was an important and, eventually, influential polemic.

The promulgation of government regulations establishing 'safe' emission levels in Europe and the US, and the negative publicity around whether illness was caused by domestic formaldehyde emissions, carried on through the 1980s. Anxious to counter this, plywood manufacturers (among other panel producers) announced 'low-emission' formulations that met new guidelines and, they claimed, reduced toxic emissions.[8] Despite these moves to adapt, the wider public remained suspicious about plywood and other panels. It is important to note that research identified many sources

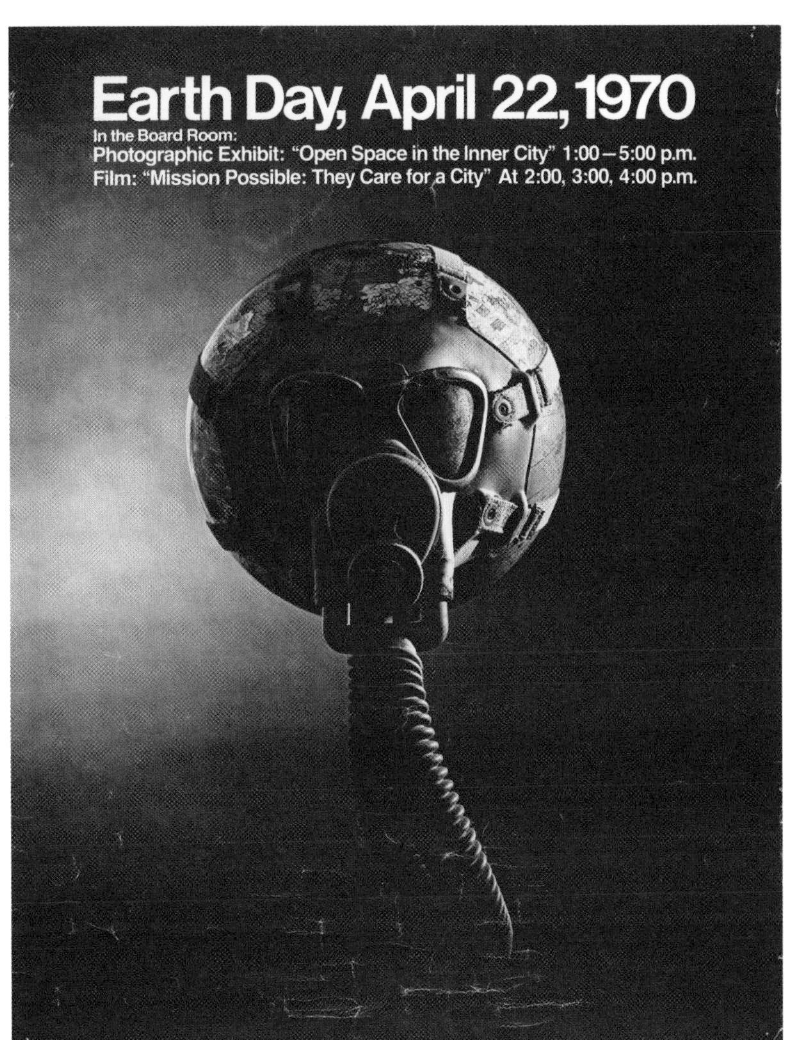

Earth Day, April 22, 1970
In the Board Room:
Photographic Exhibit: "Open Space in the Inner City" 1:00–5:00 p.m.
Film: "Mission Possible: They Care for a City" At 2:00, 3:00, 4:00 p.m.


244 (above)
**Earth Day poster**
Designed by Robert Leydenfrost with photograph by Don Brewster, 1970

of indoor formaldehyde emissions, including commonly available textiles, paints, wallpapers, glues and cleaning products. Industry also pointed out that formaldehyde emissions were generated in the natural world (by trees, for example), by smoking cigarettes and even by cooking certain foods. Good ventilation ameliorated emissions indoors but high temperature or humidity levels could cause levels to increase. Nonetheless, research consistently concluded that board products, along with UFFI, were prime contributors to indoor pollution and a threat to workers in the manufacturing industry.[9]

Standards requiring that building materials emit lower concentrations of formaldehyde led to generally lower emissions after the late 1980s and, as research continued, the levels considered safe were further reduced (especially in Japan and in Germany, and somewhat less so in the rest of the EU). The World Health Organization (WHO) formally declared formaldehyde to be a carcinogen in 2004.[10]

In spite of these steps to regulate the environmental pollution caused by plywood and other boards, ongoing industry and government complacency became clear in 2006, when evacuees from Hurricane Katrina (August 2005) in the US, living in mobile homes and trailers provided by the Federal Emergency Management Agency (FEMA), began to suffer health problems (fig. 245). The discovery by the US environmental organization the Sierra Club of unsafe levels of formaldehyde emissions in these trailers eventually led to congressional hearings (2007–08) and to US government testing (2008). It was established that these emissions came largely from plywood and particle board used for cabinet work, flooring and seating.[11]

The industry had attempted to portray the emissions problem as resolved by the time of the FEMA scandal. It was a sobering reminder of the tension between market demand for the cheapest possible prices for finished goods and the imperative to protect the environment and public health. Despite tighter standards for panel emissions, the problem continued. In 2009 a study of new homes in California – a consistent international leader in the regulation of emission levels – noted that 'nearly all homes had formaldehyde concentrations that exceeded guidelines for cancer and chronic irritation'. Residential buildings in Denmark – a country with high levels of environmental consciousness – that conformed to European guidelines for emissions were found in 2012

245 (below)
**FEMA trailers being delivered to New Orleans, December 2005**

to have air quality that did not meet WHO standards.[12] An updated version of a WHO report drawing on worldwide formaldehyde studies undertaken by both governmental and trade bodies published in 2010 noted that, in the EU, workers undertaking the 'manufacture of furniture and fixtures, except primarily of metal' suffered the most exposure to formaldehyde 'above background levels'.[13]

The Katrina episode saw the definitive tarnishing of the shiny idealism of post-war plywood. When considered alongside the impact that emissions have on people working with board products, FEMA's use of badly off-gassing trailers as emergency housing (plus their later selling on of the condemned trailers as cheap mobile home stock) also highlighted the disproportionate effect that formaldehyde emissions often have on poor and working-class people who own or live in the cheapest housing.[14]

### Geographies of production

As economies began to recover after World War II, there was a fundamental change in the worldwide plywood market, with the centre of plywood production moving from the US to Asian countries. This caused huge consternation for the US industry, with a number of public campaigns aimed at restricting the Japanese plywood trade (fig. 246). In 1950 the US produced 54.3% of the world's plywood; by 2009 the figure was down to 11%. By 1961 Japan was the second-largest producer in the world (behind the US) and would remain so until 1987, when it was overtaken by Indonesia. The combined production of Japan, Indonesia, Malaysia and China exceeded that of the US by 1991. The growth in Chinese production was especially dramatic: it doubled between 1994 and 2000, doubled again in 2001–02, exceeded US production in late 2002 and then surpassed the US's peak historic production (1987) in 2003. Chinese production doubled yet again in 2004, exceeding the combined output of all other countries by 2009. China became the world's largest consumer of plywood in 2003, having already, from the late 1990s, moved from being an importer of the material to a significant net exporter. By 2014 it was estimated that 82.6% of the world's plywood was manufactured in Asia, 10.9% in the Americas and 5.6% in Europe. As any country's consumption of plywood is highly dependent upon the construction industry, China's ongoing building boom ensures that its dominant position in the international market will not diminish any time soon. What has changed is that international furniture manufacturing has, in large measure, also moved to Asia from where it serves both export and domestic markets. Shrinking or levelling populations in Europe and North America will reinforce this trend.[15]

JAPANESE PLYWOOD
IMPORT OF FOREIGN PLYWOOD
WHAT IT MEANS TO YOU AND YOUR FAMILY


246 (above)
***Import of Foreign Plywood***
Cover of anti-Japanese trade brochure, US, 1950s

In terms of the sustainability of timber supplies there have been both positive and negative developments over the past forty years. The positive news is that it now takes less raw wood to supply an international wood market that, on average, has continued to grow year to year. Production technologies are more efficient, trees yield more pulp (for composite boards as well as for paper) than ever before, and more recycled woods and papers are used. In addition, wood composite panels that replace sawn timber with wood residues are now in use.[16] The far more devastating effect of post-1945 shifts in timber supply has been on the state of global forests, with the plywood industry contributing to a disastrous increase in deforestation and loss of rainforest.

The history of human settlement has always, to an extent, been one of deforestation. This process was greatly accelerated in the nineteenth century, as forests across the globe were systematically felled and exploited by colonial administrators and settlers. Working under the myth of an inexhaustible timber supply, much of the deforestation that took place across the British Empire in the nineteenth century was primarily aimed at clearing land for settlement and agriculture.[17] Logging in the US, including in areas that later went on to become significant to the plywood industry, also began with attempts to clear land for farming. The commercial industry expanded at the end of the nineteenth century as demand for timber increased. In the state of Oregon the number of sawmills increased from 173 to 500 in the period from 1870 to 1900. By the start of the twentieth century Oregon alone was cutting nearly 1 billion ft of wood for board annually (fig. 247).[18]

The demand for timber in the years since 1945 has continued and greatly accelerated global levels of deforestation (fig. 248). Tropical rainforests in the Philippines, Malaysia, Indonesia, Brazil and, increasingly, Papua New Guinea (fig. 249) and the Solomon Islands, have been particularly affected. Although the primary driver of global deforestation is land clearance for palm oil plantations or grazing livestock, the timber trade continues to have a large stake in the business.

Most of the tropical timber felled from the 1950s to the 1990s was exported to Japan. Japanese general trading companies set up mills in the Philippines, and then in Sabah, Indonesia, Papua New Guinea and the Solomons as stocks in each place dwindled. Much of this wood was used for plywood manufacture, including as cheap plywood for construction. Alongside Japanese exports from these countries, multinational investors

247 (right)
**Loggers**
Oregon, 1900

248 (left)

**Deforestation in Indonesia, 2014**

249 (below)

**Plywood and sawmill factory owned by the Malaysian company Rimbunan Hijau**
Papua New Guinea, c. 2008

250 (opposite)
**Zhonglin Southstar Plywood company, China, c. 2008**
Sheets of veneer being prepared for plywood manufacture

were also deeply involved in the post-war Asia–Pacific timber trade. In Indonesia, from the late 1960s onwards, companies from the Philippines, Hong Kong, Malaysia, the US, Japan, South Korea and Singapore provided funds, advice and equipment for large-scale logging. More recently, China and the EU have been the major global importers of tropical timber.[19]

In a report of 2006 estimates of the rate of Indonesian deforestation ranged between 1.9 million and 2.8 million hectares per year. The vast majority of these logs were illegally felled. The World Bank estimates that the governments of some of the poorest countries in the world lose a combined total of over US $15 billion per year to illegal logging, to say nothing of the resulting uncontrolled deforestation, loss of biodiversity, emission of greenhouse gases, and dispossession and conflict with indigenous peoples and local populations. Although attempts have been made since about 2010 to restrict the trade in illegally logged timber, these do not so far appear to be very effective.[20]

Much illegally felled timber is sold for plywood manufacture, with tropical hardwoods often used as decorative face veneers on cheap boards. As a report issued by the UK National Measurement Office in 2015 records, the complicated supply chains for plywood make this trade difficult to track: a single manufacturer might have many different veneer suppliers (fig. 250).[21] A Greenpeace report published in 2007, which looked at the import of illegal timber into the Netherlands, states:

> Plywood with a core made up of Chinese grown poplar but faced with tropical, ancient forest species, such as Okoumé from Africa or Bintangor and Red Canarium from Papua New Guinea and the Solomons is a particularly good-selling commodity in Europe. In the booming heartland of China there are thousands of small, family-run veneer mills running their machines throughout the day, stripping veneers from logs mainly for the production of cheap plywood. Their veneer is picked up by an almost as large number of plywood mills, with a few of these now emerging as larger players, which are able to flood the international plywood markets with cheap plywood, often from illegal and destructive logging operations.[22]

Despite this very dark picture of the state of the world's forests, there is evidence of some positive change. The Chinese government had, in 2013, made progress in its attempts to restrict domestic trade in illegally felled timber, and EU legislation was passed in the same year to address the import of such timber into Europe (although a meaningful impact from this has yet to be seen). As a counter to the often voracious global timber trade, there are also countries with an enviable domestic record on forestry. Among them is Finland, where 62% of forests are owned locally and managed by small stakeholders, and 26% by government, and where yields are lower than in larger, intensively forested countries. Finnish producers, for competition reasons, concentrate on higher-quality plywoods.[23]

### Selling plywood in a world looking for sustainability

Since the UN report *Our Common Future* (1987) introduced the term 'sustainable development' (defined very expansively as meaning that present-day development should never 'compromise the ability of future generations to meet their own needs'), and the 1992 UN Rio Earth Summit declared that all economic decisions should take fully into account any environmental impact, governments, businesses and world populations have, for varied and sometimes contradictory reasons, adopted sustainability as a watchword. Applying sustainable principles to materials (including plywood), and products made from such materials, has been a complex and ever-changing proposition since that time.[24]

Across the world there are a very large number of national (or, in the case of the EU, multinational) industry guidelines or product standards, as well as government regulations, that deal with issues of the sustainability of plywood, as with other materials. These can relate to all or only some of the following: sourcing of materials, use and safety of materials, methods of manufacturing, recyclability of materials, retention and auditing of records, inspection and testing regimes, product emissions, labelling and safety, and manufacturer or third-party certification of any and all of these elements. There are, unsurprisingly, vast differences between countries or regions in terms of compliance and enforcement. Yet commercial, institutional and individual consumers must make use of these regulations – however imperfect – in a globalized market to make decisions, in particular about the safety and environmental sustainability of the end product. International standards and coordination therefore remain a fundamental stumbling block to public and even trade understanding of the nature of the products they are using in manufacturing, at home or at work.

Certification schemes related to the sustainability (including legality) of forestry methods have been set up by a range of providers – non-profit organizations, for-profit companies and trade bodies – since the mid-1990s. They are intended to provide assurance to buyers of timber, and in turn to their customers, that the woods used have been

251 (above)

**'Some New Items for the Home', part I**
Jasper Morrison, installation at DAAD Gallery, Berlin, 1988. The chair was manufactured by Vitra from 1989

sustainably forested. Not all of these schemes are considered to be suitably robust and some of them work on behalf of the interests of the timber industry alone. At the time of writing, the Forest Stewardship Council (FSC), an international non-profit organization, is widely regarded as the leading such certifier, and as having contributed in a positive way to the well-being of the world's forests, although it too has been subject to criticism by both forest owners and leading environmental organizations.[25] Certification of both forests and products is a complex issue, for all parties, not least owing to the length of a supply chain that begins in the forest and ends with the sale or use of the product. Unsustainable parts of that chain are sometimes, though not always, the result of greed, contempt for environmental consequences or mere lack of resolve. Consumers also bear responsibility for demanding the cheapest possible product, if not by their words then by their behaviour in the marketplace. Inaccurate certification is embraced not only by industry or design professionals wishing to prosper in a competitive market, or resigned to living with imperfect systems, but also by consumers using it as a salve to their consciences, an easy way to avoid the complex issues around product sustainability.

An alternative to certification schemes, at least for those analyzing current products and especially contemplating new ones, is the twenty-first-century concept of life-cycle analysis, whereby the entire life of a proposed product ('cradle to grave') is assessed for its environmental, social and economic impact. Life-cycle analysis attempts to go beyond all of the elements covered in certification schemes. Instead of thinking of the ultimate end of products and materials as a 'grave', advocates of 'cradle to cradle' go still further, building recycling and reuse into the processes of design, manufacture and use. In the case of plywood, the reuse not only of offcuts (including those sold online) but also of plywood products has received some attention in recent years.[26]

Nonetheless, certification continues to be regarded by sellers of wood products – especially those who want to export to world markets – as an essential marketing tool. For consumers it provides guidance and reassurance. There is certainly a risk that any lack of vigilance of the systems could diminish the gains made so far. If the last two decades are a guide, certification schemes and, indeed, the flexible definitions of what constitute sustainable practice or materials, will be regularly redefined and repositioned.

## The rise of plywood

The building and architectural sector is the largest consumer of plywood in the world, as it has been for more than half a century. Within those practices, and the allied fields of interior and furniture design, the use of plywood is now more extensive than ever. Whereas, in certain moments of its history, plywood has been hidden, today it is routinely exposed. Its mainly light-coloured 'woodiness' is often emphasized and, at the very least, implicitly associated with classic modernism and with mid-century design – in both cases also with Scandinavian design (figs 195–196, 213 and 217). It is difficult to look through a design magazine of any kind without noticing how common the use of plywood is today. How and why did this come about?

As environmental activism of the 1970s seeped its way into popular consciousness there was, in the 1980s and 1990s, a gradual turn to 'natural' materials in affluent countries and also to simpler, less ornamented forms of design (fig. 251). Consumers, designers, makers and some manufacturers began to think more seriously about the environmental impact of their products. One reaction on the part of makers and consumers was a turn (or retreat) to the handmade or handcrafted, or (more often) that which looked handmade, often driven by a nostalgia for an allegedly simpler era.[27] Larger companies embraced the rhetoric of 'eco' or 'green' products, implying less damage and a kinder attitude to the environment. The motivations for this ranged from the sincere to the cynical, leading to the adoption of the phrase 'greenwash' to describe businesses that (exaggeratedly) market themselves on the basis of their supposed environmental credentials. Although the narrative given here is very summary, these attitudes, which have carried on to the present day, gave rise to plywood's sometimes contradictory position in the marketplace.

Plywood's appearance, as well as its name, allow it to be superficially thought of as a 'natural' material. Especially when its surface is neither stained nor laminated with other materials, it appears as wood, plain and simple. The words 'simplicity', 'clean' and 'minimal' were (and are) often applied to plywood designs, a tendency that was exemplified by 1990 in the work of the British designer Jasper Morrison (born 1959; fig. 251) and American artist Donald Judd (1928–94; fig. 252). Morrison's work has consistently been described in terms of its minimal aesthetic and truth to materials, characterized in 1989 as a turn against 1980s 'designer luxury...[in favour of] a Spartan, clutter-free existence' and a new spirit of 'ecological restraint'. This desire to reflect a concern with ecology and the 'natural' through the appearance of designed objects led to an observable increase in the use of wood over other materials, a trend that continues to the present day.[28]

Proper sourcing and certification – at least as far as the market was concerned – also allowed plywood to find a place among a group of materials seen as sustainable (despite the fact that it was still often implicated in poor environmental practice). As a material that was worked in the second half of the twentieth century with simple, handheld machine tools (such as jig saws, circular saws), and had a history in DIY, plywood also fitted well into the early twenty-first-century ethos of makerspaces. Within this context it was the rise of digital fabricating machines, specifically CNC cutters, that led to a great expansion in the use of plywood around the world.

252 (below)
**Plywood chairs**
Designed by Donald Judd, fabricated by Jeff Jamieson/Rupert Deese, Wood and Plywood Furniture, New York, 1991

## Digital platforms

A CNC (Computer Numeric Control) machine is one run entirely by a computer programme. The automated cutting of plywood is now commonly done by two different types of CNC machine: CNC routers cut both two- and three-dimensionally with rotating cutting bits called endmills, while CNC laser cutters use high-powered laser beams focused through a lens to cut two-dimensionally and on a continuous path. For industry, both types of machine allow for much faster, more complex and more precise cutting than was hitherto possible. They can also give a higher surface finish than that generated by conventional machine tools. For amateur makers, for professionals working on their own, or for design firms without their own equipment, access to CNC machines became common in the early twenty-first century through publicly accessible making spaces.[29]

The term 'makerspaces' now encompasses a range of public, non-profit and commercial sites where professional and amateurs can access equipment and expertise in order to make a range of things or to modify existing ones (fig. 253). While the types of materials and equipment available in these spaces are diverse, CNC routers and laser cutters are common in most makerspaces where woodworking is undertaken. All of the more than 1,000 digital fabrication workshops around the world called Fab Labs – based on a concept developed at Massachusetts Institute of Technology (MIT) – have, as part of their standard list of equipment, a CNC laser cutter and a CNC router (or lathe; fig. 253), in addition to everyday power tools.[30]

Any regular visitor to makerspaces would recognize that plywood is now the material most used by makers – to the extent that its texture and appearance has, without apparent intention, become an important part of the aesthetic of these spaces.[31] Although not cheap in the context of individual use (most of these makers do not buy in bulk), plywood is used in makerspaces for the same reasons that it was useful for DIY projects after World War II: it is relatively easy to handle and cut (especially with up-to-date machinery)

253 (below)
**Fab Lab, Barcelona, 2015**
With CNC cutter visible at right of photo

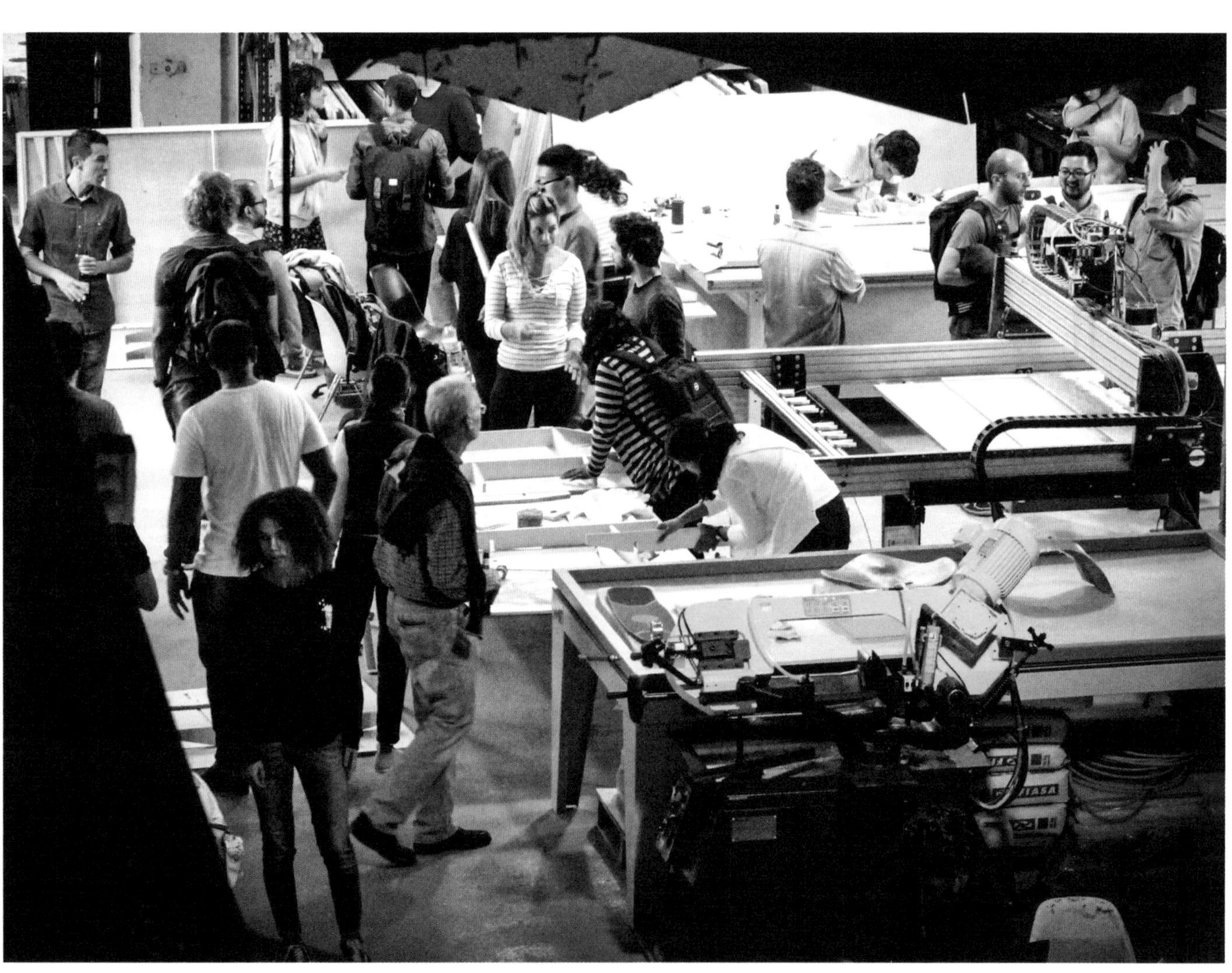

254–259 (above)

**Projects for CNC-cut plywood**
Posted on Pinterest, 2016

and is also stronger than most other board materials, meaning that it can be used to build reliable cut-out joints, and minimizing the need for additional fixtures.

The common perception of plywood as a 'natural' material, capable of being 'crafted', is also appropriate to the DIY 'fixpert' ethos of makerspaces, which are used mainly, though not exclusively, by younger people. Ideas for plywood projects are circulated not only through makerspaces themselves, but also online. A huge number of people share images of CNC-cut plywood on sites such as Pinterest (figs 254–259), or sell their items on Etsy. These projects highlight the specific aesthetic of many of the objects made in makerspaces (and increasingly, more commercially), with a noticeable focus on simple cut-out construction, visible joints and exposed edges.

The characteristics of plywood that make it especially suitable not only for individual makers, but also for companies using digital platforms to produce furniture and buildings, are its availability, structural stability and global standardization. Such companies create digital design files that can be distributed globally, the product then manufactured locally to where it will be used. This system of production – referred to as distributed manufacturing – is much more environmentally friendly than centralized manufacture. It eliminates the need for large factories or long-distance shipping, and ensures that products are produced only in the numbers required to fill demand. In order for such a system to work, a design does, however, need to be able to be produced in a standard way by different local manufacturers. Materials are key to this, and among board materials suitable for construction, plywood is one of the very few that will consistently yield the same result when cut following digital instructions.[32]

The British-based digital platform Opendesk (established 2013; fig. 260) offers furniture designs on its website. The company carries no inventory and the intention is that these designs can be freely downloaded, anywhere in the world (figs 261–262), under a Creative Commons licence. Individuals can then either make the furniture themselves, or the website will put potential purchasers (individual, corporate or institutional) in touch with local makers who can produce furniture in small or large quantities. The purchaser chooses a maker based on those criteria most important to them – price, speed of delivery, proximity and reviews – then pays the maker directly (with a commission going to Opendesk). The website originally featured designs by its architect founders but has shifted to increasingly feature other designers, who are able to submit their own projects (which are then developed by Opendesk). In the next stage of development visitors will be encouraged to modify designs on the site. Virtually all of Opendesk's designs are made from plywood.

Opendesk's original choice of plywood was based on the founders' inability to find acceptable and affordable furniture for a job that they were offered some 3,000 miles (4,828 km) away from their base. They decided to design their own and to try to find a web-based way to make it work in a system of 'distributed' or local manufacturing. They chose plywood after balancing cost, availability, the environmental credentials of possible material suppliers and, most crucially, the designers' ability to provide many makers around the world with simple digital design information and specifications that would result in the same product (taking into account the variation in measurements, drill bit sizes or machinery from country to country).

Predating the early Opendesk experiments, WikiHouse was founded in 2011. Led by Alastair Parvin (also one of Opendesk's original partners), it is now a non-profit foundation. WikiHouse is a social–architectural enterprise aimed not at selling a product but at establishing an open platform and distributed system for housebuilding for and by homeowners. Described as 'a collaborative R&D [research and development] project', it aims to arrive at inexpensive building systems capable of being rapidly erected by anyone using readily available tools. It especially aims to involve the house owner in design and construction, as s/he is the one who will care most about the building and be most affected by any health and environmental issues.

WikiHouse chose plywood for its first building system, Wren, after exploring a range of two- and three-dimensional, structurally certified materials. Plywood offered the best balance in terms of strength-to-weight ratio, consistency and price. The nature of the construction meant that WikiHouse were able to be less strict than Opendesk about specifying the precise detail and tolerances of their designs. WikiHouse aim to use the cheapest possible materials in a relatively forgiving method of construction. The Wren system (fig. 263), which is not based on either a frame system or a panel one, is conceived as a chassis of assembled plywood parts – the structure of the building – onto which components including windows, services and cladding are fitted.

Comparable to WikiHouse in both its building system (also described as a chassis system) and its extensive use of plywood, but very different in terms of approach, are the houses of the British company Facit Homes (launched in 2011). The company began with a desire to digitally manufacture houses and chose to use plywood as they wanted a sustainable building material (they use the same Wisa brand Finnish plywood, spruce in this case, as WikiHouse and Opendesk) that would lend itself to an easily assembled component system. Their approach emphasizes technology as a driver and was based on the efficiency

260 (below)
**Edie Stool (assembled and unassembled), birch plywood**
Designed by David and Joni Steiner for Opendesk, London, 2013

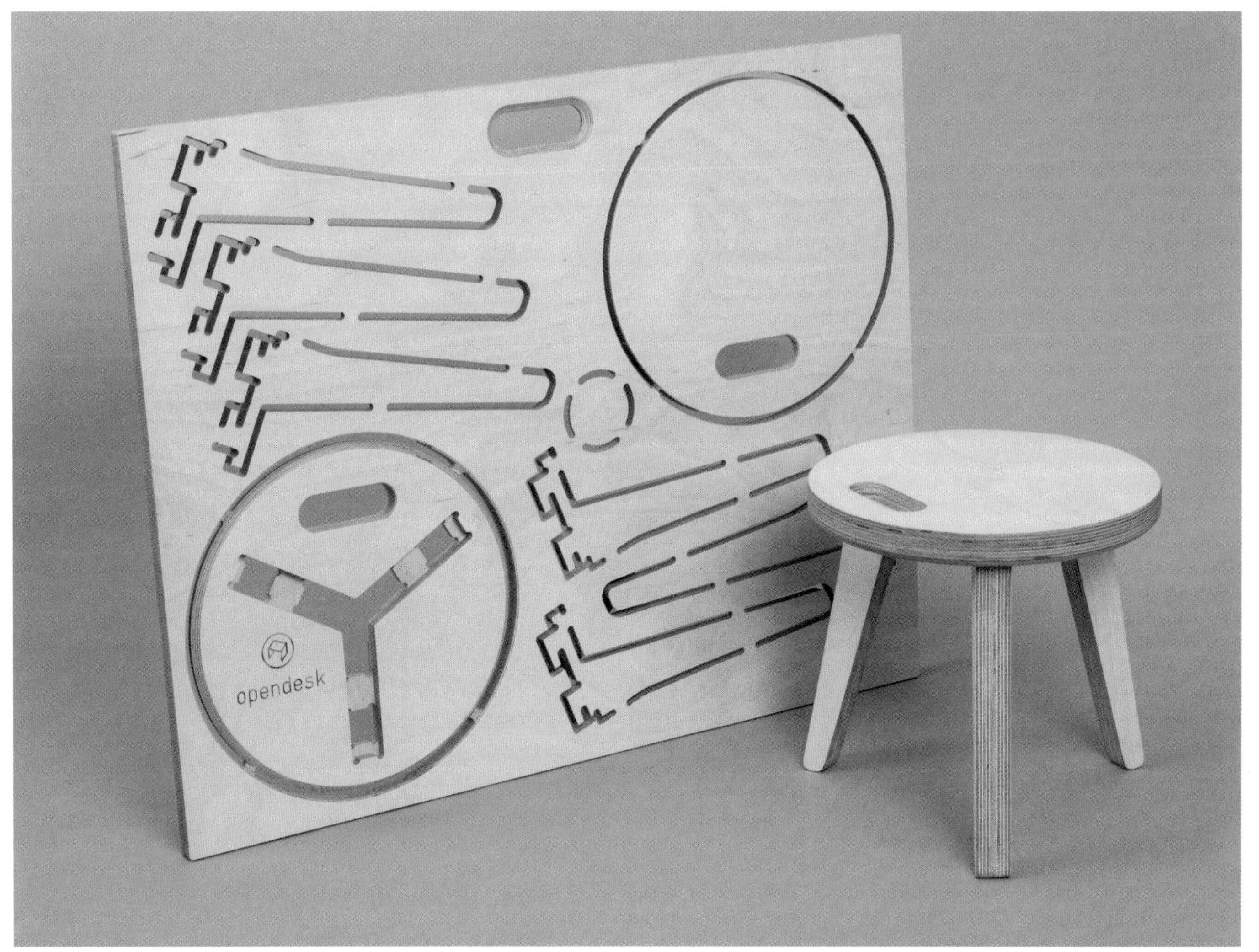

261 (right)

**Lean Desk, birch plywood**
Designed by Joni Steiner and Nick Ierodiaconou for Opendesk, London, 2013

262 (below)

**Map showing global distribution of downloads of Lean Desk (to August 2015)**

263 (opposite)

**Wren, the WikiHouse building system**
Construction stages start with the CNC cutting of parts, 2016

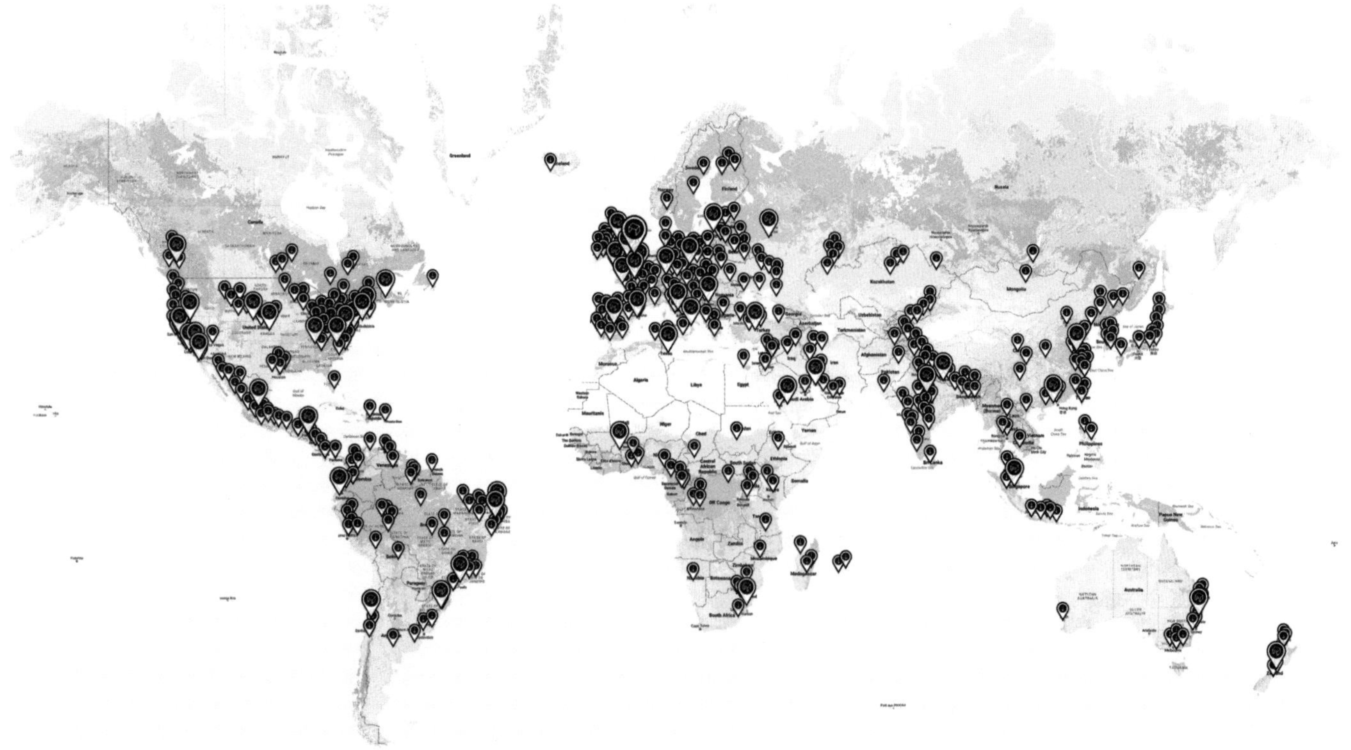

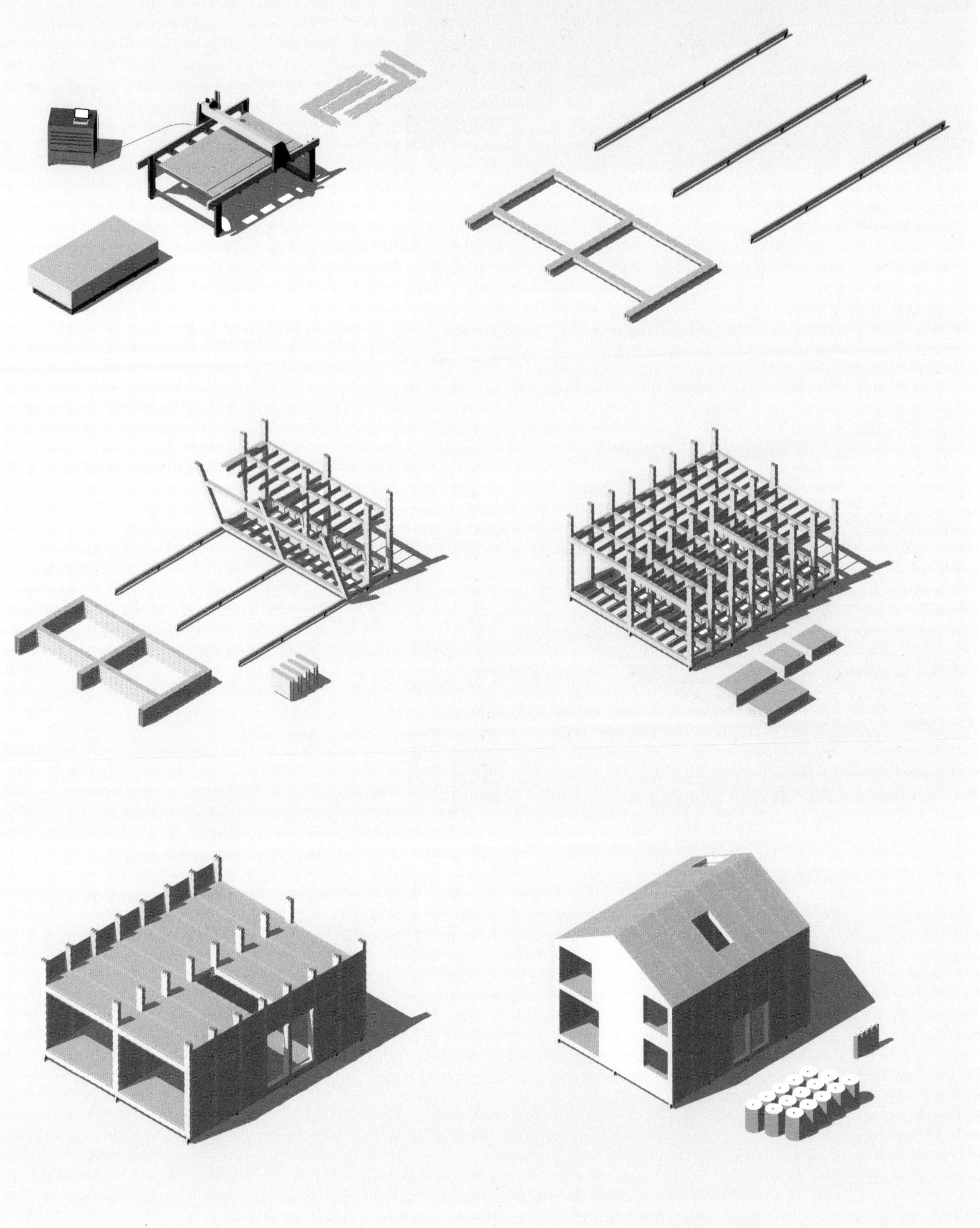

264 (top)

**Plywood construction, Facit Homes, 2013**

265 (above)

**CNC cutter transported to site, Facit Homes, 2013**

of not having to rework elements of the construction every time a new tradesperson arrived on site. Theirs is a closed system, which they feel delivers to customers precisely what they want: that every element of the final building is controlled and delivered by a single company, exactly as promised in the agreed design.

The Facit chassis is made from plywood boards that interlock to form hollow components. These, in turn, are fitted together in an integrated structural system, which the designers describe as 'big wooden lego' (fig. 264). The components are modified for each project and they are cut on site by a three-axis CNC router (fig. 265) and assembled there. The easy availability of CNC routers contributed to the choice of plywood as a building material. Rather than a prefabricated system, Facit describe their method as 'site-intensive', yet they also aim to reduce costs and to simplify construction in a way that parallels earlier prefabricated systems (see chapter 5). High-tech cutting is accompanied by low-tech assembly, as with WikiHouse.

While the buyer of an Opendesk product or the self-builder of a WikiHouse will be very aware of the plywood structure of their table or house, Facit Homes do not mention plywood at all in their marketing material. They avoid this, they say, because many homeowners perceive it as a cheap material, despite the cost of the type of plywood that they use. In the finished homes, at least in Britain, there is rarely any sign of plywood, as all surfaces of houses built to date have no exposed plywood walls.

In addition to its revival in 'prefabricated' housing systems, plywood has been used since about 2005 in a large number of experimental and temporary structures. While its lower cost is often an important reason for its selection over other building materials, plywood is also frequently used for symbolic or structural reasons.

266 (above)

**Skating shelters, Winnipeg, Canada**
Designed by Patkau Architects, 2011

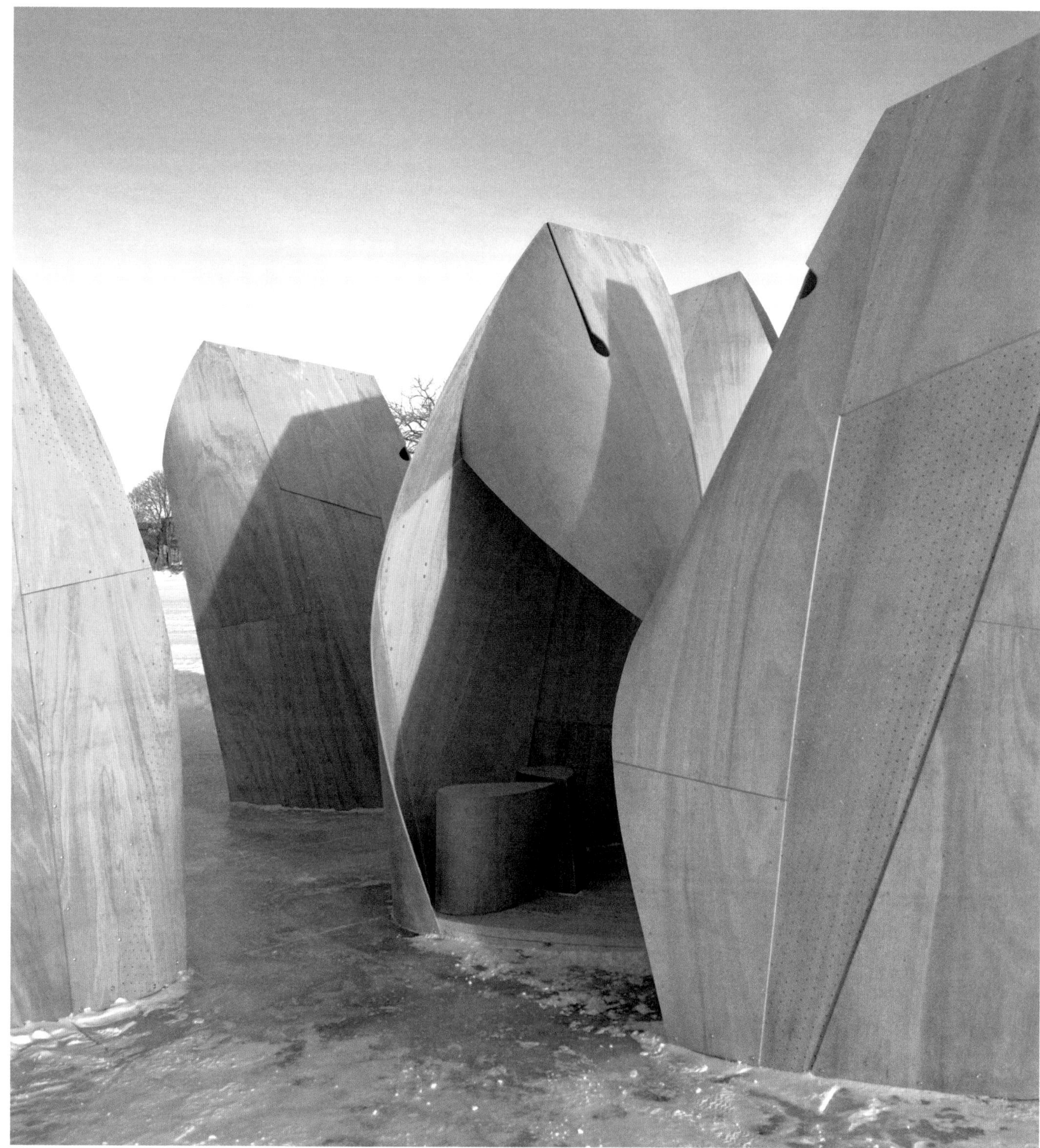

267 (above)

**Skating shelters, Winnipeg, Canada**
Designed by
Patkau Architects, 2011

A group of temporary buildings uniquely suited to the structural qualities of plywood were a set of outdoor skating shelters designed by the Canadian practice Patkau Architects in 2011. The shelters were erected on the frozen river that runs through central Winnipeg (figs 266–267), a city where winter temperatures drop to minus 30–40°C (minus 22–40°F). For this project, each shelter was built of two layers of overlapping sheets of 4 × 8 ft (1.22 × 2.4 m) 'bendy' plywood. Each sheet was 3⁄16 in. (4.76 mm) thick. The sheets were built around a triangular base and two narrow, internal, wedge-shaped supporting members. Bendy plywood is specially constructed with a thin centre layer that allows it to bend along one axis, in contrast to normal plywood, which resists any form of bending (as discussed in chapter 6, plywood can be moulded only at the stage where it is formed, from veneers layered with glue). The minimal internal structure of the shelters meant that the two halves of the shell were held in tension by being attached to each other. Six shelters of different forms were grouped in a 'village', but with the suggestion of a group of stout, monolithic creatures protecting themselves from the elements.[33]

In a similar spirit to its use for Patkau's shelters, plywood (often shaped with digital manufacturing techniques) has been one of the main materials used in architectural pavilions since about 2010. A pavilion for a 2011 'Smart Cities' exposition in Barcelona, commissioned by the Spanish utility company Endesa, was intended to demonstrate the management of solar power over a year (fig. 268). Plywood was used for the surfaces of the building, presumably owing at least in part to the association of wood with the natural world. The desire to expose as many solar panels as possible required very large, faceted surfaces in CNC-cut plywood, on both the exterior and the interior.[34]

Since 2010 the Institute for Computational Design at the University of Stuttgart has built a research pavilion each year. Intended to investigate the latest developments in computational design, simulation and production processes in architecture, three out of six of these pavilions have used plywood as their structural material. The Director of the Institute, Achim Menges, has related the recent rise of wood as an architectural material to its (relatively) sound ecological status. He draws attention to the ways in which wood's machinability, elasticity and reactivity to moisture in the air (hygroscopicity) make it particularly adaptive to the new possibilities of computational design.[35]

Equally important (although less visible) to the rise of wood as an architectural material is the increasing adoption of new kinds of so-called 'engineered wood' for structural work.[36] These products have varying degrees of proximity to plywood – plywood's closest relation among the large-scale structural timbers is laminated veneer lumber (LVL), which consists of many layers of built-up 3 mm (⅛ in.) veneer. LVL can be entirely laminated (with all of the grain running in one direction), although sometimes each fifth layer of veneer is cross-grained. LVL was used to build J. MAYER H. Architects' 2013 'Metropol Parasol', a permanent, undulating roof hovering above the Plaza de la Encarnación in downtown Seville (figs 269–270).

268 (below)
**Endesa Pavilion, Barcelona, Spain**
Designed by Institute for Advanced Architecture of Catalonia (IAAC), 2011

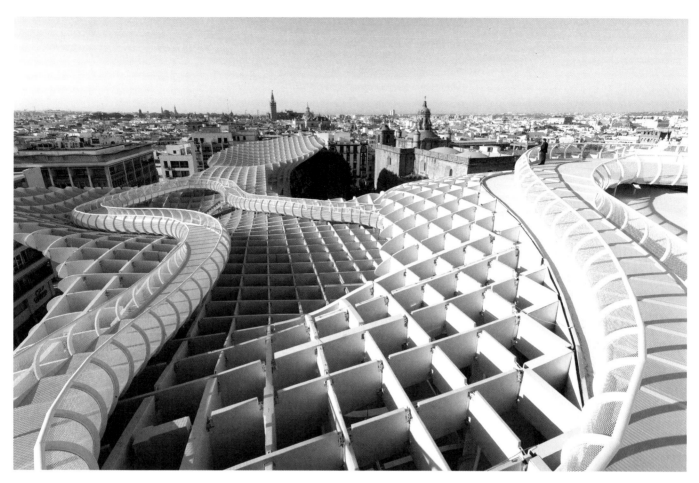

269 and 270
(above and right)

**Metropol Parasol, Seville, Spain**
Designed by J. MAYER H. Architects, 2011

The other major wood product used for structural frameworks is cross-laminated timber (CLT). Although CLT is not in fact plywood, its use in construction nonetheless merits mention, especially as it is sometimes mistakenly referred to as the raw material of 'plywood skyscrapers'. Glued, laminated, solid wood construction, especially in the form of arches and roof supports, has been used in northern Europe since at least the late nineteenth century. In the 1930s the US Forest Products Laboratory experimented with this type of construction, testing and developing the strength of curved constructional beams that they termed 'glued laminated arches' (fig. 271). Only in the 1990s was a form of CLT developed in Austria and Germany, mainly as an opportunity to use low-quality waste (solid) wood. Synthetic resin and hydraulic presses are used to press the material together under enormous force, making CLT into panels or lengths (at present) 50–500 mm (2–20 in.) thick and up to 24 m (79 ft) long – sizes that are unachievable in plywood. CLT began to be used for taller buildings only once building regulations were rewritten after 2000. In 2009 a nine-storey apartment building with CLT floors, walls, core and stairs was built in London as the (then) tallest wooden building in the world (figs 272–273).[37]

271 (left)

**First glue-laminated arch made in the US under test at the Forest Products Laboratory**
Madison, Wisconsin, 1935

272 and 273 (below, left and right)

**Murray Grove, Hackney, London**
The photo on the left shows the building under construction. Designed by Waugh Thistleton, 2008–09

**Plywood as shelter**

As has been shown throughout this book, plywood has a deeply bifurcated history – it has always been both a material used in cutting-edge design, and a mass-produced, often throwaway product. This division continues today in the stark contrast between current interest in wood as an experimental architectural material, and plywood's ongoing mass-mobilization in the construction of shelter.

As discussed in chapter 5, plywood has a long history of use in temporary, often emergency architecture. While 1930s schemes planned for the provision of finished homes, plywood's use in housing has far more often been as a temporary sheet material. Photographs taken at the so-called 'Jungle' refugee camp in Calais (fig. 274), before its destruction by French authorities in October 2016, show plywood as one of a number of materials deployed in the desperate quest to stay warm and safe. Alongside other boards such as chipboard or MDF, plywood (when available) helps to provide a more secure and weathertight structure than can be achieved simply by the use of plastic sheeting.

The reasons for using plywood in this way are the same as those that have appeared throughout this book, in relation to both highly specialized and very simple types of design – it is relatively strong, easy to build with very few (or no) tools, available in large quantities and standard sizes across the globe, often cheap, and, where it has been salvaged, frequently disposable. While often used by people to build parts of their own houses, plywood is also one of a number of materials provided in large quantities by aid organizations for emergency shelter and housing.

Since the early 2000s there has been a change in models for the provision of relief shelter, with a new focus on the idea of 'transitional housing' – an incremental approach, whereby the temporary shelters that are built (often self-built) after a disaster are intended to be gradually upgraded, or their materials recycled, into more permanent housing. Rather than relying on prefabricated structures from overseas, or the movement of people into large-scale camps, the model of transitional shelter building envisages a more organic, locally defined and locally controlled system of emergency relief.[38]

In practice, transitional housing is implemented in part through the provision of tools and construction materials so that those affected by a crisis can build or adapt structures in which they can live. Depending on the nature of the crisis, major aid organizations such as USAID (United States Agency for International Development) or the UNHCR (UN Refugee Agency) often provide 'shelter kits' for this purpose. According to UNHCR figures, the number of refugees and forcibly displaced people in the world in 2016 reached an unprecedented 65.3 million. As a 2014 'Shelter Case Studies' report notes, many of these people were and continue to be in need of housing in urban areas, meaning that shelter kits and the ability to adapt or make safe an existing structure are particularly vital to safety and survival.[39]

Plywood's inclusion in shelter kits is dependent on the nature and needs of a specific crisis. Kits given out by the UNHCR to help people insulate buildings in order to survive the 2015 Syrian winter included tools, plywood and plastic sheeting. Plywood is generally used in colder climates where heat insulation is needed (although it is sometimes replaced by other locally available or cheaper materials). It is also often used with timber framing for shelters in places that are at risk of earthquakes or hurricanes, as it is much more resilient than plastic sheeting but much less dangerous (in case of collapse) than masonry.[40]

Despite its usefulness and adaptability for shelter, plywood remains a luxury in many of the poorest or most desperate situations. Not only is plywood often hard to find, or expensive, its relative stability and permanence can make it a contentious material in situations where there is local resistance to the housing of poor or displaced people. The Grande Synthe refugee camp, near Dunkirk, northern France, provides a particularly shocking example of this. This makeshift tented settlement sprang up in the wake of the 2015 refugee crisis. Despite being described by the UK director of the international non-profit organization Médecins Sans Frontières (MSF; Doctors without Borders) as containing the worst conditions seen in twenty years of humanitarian work, French authorities resistant to the existence of the camp policed the borders of the tented settlement, refusing to allow aid organizations to bring in any more permanent building materials for the construction of safe or warm shelter. This official disavowal of responsibility for the housing of refugees, expressed by withholding of building materials, was eventually overcome by MSF, which, together with a local authority run by the Green party, managed in January 2016 to convince the French government to let them open a new camp at a nearby site, with enclosed housing for 2,500 people provided in temporary plywood shelters.[41]

274 (above)

**Shelter erected at 'Jungle' refugee camp, Calais, France, 2016**
Plywood was used alongside other materials such as plastic sheeting to construct the walls and floor

275 (right)

**Construction of Danzer 3D veneer sheet**
Each sheet is cut multiple times along its length, and the pieces then held together as a sheet with glue strips. The sheets of veneer are layered together to form a plywood that can easily be moulded in three dimensions

276 (below right)

**Comparison between a plywood sample made of five layers of conventional beech veneer (left) and one made of five layers of Danzer 3D beech veneer (right)**
The cracks and folds in the left-hand sample demonstrate the difficulty of three-dimensional moulding with conventional plywood

277–281 (opposite)

**Stages in moulding UPM Grada™ – after heat is applied the boards can be moulded**
The photos show the construction of the Dragon Skin Pavilion using this product. Designed by Emmi Keskisarja, Pekka Tynkkynen, and Kristof Crolla and Sebastien Delagrange of the architectural practice LEAD for the 2012 Hong Kong & Shenzhen Bi-City Biennale of Urbanism\Architecture

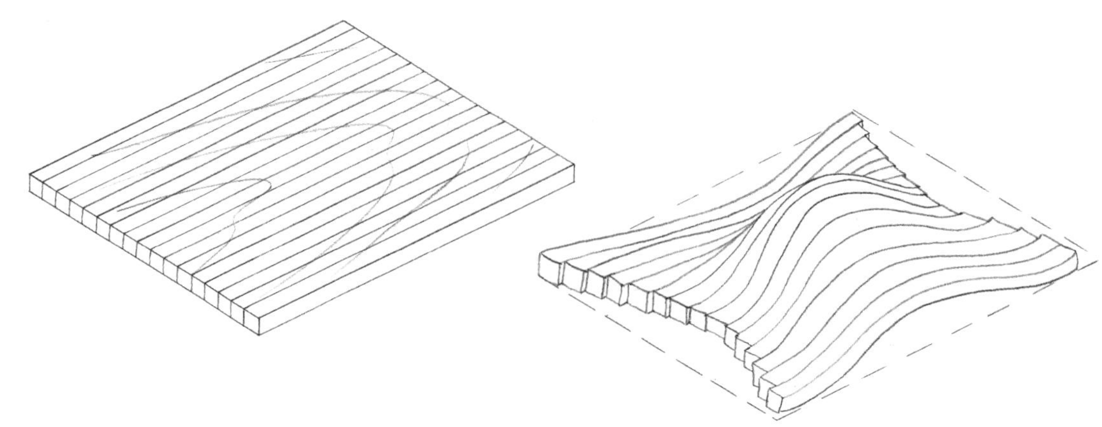

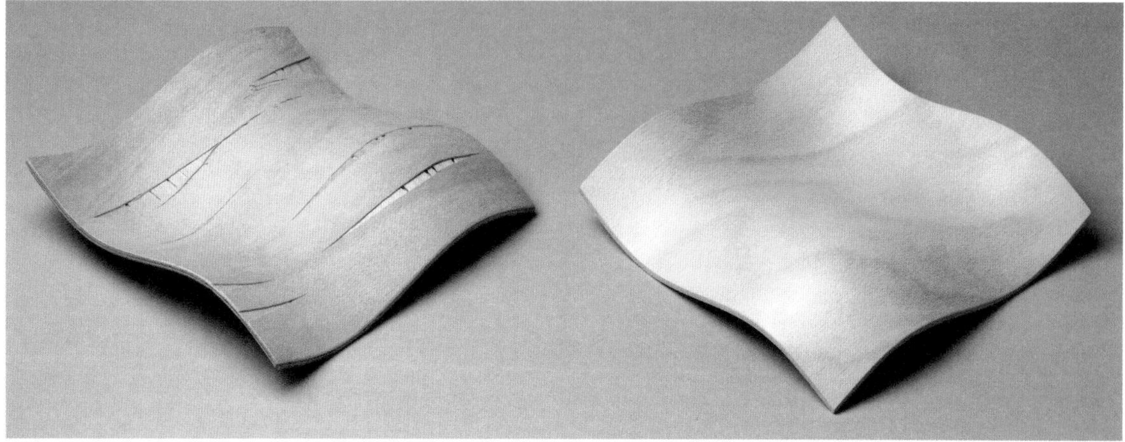

### The future of plywood

Today plywood is in use in a myriad of ways, some long-standing (for furniture and building construction) and some more recent (such as insulation in liquid natural-gas containers on ships). While the essentials of making plywood have not fundamentally changed since it was first developed, there have been some genuinely new advances in plywood technology in recent years. For example, Danzer, an Austrian-based producer of hardwood, is now selling thin sheets of veneer that can be three-dimensionally moulded.[42] This moulding is achieved by cutting a regular series of lines across each sheet of veneer, and the sheet is then held together with glue stripes applied perpendicular to the cuts. Once cut in this way, the veneer is formable in all directions – this is not possible using standard veneers (figs 275–276).

The Finnish wood producers UPM, well known for their plywoods, introduced in 2011 a board product named Grada™ (figs 277–281). This is a solid (thermoplastic) plywood that can be heated and then moulded into shape very quickly as it cools down. From a production point of view its chief advantage is that a factory can dispense with the need to handle the wet trade of gluing veneers before moulding boards. Both the Danzer and UPM products are still to be fully exploited.

With new specialist and digital applications, plywood's status within the design professions has never been higher. As it is possible to buy plywood that carries certification of its supply chain, production process and safety, it is now widely seen as a sustainable material (although, as explained above, these claims are complex and contested). The fact that it is made from wood gives it much of its appeal. In spite of this, however, plywood is for others still tainted with the 'anti-veneer' prejudice that arose in the nineteenth century – above all, the fact that it is not solid wood.

In 2015 a leading British middle-market furniture chain advertised on television with the slogan 'No Veneer in 'Ere'. In fact, the solid legs of their furniture were wrapped with a 'thin outer layer of hardwood', the leg being formed by laminating together smaller pieces of wood. In answers to an accusation of false and misleading advertising, the firm put forwards familiar arguments as to why there was 'no veneer'. Echoing the language of nineteenth- and early twentieth-century debates and court cases, they claimed that consumers would not expect 'every product to have been whittled down from a single piece of hardwood', stating that the term 'veneer' could only describe something used to hide a lesser-quality wood or engineered wood (such as plywood or MDF). The company claimed that they were not hiding any such thing – the 'oak wrap' was thicker than normal veneer, so they were within their rights to describe the furniture as '100% solid/0% veneer'. Using the almost exact words of early twentieth-century plywood manufacturers, they said that the wrapping technique 'strengthened the furniture by preventing it from expanding or contracting and reducing the chance of warping or splitting'. The Advertising Standards Authority concluded that Oak Furniture Land's claims of 'no veneer…100% solid hardwood' or even 'solid hardwood' were false.[43] It seems as though this remarkable material, so inventively used so often, will be beset by the veneer problem for a long time to come.

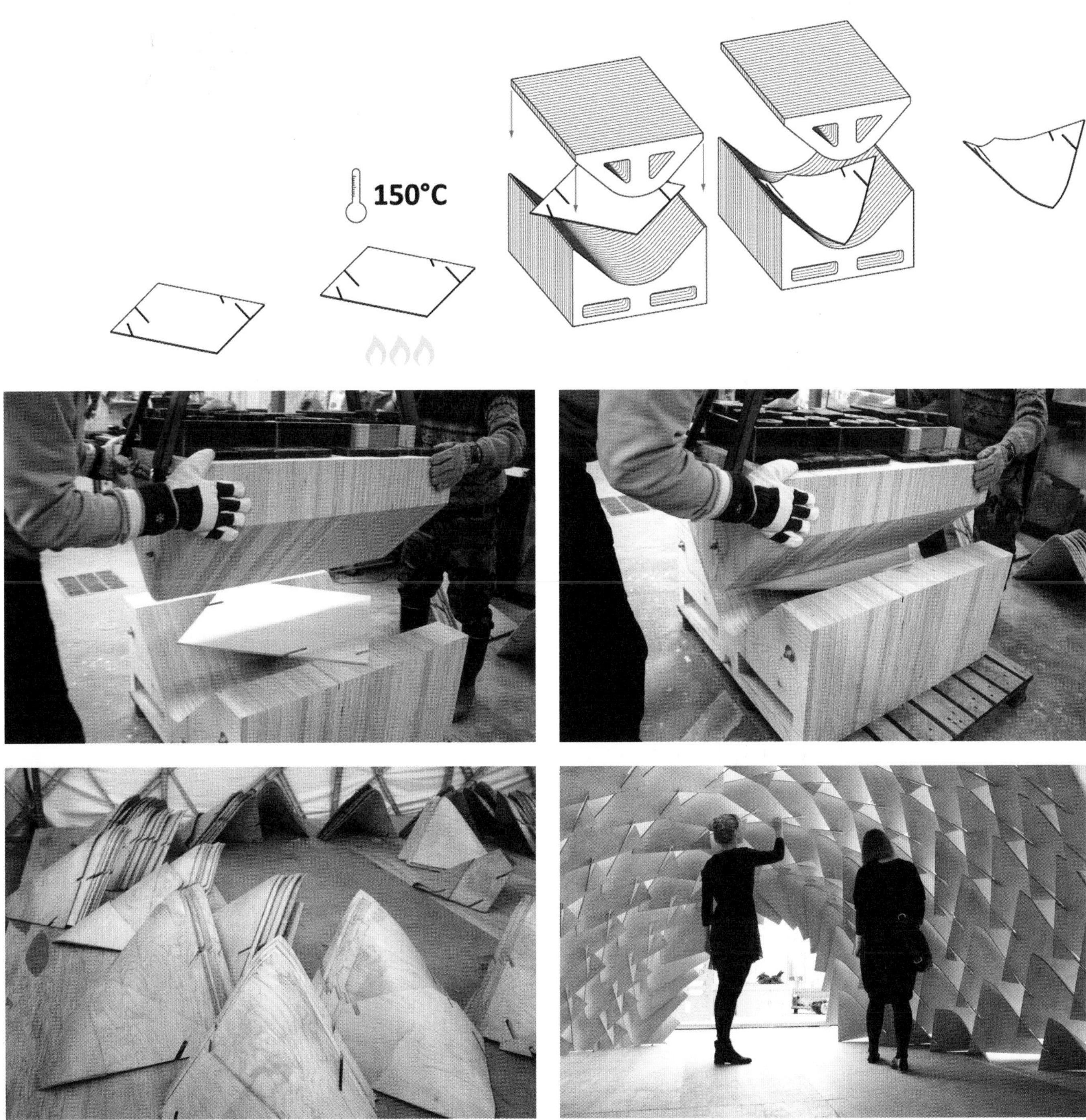

## Notes

### Introduction (pp. 6–15)

1 Relative humidity measures the amount of moisture in the air relative to the total amount of moisture the air can hold. Humidity (or absolute humidity) indicates the percentage of water vapour in the air.

2 On those materials see Meikle 1995 and Nichols 2000.

3 A notable exception to this is the exemplary book on wood versus metal aircraft, Schatzberg 1999.

4 Although shorter-lived and less influential than the US Forest Products Laboratory (FPL), a Forest Products Research Laboratory (FPRL) also operated in the UK (Buckinghamshire) between 1927 and 1988 (when it was privatized and absorbed into the Building Research Establishment). Many thanks to Gerald Moore for assistance with FPRL research.

5 The key books, all written by individuals involved in the wood or glue business and aimed at a specialist audience of practitioners and trade, were: Knight and Wulpi 1927; Mora 1932; Perry 1942; and Wood and Linn 1942 (and subsequent editions). Boulton 1920 was a series of technical essays reprinted from *Aerial Age* magazine; Wainwright 1927 concerned itself almost exclusively with plywood panelling and was almost certainly a promotional book.

6 For example, the worldwide proliferation of makerspaces (see chapter 7) since the early 2000s, the establishment in 2010 of the research club now known as the Institute of Making at the University of London, and the V&A exhibition and publication 'The Power of Making' (see Charny 2011). This was also reflected in an increasing number of books on materials, making and manufacturing. Among notable ones are: Gershenfeld 2005; Thompson 2007; Richard Sennett, *The Craftsman* (London 2008); Mark Miodownik, *Stuff Matters* (London 2013); and Forty 2012, an especially thoughtful look at concrete.

### Chapter 1 – Plywood Becomes Plywood (antiquity–c. 1900) (pp. 16–37)

1 Definitions of veneer, in terms of its thickness, vary by supplier. Precise measurements vary according to the system of measure (metric, imperial [British] or 'standard' [American]). In general, standard veneers in 2016 ranged from 0.5 mm to 0.6 mm (both 1⁄50 in.), with veneers thicker than that often described as thick-cut. The latter go up to 3 mm (1⁄8 in.), although exceptionally thick 4 mm (approximately 3/5 in.) veneers have recently become available.

2 Gale, Gosson, Hepper and Killen 2000, pp. 336–37; Wilkinson 1878, pp. 198–99; Firth and Quibell 1935, pp. 19 and 42.

3 On Greek veneer see the mention in Moss 1999, p. 71; on Roman veneered furniture see Pliny 1945, pp. 155, 535–39. Early books of plywood nearly always cited Pliny as evidence of the distinguished history of veneer and, by implication, of plywood. See, for example: Knight and Wulpi 1927, pp. 18–20, 144–45, 262.

4 Cutting from a large, solid board would also create areas of short grain that would have been highly susceptible to breakage.

5 Sheraton 1802, pp. 293–97 and pl. 25.

6 Samuel Bentham, 'Machinery for Cutting and Planing Wood', application filed 26 March 1791, issued 26 November 1791, British patent no. 1838.

7 This subject is well covered in Ostergard 1987.

8 See Ostergard 1987, pp. 14–24, 200–06, where, although the emphasis is on bending wood, numerous examples of furniture with laminated elements are discussed and illustrated. A Danish example was later published in Mirjam Gelfer-Jørgensen, *The Dream of a Golden Age: Danish Neo-Classical Furniture 1790–1850* (Copenhagen 2004), p. 248 and figs 235 and 236. The use of laminated construction 'usually of alternating grain' for, among other objects, the fronts of curved card tables was used in the US. See Benjamin A. Hewitt, Patricia E. Kane and Gerald W.R. Ward, *The Work of Many Hands: Card Tables in Federal America 1790–1820* (New Haven 1882), pp. 89–90, which refers to cat. entries 45, 47, 53, 55 and 56.

9 Khan 2005 (especially chs 1 and 2) and Macleod 1991.

10 Reingold 1960, pp. 156–57; Israel and Rosenberg 1991, p. 1095.

11 Reingold 1960, p. 158.

12 John Henry Belter, 'Bedstead', issued 19 August 1856, US patent no. 15,552. Most US patents are available on Google Patents (https://patents.google.com/).

13 The best-known example of the bed in a public collection, stamped with Belter's name and the patent date, is at the Brooklyn Museum, New York (accession no. 39.30, Gift of Mrs. Ernest Vietor). It is made in four parts, corresponding closely to the patent drawings. I am grateful to Barry Harwood of the Brooklyn Museum for confirming details of the bed's construction and for extensive discussion regarding Belter.

14 Belter's bed was unusual not because it was veneered but rather because virtually the entire bed was made of glued, cross-laminated veneers. His furniture was successfully sold to a fashionable market, and there are numerous references, both contemporary and later, to the expensive prices of Belter 'pressed work'. See, for example, Stetson 1858, p. 9.

15 See Vincent 1974. This is a short article, but nonetheless written by someone who had (unusually) carefully considered the relationship between Belter's furniture and his patents.

16 John Henry Belter, 'Making Chair Backs', issued 31 July 1847, US patent no. 5,208. The machine consisted of a large frame to hold the entire moulded seat or sofa back upright within it, fitted to a much larger table. A highly adjustable fretsaw with a blade that could be threaded directly into holes made in the back and could be positioned to cut at a very wide range of angles was an integral part of the frame.

17 In his patent Belter distinguished between a curve on a single plane, as if forming 'a portion of a hollow cylinder or cone', or a three-dimensional curve that formed 'a portion of a hollow sphere or spheroid so that a section thereof in every possible plane exhibits a curved figure'.

18 Hanks 1981, p. 53, illustrates 'one of at least five examples of Belter's "dishing"' as applied to chairs.

19 Stetson 1858, p. 9. The author, who signed Belter's three patents of 1856–60 as a witness, wrote that a patent application, presumably for using pressed work in chair backs, was filed in 1847 by Belter and rejected by the US Patent Office for unknown reasons. While Stetson's business relationship with Belter means that it is impossible to judge the truth of the claim, the later memoir of the cabinetmaker Ernest Haagen, who worked from 1853 for a competitor of Belter, described Belter as the 'original inventor' of such furniture. Haagen stated that his employer, Charles A. Baudouine, had plagiarized what was 'generally known as "Belter furniture"'. See Elizabeth A. Ingerman, 'Personal Experiences of an Old New York Cabinet Maker', *Antiques Magazine* vol. 84 (November 1963), pp. 576–80. Vincent 1974 suggests that Haagen's memory was not faultless. A slightly later British account, very possibly based on Stetson, states that Belter introduced pressed work to the world; see Charles Knight, *Arts and Sciences or Fourth Division of 'The English Cyclopaedia'* vol. 8 (London 1868), p. 606.

20 Stetson 1858, p. 9, refers to a patent by Mr Cornelius Bogaud of New York. US patent no. 8,575 was granted to Cornelius Bogard of Charlestown, Massachusetts, on 9 December 1851. Stetson's illustration (fig. 1) is a much-enhanced version of that shown in the patent, and his illustrations of two of the layers of Belter's chair backs are similarly redrawn from the 1858 patent.

21 John K. Mayo, 'Material for Roofing, Tubing, Tanks, Wainscoting, Boats and Other Structures', issued 26 December 1865, US patent no. 51,735. A dispute regarding patent fees between Mayo and the US Patent Office, which was the subject of a bill in the US Congress (H.R. 512, 1874), reveals that Mayo was an American citizen who had moved to Nova Scotia (a British Colony when the patent was originally filed in June 1865), where he had been granted citizenship and had become a subject of the British Crown. See *Reports of the Committees of the House of Representatives, First Session, 43rd Congress* vol. 1, report 53 (Washington, DC, 1874), pp. 1–3.

282 (opposite)

**Detail of teak-faced plywood chair**
Designed by Grete Jalk, manufactured by Poul Jeppesen, Denmark, 1963 (see p. 165)

22 Patent Act of 1793, Ch. 11, 1 Stat. 318–323 (21 February 1793), section 3.

23 This paragraph and the next one draw on Dodd 1991, pp. 1013–14 (on Burr v. Duryee, 1863) and pp. 999–1017, on the subject of reissues in general; and Israel and Rosenberg 1991, pp. 1096–97.

24 'An Act concerning Patents for Useful Inventions' (the US Patent Act of 3 July 1832), cited in Dodd 1991, p. 1001 (quotation), and pp. 1004–08 on the last point.

25 Such bridges were normally rectangular and built in the early nineteenth century in wood lattice in North America and, in the 1840s, in solid wrought-iron plates by the British engineer Robert Stephenson in Wales (two examples), England and Canada. While the concept engendered much initial enthusiasm within the British engineering community especially, the design principles were in many ways uneconomic compared with those of more common lattice or truss bridge construction. See Gregory K. Dreicer, 'Building Bridges and Boundaries: the Lattice and the Tube, 1820–1860', *Technology and Culture* vol. 51: no. 1 (January 2010), pp. 126–63, and Michael R. Bailey (ed.), *Robert Stephenson: The Eminent Engineer* (Aldershot 2003).

26 'Pneumatic Locomotion', *New York Times* (16 September 1867), p. 8. Other contemporary accounts are reprinted in Beach 1868, ch. 5. Although there are many subsequent mentions of the exhibition in the context of the building of this first New York City subway, few note, let alone focus on, the use of plywood. A recent popular book describes Beach's larger project: Doug Most, *The Race Underground* (New York 2014), ch. 1.

27 *Scientific American* (19 October 1867), reprinted in Beach 1868, p. 41.

28 While Gardner's patents and related court cases are all easily accessible (and have been so for decades), and a large 1884 catalogue of his firm is at the Winterthur Library, Winterthur, Delaware, very little of note has been published on the firm. The standard secondary source is Ames 1971. The most significant research, especially that into the firm's origins and early years, as well as into the very revealing R.G. Dun credit reports of Gardner and his competitors (Baker Library, Harvard University, Cambridge, MA), was undertaken by Barbara Pisch who kindly shared her MA paper (2012). I am grateful to Barry Harwood for bringing this to my attention.

29 Two thirds of his right to the patents were assigned to Gardner & Gardner, and in subsequent amendments known as reissues these were assigned to individual family members as the ownership of the business changed.

30 He states in the first patent that 'in practice the layers of veneering and canvas may be increased in number, if desired' (George Gardner, 'Improvement in Chair Seats', issued 21 May 1872, US patent no. 127,044).

31 By this time George Gardner had apparently been bought out by his brothers Oliver and William, both of whom (along with Jane E. Gardner, Oliver's wife) were listed as assignees of the patent. Pisch 2012, p. 19.

32 Herz catalogues and products have not been found yet, although a group of later patents (1890–1902) exist and there are mentions of the firm's products in the 1880s (three-ply parquet flooring and veneer seating, see: Herz & Co. advertisement, *The American Architect and Building News* vol. 8: no. 258 (30 October 1880) p. ii, cited in Pisch 2012, p. 46). Pisch 2012, p. 47, notes reports of an 1882 fire at Herz's factory in which losses amounted to about $40,000, highlighting the large scale of his business: 'A Chair Manufactory Burned', *New York Times* (21 November 1882), p. 5.

33 Gardner and others v. Herz, US Supreme Court 118 U.S. 180, decided 10 May 1886. See: https://www.law.cornell.edu/supremecourt/text/118/180 (accessed 23 June 2016): the case referred to by Pisch 2012, p. 49. Given that patent reissues would not extend the original term of a patent, Gardner's original patents were due to expire in 1889 in any case.

34 For evidence of the extent to which the firm was increasing its production and product range in this period, see the R.G. Dun reports, reprinted as an appendix to Pisch 2012.

35 Gardner & Company 1884, copy held at the Winterthur Library. R.G. Dun entries refer to a 'Large business principally confined to... Railroad companies' (June 1880) and 'Adding largely to their business by making a speciality of car work' (August 1883). Pisch 2012, appendix of R.G. Dun reports.

36 The Cole patent model achieved a certain status when it was published in Siegfried Giedion, *Mechanization Takes Command* (New York 1948), p. 504, and subsequently acquired by the Museum of Modern Art, New York, in 1956. Israel and Rosenberg 1991, pp. 1096–98, writing about American patents, suggest that such patents often reflect not practical invention but only something that the patentee thought could be made. They caution that only access to full (and rarely surviving) patent application records, which reveal negotiation with the Patent Office, offers a full picture of the invention and the applicant's possible intentions.

37 In 1888 a Veneer Seat Manufacturers' Association was formed in order to promote and regulate the trade. The founding of this Association suggests the size that the business in plywood seats had reached by this point. 'Perforated Chair Seats. Their Manufacturers Combine in Order to Raise Prices', *New York Times* (17 October 1888), p. 9, cited in Pisch 2012, p. 30. Pisch (p. 32) states that the Gardner family were bought out of their business by a rival firm, Frost, Peterson & Co., in the late 1880s.

**Chapter 2 – Manufacturing Plywood (1807–c. 1910) (pp. 38–53)**

1 The hand cutting of veneer continued in Britain only in small workshops and for special uses and customers. As far as the woodworking industries and the trade of the professional sawyer were concerned, hand cutting ceased in the mid-nineteenth century. See below, n. 9.

2 Quotation from Mayhew 1850, p. 5. Marc Isambard Brunel, 'Cutting Veneers', application filed 23 September 1806, issued 23 March 1807, British patent no. 2968; Samuel Bentham, 'Machinery for Cutting and Planing Wood', application filed 26 March 1791, issued 26 November 1791, British patent no. 1838; Samuel Bentham, 'New and Improved Methods and Means of working Wood, Metal and other Materials', issued 23 April 1793, British patent no. 1951. Brunel's veneer cutter was built by the civil engineer Henry Maudslay (1771–1831). Bentham, Brunel and Maudslay collaborated from 1801 to build blockmaking machinery for the Royal Navy at Portsmouth, Hampshire. See: Carolyn Cooper, 'The Portsmouth System of Manufacture', *Technology and Culture* vol. 25: no. 2 (April 1984), pp. 182–225.

3 Description of a 'flat cutting-machine' in George Koch, 'Improvement in Veneer-Cutters', issued 5 July 1870, US patent no. 105,092; Powis Bale 1880, pp. 2–3, on Bentham's importance; James Borthwick, owner of a sawmill at Leith, near Edinburgh, ordered saws and equipment from Brunel in 1810, as well as designs for new buildings, see Thom 2010, p. 60; Phillips 1817, p. 46, describes Brunel's sawmill.

4 Phillips 1817, p. 46. Mechanical veneer saws have always had much larger blades than saws for normal wood cutting. Early nineteenth-century examples of such saws, inevitably following Brunel and Bentham, survive in the Technical Museums of Vienna (1816) and Slovenia (1824).

5 The claim that Immanuel Nobel (Swedish inventor and father of Alfred Nobel) invented the rotary lathe is widely repeated on the internet. No book on the Nobel family supports this claim nor is this (so far) documented in the Nobel Archive. Thanks to Denise Hagströmer for assistance with Nobel research. On Faveryear: Dorothy Jean de Val, 'Gradus ad Parnassum: the Pianoforte in London, 1770–1820', PhD thesis (University of London, King's College, 1991), p. 24, and David Rowland, 'Clementi's Music Business' in Michael Kassler (ed.), *The Music Trade in Georgian England* (Farnham and Burlington 2011), p. 155.

6 Kermik 1998, p. 42 and n. 26, states that 'some Russian and Estonian

researchers have associated the invention of rotary cutting technology', specifically small-scale rotary cutters for making pencils, with the Tallinn firm of Luther, Buller, Mickwitz & Ko. However, these sources date from 1902 and from the 'later Soviet era'. It is worth noting, however, that no other patents assigned to Faveryear are known, which seems surprising for an entrepreneur who had (apparently) designed such an innovative and commercially useful machine.

7 See Henry Faveryear, 'Machine for Cutting Veneers, & c.', application filed 25 December 1818, issued 24 June 1819, British patent no. 4324. The Bavarian account of 'Everyear', also 'Ewarpear' or 'Faveryer', published the year before the patent, was in Spaun, 'Hölzerne Fournier-Platten von einigen hundert Schuhen Länge, und 4 bis 5 auch mehrschubiger Breite', *Wöchentlicher Anzeiger für Kunst- und Gewerbe-Fleiss in Königreich Bayern* vol. 3: no. 35 (30 August 1817), col. 537. A correspondent wrote to the same magazine (Faber, vol. 3: no. 40 [4 October 1817], cols 597–99) that cabinetmakers in Fürth (northern Bavaria) had already developed a similar peeling method, although not to the same degree as Everyear. *Jahrbücher des k.k. polytechnischen Instituts in Wien* vol. 3 (1822), p. 309ff, pl. III. Articles cited by Georg Himmelheber, *Biedermeier Furniture* (London, 1974), pp. 93–94, though without identifying 'Everyear' or realizing that the Viennese example was a direct copy of Faveryear's. Thanks to Dr Hubert Weitensfelder for information about the model, which survives in the Technical Museum of Vienna (inventory no. 59678).

8 Holtzapffel 1843, p. 154. Despite the occasional use of the word 'lathe' for the rotary cutting machine, owing to the turning of the log (e.g. George Dodd, 'Wood, and How to Cut It', *Household Words* vol. 6 [19 February 1853], p. 543), most nineteenth-century accounts describe rather than name the machine, and it would appear that the terms rotary peeler or lathe are mainly twentieth-century uses.

9 Mayhew 1850, p. 5, quoting (at length) a former sawyer. Advertisement in *Scientific American* vol. 10: no. 12 (18 March 1864), p. 19. The observation of steam power being more common in the UK than in the US comes from Mayhew 1850, p. 5.

10 *London* 1811, p. 329, on the pricing of labour for supplying engine- or mill-cut veneer rather than that cut by a sawyer (no such distinction in the 1803 edition but identical in the editions of 1824 and 1836 with same page reference). *Edinburgh* 1811 has no mention of machine-cut veneers but the edition of 1821 does, where the same price differential as London applied. The sawyer interviewed in Mayhew 1850, p. 5, explained that Brunel's machine could cut eight veneers to the inch in 1810, the same or slightly better than an expert sawyer (who would normally cut six to the inch), but that within a short time the machine could cut fourteen to the inch, which no sawyer could. 'When they first set up [1810] they had 6*d*. [pence] a foot for cutting veneer, and now [1850] they have only 1*d*.'

11 On deals see Bowett 2012, pp. 292–95, especially. The years leading up to Faveryear's patent also saw more cutting of veneers from native British woods, owing to disruption to supplies of imported mahoganies and rosewoods caused by the Napoleonic Wars (1803–15). The production of furniture expanded at the bottom of the market, as those with less money bought increasingly available cheap furniture, some of it veneered. Native British woods were described as 'having of late [by the late 1840s] come into much more frequent use as veneers' in Mayhew 1850, p. 5.

12 Contemporary testimony on this comes from Mayhew 1850, p. 7.

13 On this subject (although not on French) see Hounshell 1984, pp. 127–46. On French see 'Built-up Veneer Work', *The Furniture Gazette* vol. 2: no. 43 (31 January 1874), p. 109 (reprinted from *The Boston Cabinet-Maker*). On sewing machines in the home see Douglas 1982.

14 'Built-up Veneer Work' 1874 mentions five patents, of which three have been found including an 1880 patent that makes no mention of materials ('Sewing Machine Cover', issued 7 June 1870, US patent no. 103,863; 'Improvements in Bindings for Sewing-Machine Covers', issued 29 April 1873, US patent no. 138,324; 'Sewing Machine Case', issued 26 October 1880, US patent no. 11,999). See also 'Improved Sewing Machine Cover', *Scientific American* vol. 24: no. 4 (21 January 1871), p. 54.

15 The following paragraphs rely on Hounshell 1984, pp. 132–46. See also Perry 1942, p. 29, and the first-hand account of a visit to the factory in Truax 1919.

16 The precise design of the case varied over the years. Two variations are seen in the 1893 Singer catalogue, Hagley Library Trade Cat.S617 1893 c. 1 at http://digital.hagley.org/cdm/ref/collection/p268001coll12/id/8452 (accessed 11 May 2016). Singer sewing machines are dateable by their serial numbers. Dozens of websites selling these, as well as the survival of so many examples, indicate the longevity of the cases in the twentieth century.

17 The 1919 information from Truax 1919.

18 Hounshell 1984, pp. 144–45. In terms of comparison, the volume of plywood seats and backs made by the Thonet furniture company may well have been extremely high by the very early twentieth century, based on overall production figures of 875,000 in 1890, 1 million in 1900 and 1.8 million in 1913 (these were mainly chairs). Sales figures from Wilhelm Franz Exner, *Das Biegen des Holzes* (4th edition, Leipzig 1922), pp. 41–43.

19 Francis A. Walker (ed.), *United States International Exhibition 1876, Reports and Awards* vol. 4 (Washington, DC, 1880), pp. 728 (list of members of Committee) and 735 (Gardner citation).

20 'Die Holzindustrie in den Verein. Staaten', *Deutsche Industrie-Zeitung* vol. 24 (13 June 1877), p. 233, on veneer cutting. The 1880 display was at the Lower Austrian Trade Exhibition; on this and the warning see *Bericht über die Niederösterreichische Gewerbe-Aussstellung in Wien 1880* (Vienna 1881), p. 76, cited by Graham Dry in his seminal article, 'The Development of the Bent-wood Furniture Industry 1869–1914' in Ostergard 1987, p. 90, n. 104. The initial Thonet manufacture was made only upon special request owing to the desire not to put their cane weavers out of work, according to Herm. Schuldt jr., 'Ueber [sic] amerikanische Holzfournier-Sitze', *Kunst und Gewerbe: Wochenschrift zur Forderung deutscher kunst-Industrie* vol. 15: no. 1 (1881), p. 43, also cited by Dry in Ostergard 1987, p. 90, n. 104. Dry's conclusion that Thonet began this manufacture in 1877 remains unproven. The first known Thonet catalogue showing the veneer seats was published in 1885; see Eva B. Ottilinger (ed.), *Gebrüder Thonet* (Vienna 2003), pp. 129–30, 132–33. Schuldt is apparently also the source of the mistaken idea that Carl Wittkowsky was producing plywood seats in the early 1870s (Dry 1987, p. 90, n. 104), although his first German patent was granted in 1884 (see Kollmann 1962, p. 3). Pisch 2012 first noted that Wittkowsky held US patents starting in 1884.

21 On the Luther company in the nineteenth century see Kermik 2004, pp. 13–51. He cites K. Kala, O. Karma and T. Karjahärm, *Tallinna Vineeri-ja Mööblikombinaat 1877–1977* (Tallinn 1977) (hereafter TVMK), p. 8, and Estonian State Archive 4357, 1/10 for the production figures. The authors of TVMK 1977 discovered archival material in the Estonian State Archive also published by Kermik related to Luther and its UK arm, Venesta. Kermik 2004 refers to two private archives in Britain: the Luther Archive and the Rutherford Archive. At the time of writing, these have been lost except for selected photocopies generously shared by Kermik. These publications have made Luther the best documented of nineteenth- and early twentieth-century firms. See also Kermik 1998. Luther's contribution to the development of European plywood was recognized in Pevsner 1939, p. 129.

22 Production figures from Kermik 2004, pp. 21, 23. Kermik does not state when the Gardner-type furniture with continuous plywood seat/backs was introduced. However, he dates illustrations of certain pieces of furniture to 1886 (pp. 26, 169–70), the year after

Luther's plywood seats were first made, and writes that the furniture must have first been made before 'the factory started to produce office furniture' in 1888 (p. 29).

23 At a time when there would have been no motivation to praise a private company, a Soviet-era article that lists the year and number of plywood factories in Russia credits Luther as the first, writing that 'Following his [Luther's] example, the plywood industry in Russia started to develop'. See A. Kirlov, 'Эссе по истории производства фанеры/ Esse po istorii proizvodstva faneri', *Лесопромышленное дело/ Lesopromyshlennoe delo* ['Essay on the History of Plywood Production', *Timber Industry Magazine*] nos 11–12 (June 1923), p. 9.

24 None of these products is known to have been made.

25 'Built-up Furniture', *New York Sun* (18 February 1898), p. 18; Perry 1942, p. 31, cites the Indianapolis Cabinet Company making desk tops about 1883, others by 1890, and it being standard practice soon after. Interestingly, as late as 1928 in Germany, during a push for greater standardization of plywood, a leading plywood journal argued in a series of articles against the 'inefficient' production of plywood by independent joiners and small workshops; see, for example, 'Sperrholz und Fournier in der Möbelfabrikation: Eckverbindungen von Sperrholz', *Sperrholz und Fournier* no. 15 (1928), pp. 496–98.

26 'Veneer and Panel Manufacturers' Association', *Hardwood Record* vol. 21: no. 5 (25 December 1905), p. 18. An Association of German Plywood Merchants was founded in 1920. See 'Tagungen. Verband der deutschen Sperrholzhändel, seine Entwicklung...', *Sperrholz und Fournier* no. 12 (1928), pp. 415–16. A Soviet-era Plywood Trust was established in 1922 in an effort to resurrect the Russian plywood industry, still incapacitated after the Revolution of 1917. See Prof. M. Deshevoy, 'Лесная промышленность на всесоюзной выставке/ Lesnaya promyshlennost' na vsesoyuznoy vystavke', *Лесопромышленное дело/Lesopromyshlennoe delo* ['Timber Industry in the All-Soviet Union Exhibition', *Timber Industry Magazine*] nos 19–20 (October 1923), pp. 44–45.

27 Kermik 2004, pp. 43–51, on Luther boards; p. 45 mentions 'a number of mills in Eastern Europe' and the appearance of 'lower quality boards...on the market'. N. 84 refers to a letter of Christian Luther's to the firm's UK representative, E. Archer (17 April 1901), although this may concern a different topic. On Kostovich see: *Записка о развитии товарищества эксплуатирующего патенты Костовича и его преобразование в акционерное общество (под названием) 'Ассоциация по обработке металла и древесины'/ Zapiska o razvitii tovarischestva ekspluatiruyushego patenti Kostovicha i ego preobrazovanie v aktsionernoe obschestvo (pod nazvaniem) 'Assotsiatsia po oobrabotke metalla i drevesini' [Note on the development of the partnership exploiting Kostovich's patents and on its conversion to a stock company (called) 'Association for metal and wood processing']* (St Petersburg 1891); and A.N. Guryev, *Записка о производстве арборита / Zapiska o proizvodstve arboreta [A Note on Production of Arboryte]* (St Petersburg 1903), an entire book on the subject, presumably promotional.

28 On Blomberger see Schäfer and Zandonella 1993, a celebratory company history. On *Tischlerplatten* see Schmidt [co-founder of the Deutsche Werkstätten] 1933, pp. 87–89, which dates Kummel's development to 1898 (and also credits Luterma [A.M. Luther] as the first producers of plywood seats for German-made chairs); Kollmann 1962, p. 6, suggests Kummel's development took place in 1910; see Wood and Linn 1942, pp. 117–18 (on imports to Britain possibly during the nineteenth century and, more reliably, in the early twentieth century); and on their use during the 1930s see Harrod 2008, pp. 19–22.

29 C.W. Luther, 'Waterproof Glue', issued 1 October 1896, British patent no. 21,774. Luther's new glue was mentioned by Pevsner 1939, p. 129. It seems unlikely that this form of thermoplastic plywood was successfully manufactured at this time, given that there is no subsequent evidence of its use. Indeed, only in 2008 was a version of this first developed for the market (see pp. 208–09).

30 The detailed history of plywood board remains to be written. Clues to the gradual standardization and to the increase of plywood board sizes are to be found in trade advertisements, price-lists and accounts such as Wood and Linn 1942, pp. 96–98 (on hot press sizes), p. 301 (importation of large boards), pp. 412–13, and, slightly revised, 1950, pp. 472–73 (on tea and rubber chest sizes). It seems likely that small board sizes increased meaningfully between 1914 and 1930. I am grateful to Jyri Kermik for conversations on this matter.

31 Koponen 2001, pp. 16, 44–45, which includes comments on Luther's connections to Finland and on the fundamental importance of the tea crate business for the first Finnish plywood company, Wilh. Schauman Fanerfabrik Ab, as well as the four others founded between 1913 and 1918; and Kermik 1995, pp. 102–03, which explained that a Luther employee sacked for his Bolshevik politics went to work for Schauman in its early days.

32 Nick Hall, *The Tea Industry* (Cambridge 2000), ch. 4, p. 3, claims that plywood tea chests had started to replace solid wood ones by the 1870s, although no reference is given. A 'Plywood Chest Association' was not formed in the UK until 1932. It was started by a group of tea chest manufacturers and distributors who intended to establish a quota-selling scheme and synchronize distribution. Papers relating to the Association (1927–72) are held in the London Metropolitan Archives (CLC/B/179).

33 *First Fifty* 1948, pp. 3–4, describes a chest 'first patented by Mr Arthur Andrews'. The patent has not been located at the time of writing. Unless otherwise noted, all quotes in this section come from *First Fifty* 1948, pp. 3–7.

34 The E.H. Archer story comes from *First Fifty* 1948. Kermik 2004, pp. 47–49 draws upon this but also on the recollections of Y.M. Luther (p. 47, n. 92), the Rutherford and Luther Archives (see n. 21), the Luther papers in the Estonian State Archive, and TVMK, p. 12. The last offers the beach discovery story.

35 Letter quoted in Kermik 2004, p. 51, n. 108, box sizes p. 49. Tea chest characteristics from 'Tea-Chest Manufacture in India', *Scientific American* vol. 118: no. 17 (27 April 1918), p. 396.

36 Reports of national and international trade figures are notoriously difficult to compare, not least owing to different methods of presenting information and the fact that plywood is not always separated from general wood exports and imports. There is, however, sufficient corroborative reporting in contemporary wood trade journals to generalize. See J.B.B. Stryker, 'A Comparison with European Methods', *Veneers* (February 1914), p. 13 (American); S.F. Cornwall, 'The Plywood Trade', *Timber Trades Journal* (28 March 1914), pp. 573–76 (British); and A. Kirlov, 'Эссе по истории производства фанеры/ Esse po istorii proizvodstva faneri', *Лесопромышленное дело/ Lesopromyshlennoe delo* ['Essay on the History of Plywood Production', *Timber Industry Magazine*] nos 11–12 (June 1923), p. 9 (Russian). 'Der internationale Sperrholzverkehr 1935', *Holztechnik* vol. 16: no. 7 (5 April 1936), pp. 113–14, showed that Russia was Europe's largest exporter and Finland a close second in 1934 and 1935, both nearly doubling that of Poland, the third largest European exporter (the US was omitted as it published data only on the value rather than cubic metreage of its wood exports). 'England' was described as the buyer of 56% of all European exports in 1935, eclipsing Holland and Germany by a factor of eight. However, the Russian Revolution led to a decline in the quantity and quality of Russian plywood exports and, for this reason, Britain imported more Finnish than Russian plywood by 1935. On Finnish exports see the useful table in Rinne 1952, p. 28, covering 1920–1960 and Koponen 2001, which states (pp. 44–45) that most Finnish plywood produced between 1912 and 1918 was exported to Britain, that during the 1930s Finland was 'the largest plywood producing nation in the world', and that the UK was the largest buyer of Finnish plywood between 1912 and the early 1950s.

37 Kermik 2004, p. 51 (60,000), p. 65 (import duty).
38 See 'Equipment for Tea Chest Plant', *Veneers* vol. 9: no. 9 (September 1915), p. 26; 'Tea-Chest Manufacture in India' 1918, p. 396; 'Plywood Box Industry of Dutch East Indies', *The Timberman* (November 1925), p. 213; 'Plywood Industry. Plea for Protection', *The Times of India* (13 August 1927), p. 12; 'Rectangular Plywood Containers', *Indian Forest Leaflet* no. 26-1942 (Dehra Dun 1942).
39 A French account of an expedition to the South Pole, published in 1910, writes that: 'An expedition blessed with a very large budget would be well advised to pack its provisions in Venesta cases, a solid, watertight, light material.' Dr Jean Charcot, *Le Pourquoi-pas? Dans l'Antarctique. Journal de la deuxième expedition au pole sud 1908–1910* (Paris 1910), p. 18.
40 On Venesta board standards see Kermik 2004, p. 49. E.H. Shackleton, *The Heart of the Antarctic* (London 1909), pp. 8, 126–27, 143–45, 150, 217–18. Shackleton wrote (p. 8) that he ordered boxes measuring 30 × 15 in. (76 × 38 cm); that each weighed 4 lbs (1.8 kg) less than an 'ordinary packing case', resulting in huge savings in weight; and (p. 113) that the 'Venesta cases could withstand the roughest treatment without breakage or damage to the contents'. *Polar Times*, see: H.G.R. King (ed.), *Diary of the Terra Nova Expedition... 1910–1912* (London 1972), p. 181. Boots, see: diary entry for 1 July 1911 published online by the Scott Polar Research Institute, University of Cambridge, at http://www.spri.cam.ac.uk/museum/diaries/scottslastexpedition/1911/07/01/1-7-1911/ (accessed 27 September 2016).

**Chapter 3 – The Veneer Problem (1850s–1930s) (pp. 54–71)**

1 [Francis] September 1850, p. 244.
2 Dickens 1884, p. 5.
3 Frederick Litchfield, *Illustrated History of Furniture* (London 1892), p. 237.
4 This differs from the otherwise excellent view offered in Knowles 1985, p. 88.
5 A 1787 book of literary criticism characterizes the Enlightenment idea of Bel-Esprit as 'purely superficial, with no depth...in general a sort of veneer (with all that that implies)'. The following year, an author is criticized for writing tiring 'constant declamations...[which] are clearly only a veneer applied without art'. Jean-Antoine Rigoley de Juvigny, *De la décadence des lettres et des moeurs, depuis les Grecs et les Romains jusqu'à nos jours. Par M. Rigoley de Juvigny,...Seconde edition* (Paris 1787), p. 186, and Charles Palissot de Montenoy, *Oeuvres de M. Palissot, lecteur de S.A.S. M.gr le duc d'Orléans. Nouvelle édition, revue et corrigée. Mémoires pour servir à l'histoire de notre littérature depuis François Ier jusqu'à nos jours / Tome premier [- quatrième]* (Paris 1788), p. 377. Such pejorative uses of the term became more common in early nineteenth-century France, where a story is said to be obstructed by 'a fatuous device thrown on to a fable, an embellishment of veneer...' and a selection of poetry is decried as 'bad verse, cold adulations in veneer'. Examples also arose increasingly in short stories ('this life of veneer disappeared behind something better') and novels ('this passion is... nothing more than an affectation, that which we would call veneer'). Népomucène-Louis Lemercier, *Cours analytique de littérature générale...* vol. 4: part 3, section 2 (Paris 1817), p. 230; Jean François de La Harpe, *Lycée, ou Cours de littérature ancienne et modern* vol. 12 (Paris 1825), p. 335; 'Le Pressentiment' in *Les cent-et-une nouvelles nouvelles des Cent-et-un, ornées de cent-et-une vignettes* vol. 2 (Paris 1833), p. 380; and Arnould Frémy, *Une fée de salon* vol. 1 (Paris 1837), p. 244.
6 I am grateful to Adam Bowett for bringing this to my attention.
7 [Francis] September 1850, p. 244. The subsequent essays in the series were published in: October 1850 (pp. 437–45), February 1851 (pp. 147–52), April 1851 (pp. 472–76), September 1851 (pp. 33–39) and January 1852 (pp. 87–94). The essays were published anonymously, but George Henry Francis was identified as their author from at least the 1860s (see the obituary published for Francis in *Public Opinion* vol. 10: no. 259 [8 September 1866], p. 277). Knowles 1985 offered a valuable and original exploration of the *Fraser's* essays. The essays have been described in Peter Gurney, *Wanting and Having. Popular Politics and Liberal Consumerism in England, 1830–70* (Manchester 2015), pp. 301–23, which does not cite Knowles.
8 [Francis] September 1850, pp. 238 and 239.
9 [Francis] September 1850, p. 241.
10 [Francis] September 1850, p. 244.
11 Joseph Stirling Coyne, *The Man of Many Friends* (London 1855); Alfred, Lord Tennyson, 'The Princess' (1847) in Adam Roberts (ed.), *Alfred Tennyson: A Critical Edition of the Major Works* (Oxford and New York 2000), p. 120; William Bayle Bernard, *The Evil Genius* (London 1856), p. 39; 'British Institution', *The Times* (6 February 1865), p. 5; 'Recent Novels', *The Times* (22 October 1884), p. 10; Westland Marston, *The Favourite of Fortune* (London 1876), p. 91.
12 J.T. Trowbridge, 'Half-Hours with Father Brighthopes: VIII' in *Our Young Folks: An Illustrated Magazine for Boys and Girls* vol. 2: no. 11 (November 1866), p. 681.
13 'Company Manners' in *All the Year Round* vol. 20 'New Series' (21 November 1868), p. 568; Frances Eleanor Trollope, ch. 8 of 'Veronica' in *All the Year Round* vol. 2 'New Series' (28 August 1869), p. 292.
14 Bartley Theodore Campbell, 'The Galley Slave' (1876) in Napier Wilt (ed.), *The White Slave and Other Plays by Bartley Campbell* (Princeton 1941), p. 140; Edward Payson Roe, *What Can She Do?* (New York 1873), p. 012.
15 Untitled article, *The Times* (30 December 1865), p. 8; untitled article, *The Times* (26 May 1877), p. 11; 'The Tithe System in Asia Minor', *The Times* (18 October 1879), p. 4; 'The Chinese in Central Asia', *The Times* (27 January 1881), p. 3; 'We have lately printed some very forcible appeals', *The Times* (5 February 1883), p. 9; 'The name of ISMAIL PASHA has been little', *The Times* (3 June 1886), p. 9; Louis S. Jackson, 'Indian Criminal Procedure', *The Times* (3 March 1883), p. 8.
16 The quotations are from the 1887 Trade Descriptions Act, sections 2, 3 and 2, sub-section 3 respectively.
17 'What is Walnut? Important Decision in Manchester', *Furniture Record* (UK) (3 July 1903), p. 6 (report); 'What is Walnut?', *Furniture Record* (UK) (10 July 1903), p. 20; 'What is a "Solid Walnut Suite"?', *Furniture Record* (UK) (10 July 1903), pp. 24–25 (editorials and letters). The *Furniture Record* was at odds with its readership on this question, urging that all descriptions be understood by the purchaser.
18 'What is Solid Walnut? A Dispute in Liverpool', *Furniture Record* (UK) (21 October 1904), p. 405; see also p. 402.
19 In addition, individuals in the trade and in trade journals had been calling for the involvement of the key UK trade union organization, the National Council of Furnishings (sometimes, Furniture) Trades, to help resolve the issue once and for all. Unfortunately, as the Council represented both manufacturers and retailers, the range of views held was described as too diverse to arrive at agreement.
20 'What is a "Solid Walnut" Robe?' [*sic*], *Cabinet Maker and Complete House Furnisher* (1 February 1913), p. 145.
21 'The "Solid Mahogany" Question Again', *Cabinet Maker and Complete House Furnisher* (19 August 1922), p. 356; 'What is Solid Mahogany?', *Furniture Record* (UK) (25 August 1922), p. 210; '"Solid Mahogany" Question: A Provincial Opinion', *Furniture Record* (UK) (25 August 1922), p. 216; '"Solid Mahogany". The Need for Definition', *Furniture Record* (UK) (25 August 1922), p. 218; 'Solid Mahogany Question: The Newcastle Case', *Furniture Record* (UK) (1 September 1922), p. 260; with articles in the same journals following.
22 On the post-war economy see Solomus Solomou, 'Business Cycles', in Joel Mokyr (ed.), *The Oxford Encyclopedia of Economic History* vol. 1 (Oxford and New York 2003), pp. 301–07, especially 305. 'Deadlock in the "Solid Mahogany" Question', *Cabinet Maker and Complete House Furnisher* (14 October 1922), p. 64.
23 Quotations in this paragraph from 'Built-up Furniture' first published in the daily newspaper the *New York Sun* (18 February 1898), p. 18, with excerpts reprinted in the British *Furniture and Decoration & the Furniture Gazette* (15 June 1898), p. 113; and 'Trade Notes/

Best Furniture is Veneered', *Furniture Record* (UK) (19 December 1902), p. 641. See also E.V. Knight, 'Advantages of Built-up Over Solid Stock in the Manufacture of Furniture and Case Goods', *Veneers* vol. 6: no. 7 (July 1912), p. 11: '*Veneered furniture* costs more, lasts longer and is more beautiful in every particular than is furniture made from solid stock.'

24 See, for example: 'Prospects for Veneer Extension', *Veneers* (May 1907), pp. 10–11 (on boxes and packaging); 'Some Problems of Veneer Making', *Hardwood Record* vol. 22: no. 9 (25 August 1906), p. 18 (on panels); 'That "Solid" Misconception', *Grand Rapids Furniture Record* vol. 45 (November 1922), pp. 292–93 (on case goods).

25 For example, 'Plywood for Wall Covering', *Veneers* vol. 13: no. 11 (November 1919), p. 12; Philip Faulkner, 'Veneer Coming into Its Own', *Veneers* vol. 14: no. 1 (January 1920) p. 28.

26 Virtually all of the patents mentioned in chapter 1 make these points, as do most articles and all books on plywood.

27 Letter to the editor, *Veneers* (December 1907), p. 18.

28 Advertisement for Edwards Cassavetti & Conrad Ltd, London, *Timber Trades Journal* (29 December 1906), p. 948, offering 'oak, birch, alder & c.' ply wood. Reproduced as fig. 75.

29 The term is used in *Scientific American* vol. 57: no. 4 (1887), p. 58, referring to and quoting from US patent no. 365,513 ('Bottle Casing', application filed 16 April 1887, issued 28 June 1887), in which the term 'three-ply veneer' is used. Figs 75 and 76 show its use in 1906 and 1907 respectively. For typical uses of the latter term at this time see articles in *Veneers* magazine: 'New Laminated Case Construction' (10 October 1908), p. 42; 'Built-up Panels in England', (December 1909), p. 11; '"Veneers" a Misnomer' (June 1910), p. 12; and 'Veneers in Automobile Manufacture', *Hardwood Record* vol. 29 (25 March 1910), p. 30.

30 'The Veneer and Panel Business', *Hardwood Record* vol. 23: no. 5 (25 December 1906), pp. 13–14, divides the American panel business into three classes: 'The manufacturer who makes sawed, sliced and rotary cut veneers only; the manufacturer who makes veneers and built-up stock or panels; and the manufacturer who buys his veneers and makes panels only.'

31 Magazine of the *Deutsche Holzarbeiter Verband*, see 'Die Behandlung von Tischplatten zu Auszugstischen', *Fachblatt für Holzarbeiter* no. 8 (1906), p. 62; 'Fachschuldirektor Reineking: Moderne Formen im Möbelbau', Fachblatt für Holzarbeiter no. 1 (1907), pp. 4–5; E. Augst, 'Furniere und Furnieren (Schluß)', *Fachblatt für Holzarbeiter* no. 11 (1909), p. 250; and E. Augst, 'Konstruktion und Erhaltung der Tischlereierzeugnisse', *Fachblatt für Holzarbeiter* no. 4 (1910), pp. 80–81. On Swedish usage see Joachim Bittner, 'Furniere-Sperrholz-Schichtholz', part 1 in H. Haacke (ed.), *Werkstattbücher* vol. 76 (1939), p. 4. *Starkholz* seems to have been used outside of the traditional wood trades, for example, 'Rubrik Eisenbahntechnische Rundschau', *Der Waggonbau und Lokomotiv-Bau* (28 April 1921), p. 136.

32 'About European Veneering Methods', *Veneers* vol. 9: no. 7 (July 1915), p. 9.

33 For example, 'The Aircraft Industry will find all their plywood... Siberian & General Trading Co...', *Cabinet Maker and Complete House Furnisher* (17 October 1917), p. 77; 'Plyol. The Best Cement for Three-Ply Veneering, etc.', featuring a trademark of an aeroplane propeller, Plyol, London, *Furniture Record* (UK) (30 November 1917), p. 465; 'Ash for Aeroplane Work/Plywood...', advertisement of C. Jennings & Co., Bristol, *Cabinet Maker and Complete House Furnisher* (2 March 1918), p. 236; 'The London Plywood Manufacturing Co... Speciality: Plywood for Aircraft', *Furniture Record* (UK) (12 July 1918), p. 31; 'Aeroplane Stamping in 3-Ply Wood', A.W. Ross, London, *Cabinet Maker and Complete House Furnisher* (20 July 1918), p. 53; or 'Y. Goldberg Manufacturer of Plywood for Aircraft Construction', London, *Cabinet Maker and Complete House Furnisher* (16 November 1918), p. 153 (which would have gone to press before Armistice Day [11 November 1918] but which, weeks later in the issue of 21 December, p. 290, was changed to 'Plywood Manufacturer for Furniture and Aircraft Construction' and by 15 February 1919, p. 223, omitted any mention of aircraft in favour of 'Plywood for Cabinet Manufacture, Panelling Table Tops, Office Furniture, & c.').

34 Observer, 'Furniture Buyers Balk at Veneers', *Veneers* vol. 17: no. 4 (April 1923), p. 26, and 'Some Excellent Advertising', *Veneers* vol. 17: no. 5 (May 1923), p. 41.

35 E.A.U., 'Pride in Plywood', *Veneers* vol. 27: no. 6 (June 1923), p. 42, and A.W.H., 'There is no Sham in Plywood', *Veneers* vol. 27: no. 7 (July 1923), p. 35, both typical of the era.

36 'Trade Commission Become Interested in Furniture Trade's Terms', *Furniture Record* (US) vol. 49 (October 1924), p. 224, reporting on an 8 September hearing in Chicago.

37 'Name the Woods', *Furniture Record* (US) vol. 49 (November 1924), p. 263.

38 'Exhibit 9, Statement of Trade Practice Conferences, Retail Furniture', *FTC Annual Report* 1926, pp. 166–67, text of an 'Announcement' made on 7 January 1926. Ten other significant points further interpreted the rules.

39 'Petition for Reopening of Hearing on Furniture Standards', *Hardwood Record* vol. 60: no. 11 (25 March 1926), p. 13. See also W.V. Morrow, 'Manufacturers Object to New Trade Terms', *The Furniture Manufacturer and Artisan* (April 1926), p. 42. In a demonstration of the differing interests of manufacturers and retailers, reflected also in the inability to reach an agreed terminology in the UK (see p. 62), it was the retailers that introduced the language regarding veneered furniture. See 'Uniform Wood Designations Now Before Federal Trade Commission', *Furniture Record* (US) vol. 51 (December 1925), p. 337.

40 This was made explicit in a memorandum following up on the petition of the Furniture Manufacturers' Association of Grand Rapids as reported in 'Wants Veneered Furniture in Right Light', *The Furniture Manufacturer and Artisan* (May 1926), p. 41.

41 FTC Annual Report 1927 (covering 1 July 1926–30 June 1927), p. 12. Proceedings were initiated against them.

42 Docket 1396, 'Complaint', FTC v. Berkey & Gay, 15 September 1926, pp. 1–3. Nearly identical language was used in all the complaints that carried Docket numbers 1397–1414 and the case against all was, by agreement between the FTC and all parties, referred to as FTC v. Berkey & Gay. The number of firms involved in this case varied as some elected to comply with the FTC rules during the course of the case, while additional firms were charged subsequent to the complaint described as 'FTC v. Berkey & Gay'. The numbers involved are detailed in the FTC *Annual Reports*. Confusingly, the 1929 *Annual Report* (p. 81) refers to both twenty-six cases and to twenty-five.

43 *Official Report of Proceedings Before the Federal Trade Commission*, RG122, Docket 1396-1422 Inclusive Testimony (Box 969).

44 The face veneers of walnut or mahogany were, by the admission of the manufacturers, generally 1⁄28 in. (0.8 mm) thick, sometimes (in the case of European veneers) even 1⁄35 or 1⁄40 in. (0.7 or 0.63 mm). This led a FTC lawyer to describe such veneers as 'a tissue of...wood', which clearly could not be used to describe the bulk of the wood from which a piece of furniture was made. FTC, Brief, 1927, p. 13 and Testimony 1, part 1, p. 127, testimony of Mr Widdicomb of John Widdicomb Company.

45 FTC Reply Brief, 24 March 1928, p. 14, RG 122 Docket 1396. The memorandum in this brief was a quotation from an earlier memorandum sent by attorneys for the Grand Rapids respondents. The manufacturers also occasionally employed a seemingly contradictory argument in order to bolster their case against accusations of deceiving consumers by stating that 'consumers are generally conversant with the superiority of veneered furniture'. Respondent Brief, 8 December 1927, Dockets 1396–1422 inclusive, p. 32 copy consulted in RG 122 Docket 1396.

46 Such an argument proved counterproductive as the FTC cited the respondents' adherence to the Grand Rapids Furniture Manufacturers' Association guidelines as proof that they were

not following the FTC rules. See RG 122 Docket 1396, Reply Brief, Reply Appendix, p. 4. Quotations from 'Brief on Behalf of Respn', 8 December 1927 (FTC date stamp 29 February 1928), pp. 13, 16, 17, 20.

47 US Court of Appeals for the Sixth Circuit – 42 F.2d 427 (6th Cir. 1930), 2 July 1930, formed part of the FTC papers at RG122 Docket 1396, Appeal Court Ruling and Mandate but is also available at http://law.justia.com/cases/federal/appellate-courts/F2/42/427/1491870/ (accessed 11 July 2016). Contemporary law journals pointed out both that the US Supreme Court might have overturned the decision and that other courts, faced with the same evidence, had ruled in favour of the FTC. See V.R., 'Federal Trade Commission: Recent Interpretation of the Federal Trade Commission Act', *Michigan Law Review* vol. 32: no. 8 (June 1935), pp. 1149–50, and 'Scope of the Jurisdiction of the Federal Trade Commission over False and Misleading Advertising', *Yale Law Journal* vol. 40: no. 4 (February 1931), p. 624 including n. 33.

48 Thomas Perry, 'Plywood Makes Better Furniture and Here's Why', *Furniture Record* (US) (April 1926), pp. 40, 42–44, 90–91. The author was an engineer who studied at Massachusetts Institute of Technology (MIT) and went onto work for numerous plywood companies and a glue company and was, before 1926, President of the Plywood Manufacturers' Association. In 1942 he published the book *Modern Plywood*.

49 G. Baseden Butt, 'Plywood – Potentialities of a New Material in Furniture Construction', *Good Furniture* vol. 28 (March 1927), p. 128, and Butt, 'Possibilities of Plywood Not Yet Scratched', *Furniture Manufacturer* vol. 34 (August 1927), p. 56.

50 In fact, the first book on plywood was Boulton 1920, although it consisted solely of articles from *Aerial Age* magazine on the use of plywood in aircraft. It was therefore an effort to disseminate technical information to a specialist audience rather than an exercise in promoting the status and use of plywood.

**Chapter 4 – 'Plywood Flies and Fights' (1911–1945) (pp. 72–103)**

1 'Plywood Flies and Fights', *Fortune* vol. 25: no. 3 (March 1942), pp. 74–77.

2 Chernenko 2001, p. 32.

3 'Птица Капитана Костовича/Ptitsa Kapitana Kostovicha' ['Captain Kostovich's Bird'], *Огонёк/Ogonyok* no. 22 (1882), p. 448. Chernenko 2001, pp. 27–28; this and other plywood projects referred to in the next two paragraphs here are on pp. 22–60. This monograph usefully quotes from numerous contemporary sources, as well as from secondary ones.

4 This patent has not been located, although the British patent referred to in the next sentence is Ogneslav Kostovits, patent for 'Improvements in the Manufacture of Various Articles of Wood', application filed 4 April 1884, issued 2 January 1885, British patent no. 5942.

5 The use of plywood for masts only seems to have seen commercial application in the 1940s and 1950s, when US Plywood used hollow plywood tubes to make demountable telegraph masts for the US Army. See 'Plywood Radio Masts for Signal Corps', *Bell Laboratories Record* vol. 23: no. 1 (January 1945), p. 22.

6 Chernenko 2001, pp. 58, 60. A British writer in 1910 stated that 'one of the most remarkable of dirigible vessels [is] now under construction' by Kostovich, and described its design: see Hearne 1910, p. 300, although it is not mentioned in the 1909 edition of the same book which carried the title *Aerial Warfare*. Kostovich (spelled Kosztovits) filed an American patent application, no. 830,084, issued 4 September 1906, for an 'Apparatus for Manufacturing Casks', which used plywood moulded on a bending machine.

7 Kollmann, Kuenzi and Stamm 1975, p. 156. Schütte Lanz's designs were copied in the UK during World War I for the unsuccessful R31 and R32 airships, built by the Short Brothers. The Short Brothers were given information about the construction of the airships, plus a recipe for Schütte Lanz's casein glue, by a man called Muller who defected to the UK and identified himself as an ex-employee of the company (see Brian J. Turpin, 'His Majesty's Rigid Airships 1917–1921, part one', *Cross and Cockade* vol. 37: no. 2 [2006], pp. 71–86).

8 Elmendorf 1919, p. 8, wrote: 'Plywood is being used extensively in many airplanes; in particular for fuselage sides, bulkheads, engine bearers, wing rib webs, gusset and thrust plates, flooring, diaphragms, and at times for partially covering wings, in particular at the leading edges. In some machines, stabilizer, elevator and rudder surfaces are covered with thin plywood.' At the time of writing this thesis Elmendorf was also an engineer at the US Forest Products Laboratory and a consultant for the Haskelite company; he also taught at the University of Wisconsin.

9 'The Antoinette Monoplane', *Flight* (23 October 1909), pp. 662–63, 681–83, and Suplee 1919, p. 946.

10 A particularly prominent example of this comes from the British Saunders Company (based on the Isle of Wight), which began by manufacturing stitched plywood boat hulls in the 1890s. They moved into seaplane construction in the 1910s (see 'The Consuta System in Aviation', *Flight* [6 February 1919], p. 184). The French Deperdussin company designed plywood boats as well as planes, and the French plywood sidecar designer Georges Lévy went on to manufacture seaplanes (essentially transferring the form of the sidecar to act as a seaplane float).

11 'Russian Military Aviation', *The Aeroplane* (19 September 1912), p. 296. No detailed accounts of Steglau's plane survive, although the 1916 book *Aerial Russia* describes it as having been built entirely of wood 'even the wings being constructed of three-ply wood instead of fabric' (Roustam-Bek 1916, p. 38).

12 Shavrov, *History of Airplane Designs in the USSR up to 1938* (Russia 1969), pp. 12–13. Some sections of the book were translated into English for the US Department of the Army (within the US Department of Defense), translation dated 24 July 1974 (Army Foreign Science and Technology Center Charlottesville, VA, accession no. AD0786845). In a paper about the design of the S-6 and S-9, Sergei Sikorsky states that a plywood-clad fuselage was used on the S-6A in order to eliminate the tail boom from Sikorsky's original, and inefficient, S-6 design (paper held in the Igor I. Sikorsky Historical Archives, Stratford, CT).

13 Woodman 2004, p. 77. Woodman notes (without a reference) that the plywood used was Kostovich's patented 'Arborit'. Thanks to Sergei Sikorsky and the Sikorsky Archives for kindly supplying a copy of the paper referred to in n. 12, and for drawing Woodman's article to my attention.

14 Of which number 1,213 served in France before the war ended. The DH-4 then became the mainstay of the US Postal Service. The number of de Havilland planes ordered comes from the Smithsonian National Air and Space Museum, Washington, DC, see https://airandspace.si.edu/collection-objects/de-havilland-dh-4 and http://www.centennialofflight.net/essay/Dictionary/DH4/DI74.htm (accessed 12 May 2016).

15 'Veneer Panels for Aeroplanes', *Furniture Record* (US) (28 March 1918), p. 270, quoting 'an examination of the specifications' for contracts let by the government for 3,000 aeroplanes, which may well have referred to the DH-4.

16 Plywood webs were also employed in the wing ribs (see Elmendorf and Wirka 1919). 'The De Havilland IV Biplane', *Flight* (20 June 1918), p. 677.

17 Elmendorf 1921, p. 109, and Butler 1919. Nelson 1971 provides a useful summary of the entire Aircraft Program, pp. 71–76 drawing especially on Allen 1919.

18 Allen and Truax 1920, based on FPL reports written by the authors, and Elmendorf 1919, pp. 5–6 (including on secrecy), 55–61; and Allen 1919, pp. 22–26, for this and the following paragraph. The company making the casein glue was not named in FPL papers but could well have been the Haskell company, with which the FPL had numerous meetings at this time. The history of the Haskell companies deserves to be written. Haskell Manufacturing was initially founded in Ludington, Michigan, in about 1916. A second factory was built in Grand Rapids, Michigan. From 1918 the canoe business was based in Ludington while the

Grand Rapids factory was devoted to military and other plywood. By 1918 the Grand Rapids company was refered to as the Haskelite Manufacturing Company (see Sponsler 1918, one of numerous FPL documents recording contact with the Haskelite company during World War I and afterwards).

19 This paragraph also draws on Elmendorf 1919, p. 5, and Allen 1919, pp. 22–26. Allen and Truax 1920 (Truax, like Elmendorf, was an FPL engineer) summarizes glue technology after the war. The Elmendorf thesis is a useful summary of his work at the FPL.

20 In 1929 a German Research and Information Centre (Forshungs und Beratungsstelle für Sperrholz) was founded in Berlin.

21 The end of the war limited further application. On FPL testing see Elmendorf 1919, *passim*, and Elmendorf 1920, summarized on pp. 109–22. On wing ribs see the brief summary in Allen 1919, p. 31, and the more detailed series of reports by Elmendorf and Wirka 1919.

22 For example, as early as 1921 the German magazine *Der Waggon und Lokomotiv-Bau* 1 (6 January 1921), p. 37, cites the FPL's work (mentioned in a publication entitled *Der Holzkäufer* on 'so-called *Starkholz*' [strong wood]), presenting the American word as plywood. It is very possible that this arose owing to the FPL's publication that year of a Technical Note on plywood (see FPL 1921). Quotation from 'The Post-War Veneer Business', *Veneers* (November 1918), p. 15.

23 Armand-Jean-Auguste Deperdussin, 'Procédé de fabrication de coques pour aeroplanes, embarcations et autres analogues', application filed 12 April 1911, issued 21 June 1911, French patent no. 428,412. A second patent, 'Fuselage pour aéroplanes', application filed 22 April 1912, issued 29 June 1912, French patent no. 442,814, showed a rotating mould for easier veneer application, and refined the moulding technique.

24 The patent does not describe the finish used on this textile, and contemporary articles only describe it as 'glued and varnished' ('Le "monocoque" Deperdussin', *L'Aérophile* [15 September 1912], p. 410). Planes of this period were most often covered with 'doped' textiles: dope being a cellulose nitrate or acetate-based product.

25 Description of the plane's 'torpedo-type body' published in 'The 100-H.P Deperdussin Racing Monoplane', *Flight* (10 February 1912), p. 119. Description of reduction in air resistance in Paul J. Palmer, 'Practical Aeroplane Design', *Aircraft* (May 1914), p. 311. 1913 world speed record reported in 'Le Meeting d'Aviation de Reims', *Le Sport Universel Illustré* (5 October 1913), p. 641.

26 Other early experiments with monocoque-type fuselages include a British patent issued to Louis Beauclerc Goldman in 1910 ('Improvements in Aerial Machines', application filed 10 April 1909, issued 13 April 1910, British patent no. 8687) for a plane with a rounded, enclosed fuselage 'formed of the combination of a hollow hemisphere, a hollow cylinder and a hollow cone'. Although it is not clear whether this plane was ever built, it received prominent attention in the British press (see, for example: 'Future Developments in Flying Machines' in Hearne 1910, p. 298). In 1911 Handley-Page exhibited a plane subsequently described as follows: 'The rear portion of the fuselage was a beautifully finished mahogany monocoque, and for the rest the machine was characterised by the crescent-shaped plan form with upturned wing-tip trailing edges.' ('A "Page" of History', *Flight* [22 June 1939], p. i).

27 Eugène-François Ruchonnet, 'Fuselage indéformable pour appareils d'aviation', application filed 3 June 1911, issued 12 August 1911, French patent no. 430,578. 'Mort de Ruchonnet', *La Revue Aérienne* (25 January 1912), pp. 51–52.

28 'Le Salon d'Aviation', *Le Journal* (30 October 1912), p. 2.

29 'Détails de la construction des Appareils du Salon', *L'Aérophile* (1 December 1912), p. 538.

30 Walter A. House. 'Some Facts Regarding a "Challenger"', *Aircraft* (March 1914), p. 280.

31 W.E. de B. Whittaker, 'Military Requirements and the Paris Show', *The Aeroplane* (7 November 1912), p. 462.

32 Both terms appear, for example, in Mann 1918, p. 16; in Aeronautical Research Section 1918, pp. 5, 63–64; and in Woodhouse 1920, pp. 170–71. The same sources were used for the next paragraph.

33 The subject of plywood monocoques, like materials in general, is not well covered in historical aircraft literature, with one notable exception: Schatzberg 1999, ch. 6, not only summarizes the facts concerning (mainly) American monocoques but contextualizes this history within his wider subject of how the symbolism of metal as a future-looking material led military procurers as well as aeroplane professionals to abandon wood in metal's favour, despite its being an unproven material for aeroplane construction.

34 While the Deperdussin type of monocoque had been mooted for military use, monocoques of all types – as opposed to box girder aircraft merely clad with plywood – were described as being able to withstand damage by artillery or bullets owing to the lack of parts such as struts or wires. They also avoided the problem of stretched fabric ripping and becoming entangled around control wires. Monocoques with minimal internal support, however, were superior to semi-monocoques as damage to supporting elements could weaken the fuselage. On the other hand, semi-monocoques with internal ribs and longerons allowed for a lighter external skin.

35 Aeronautical Research Section 1918, pp. 5–30. A US Air Force entirely separate from the Army was not established until 1947.

36 In fact, the US Army built a monocoque racing plane after the war that won the main American aerial competition in 1920. This success led private American companies to also pursue monocoques. See Schatzberg 1999, p. 117.

37 See 'Some Thoughts on Fuselage Construction', *Flight* (18 May 1916), p. 417; 'An Albatros Fighting Biplane', *Flight* (28 February 1918), pp. 222–27 (both of which mention the relevance of boat building to these aircraft); and the Albatros CV described in Woodhouse 1920, pp. 170–71.

38 Mikesh 1980, pp. 33–36.

39 Suplee 1919, p. 947. The British and French used 'plywood in flat or slightly cured sheets, nailed on as a mere covering', while in German planes it was 'formed and united in an integral part of the structure'. The other successful German semi-monocoque of World War I was the Pfalz D.III, built much more on Deperdussin principles. The D.III was described in the French press in 1918 as an oval fuselage supported on the interior with bulkheads, the skin built in a two-part mould from bands of cross-grained wood, each 9 cm wide. 'L'Avion allemande PFALZ D.III', *L'Aérophile* (1–15 July 1918), pp. 194–98.

40 A 1920 advertisement highlights the need for a change to a more marketable name, when it describes how to pronounce Loughead ('Lock-heed'). An article published in *Popular Aviation* magazine in 1931 states: '...did you know that Lockheed assumed its present name because the Loughead brothers who started the company were tired of being called "log-heads?"'. 'Can You Say "Szekely"? Here's How', *Popular Aviation* vol. 9: no. 1 (July 1931), p. 11.

41 Mikesh 1980, p. 5. This Albatros D.Va is now in the collection of the National Air and Space Museum in Washington, DC (Gift of George K. Whitney, inventory no. A19500092000), and the only other surviving example of a D.Va is held at the Australian War Memorial in Canberra (inventory no. RELAWM04806).

42 An article published in 1920 describes 'traces of the well-known German Albatros having been used as a model' ('An American Single-Seater with Novel Features', *Flight* [5 August 1920], p. 864). See also D. Paul and D. Pratt, 'History of Flight Vehicle Structures 1903–1990', *Journal of Aircraft* vol. 41: no. 5 (Sept–Oct 2004), p. 969.

43 Malcolm Loughead, patent for a 'Process of Manufacturing Curved Forms of Plywood or Fibrous Compositions', application filed 12 August 1919, issued 8 August 1922, US patent no. 1,425,113. Loughead assigns one-quarter rights each to his brother Allan and their collaborators John K. Northrop (then draughtsman) and

Anthony Stadlman (then shop superintendent).

44 The details of glue, cloth and pressure were clearly shared by the Lougheads at the plane's launch at the San Francisco Aeronautical Show in Spring 1920. See 'The Loughead Sport Biplane', *Aviation* vol. 8: no. 9 (1 June 1920), p. 367, cited in Schatzberg 1999, p. 117; and also 'An American Single-Seater with Novel Features', *Flight* (August 1920), pp. 864–65, which mentions a connection with the design of the German Albatros aircraft, and Patricia Groves, 'Loughead Sport-Biplane Model S-1 History' *American Aircraft Modeler* (October 1972), pp. 40–46, available at http://www.airplanesandrockets.com/airplanes/loughead-sport-biplane-model-s-1-history-oct-1972-AAM.htm (accessed 1 June 2016), an article based on interviews with Loughead collaborators John K. Northrop and Anthony Stadlman.

45 This was owing to the fact that the S-1, introduced in 1920, failed to sell in a market filled with cheaper aeroplanes, including surplus military ones.

46 Vultee 1928 and, in greater detail, in the unpublished Floyd 1940. See also Hardecker 1929 and 'Plywood in Aircraft Construction', *The Timberman* (January 1929), p. 161, on the Vega.

47 By this time, Sitka spruce was well established as the most desirable wood for aeroplane construction. It grew very tall and straight, had an excellent strength-to-weight ratio (especially important for aircraft) and was easy to work. The inner and outer longitudinal layers were each about $\frac{1}{24}$ in. (1.06 mm) thick, the middle layer $\frac{1}{16}$ in. (1.58 mm), and the finished shell, with fabric and glue added, between $\frac{5}{32}$ and $\frac{3}{16}$ in. (4–4.76 mm). The longitudinal pieces were originally 25 ft (7.62 m) in length, made from veneer spliced together with scarf joints, and tapered from 1 in. (25.4 mm) wide at each end to 6 in. (152.4 mm) at the centre.

48 Neither the 1919 patent nor Vultee's description of the Vega process included mention of heat being used in the moulding process.

49 Vultee 1928, p. 453, on wind resistance; Floyd 1940 on the three Lockheed models.

50 See James L. White, *Rubber Processing: Technology, Materials and Principles* (Munich 1995), pp. 521–28, on early developments. In the nineteenth century a patent issued to Caleb Burnap describes the use of fluid-pressure moulding via water to press veneers into plywood ('Bending Wood', issued 27 September 1853, US patent no. 10,056); and Edward Knight includes what appears to be a bag-moulding veneer press in his 1870 encyclopedia of machinery (Edward H. Knight, *Knight's American Mechanical Dictionary. Volume III – REA-ZYM* [Boston 1882], p. 2701).

51 The crash of a Fokker Trimotor (metal) aircraft with wooden wings carrying a famous university football coach (Knute Rockne) in Kansas in 1931 provided the argument for dispensing with the use of wood in aircraft. See Schatzberg 1999, pp. 132–34, 154. Schatzberg tells the story of the 'progress ideology' of metal in exemplary detail and in particular through US military and other government records. British comment from Goff 1943, p. 263.

52 See Kollmann, Kuenzi and Stamm 1975, p. 57, and Schatzberg 1999, p. 176. The FPL had first attempted the creation of a dry sheet glue to coat 'very thin plywood' in 1918 using tissue paper (as a substitute for linen) coated with blood albumin glue but this was unsuccessful. See Sponsler 'Gluing' 1918 and Sponsler 'Thin Plywood' 1918; Allen 1919, p. 25; Allen and Truax 1920, pp. 17–18.

53 See Elmendorf 1933, pp. 6–11. The American firm was the Resinous Products Company, Philadelphia, which advertised widely in the wood trade and aircraft press. Their informational booklets found wide circulation in the international plywood trade. Elmendorf suggests that the near expiration of the McCain patent opened the American market to Tego film. The sale date of late 1935 comes from Perry 1947, p. 58 (Perry worked for Resinous Products Co.). Perry 1952, p. 791, states that Rohm & Haas manufactured Tego film in the US from 1937. Schatzberg 1999, pp. 180–81, also discusses the research of the German scientist Otto Kraemer.

54 N.A. de Bruyne, 'Plastic Progress', *Flight* (12 January 1939), pp. a–c. See 'Dry Glue Panels Announced', *The Timberman* (December 1934), pp. 30–31. Plywood swimming costumes were revisited as a marketing device in the 1930s, and a group of photographs dated 1935 are held in the Timberman archive at the Oregon Historical Society, Portland (Box 24). An example of one of the costumes survives in the collections of the Aberdeen Museum, Washington State. Many thanks to Dave Morris for information about this swimming costume.

55 Joseph L. Nicholson, 'The Plywood Plane is Here', *Forbes* vol. 46: no. 9 (1 November 1940), pp. 14–25, 31.

56 F.R. Seekins, 'The Vacuum Veneering Process', *Veneers and Plywood* (May 1936), pp. 8–9, refers to it as 'a new method of laying veneers'.

57 A good, general description of the processes is Heebink 1943, revised in 1953. See Taylor 1943 for a detailed contemporary description of the Vidal process. Schatzberg 1999, pp. 181–90, describes the Duramold and Vidal processes in terms of the aircraft projects they were developed or used for. The individual processes are described but not named by Perry 1943, which reappears in other American and British journals. Harrod 2008, p. 28, suggests that the Deutsche Werkstätten's *vergütetes Holz* (improved wood) was an analogous process.

58 See, for example: 'Molded Airplanes for Defense', *Modern Plastics* vol. 17: no. 11 (July 1940), pp. 25–29, 78–82; Nicholson 1940; Harold P. Moon, 'Development of a Plastic Molded Airplane', *Aviation* (January 1941), pp. 44–45, 140–45.

59 For examples of FPL research see: Trayer 1930, pp. 165–67; Brouse 1940; Wilson 'Wood' 1940; Wilson 'Report' 1940. For a report prepared by North American Aviation for the US Army Air Corps, see Beach 1941.

60 Hughes Hercules press release (about 1944, the date blacked out in the original), held at the US Forest Products Laboratory Library in Madison, Wisconsin (333/H87). See Schatzberg 1999, pp. 206–12. For a contemporary account of the plane: 'Looking Inside the World's Largest Plane', *Popular Science* vol. 147: no. 3 (September 1945), pp. 94–96. A number of general histories of the Spruce Goose have been published, for example: Charles Barton, *Howard Hughes and his Flying Boat* (rev. edition, Vienna, VA, 1998) and Graham M. Simons, *Howard Hughes and the Spruce Goose* (South Yorkshire 2014).

61 This argument appears in many publications, for example Nicholson 1940, p. 15.

62 Schatzberg 1999, pp. 199–206 documents the background to this failure.

63 The most comprehensive book on the Mosquito is Sharp and Bowyer 1971, which, despite being based on (sadly, unreferenced) archival sources, and containing extensive information and statistics on specifications, performance, subcontractors and missions, contains barely any detailed information on materials and construction. On this subject see Goff 1943 with other essential details in 'The Mosquito', *Wood* (July 1943), pp. 143–49. Kollmann, Kuenzi and Stamm 1975, pp. 56–93, offer a detailed technical view on synthetic glues and also brief histories of each type with useful references. See also the account in Schatzberg 1999, pp. 212–17, which cites other sources.

64 These qualities of the Albatross construction noted at the time in H.J. Gough, 'Materials of Aircraft Construction', *Journal of the Royal Aeronautical Society* vol. 42: issue 335 (November 1938), pp. 930–32.

65 There were different glues used depending upon production date and location of manufacture. By the time details of the plane's design were first published (1943) different synthetic resins were used; 'The Mosquito', *Wood* (July 1943), p. 145 cites the use of urea formaldehyde Beetle cement, as does James Montagne, 'Producing "Mosquito" Bombers in Canada', *Veneers and Plywood* vol. 37: no. 11 (November 1943), pp. 8–10; 'The Plywood Airplane is a Tego-Bonded Airplane', advertisement published in *Veneers and Plywood* (December 1943), p. 5, and Thomas Perry (whose firm supplied glues), 'Plywood as Used in the "Mosquito" Plan", *Veneers and Plywood* (January 1945), p. 9, explains that in the Canadian production flat plywood pieces were glued with Tego film, sharply

curved parts were bag moulded with Amberlite PR-14 resin, and that for the attaching of wood and plywood parts Uformite CB-552 resin adhesive was used. An article in *Aerospace*, based in part on an (unreferenced) interview with one of the Mosquito designers, states that casein was replaced by a synthetic glue known as 'Beetle' (invented by de Bruyne) in 'about 1942'. A letter written in response to the article, by a former chargehand inspector, states that synthetic glue started to be used on the Mosquito fuselage from 1942, when Harris Lebus became subcontractors. Harris Lebus had been using synthetic glue (both cold and heated) since at least 1941. See 'First Composite Combat Aircraft', *Aerospace* (November 1990), pp. 16–20, and 'Mosquito's German Glue' (letter), *Aerospace* (January 1999), p. 27.

66 Wartime articles on the Mosquito rarely referenced the source of materials but, later, the use of solid Canadian spruce and Canadian and American birch veneers were widely discussed. See James Montagnes, 'Producing "Mosquito" Bombers in Canada', *Veneers and Plywood* vol. 37: no. 11 (November 1943), pp. 8–10; Connor 2014 (an erratically referenced family memoir), pp. 100–03, on exports of Wisconsin plywood and veneers from the Roddis Lumber and Veneer Company as well as the Lullaby Furniture Company to de Havilland; and Sharp and Bowyer 1971, p. 81, for quantities produced at each factory and pp. 433–39 for a list of subcontractors.

**Chapter 5 – Building the Modern World (1920s–1940s) (pp. 104–145)**

1 Sometimes these forms were lined with special paper, in order to give a smoother finish to the moulded concrete and make the formwork easy to remove and re-use. Wynn 1926, pp. 281–86.

2 See 'Douglas Fir Plywood Concrete Forms', *The Timberman* (November 1929), p. 210; J.E. Hyler, 'Plywood in Concrete Construction', *Veneers* (May 1931), pp. 18–19; P.S. Hill, 'Plywood as a Building Material', *Veneers* (August 1933), pp. 8–9; 'Plywood Formers', *Wood* (June 1941), p. 132; Wynn 1939, pp. 281–83. The 1926 edition does not mention plywood (the 1930 edition has not been found). Recent statistics are from http://www.performancepanels.com/concrete-form-panels-faq (accessed 18 September 2016). Perry 1942, p. 34; on wage costs see J.A. Emmett, 'Plywood-built Forms in Cement Construction', *Veneers and Plywood* (December 1935), p. 11, and Forty 2012, pp. 235, 238.

3 '"Mulberry" Wood', *Wood* (March 1945), pp. 70–72; 'Plywood for Concrete Forms', *Veneers* vol. 45: no. 7 (July 1951), p. 18; Wood and Linn 1942, p. 423 and 1950 (rev. edition), p. 484, described the use of resin-bonded ply shuttering as 'increasing rapidly' and in the 1960 edition, p. 419, as 'universal'; and Cour 1955, p. 115 ('standard material').

4 See chapter 2, n. 27.

5 See 'The Incursion of Veneers', *Hardwood Record* vol. 21: no. 8 (10 February 1906), pp. 7–8 (on door makers embracing 'three or five ply veneered panels'); 'Utilization of Hardwood – Flush Veneered Doors', *Hardwood Record* (10 September 1909), pp. 19–20; 'On the Use of Plywood', *Woodworker* vol. 38: no. 485 (April 1934), p. 132; Baseden Butt, 'A Perfect Home in a Victorian House', *Woman's Magazine Annual* 1935 (London 1935), pp. 760–62; R.G., 'Evolution of the Door', *Wood* (January 1936), pp. 12–16; and Perry 1942, pp. 243–46.

6 Such use of plywood seems to have begun about 1905. Plywood wall panelling was used on numerous well-known British ocean liners including the RMS *Mauretania* (1906), *Titanic* (1911) and *Olympic* (1911). See also 'Veneers for Interior Decoration', *Cabinet Maker and Complete House Furnisher* (21 November 1908), p. 265, in which the British magazine refers to the use of cross-grained veneers on solid wood as 'first attempted as an experiment...and now a dining-room of a Fifth Avenue house in New York is being lined entirely as regards its walls and ceilings, with veneers'. Shirley B. Wainwright's *Modern Plywood* (London 1927) was published to promote the use of plywood for interior wall panelling. Aimed at architects and interior designers, it was probably commissioned by a trade association or distributors of plywood and 'laminboard', which is particularly promoted in its pages.

7 Wilk 1993, including pp. 41–42 on Wright's preference for swamp cypress and, in this instance, his use of hollow-core or 'egg-box' plywood, in which the core was made up of veneers arranged in a rectilinear or hexagonal veneer construction perpendicular to the outer veneer layers, which were faced in cypress. Hollow-core was, and continues to be, used for some door construction.

8 Some of these products were sold for other uses too. Wall panelling was the only plywood application given its own chapter in Wood and Linn 1942 (and also in the revised editions of 1950 and 1960).

9 The murals, 'Conquering the West by Water' and 'Conquering the West by Land', were designed by Herman Volz and painted by Works Project Administration artists.

10 Fifty-seven buildings noted in *Architectural Forum* (June 1939), p. 84 (advertisement for Laux Plywood Finishes); William Jennings, 'Plywood: 8,000,000 Square Feet at Treasure Island', *Architect and Engineer* (February 1939), pp. 53–55, and claim of 10 million square feet in pl. 5; 'Mr Creel and the Indians Put on a Smash Hit', *The Coast* (March 1939), p. 10 ($6.90); 'Plywood goes to the Fair', *Veneers and Plywood* (July 1939), p. 7; Alfred Frankenstein, 'Pageant of the Pacific', *Magazine of Art* 32 (March 1939), pp. 132–34; and F.A. Gutheim, 'The Buildings and the Plan', pp. 135–39, and 'Golden Gate International Exposition 1939', pp. 51–57 (California Group and Federal Building), 58–59 (Hall of Floriculture), and p. 52 ('U.S. Government Building'), *Architectural Record* (April 1939).

11 West Coast producers of plywood, virtually all of whom used Douglas fir, led not only plywood production but also what were described as meagre American exports ('only a fraction of 1 percent of the output' of the entire American plywood industry) even before the Depression hit. See E.B.M., 'The Plywood Export Business', *Veneers* (March 1929), pp. 23–24.

12 Cour 1955, pp. 104–14, on W.E. Difford and the DFPA, an official history with little contextualization. See also US Department of Commerce, Bureau of Standards, *Douglas-Fir Plywood, Commercial Standard CS45-33* (Washington, DC, 1933) and subsequent revisions CS45-36 (1936), CS45-38 (1938) and CS-45 (1945).

13 Joseph P. Cusker, 'The World of Tomorrow', in Helen A. Harrison, *Dawn of a New Day, the New York World's Fair 1939/40* (New York 1980), pp. 4–6; *The House of Plywood, Demonstration House No. 2*, pamphlet (New York 1939); 'Modern Houses Top NY Fair... A House-by-House Presentation of the Town of Tomorrow', *Architectural Forum* (July 1939), pp. 63–72, 34 [*sic*]; Kelly 1951, p. 170, noting the DFPA's 'promotional activities on behalf of prefabrication since 1938'; *Dri-Bilt with Plywood. A Better Way to Build!*, promotional brochure (Tacoma 1939), https://archive.org/details/DouglasFirPlywoodAssociation (accessed 24 August 2016); and Cour 1955, pp. 104–14.

14 'Aging Trylon due for rejuvenation: 700-foot theme tower, gray and falling apart, to be subject of conference', *New York Times* (10 November 1939), p. 23; 'Fair turns ground for typical homes...Trylon nearly covered; new plywood coat is put on – workmen busy preparing for opening on May 11', *New York Times* (29 March 1940), p. 20; 'The "Forty Fair"', *New York Times* (10 May 1940), p. 132; 'Trylon gets new coat for 1940 Fair', *Engineering News Record* (21 March 1940), pp. 4–5.

15 Pearson 1978, pp. 176–84; Mackeith and Smeds 1992, pp. 137–50; and Sarah Menin, 'Embracing Independence: The Finland Pavilion, New York, 1939', in Anderson, Fenske and Fixler 2012, pp. 141–69.

16 Albert Baxter, *History of the City of Grand Rapids* (New York 1891), pp. 500–01; *The Australasian Ironmonger* (1 May 1890), p. 131; and Margaretta Jean Darnall, 'Innovations in American Prefabricated Housing: 1860–1890', *Journal of the Society of Architectural Historians* vol. 31: no. 1 (March 1972), pp. 51–55, on earlier, non-plywood panel houses. The Scottish landscape gardener and designer J.C. Loudon in *An Encyclopedia of Cottage, Farm, and*

*Villa Architecture* (London 1836), p. 256, had proposed a portable cottage, albeit not factory-produced. A new edition of Loudon (*An Encyclopedia of Cottage, Farm, and Villa Architecture and Furniture*; London 1857), pp. 251–56, illustrated a portable cottage for the 'Use of Emmigrants and Others', as well as on pp. 256–57, one 'used as a Substitute for a Country Residence' and two versions of an 'Ambulatory Cottage'.

17 Mott T. Greene, *Alfred Wegener: Science, Exploration, and the Theory of Continental Drift* (Baltimore 2015), pp. 283–84. Many thanks to John Burman for bringing this reference to my attention.

18 Dr A. Tilmant, 'Laboratoires Automobiles de Bacteriology', *Automobilia* (15 November 1919), pp. 44–45.

19 Perry 1942, p. 248.

20 See Harrod 2008, pp. 10–13. Those illustrated here appear in the marketing publication Deutsche Werkstätten 1925–27. Deutsche Werkstätten 1934 publishes a group built in Hellerau in 1934 in which the use of 'brushed Oregon', probably referring to Douglas fir or pine, was mentioned. On the plywood tents see the full catalogue in the Finnish National Library (Digital Collections of National Library of Finland), http://digi.kansalliskirjasto.fi/pienpainate/binding/341800?page=1 (accessed 12 June 2016), the cover of which is fig. 159; and Koponen 2001, pp. 96–97.

21 Michael L. Dolfman and Denis M. McSweeney, '100 Years of US Consumer Spending', US Bureau of Labor Statistics Report 991 (rev. edition, Washington, DC, 2006), pp. 15, 19, http://www.bls.gov/opub/uscs/1934-36.pdf (accessed 23 August 2016). House building decline from Joseph M. McCarthy, 'Prefabrication of Houses', *The Timberman* (July 1936), p. 11.

22 A short history of Government-Sponsored Enterprises (related to the financing of housing) is published by the (since renamed) Federal Housing Finance Agency at http://fhfaoig.gov/LearnMore/History (accessed 23 August 2016).

23 'Purpose of the FPL Work', 20 September 1934, cited in Koning 2010, p. 5; Trayer 1935; and Nelson 1971, p. 112. The FPL had been testing the strength of frame-wall construction since at least 1929. See 'Tests of Frame Wall Construction', *Engineering News-Record* (24 October 1929), pp. 656–67, and Trayer 1934. FPL *Annual Report* 1933, p. 7, described 'lumber for building and manufacturing purposes' as using 50% of all timber cut from American forests.

24 'Tomorrow's Wood Unit House to be Displayed at Madison Home Show', *Wisconsin State Journal* (10 March 1935) and 'A New Idea in House Construction', *The Log of the Lab* (10 May 1935) (internal FPL publication). The history of FPL research leading to the house is to be found in its Projects files, summarized in its unpublished Research Program reports (which were irregularly written during the Depression era). The formal research on the unit house began in 1932 (Project 289-1), although work on plywood panels in floors and walls had begun as early as 1927 (Project 273-1) and was published first in 1929, see 'Tests of Frame Wall Construction', *Engineering News-Record* (24 October 1929), pp. 656–67, and, before the first unit house was erected, in Trayer 1934.

25 Wood and Linn 1942, pp. 96–98, discuss changes to panel sizes during this period.

26 Trayer June 1935 (unpublished); the main published report was Trayer May 1935. Additional information on the response was included in Luxford 1937, revised versions October 1958 and 1965. In 1935 synthetic glue was still considered to be too expensive for house building, see Joseph M. McCarthy, 'Prefabrication of Houses', *The Timberman* (July 1936), p. 26.

27 The terms were widely used in FPL documents and press articles although the patent for the 1935 system referred to 'stressed-covering panels'. See John A. Newlin and George W. Trayer, 'Prefabricated Building and Building Construction' (for 'the free use of the Public in...the' US), application filed 28 November 1936, issued 28 February 1939, US patent no. 2,148,575.

28 Holabird & Root had been architects of the FPL's 1931 building. The 1937 and 1938 houses were referred to in Luxford 1937.

29 Eleanor Roosevelt diary, https://www.gwu.edu/~erpapers/myday/displaydoc.cfm?_y=1937&_f=md054794 (accessed 21 September 2016).

30 Bruce and Sandbank 1943, p. 13, for 'most widely known' and 'enormous effect'; Kelly 1951, pp. 33, 181, 227, 233, 311 and 326; for a more contemporary view, Bemis 1936, vol. 3, pp. 429–31; and Harrison, Albery and Whiting 1945, pp. 53–53 for a British view ('extensively used in the States and experimental structures are erected in this country').

31 Modifications such as the addition of metal stiffening shoes for the end panels.

32 See Harrison, Albery and Whiting 1945, unpaginated 'Case Sheet' for Gunnison following p. 71 on relationship to FPL system; 'Prefabricated MagicHomes', *Architectural Forum* vol. 65 (September 1936), pp. 248, 250, 252, on the founding circumstances of Gunnison, Perry's role and its intended buyers; and Kelly 1951, pp. 62–63, on the polls.

33 Hines 1982, pp. 163 and 166–68.

34 See Hines 1982, pp. 129–30; 'Exhibition House Group', *Architectural Forum* vol. 65: no. 7 (1 July 1936) pp. 38–39; 'Plywood Model House, Los Angeles, California, Richard J. Neutra, Architect', *American Architect and Architecture* 149 (September 1936), pp. 24–25; and Edward R. Ford, *The Details of Modern Architecture* (Cambridge, MA, 1996), pp. 87–101, on related Neutra building systems. The plywood house was a smaller version of Neutra's entry (awarded second prize) into the General Electric Home Electric (small house) Competition of 1935, see 'The House for Modern Living', *Architectural Forum* vol. 64: no. 4 (April 1935), p. 275.

35 Richard and Dion Neutra papers, 1925–1970, Charles E. Young Research Library, UCLA, Box 98, Folder 9. Description of the 'Super Plywood Model House' by Richard J. Neutra (undated).

36 In 1951 the house was sold to a new owner and, three years later, the plywood was described by Neutra's wife, Dione, as having 'lasted and [given] service'; letter from Dione Neutra to Robert E. Hamill, 22 February 1954, Richard and Dion Neutra papers, 1925–1970, Charles E. Young Research Library, UCLA, Box 98, Folder 9.

37 'Your Home of the Future', *Popular Mechanics* (October 1942), p. 75.

38 Kelly 1951, pp. 51, 57 and 61.

39 Bruce and Sandbank 1943, pp. 15–16; Harrison, Albery and Whiting 1945. The best-known TVA plywood house project was at Oak Ridge, Tennessee, where houses were built for workers on the atomic bomb development. Archival material relating to the TVA is held at the US National Archives at Atlanta, Georgia. Thanks to Jennifer Sale Crane for information on TVA prefabricated houses.

40 Wurster 1941 contains the most detailed description of the manufacturing and gluing process, and also an advertisement for Laucks construction glues, where casein is specifically mentioned; the article cited in Treib 1995, pp. 146–51, on Vallejo. See also 'Plywood City', *Western Building* (October 1942), pp. 4–6, for details of Plywood Structures methods. Notes, contracts, drawings and photographs of the project are found in the Wurster, Bernardi and Emmons Collection, Manuscript Boxes 210–223, Environmental Design Archives, UC Berkeley. In between the two schemes Wurster built twenty-five experimental units, some two-storey, in both wood frame and masonry construction with prefabricated infill panels.

41 The story of Goldberg's prefabrication is told in full in Ryan 2011. See in particular: Elizabeth A.T. Smith, 'Space, Structure and Society', pp. 18–61, and Alison Fisher, 'The Road to Community', pp. 62–97. Fisher in Ryan, p. 66. Many thanks to Geoffrey Goldberg for sharing information and archival material relating to his father's work with plywood.

42 The other three company founders were the architect Gilmer Black, the lawyer Edwin Ashcraft and Ross J. Beatty Jr, who owned the land on which the Melrose Park houses were built.

43 Goldberg wrote: 'Standard Houses Corporation...believe we can make a profitable business of giving the American working classes scientifically planned living

accommodations at prices the family of modest income can afford to pay.' Standard Houses 1937. US $4,000 to $7,000 is equivalent to $67,455.28 to $118,046.74 in 2017: https://www.bls.gov/data/inflation_calculator.htm (accessed 10 February 2017).

44 'Factory Houses for $2995', *Architectural Forum* vol. 72: no. 1 (January 1940), p. 66. In an oral history interview recorded by the Art Institute of Chicago in 1992, Goldberg noted that the plywood for the houses was supplied by the US Plywood Corporation, which had recently gone public. 'Oral History of Bertrand Goldberg', interviewed by Betty J. Blum. Complied under the auspices of the Chicago Architects Oral History Project, The Art Institute of Chicago, 1992 (revised edition 2001), p. 103: http://digital-libraries.saic.edu/cdm/ref/collection/caohp/id/3933 (accessed 17 July 2016).

45 Bertrand Goldberg and Gilmer V. Black, 'Technical Information Relative to the Manufacture of Prefabricated Plywood Houses by Standard Houses Corp.', undated [1940], Goldberg Family Archive. Standard Housing managed to generate a good amount of publicity around their sale and this, combined with their cheap price ($2,995 per house, including land), meant that 3,000 visitors reportedly came to see the five houses the day they were put on the market – only nine applications were put in to buy, but all five sold that day. 'Factory Houses for $2995', *Architectural Forum* vol. 72: no. 1 (January 1940), p. 67.

46 For the Indian Head project ten different architects were asked to design houses for a single site – this was intended to test different models of demountable housing. The other architects who designed for the site included Walter Gropius and Frank Lloyd Wright.

47 Letter from Bertrand Goldberg to John Ihlder (Administrator, National Capital Housing Authority), 22 September 1943, p. 9. Goldberg Family Archive.

48 These boards are not dated but are likely to have been made in 1944, as they state that the company is seven years old. Standard Houses designed their factory production methods in agreement with unions. It was very unusual at this time for unions to work on prefabricated housing. See 'Oral History of Bertrand Goldberg', p. 110.

49 'New Freight Car Passes Rail Tests', *New York Times* (19 December 1950), p. 59: '...a monocoque construction of plywood, [which] not only can save the nation many tons of critical steel and many man-hours of labor in construction and maintenance, but in performance tests has shown itself superior to the conventional steel freight car.'

50 Bertrand Goldberg, 'Wooden Cellular Laminated Railway Car', application filed 27 April 1951, issued 23 June 1953, US patent no. 2,642,817.

51 Pressed Steel Car Company publicity material, c. 1951. Goldberg Family Archive.

52 'Plywood and plastics make portable home for fast relocation', *Wall Street Journal* (9 May 1952), p. 2.

53 The story of Deskey and the Sportshack is told by Jeffrey L. Meikle, 'Donald Deskey Associates', in Hanks with Toher 1987, pp. 124–30, based on transcripts of historic interviews with Deskey and the following sources cited: US patent no. 2,286,068, applied for 25 May 1940, issued 9 June 1942 and the advertisement illustrated as fig. 188 in this book. The announcement of Week-end Cabins and colour images of the Metropolitan (Met) Museum interior and model were in Robert W. Marks, 'Donald Deskey's Sportshack', *Esquire* (August 1940), pp. 68–69. A story of the invention of Weldtex different than that told by Deskey was given by Lawrence Ottinger of the US Plywood Corporation in Alva Johnston, 'Profiles. The Plywood Baron II', *The New Yorker* vol. 21 (29 December 1945), pp. 30, 32.

54 The Met Museum installation and also the *Collier's* (magazine) House of Ideas, built on an outdoor terrace at Rockefeller Center in New York, are illustrated in a Weldtex catalogue, *Weldtex/for Walls which Grow Old Gracefully/Created by Donald Deskey...* (New York [undated but almost certainly 1940s owing to the way they were described]). Although the World's Fair version was described as 'being built' for the 'America at Home' exhibition (according to Talbot F. Hamlin, 'Interior Decoration, 1940', *Pencil Points* [July 1940], pp. 433–34), no photographs of it have been found.

55 Kelly 1951, pp. 57, 61 and 79.

**Chapter 6 – Plywood Shows its Face (1930s–1980s) (pp. 146–181)**

1 A dominant market for plywood also started to develop in Asia from the 1950s, especially in Japan. See chapter 7.

2 After the death of Korhonen in 1935 manufacturing continued in the same factory but by a new firm founded by Aalto; his wife, the architect Aino Marsio-Aalto; Marie Gullichsen; and Nils Gustav Hahl. See Stritzler-Levine and Riekko 2016. For a less well-documented but still relevant view see Göran Schildt, 'The Decisive Years' in Pallasmaa 1984, pp. 65–82, especially and also Tuukkanen 2002, chs 1 and 2.

3 On the 'Wood Only' exhibition see 'Standard Wooden Furniture at the Finnish Exhibition', *Architectural Review* 74 (December 1933), p. 220; 'Finnish Furniture', *The Times* (17 November 1933), p. 13; and Harry Charrington, 'Retailing Aalto in London before Artek', in Stritzler-Levine and Riekko 2016, pp. 101–42. On Summers see Deese 1992, based in part on interviews with Summers's widow. On Pritchard see Pritchard 1984 and Grieve 2004. The fact that the Luther stool was marketed without the name of a designer (a then barely decade-old marketing technique and mainly in the modernist furniture business) indicates that it might well have been designed within the Luther company.

4 In the arm/frame pieces all of the force is acting on one plane. The single-grain direction (along the length of the arm) is perpendicular to these forces. Cross-graining the frame would weaken its structure, as the single direction of the force means that the short grain layers would not be resisting any of the weight put on the chair by the sitter. The seat, which has a wider surface area and joins to the frame in four places, has forces acting on it in two directions (lengthways and crossways), and this is why plywood's cross-graining is better able to resist the weight and resulting stresses. A laminated seat, on the other hand, would tend to split along the grain. Aalto's plywood seat was made of seven layers of 1–1.2 mm-thick veneer (8 mm thick in total), while the arms were made of four layers of laminated veneer, 3 mm (the two outer layers) and 5 mm (the two inner veneers) thick (16 mm in total). Breuer's Short Chair seat is made of five layers of 1.5–2 mm-thick veneer (7.5 mm in total). The frame is made of ten layers of laminated veneer 1.5–2 mm thick (17.5 mm in total). All measurements taken from the chairs shown in figs 195 and 201.

5 Breuer's laminated arms and base were of similar thickness to Aalto's (though Breuer used ten veneers while Aalto used only four). The abrupt curve of Breuer's arms required a fin-like brace beneath. His seat was mortised into the top of the arm and to the leg. In his cantilever chair Aalto had also mortised the seat into both the back and into the frame below.

6 The process is described in Deese 1992, p. 188. A very short contemporary film of the chair's making exists in private hands. Breuer's parts were moulded in heavy convex/concave moulds, as were Aalto's seats. However, Aalto's arms, in the form of a stack of veneers with wet glue, were bent onto a former or convex mould (as seen in fig. 197) and then clamped in place to dry.

7 Kevin Davies's pioneering article published sales figures for Aalto furniture: Davies 1998, pp. 145–56, n. 12, for the 40–50% source. He noted as an explanation that per capita income in Britain was higher than that of any continental European country during this period. Further details on Artek exports was published in Ólafsdóttir 1998. The Pritchard claim is made in the unpublished draft 'History of the Isokon Furniture Company' (27 April 1944), p. 2, and in a letter, Jack Pritchard to Frederick Fyleman (13 December 1943), p. 2, both Pritchard Papers, University of East Anglia Library, PP/18/1/1/30 and PP/18/9/4/2. An Isokon royalty statement sent to Breuer for 1937 listed sales of 89 Long Chairs, 18 Nesting Tables and 7 Short Chairs

(Pritchard Papers, PP/18/7/5/9). In a letter to Venesta, Pritchard wrote that Isokon had been selling three to six Long Chairs per week in May 1938, Pritchard to E. Reid, Venesta (16 May 1938), Pritchard Archive, file 18, case 7 (file notation when Pritchard Papers were in their previous location at the University of Newcastle). In 1939, 50 'hand made' [*sic*] or 'prototype models' of the Penguin Donkey were sold 'at full price within a week or two of the declaration of war' ('History of the Isokon Furniture Company', p. 2, Pritchard Papers PP/18/1/1/30). Deese 1992, p. 196, noted the lack of any Makers of Simple Furniture sales figures for 1935–37 and that while there was sufficient success to finance the purchase of Summers's first house there was not enough to expand the firm's operation. An extant order book for the first half of December 1939 showed 100 pieces on order.

8 For published examples of Charles Eames's recognition of Aalto and Breuer see Ostroff 2015, pp. 188, 276, 359, 373, and (for Aalto and Organic Design) especially 374, among others. Neuhart and Neuhart 2010, p. 257, claims a special place for Breuer apparently based on conversations with Charles Eames. Neuhart and Neuhart 2010 might be said to have finally begun this process but the authors were throughout motivated by a desire to take away from both Charles and (especially) Ray Eames credit for their work in favour of individuals working in their office. And in much of their contextualizing, they insufficiently understood their sources; for example, they overstate the extent of the use of resin-bonded plywood in 1930s America and, equally, the state of 'assembly-line machine production' using Duramold and Vidal moulding (both p. 259), and they suppose knowledge of the techniques used for the Mosquito aeroplane at a time before the plane had flown or been publicized (p. 294).

9 The 1940 MoMA competition 'Industrial Design' was subsequently referred to by the 1941 exhibition title 'Organic Design in Home Furnishings'. Noyes 1941, pp. 11–13. The type of glue used is unclear. The MoMA catalogue reproduces a photograph of a sheet of glue film being used while Neuhart and Neuhart 2010, p. 293, state it was urea and formaldehyde, which starts as a powder and must be applied as a paste. The chair backs were initially intended to be exposed plywood, but ended up being upholstered in order to hide the cracks and patches in the veneer (Neuhart and Neuhart 2010, p. 276).

10 Noyes 1941, pp. 7–8, 11.

11 With a completely novel design, a new type of product to mould, and little time between the announcement of the competition and the exhibition of the final results, the chairs were apparently sold at a mark-up of no more than 10% rather than the normal 100%. See letter from Eliot Noyes (MoMA) to Eero Saarinen, 5 August 1941 (courtesy of the Eames Office LLC, with thanks to David Hertsgaard).

12 On the matter of credit for the sculptures, Demetrious 2001, p. 42, wrote: 'Though at times credited just to Ray, these sculptures were, in fact, the work of both of them, as much as of [*sic*] the later furniture, which was often credited just to Charles.' The sculpture in fig. 206 was, like many published at the time, credited to Ray alone. On this issue see Kirkham 1995, ch. 5, n. 37. Charles Eames had worked in a printing shop and a steel mill as a boy (his father had died when he was young), and he later undertook construction work and carving as part of his architectural work. See Demetrious 2001, pp. 52, 54–55, 59–60.

13 Six or seven layers, depending upon how they are counted. Mahogany or birch on the faces, gum on the inside. Final splint between 3⁄16in. (4.76 mm) and ¼in. (6.35 mm) wide. See the brochure published in Ince 2015, pp. 30–31; also Neuhart and Neuhart 2010, pp. 305–10, 325–45. The splints were relatively waterproof, made with a melamine-urea-formaldehyde glue and sprayed with a synthetic resin varnish after moulding.

14 The Eameses made parts for the Vultee BT-15 trainer and the Airborne Transport CG-16 'Flying Flatcar' glider, among others. See Neuhart and Neuhart 2010, pp. 322–23. The MoMA exhibition was illustrated in Kirkham 1995, p. 215, although it was not made clear that the plywood parts shown were not made by the Eameses but instead by other manufacturers. The Eameses returned to the shell form in the much more suitable material of fibreglass-reinforced plastic in 1951.

15 On Eames and zoomorphism see Wilk 1987, p. 168; Wormley quotation in Betty Pepis, '3 Stress Faults in Modern Design', *New York Times* (6 April 1950), p. 44.

16 Discussion between Robin Day and the author, October 1991 (exact date unrecorded). Kirkham 1995, p. 228, refers to 2,000 DCM chairs being manufactured each month by 1951. For a reference to Charles Eames' [*sic*] plywood and steel side chair as one of the top ten designs of all time: 'Designers' Choice', *Time* vol. 73: no. 2 (12 January 1959), p. 60.

17 Robert W. Marks, 'On wings of wood. Plastic plywood, that miracle substance of planes, will create new automobiles, homes and countless things after the war', *Esquire* (July 1942), p. 133.

18 The Korean War had stretched expanding, but much in demand, US plywood supplies (Finland too was a major exporter to that war effort). After the war aid to South Korea included additional American and Finnish plywood. On Finland see Koponen 2001, p. 47. On the US see: 'Korea to get more lumber', *New York Times* (26 March 1954), p. 36; Charles Wilson, 'US mobilisation. Resume of second quarterly report', *Northern Advertiser* (24 August 1951), p. 11.

19 See, for example: Wangaar and Tigelaar 1945; Seborg and Fleischer 1945; Chown and Falk 1946; Myers 1945.

20 *Wartime Technological Developments* 1945, p. 32.

21 Bulkheads that divided the boat hulls into watertight compartments were to have been made of plywood too, but this was deemed less of a priority than the material's allocation for aircraft use and they were instead made of solid mahogany planks cross-grained for extra strength. An unusually informative film on the scheme showing the production of a boat, 'The Story of the Fairmile Patrol Boat' narrated by Vice Admiral C.V. Usborne, is in the collection of the Imperial War Museum (ADM 5022), and online at www.iwm.org.uk/collections/item/object/1060013115 (accessed 22 June 2016).

22 Instead of there being only nineteen UK boat yards that could handle all steps in the making of such ships, ninety-five yards (spread from Scotland to the south coast of England) became available under the decentralized system. Admiralty papers relating to the Fairmile Marine Company are at the National Archives, Kew, London. The draft agreement (22 February 1940) between Noel Macklin and the Admiralty summarized the orders placed to date (495 in total) and agreed that a new company (a 'shadow factory') would be set up on behalf of the Admirality (NA/ADM 116/4836). The Fairmile Marine Company was incorporated on 12 August 1940 (NA/TS 32/449). It refers to plywood 'as one of the bottlenecks of the present war since such immense quantities are needed for aircraft construction'.

23 For a comprehensive account of the role of the PT boat in World War II, see Curtis L. Nelson, *Hunters in the Shallows: A History of the PT Boat* (Washington, DC, and London 1998). For plywood's use in US PT boats, see: *Detail specifications for building Motor Torpedo Boats PT 565-624 (80-Foot) for the United States Navy Bureau of Ships* (Washington, DC, 31 March 1944). Thanks to Don Shannon, PT Boat Curator, Battleship Cove Museum (Fall River, MA) for drawing my attention to this document and for help with questions about the construction of PT boats.

24 John Steinbeck, *Once There Was a War* (New York 1958), pp. 201–03 (brought to my attention by Peter Bell), and '"Plywood Navy", Our Coastal Forces', *The Manchester Guardian* (20 August 1942), p. 3. See also 'PT-Boats Shepherd Invaders to France', *New York Times* (7 June 1944), p. 3, referring to 'the plywood navy'.

25 See: 'The Navy's Watch on the Rhone', *Popular Mechanics* vol. 83: no. 6 (June 1945), pp. 1–5; 'Plywood PT Boats...' *Popular Science* vol. 145: no. 6 (December 1944), p. 176; 'Their Shields Were Plywood', *New York Times* (13 September 1942),

p. BR1; 'PT Boats', *New York Times* (31 January 1943), p. E10; and 'Reflections Point to Boat of Future' *New York Times* (12 January 1941), p. 59.

26 'Trend Toward Use of Plywood Noted', *New York Times* (12 January 1947), p. S7, which mentions 'commonplace' but also the importance of the introduction of exterior-grade plywood in 1936 in 'pioneering' boat building. Perry 1942, p. 231, cites 1938 as the year that plywood use in boats became 'impressive' owing to the availability of Tego-bonded plywood distributed by the US Plywood Corporation, which promoted the use of plywood in boats. Plywood had been used in a limited way in boatbuilding since the early twentieth century: for Luther's Venesta canoe (1899) and the Haskell canoe (1917), for yachts – including Sir Thomas Lipton's trans-Atlantic racing yacht (1914), inspired by tea crates used by his eponymous firm and aeroplane designer Anthony (Anton) Fokker's futuristic 'QED' (1938) – for small rowboats and, especially, for speedboats once streamlining took hold in the 1930s. See Kermik 2004, p. 63, for the Venesta canoe (possibly made to promote Luther's 'waterproof' glue, see chapter 2); 'Veneer in Boat-building', *Veneers* (November 1914), p. 8, and Joseph Brinker, 'Racing for "America's" Cup: When Sport Becomes a Science', *Popular Science* vol. 97: no. 1 (July 1920), pp. 17–22, on Lipton's Shamrock IV; 'Fokker's "QED"', *Life Magazine* (22 August 1938), p. 17; and J.A. Emmett, 'Boatbuilders Turn to Plywood', *Veneers* (April 1935), pp. 8–9, on streamlined speedboats.

27 'Wagemaker Wolverine Boats' catalogue, 1949, held in the collections of the Western Michigan University Archives and Regional History Collections, Kalamazoo. Thank you to Lynn Houghton for providing access to a scan of this catalogue.

28 Riva's first experiment with plywood was in 1948, where he used it in the construction of a speedboat called the BF Lungo. Piero Gibellini, of the Riva Historical Society (RHS), has written about the design of this boat in the Riva Historical Society magazine: 'BF Lungo', *Vivariva* 35 (Winter 2012), pp. 44–46.

29 By the end of 1958, 177 plywood hulls had been built for the Florida (the first all-plywood model), Super Florida, Ariston and Tritone models.

30 There is no comprehensive book on Riva's history. The information on this page comes from the following: interview with Mariella di Vito and Piero Maria Gibellini of the RHS (20 September 2016), and with Ricardo Sassoli of Riva (20–21 September 2016), both conducted by Lucia Savi. The company's 'Technical Registry', now in the RHS, lists every version of every Riva model including the types and species of wood used and for which parts. This is transcribed in Piero Gibellini, '8. Woods PMG' *Vivariva* 33 (2011), pp. 14–19. '7. Marine Plywood' in the same issue, pp. 12–13, recounts the origins of the Riva–Lodi partnership, drawing on other published sources. The RHS also holds two Technical Services Bulletins (13 and 23), which describe in detail the plywood being used in 1958: this was Finnish beech sandwiched between Nigerian cedar on the interior side and Grand Bassam (Ivory Coast) mahogany on the outer side. The Riva company retains one of its original moulds for the Aquarama, together with materials samples and a photographic archive.

31 Undated (1960s) Riva catalogue, RHS archives.

32 The underside of the chassis was sprayed with a bituminous sealing material. Costin called his non-shell chassis 'monocoque' as the stresses were evenly distributed across the chassis rather than through the body, despite its not being a closed, single-shell structure, as in aircraft. His de Havilland background was almost always mentioned in press accounts of the cars, even after he had left the firm. See 'The Marcos 1800' *Motor Sport* (April 1965), pp. 247, 249–50; 'Marcos 1600 GT', *Automobile Engineer* (July 1968), pp. 301–03; and Alan Baker, 'Return of the Wooden Motor Car', *New Scientist* (20 January 1972), pp. 159–61.

33 The Marcos name combined those of the designers and partners Jem Marsh and Frank Costin. By 1962 both had left the firm (at least temporarily) but the GT cars were made with the plywood Costin chassis. Fig. 225 is from a series of early Gullwing images. See sources in n. 32 above.

34 Cover of *Time* magazine headlined 'Do-It-Yourself. The new billion-dollar hobby' (2 August 1954) and lengthy article 'The Shoulder Trade', pp. 62–68, suggest the economic importance of DIY in the US as does 'Plywood Thrives on Do-It-Yourself', *New York Times* (5 September 1954), Section 3, pp. 1 and 7. Scores of articles on plywood in DIY are to be found in magazines including *Popular Mechanics* (published from 1902), *Popular Science* (published from 1872), *The Family Handyman* (published from 1951) and, in Britain, *Practical Householder* (published from 1955) and *Do It Yourself* (published from 1957). Home decorating magazines encouraged house modernization and published how-to books and pamphlets. See Goldstein 1998 and Atkinson 2006.

35 W.P. Matthews broadcast on DIY on BBC radio in the 1930s and then BBC television from 1946/7 to 1955. See obituary 'Barry Bucknell', *The Guardian* (27 February 2003) at https://www.theguardian.com/news/2003/feb/27/guardianobituaries (accessed 2 October 2016). In addition to DIY elements of the Ideal Home Exhibition (founded 1908) in London, the first annual New York DIY show was in March 1953 (see Betty Pepis, 'Householders get a self-help show', *New York Times* [17 March 1953], p. 53), the first Los Angeles show was the same year ('The Shoulder Trade', *Time* vol. 64: no. 5 [2 August 1954], p. 64), and London's *Practical Householder* exhibition at Earls Court and the *Do It Yourself* (magazine) exhibition at Olympia were both inaugurated in 1958.

36 For example 'Flying Water Bugs', *Popular Mechanics* vol. 85: no. 4 (April 1946), pp. 96–100, on use of phenolic resins during and after war enabling faster boat speeds (but not a how-to article); and 'Radio Toasts Wood Sandwiches for Car Bodies', *Popular Science* vol. 155: no. 4 (October 1949), pp. 174–76. See also post-war intelligence reports referenced in n. 19.

37 'In the Mood for Modern Living', *Practical Householder* (May 1961), p. 458, advised on the practical advantages of plywood for the amateur. Joseph Nolan, '"Do-it" on parade', *New York Times* (20 March 1955), p. X31, on the four Ps.

38 A number of academic articles have been published on the history of the Mirror dinghy, most notably Jackson 2006. See also Dingle 1999, pp. 121–27; Richard Blundel, '"Little ships": the co-evolution of technological capabilities and industrial dynamics in competing innovation networks', *Industry and Innovation* vol. 13: no. 3, pp. 313–34. £63 11s. was equivalent to about £1,200 in 2016 prices; see http://www.bankofengland.co.uk/education/Pages/resources/inflationtools/calculator/flash/default.aspx (accessed 4 November 2016). At the end of 1962 the average annual salary for manual workers was 317s. 3d.; see http://hansard.millbanksystems.com/written_answers/1963/mar/21/manual-workers-average-weekly-earnings (accessed 4 November 2016). Boat kits were also sold by well-established boat companies; see '103 Models in Chris-Craft Line, Not Counting Prefabricated Kits', *New York Times* (13 January 1952), p. S11, where kits are described as 'a relatively new development for the firm'.

39 Mirror dinghy brochure, c. 1963. Thanks to Martin Egan for kindly lending his copies of early Mirror dinghy advertising material, and for advice and help on the history of the boat.

40 Bucknell apparently got the idea for this method of construction from kayak building (Dingle 1999, p. 123), although it also has relationships to a longer history of boat building – in the late nineteenth century Samuel Saunders made very early plywood-hulled boats in his shipyard on the Thames. His patent of 1898 specifies the use of wire, 'threaded or laced' through holes drilled in the hull, both to hold the layers of veneer together and to secure solid elements such as battens, in the place of nails. Samuel Edgar Saunders, 'Improvements in Building Boats, Carriages, Panels and Other Articles', application filed 4 January 1898, issued 31 December 1898, British patent no. 222.

41 Mirror dinghy building instructions, reissued 2004: http://www.

ukmirrorsailing.com/images/building_a_mirror_dinghy/mirror_canadian_building_instructions.pdf (accessed 25 October 2016).

42 In 1999 the Mirror dinghy was the most registered sailing dinghy in the Australian state of Victoria. Dingle 1999, pp. 123–24.

43 The history of surfing was, from the nineteenth century onwards, deeply implicated in the history of colonialism. See Isiah Helekunihi Walker, *Waves of Resistance: Surfing and History in Twentieth-century Hawai'i* (Honolulu 2011). For a very good account of the migration of surfboard designs across the Pacific, see Gibson and Warren 2014. Hi Sibley, 'Surf sleds and boards. Simple ways to build them – one type is only a piece of plywood, yet it gives thrilling sport', *Popular Science* vol. 112: no. 6 (June 1928), pp. 79 and 98. Prior to the development of hollow construction surfboards had been made from shaped planks (or a single piece) of solid wood, usually redwood in California and Hawai'i.

44 Tom Blake, 'Water sled', application filed 18 April 1931, issued 16 August 1932, US patent no. 1,872,230. For early references to the use of plywood in Tom Blake boards see plans for a board design using plywood, dated 1937 (Lynch and Gault-Williams 2001, p. 99); and brochure for the Thomas Rogers Company, c. 1937: design nos 4, 5, 6 and 7 specify mahogany side rails planked with Weldwood waterproof 3-ply panel (Lynch and Gault-Williams 2001, p. 97). Blake worked with Rogers to commercially produce boards from 1932 to 1937. DIY plans for a Tom Blake board with plywood planking published in *Popular Science* vol. 134: no. 6 (June 1939), pp. 174–76 (see fig. 235). Thanks to Geoff Cater for information and references relating to the construction of Tom Blake's early plywood boards.

45 'Make a Super Surfboard for £4', *Boy's Own Paper* (May 1965), pp. 8–11. £4 was equivalent to £71.08 in 2016: http://www.bankofengland.co.uk/education/Pages/resources/inflationtools/calculator/default.aspx (accessed 10 February 2017). Thanks to Kevin Cook, of the Museum of British Surfing, for bringing this project to my attention. The Museum of British Surfing have in their collection Blandford's own hollow board, plus a board made using the *Boy's Own* plans.

46 For a detailed history of skateboard design, see Borden 2001, ch. 2.

47 Borden 2001 is the best and most comprehensive history of skateboarding, architecture and design. See pp. 174–76 for an account of the early 1980s closure of skateparks.

48 On Rampage ramps see Angiulo 1977, p. 64 and Borden 2001, p. 77. Articles on ramp building state that it is best to layer three sheets of very thin ply (specifying that between 20 and 30 sheets will be needed), which will curve easy to the shape of the ramp. Alternatively (if a thicker grade is used), they recommend cutting parallel half-depth lines into the underside of the wood to accommodate bending. For examples of these articles, see 'Ramp Raging', *Thrasher* (July 1981), pp. 10–13; 'Ramp Building', *Thrasher* (August 1981), pp. 20–21; letter from Christian Eggers, West Germany, published in *Thrasher* (January 1982), p. 27; interview with Steve Caballero, *Thrasher* (February 1982), pp. 34–37; Wayne Lyons, 'The Cherry Lane Ramp', *Thrasher* (August 1982), pp. 30–31; letter from Pol Philippe Castagne, Belgium, published in *Thrasher* (May 1983), p. 29.

49 'Ramp Building. Part II. Smaller Ramps and Superstructures', *Thrasher* (April 1983), p. 37.

50 Elaine Tyler May, *Homeward Bound: American Families in the Cold War Era* (New York 1988), pp. 165–66, cited in Goldstein 1998, p. 38.

51 The model shown in fig. 238 was made for the State of Montana in about 1962. It is one of a group of models, all made to represent the designs in the US Defense Department's 1962 booklet 'Family Shelter Designs'. This group of models was used by the State in public displays and at events such as state fairs. The models were intended to encourage people to build their own DIY fallout shelters. The models were acquired for the V&A in 2016, from a private collector in Montana (Museum nos: CD.19–2016 to CD.25–2016). One other incomplete set of the models is known to survive in the collection of the Museum of Nuclear History in Washington State. For a good account of DIY shelter building during the Cold War, see Sarah A. Lichtman, 'Do-it-yourself Security: Safety, Gender, and the Home Fallout Shelter in Cold War America', *Journal of Design History* vol. 19: no. 1 (Spring 2006), pp. 39–55.

**Chapter 7 – The Fall and Rise of Plywood (1960s–today) (pp. 182–209)**

1 The main uses of plywood in the US in the 1960s were, first, construction and, second, furniture and cabinetwork; see Panshin et al 1962, p. 169.

2 On the early history of boards and also subsequent history of the competition to plywood from other boards see Zerbe et al 2015 and, on the market, Haynes 2003.

3 There are some products sold where the constituent elements of particleboard are moulded into curved or even three-dimensional shapes: for example, the Thomson company's Saba brand produced a television designed by Philippe Starck (1994) encased in multi-part, curved, high-density (compressed) 'wood' and, at the time of writing, Chinese companies are selling 'presswood' pallets, said to be half the weight of ones made from solid wood. Numerous examples can be seen on www.alibaba.com.

4 The term 'petrochemical house' was coined by Ore 2011, p. 263. Mixed with a hardening agent and applied cold UF adhesive was, since 1945 (and remains by a considerable margin), the most popular glue for all types of panel manufacture. For a contemporary view see Perry, *Modern Adhesives* 1947, pp. 69–73 and, on its history, Kollmann, Juenzi and Stamm II 1975, pp. 68–69.

5 For example, O. Wittmann, 'Die nachträgliche Formaldehyddabspaltung bei Spanplatten', *Holz als Roh- und Werkstoff* vol. 20: no. 6 (June 1962), pp. 221–24, and Peter A. Breysse, 'Chipboard-Formaldehyde', *Occupational Health Newsletter* vol. 10 (1961), pp. 1–4, the latter cited in Ore 2011, p. 278; on Breysse as an advocate in the popular press see 'Built-In Fumes Plague Homes', *New York Times* (7 May 1978), section 3, p. 1.

6 On industry recognition see, for example, H.G. Freeman and W.C. Grendon, 'Formaldehyde Detection and Control in the Wood Industry', *Forest Products Journal* vol. 21: no. 9 (September 1971), pp. 54–57, where it was noted that 'limits for use [of formaldehyde] have been established to protect the health of employees while still enabling the use of adhesives that allow us to make a quality product at a feasible production rate'; the entire issue of that journal was devoted to 'Environmental Control'. Citations of early research and action are found in the scientific literature, see Nestler 1977; T. Salthammer, S. Mentese and R. Marutzky, 'Formaldehyde in the Indoor Environment', *Chemical Review* vol. 110: no. 4 (14 April 2010), pp. 2536–72; and R. Marutzky, 'Release of Formaldehyde by Wood Products' in A. Pizzi (ed.), *Wood Adhesives: Chemistry and Technology* vol. 2 (New York 1989), pp. 307–88. Canada banned the advertising, sale or importation into Canada under item 34, Part I of Schedule I to the *Hazardous Products Act* in December 1980.

7 Ore 2011, pp. 280–85 especially; 'Formaldehyde: review of scientific basis of EPA's carcinogenic risk assessment. Hearing before the Subcommittee on Investigations and Oversight of the Committee on Science and Technology, US House of Representatives', Ninety-seventh Congress, second session, 20 May 1982; the accusation was from an environmental biochemist from the University of California attached to the Environmental Defense Fund, see 'Built-In Fumes Plague Homes', *New York Times* (7 May 1978), section 3, p. F1.

8 In 1980 the US National Academy of Science advised maintaining the lowest practical formaldehyde concentrations. In 1982 the US Department of Housing and Urban Development issued product standards for panel products containing formaldehyde, many European countries (Austria, Denmark, Germany, Sweden) adopted a new E1 emissions class for products in 1985 (and subsequently made more stringent in Germany), and in 1987 the US Environmental Protection Agency (EPA) ruled that formaldehyde was 'probably' a carcinogen in mobile

homes and in conventional homes using a great deal of pressed boards. On European standards see C. Hill, A. Norton and A. Kutnar, 'Environmental Impacts of Wood Composites and Legislative Obligations', in Ansell 2015, pp. 325–28.

9 In addition to the information cited in the previous note, see M.S. Cohn, *Revised Carcinogenic Risk Assessment of Urea Formaldehyde: Foam Insulation: Estimates of Cancer Risk due to Inhalation of Formaldehyde Released by UFFI*, Consumer Product Safety Commission (Washington, DC, 1981) and for an overview of 1980s and also later research James A. Swenberg et al, 'Formaldehyde Carcinogenicity Research: 30 Years and Counting for Mode of Action, Epidemiology, and Cancer Risk Assessment', *Toxicological Pathology* vol. 41: no. 2 (February 2013), pp. 181–89.

10 Lower emissions since the late 1980s are referred to in World Health Organization, IARC Monographs on the Evaluation of Carcinogenic Risks to Humans, vol. 62: *Wood Dust and Formaldehyde*, 1995, online at https://monographs.iarc.fr/ENG/Monographs/vol62/mono62.pdf, p. 341, and reprinted in the 2006 edition of the report, p. 235.

11 'Assisting Residents of Toxic Trailers Led to Recognition of Additional Dangers of Formaldehyde', link at http://www.sierraclub.org/toxics (accessed 10 September 2016). R. Maddalena, M. Russell, D.P. Sullivan and M.G. Apte, 'Aldehyde and Other Volatile Organic Chemical Emissions in Four FEMA Temporary Housing Units – Final Report', Ernest Orlando Lawrence Berkeley National Laboratory, Report LBNL-254E (November 2008), *passim*, table 3, lists surface materials in the four brands of units.

12 F.J. Offermann, 'Ventilation and Indoor Air Quality in New Homes', California Air Resources Board and California Energy Commission, PIER Energy-Related Environmental Research Program, Collaborative Report CEC-500-2009-085 (2009); and Barbara Kolarik et al, 'Concentration of Formaldehyde in new Danish Residential Buildings in Relation to WHO Recommendations and CEN Requirements', *Indoor + Built Environment Journal* vol 21: issue 4 (August 2012), pp. 552–61.

13 World Health Organization, IARC Monograph, 'Chemical Agents and Related Occupations. A Review of Human Carcinogens', vol. 100 F (2010); see http://monographs.iarc.fr/ENG/Monographs/vol100F/mono100F-29.pdf, p. 403 (accessed 17 January 2017).

14 Ore 2011, pp. 285–86.

15 The 1950 figure is from Roger A. Sedjo and Samuel J. Radcliffe, 'Postwar Trends in US Forest Products Trade', Research Paper R-22 (Washington, DC, 1980), p. 100. The percentages for 2014 production come from FAOSTATS, http://faostat3.fao.org/browse/F/*/E (accessed 10 November 2016). All other statistics in this paragraph are from J. Presemon, D.N. Wear, M.O. Foster, *The Global Position of the US Forest Products Industry* (Asheville, NC, 2015), pp. 17–18, based on UN Food and Agricultural Organization data.

16 Adjani 2011, pp. 53–55, especially.

17 S. Ravi Rajan, *Modernizing Nature. Forestry and Imperial Eco-Development 1800–1950* (Oxford and New York 2006), pp. 7–12.

18 These levels of logging had a negative impact not only in terms of loss of forest cover and biodiversity, but also because of the polluting effects of saw mills. Water sources were particularly affected, in part because of they were so regularly blocked by large log jams (often relieved through explosions) and also because of the use of damming to regulate stream flows and flush logs down a river according to daily or weekly schedules. Joseph E. Taylor III, *Making Salmon. An Environmental History of the Northwest Fisheries Crisis* (Seattle 1999), pp. 56–57.

19 On the use of cheap tropical plywood for construction see Dauvergne 1997, pp. 18–20. On global corporate investment in the Indonesian logging industry see Dauvergne 1997, p. 15 and Christopher M. Barr, 'Bob Hasan, the Rise of Apkindo, and the Shifting Dynamics of Control in Indonesia's Plywood Sector', *Indonesia* vol. 65 (April 1998), pp. 1–36. On the EU and China as major importers of tropical wood see 'Changing International Markets for Timber and Wood Products', EFI Policy Brief 5 (2010), and William Laurence, 'China's appetite for wood takes a heavy toll on forests' (November 2011), http://e360.yale.edu/feature/chinas_appetite_for_wood_takes_a_heavy_toll_on_forests/2465/ (accessed 10 October 2016).

20 'Forest Crime File. Kayu Lapis Indonesia the untouchable god of Indonesian ancient forest destruction', Greenpeace report (April 2006), http://www.greenpeace.org/international/Global/international/planet-2/report/2006/4/kayu-lapis-crime-file.pdf (accessed 3 September 2016). For World Bank figures on illegal logging, see EU FLEGT Facility 2010, p. 4.

21 Pillet and Sawyer 2015, p. 5.

22 'Crime file. Partners in crime: how Dutch timber traders break their promises, trade illegal timber and fuel destruction of the paradise forests', Greenpeace report (April 2007), pp. 5–6, http://www.greenpeace.nl/Global/nederland/report/2010/6/partners-in-crime-how-dutch.pdf (accessed 3 September 2016).

23 On Chinese government efforts see Wellesley 2014. Although the EU introduced new legislation to restrict the trade in illegal timber in 2013, there have been doubts raised about the efficacy of their implementation, see 'Europe failing to use legal armoury against illegal logging', Greenpeace media briefing (February 2016); Arthur Nelsen, '"No evidence" that EU's illegal timber policy is working', *The Guardian* (10 February 2016), published at: https://www.theguardian.com/environment/2016/feb/10/no-evidence-that-eus-illegal-timber-policy-is-working (accessed 28 October 2016). Finland also has a long tradition of forest research and management and 14% of Finns own forest land. 20% of Finnish exports come from forests. See the Finnish (government) Forest Research Institute (Metla) website: http://www.metla.fi/metla/index-en.htm. Data on Finnish forest ownership is at http://www.smy.fi/en/forest-fi/graphs/forest-owners/ (Finnish Forest Association).

24 The report was *Our Common Future, World Commission on Environment and Development* (Oxford 1987); a summary is published at http://www.un.org/geninfo/bp/enviro.html. The Rio declaration is at http://www.unep.org/documents.multilingual/default.asp?documentid=78&articleid=1163 (both accessed 11 November 2016).

25 2016 examples of each are Pentti Linnamaa, 'Point of view: Forest certification ensures confusion instead of sustainability', published on the website of the Finnish Forest Association (http://www.smy.fi/en/artikkeli/point-of-view-forest-certification-ensures-confusion-instead-of-sustainability/), and the Greenpeace article on 'The Forest Stewardship Council (FSC)' (http://www.greenpeace.org/international/en/campaigns/forests/solutions/alternatives-to-forest-destruc/), which includes links to 'FSC at Risk: Progress Report' (both accessed 17 January 2017). See also the website https://fsc-watch.com/.

26 Braungart McDonough 2002. A description of life cycle assessment of wood composites is found in Hill, Norton and Kutnar, pp. 314–19. Thanks to Daniel Charny of From Now On and Kingston University for discussions on this subject.

27 Svetlana Boym, *The Future of Nostalgia* (New York 2001), p. 10, has argued that 'new technology and advanced marketing stimulate ersatz nostalgia – for things you never thought you had lost – and anticipatory nostalgia – for the present that flees with the speed of a click'.

28 See Rick Poyner, 'Excess is a Bore', *Blueprint* (November 1989), p. 28 (quotations), and Mike Jones, 'Calming Influences', *Design* (June 1992), p. 30, which refers to 'A new sense of calm, nineties rationalism' in an article that includes Morrison's work. On the Morrison project in fig. 251 see Peter Dormer, *Jasper Morrison* (London 1990), pp. 61–62. Judd produced furniture in solid wood from the late 1970s and plywood starting in 1990. Some of the latter chairs were based on designs of the early 1980s. An early example of the turn to recyclable materials (including wood) in mass-produced, commercial office furniture was the Picto chair designed by ProduktEntwicklung Roericht and

manufactured from 1992 by the German company Wilkhahn, a firm with a notable commitment to sustainable manufacture (see http://collections.vam.ac.uk/item/O112497/picto-chair-model-2067-office-chair-produktentwicklung-roericht/). The trend towards wood is observable in design magazines of the last three decades and in the objects shown at international design trade fairs. See, for example, Natre Wannathepsakul's timber supplement, published in *Blueprint* (January 2011), pp. 79–83, which describes a growing interest in wood as a material for both architecture and furniture design: 'As environmental concerns dominate our era, architects are forced to consider carbon footprints. Sustainability and technological innovation create a strong foundation for timber's appeal and versatility in the 21st century'. At a more commercial level, *The Telegraph*'s 2012 summary of trends at the Milan Furniture Fair noted a growing 'fetishisation of wood, a trend that has been building for some time': http://www.telegraph.co.uk/lifestyle/interiors/9245501/Milan-Furniture-Fair-in-pictures.html?frame=2210929 (accessed 19 January 2017).

29 Videos of these machines can be found online and their industrial use is described in Thompson 2007, pp. 182–86, 248–50.

30 See 'Is it a Hackerspace, Makerspace, TechShop, or FabLab?' (22 May 2013), http://makezine.com/2013/05/22/the-difference-between-hackerspaces-makerspaces-techshops-and-fablabs/ (accessed 21 September 2016). Fab Labs, founded in 2005 by the MIT Media Lab as a global outreach project, contain a very specific kit of parts (see Gershenfeld 2005) and http://fab.cba.mit.edu/; makerspaces, derived from hackerspaces (Germany 1995), are less prescribed and are now also run by for-profit companies. See also Dellot 2015 and Halligan and Charny 2016. On modification see, for example, http://www.ikeahackers.net/, where much plywood is used.

31 Interview with Daniel Charny, August 2016.

32 This and the following paragraphs are is based on interviews with those in the field including Daniel Charny, Joni Steiner of Opendesk, Alastair Parvin of WikiHouse and Bruce Bell of Facit Homes. I am grateful to all of them for their time and interest.

33 See *Patkau Architects* 2017.

34 https://iaac.net/research-projects/solar-house/endesa-pavilion/ (accessed 15 October 2016).

35 http://icd.uni-stuttgart.de/?p=12965 (accessed 14 November 2016); Menges, Schwinn and David Krieg 2017, p. 98.

36 The term engineered wood – used no later than 1952 with reference to plywood (see Perry 1952) – began to gain some currency in the 1980s and started to become common for marketing purposes in the 1990s. The trade body, the American Plywood Association, changed its name in 1994 to APA – The Engineered Wood Association and today the term is widely used, especially for flooring and architectural elements made of a variety of glued woods.

37 See T.R.C. Wilson, *The Glued Laminated Wooden Arch*, US Department of Agriculture Technical Bulletin no. 691 (Washington, DC, October 1939), a summary of the FPL research project. Andreas Jordahl Rhude, 'Structural Glued Laminated Timber: History of its Origins and Early Development', *Forest Products Journal* vol. 46: no.1 (January 1996), p. 15; E. Karacabeyli, *CLT handbook: Cross-laminated Timber* (Pointe-Claire, Canada, 2013); and Valentine Low, '35-storey skyscrapers…built out of plywood', *The Times* (5 June 2015), p. 23.

38 See Joseph Ashmore and Corinne Treherne, Brigitte Rohwerder, *Transitional Shelters: Eight Designs* (Geneva 2011), http://www.ifrc.org/PageFiles/95186/900300-Transitional%20Shelters-Eight%20designs-EN-LR.pdf (accessed 3 October 2016); Bill Flinn, 'Changing Approaches to Post-disaster Shelter', *Humanitarian Exchange* no. 58 (July 2013), pp. 38–39, http://odihpn.org/magazine/changing-approaches-to-post-disaster-shelter/ (accessed 10 September 2016); Victoria Maynard, Elizabeth Parker and John Twigg, *The effectiveness and efficiency of interventions supporting shelter self-recovery following humanitarian crises: an evidence synthesis protocol* (Oxford 2016), pp. 8–20, https://assets.publishing.service.gov.uk/media/57a0895d40f0b652dd0001b0/OX-HEP-Shelter-Print.pdf (accessed 10 September 2016); 'Transitional Shelter in Post-disaster Contexts', GSDRC research report 1387 (22 July 2016), http://www.gsdrc.org/wp-content/uploads/2016/08/HDQ1387.pdf (accessed 10 September 2016).

39 For global refugee figures see: http://www.unhcr.org/uk/figures-at-a-glance.html (accessed 1 November 2016); *Shelter Projects 2013–2014*, p. x.

40 On winter shelter kits in Syria see 'Syria and Iraq situations, final report, 2015–2016 UNHCR regional winter assistance', http://www.unhcr.org/turkey/uploads/root/unhcr_regional_winter_assistance_final_report_-_2015-2016.pdf (accessed 29 May 2016). On plywood for post-earthquake and hurricane shelters see International Federation of the Red Cross and Red Crescent Societies, 'Post-disaster Shelter: Ten Designs', http://www.sheltercasestudies.org/files/tshelter-8designs/10designs2013/2013-Postdisaster-shelter-10designs-Haiti-1.pdf (accessed 29 May 2016).

41 http://www.msf.org.uk/article/refugee-crisis-msf-granted-permission-new-camp-northern-france (accessed 10 September 2016).

42 Sold as '3D veneer', it was first developed by Reholz GmbH, which was purchased by Danzer in 2008.

43 Oak Furniture Land's advertisements could be seen on YouTube until recently. In October 2016 the UK Advertising Standards Authority upheld a complaint (Complaint Ref: A16-339625) that they had misled consumers with the slogan as they used 'oak wrap' made from thin pieces of wood glued together to cover the legs of furniture. The judgment is online at https://www.asa.org.uk/Rulings/Adjudications/2016/10/JB-Global-Ltd/SHP_ADJ_339625.aspx#.WCjgAy2LSUk (accessed 2 February 2017), and was reported widely in the national and regional UK press. The firm would not allow use of an image of their advertisement in this book without having approval of the text. The ASA, an industry body, would not respond to requests to read the testimony and documents submitted in the case. Typically, oak furniture wrap is a vinyl product, although not in this case.

## Selected Bibliography

In order to make the bibliography as useful as possible, it has been divided into unpublished and published material. It is organized by author and, if there is more than one citation by the same author(s), by date. Some authors will be found in both the published and unpublished sections. A separate list of magazines and journals indicates where a long run has been consulted. US Forest Products Research Laboratory is abbreviated throughout as FPL.

### Magazines and journals


*Aerial Age Weekly*
*Aero Digest*
*Architectural Forum*
*Architectural Review*
*Cabinet Maker and Complete House Furnisher*
*Design*
*Fachblatt für Holzarbeiter*
*Flight*
*Furniture Age*
*Furniture Gazette*
*Furniture Manufacturer and Artisan*
*Furniture Record (both UK and US)*
*Good Furniture*
*Hardwood Record*
*Лесопромышленное дело/ Lesopromyshlennoe delo [Timber Industry Magazine]*
*New York Times*
*Popular Mechanics*
*Popular Science*
*Practical Householder*
*Scientific American*
*Sperrholz und Furnier*
*Svensk Trävaru*
*Timber Trades Journal*
*Timberman*
*Veneers and Plywood*
*Wood*


### Unpublished sources


Shirley W. Allen, 'A History of War Cooperation Between the Bureau of Aircraft Production and the Forest Products Laboratory' (Madison, WI, 1919)

Shirley W. Allen, 'A History of the War Activities of the Forest Products Laboratory' (Madison, WI, 1919)

W.I. Beach, 'The North American Program for Wooden Aircraft Structures', report prepared by North American Aviation for the US Army Air Corps, report NA-5157 (Washington, DC, 1941, declassified 1950)

Don Brouse, 'Comments on Visit to Aircraft Factories at Wichita, Kansas, October 14 to 16, 1940', FPL Project 302-4

O.M. Butler, 'War Activities of the Forest Products Laboratory', FPL MS 0-98/B97W, marked 'For Publication in "Yale Forest News"', date stamped 2 March 1919

Armin Elmendorf, 'The Design of Plywood for Aircraft', ME thesis (University of Wisconsin 1919)

Armin Elmendorf, 'Plywood Developments in Germany', report prepared for the FPL (Madison, WI, 9 December 1933)

Armin Elmendorf, Willard S. Wilder, W.S. Broome and R.E. Johnston, 'Tests on Substitutes for Linen in Airplane Construction', first progress report, FPL Project L-225-10 (Madison, WI, 9 April 1918)

Armin Elmendorf and Raymond Wirka, 'Strength Tests on Airplane Wing Ribs', FPL Project L-225-2, (Madison, WI, April, July and November 1919)

T.N. Floyd, 'Early Lockheed Plywood Construction', report R-114 (rewritten from Haskelite Report no. 702) (1 April 1940), Lockheed Martin Archives

FPL, 'Recent Progress in Wood Research at the U.S. Forest Products Laboratory', (Madison, WI, August 1930)

FPL, 'Recent Progress on Housing Research at the Forest Products Laboratory' (Madison, WI, September 1938)

FPL, 'Advance Progress Report on Forest Products Laboratory Wood, Plywood, and Glue Research and Development Program Prepared for the Ninth Conference of the ANC Executive Technical Subcommittee on Requirements for Wood Aircraft and Wood Structures in Aircraft...' (Madison, WI, June 1943)

Jyri Kermik, 'A.M. Luther: A Case Study of the History and Form of Plywood 1877–1940', PhD Thesis (Royal College of Art, London, 1998)

R.F. Luxford and Don Brouse, 'Three-year Service Test of Plywood in Forest Products Laboratory Prefabricated House No. 1', FPL Project L-289-1 (Madison, WI, 1935)

Barbara Pisch, 'Gardner & Co.: Perforated-Plywood Seating Pioneers', unpublished paper written for the MA Program in the History of Decorative Arts and Design, New School/Cooper-Hewitt Museum, New York, 2012

C.L. Sponsler, 'A Method of Gluing Thin Veneer', FPL Project L-225-9 (Madison, WI, 1918)

C.L. Sponsler, 'Thin Plywood Manufacture by the Dry Glue Process. Memorandum on the Installation of the Method in the Haskelite Manufacturing Corporation's plant at Grand Rapids, Mich.', FPL Project L-225-9 (Madison, WI, 1918)

William A. Taylor, *The Vidal Process of Molding Fibrous Materials* (New Jersey October 1943)

George W. Trayer, 'A Prefabricated Wood House System', office report, FPL Project L-289-1 (Madison, WI, date stamped 1 June 1935)

T.R. Truax, 'Memorandum on a Visit to the Singer Manufacturing Company's Cabinet Factory at South Bend, Indiana', unpublished memorandum, FPL Project 157 (Madison, WI, 1919)

Thomas R.C. Wilson, 'Wood in Airplane Construction', FPL Project 302-4 (Madison, WI, 17 September 1940)

T.R.C. Wilson, 'Report of Visits to Western Aircraft Plants, September 30 to October 18, 1940', Field Trip Report, FPL Project L-302-4 (Madison, WI, 1940)

Carlile P. Winslow, 'Forest Lands and Forest Industries', address given before Central States Forestry Congress (17 November 1932)

Carlile P. Winslow, 'Airplanes: Current Interest and Progress in the Use of Forest Products in Aircraft Construction', report for FPL (Madison, WI, 1940)


### Published sources


Judith Adjani, 'The Global Wood Market, Wood Resource Productivity and Price Trends: an Examination with Special Attention to China', *Environmental Conservation* vol. 38: no. 1 (March 2011), pp. 54–55, 57

Aeronautical Research Section, 'Veneer Fuselage Construction and Tests. Part I: Investigations of a Series of Bodies for Two-seater Combat Machines – Conclusions and Design Recommendations', *The Bulletin of the Experimental Department Airplane Engineering Division U.S.A.* vol. 2: no. 1 (October 1918), pp. 5–29

L.E. Akers, *Particle Board and Hardboard* (London 1966)

S.W. Allen and T.R. Truax, *Glues Used in Airplane Parts*, National Advisory Committee for Aeronautics report no. 66 (Washington, DC, 1920)

Kenneth Ames, 'Gardner & Company of New York', *Antiques* vol. 100: no. 2 (August 1971), pp. 252–55

Stanford Anderson, Gail Fenske and David Fixler, *Aalto and America* (New Haven 2012)

Mick Anguilo, 'On the Rampage', *Skateboarder* vol 4: no 3 (October 1977), pp. 60–69

Martin P. Ansell (ed.), *Wood Composites* (Cambridge 2015)

Paul Atkinson, 'Do It Yourself: Democracy and Design', *Journal of Design History* vol 19: vol. 2 (Spring 2006), pp. 1–10

Alfred E. Beach, *The Pneumatic Dispatch* (New York 1868)

Sandra Beebe, *The Company by the Bay* (Springfield, OR, 1988)

Albert Farwell Bemis, *The Evolving House* (Cambridge, MA, 1936)

Barry Bergdoll (ed.), *Home Delivery: Fabricating the Modern Dwelling* (New York 2008)

Douglas Booth, 'Surfing: the Cultural and Technological Determinants of a Dance', *Culture, Sport and Society* vol. 2: no. 1 (1999), pp. 36–55

Iain Borden, *Skateboarding, Space and the City. Architecture and the Body* (Oxford and New York 2001)

B.C. Boulton, *The Manufacture and Use of Plywood and Glue* (London 1920)

Adam Bowett, *Woods in British Furniture Making 1400–1900* (London 2012)

Michael Braungart and William McDonough, *Cradle to Cradle: Remaking the Way We Make Things* (New York 2002)

Don Brouse, 'Methods of Increasing Durability of Plywood', FPL report R1125 (Madison, WI, 1932)

Alfred Bruce and Harold Sandbank, *A History of Prefabrication* (New York 1943)

G.T. Chernenko, Жизнь И необыкновенные изобретения капитана костовича/*Zhyzn' i neobyknowniye izobreteniya kapitana Kostovicha [Life and Extraordinary Inventions of Captain Kostovich]* (St Petersburg 2001)

W.R. Chown and E. Falk, *Investigation of Targets Connected with the German Plywood Industry*, BIOS final report no. 529, prepared by British Intelligence Objectives Sub-Committee (London 1946)

Sara Witter Connor, *Wisconsin's Flying Trees in World War II* (Charleston, SC, 2014)

Robert M Cour, *The Plywood Age* (Portland, OR, 1955)
Peter Dauvergne, 'Globalisation and Deforestation in the Asia-Pacific', Working Paper No. 1997/7 (Canberra November 1997)
Kevin Davies, 'Finmar and the Furniture of the Future: the Sale of Alvar Aalto's Plywood Furniture in the UK, 1934–1939' *Journal of Design History* vol. 11: no. 2 (1998), pp. 145–56
Martha Deese, 'Gerald Summers and the Makers of Simple Furniture', *Journal of Design History* vol. 5: no. 3 (1992), pp. 183–205
Benedict Dellot, 'Ours to Master. How makerspaces can help us master technology for a more human end', Royal Society of Arts (RSA) report (London 2015) https://www.thersa.org/globalassets/pdfs/reports/rsaj3881_ours_to_master_report_11.15_web.pdf (accessed 21 September 2016)
Eames Demetrious, *An Eames Primer* (London 2001)
Deutsche Werkstätten, *De-We Plattenhaus*, marketing publication (Dresden [1925–27])
Deutsche Werkstätten, *Die Neue Zeit, Holzhäuser der Deutschen Werkstätten*, marketing publication ([Hellerau] 1934)
Lionel Devlieger (ed.), *Behind the Green Door. A Critical Look at Sustainable Architecture through 600 Objects by Rotor* (Oslo 2014)
Charles Dickens, *Our Mutual Friend* (Chicago and New York 1884)
Tony Dingle, '"I'd rather be sailing": the Postwar Boom in Dinghy Sailing', *The Great Circle* vol. 21: no. 2 (1999), pp. 121–27
Kendall J. Dodd, 'Pursuing the Essence of Inventions: Reissuing Patents in the 19th Century' *Technology and Culture* vol. 32: no. 4 (October 1991), pp. 999–1017
Diane M. Douglas, 'The Machine in the Parlor, A Dialectical Analysis of the Sewing Machine', *Journal of American Culture* vol. 1: no. 5 (1982), pp. 20–29
David Edgerton, *Shock of the Old: Technology and Global History since 1900* (London 2008)
David Edgerton, *England and the Aeroplane: Militarism, Modernity and Mechanics* (London 2013)
*The Edinburgh Book of Prices for Manufacturing Cabinet-Work* (Edinburgh 1811 and 1821)
Armin Elmendorf, 'Data on the Design of Plywood for Aircraft' in *Annual Report of the National Advisory Committee for Aeronautics* (Washington, DC, 1921), pp. 109–22
EU FLEGT Facility, 'Changing International Markets for Timber and Wood Products', European Forest Institute Policy Brief 5 (Joensuu 2010), http://www.efi.int/files/attachments/publications/efi_policy_brief_5_eng_net.pdf (accessed 30 August 2016)
*Our First Fifty Years. The Story of Venesta Limited 1898–1948* (London 1948)
Adrian Forty, *Concrete and Culture* (London 2012)
FPL, 'Gluing Veneer at High Moisture Content', Technical Note no. F-11 (Madison, WI, 1919)
FPL, 'Calculation of Pressure in a Hydraulic Veneer Press', Technical Note no. F-25 (Madison, WI, 1919)
FPL, 'Tests for Water Resistance of Plywood', Technical Note no. F-26 (Madison, WI, 1919)
FPL, 'Thin Plywood', Technical Note no. F-29 (Madison, WI, 1919)
FPL, 'Effect of Oils on Strength of Glues in Plywood', Technical Note no. 99 (Madison, WI, 1920)
FPL, 'Effect of Varying the Number of Plies in Plywood', Technical Note no. 132 (Madison, WI, 1921)
FPL, *Wood Handbook. Wood as an Engineering Material* (Washington, DC, 1935, revised 1940, 1955, 1974, 1987, 1999, 2010)
FPL, 'Research in Forest Products: Annual Report of the Forest Products Laboratory' (Madison, WI, 1938)
FPL, 'The Forest Products Laboratory: A Brief Account of its Work and Aims' (Madison, WI, 1938)
FPL, 'Glues for Use in Aircraft', report 1337 (Madison, WI, October 1941)
FPL, 'Wood Goes to War', report D1426 (Madison, WI, December 1942)
FPL, 'Wood's Technological Coming-of-Age', report 1442 (Madison, WI, December 1943)
FPL, 'The Use of Wood for Aircraft in the United Kingdom: Report of the Forest Products Mission', report 1540 (Madison, WI, June 1944)
FPL and Army-Navy-Civil Committee, 'ANC Bulletin: Design of Wood Aircraft Structures', ANC-18 (Washington, DC, June 1948)
FPL, 'Properties of Ordinary Wood Compared with Plywood', Technical Note no. 131 (Madison, WI, 1952)
FPL, *The Forest Products Laboratory – A Golden Anniversary Record, 1910–1960* (Madison, WI, 1960)
[George Henry Francis], 'The Age of Veneer', *Fraser's Magazine* (September 1850, pp. 237–45; October 1850, pp. 437–45; February 1851, pp. 147–52; April 1851, pp. 472–76; September 1851, pp. 332–39; January 1852, pp. 87–94)
Rowena Gale, Peter Gosson, Nigel Hepper and Geoffrey Killen, 'Wood', in Paul T. Nicholson and Ian Shaw, *Ancient Egyptian Materials and Technology* (Cambridge 2000), pp. 334–71
Gardner & Company catalogue, *Perforated Veneer Seats, Chairs, Settees, etc* (New York September 1884)
George A. Garratt, 'Wood in War and Peace', US Forest Products Laboratory report R1460 (Madison, WI, October 1944)
Neil A. Gershenfeld, *Fab: the Coming Revolution on Your Desktop – from Personal Computers to Personal Fabrication* (New York 2005)
Chris Gibson and Andrew Warren, 'Making Surfboards: Emergence of a Trans-Pacific Cultural Industry', *The Journal of Pacific History* vol. 49: no. 1 (2014), pp. 1–25
Wilfred E. Goff, 'The De Havilland Mosquito', *Aircraft Production*, Part I (June 1943), pp. 263–74, and Part II (July 1943), pp. 315–27.
Carolyn M. Goldstein, *Do It Yourself* (Washington, DC, 1998)
Alastair Grieve, *Isokon* (London 2004)
Dee Halligan and Daniel Charny, 'Cultural roles of makerspaces (and roles of making in cultural spaces)', interim report (September 2016), http://www.fromnowon.co.uk/news/new-research-cultural-roles-of-makerspaces-and-makings-role-in-cultural-spaces (accessed 21 September 2016)
David A. Hanks, *Innovative Furniture in America from 1800 to the Present* (New York 1981)
David A. Hanks with Jennifer Toher, *Donald Deskey* (New York 1987)
John F. Hardecker, 'Veneers Employed in Mass Airplane Construction', *Veneers* (March 1929), pp. 18–20
Richard Harris, *Building a Market: The Rise of the Home Improvement Industry, 1914–1960* (Chicago and London 2013)
D. Dex Harrison, J.M. Albery and M.W. Whiting, *A Survey of Prefabrication* (London 1945)
W. Owen Harrod, 'Unfamiliar Precedents: Plywood Furniture in Weimar Germany', *Studies in the Decorative Arts* vol. 15: no. 2 (Spring–Summer 2008), pp. 2–35
Richard W. Haynes, 'An Analysis of the Timber Situation in the United States: 1952 to 2050', General Technical Report PNW-GTR-560 (Portland, OR, 2003)
R.P. Hearne, *Airships in Peace and War* (2nd edition, London 1910)
Bruce G. Heebink, 'Bag-molding of Plywood', FPL report R1431, revised as report R1624 (Madison, WI, 1943, revised 1953 as 'Fluid-Pressure Molding of Plywood')
Bruce G. Heebink, 'Summary of Methods of Bag-Molding', FPL report 1347 (Madison, WI, April 1943)
Bruce G. Heebink, Alvin A. Mohaupt and John J. Kunzweiler, 'Fabrication of Lightweight Sandwich Panels of the Aircraft Type', FPL Project 580 A-1, report 1574 (Madison, WI, 1947, revised March 1954)
Otto C. Heyer and R.F. Blomquist, 'Stressed-Skin Panel Performance After Twenty-Five Years of Service', FPL report FPL-18 (Madison, WI, December 1964)
Thomas Hines, *Richard Neutra and the Search for Modern Architecture* (New York 1982)
Charles Holtzapffel, *Turning and mechanical manipulation intended as a work of general reference and practical instruction on the lathe, and the various mechanical pursuits followed by amateurs, Vol. I* (London 1843)
David Hounshell, *From the American System to Mass Production, 1800–1932* (Baltimore 1984)
Frank H. House, *Timber at War* (London 1965)
Catherine Ince with Lotte Johnson (eds), *The World of Charles and Ray Eames* (London 2015)
Paul Israel and Robert Rosenberg, 'Patent Office Records as a Historical Source: the Case of Thomas Edison', *Technology and Culture* vol. 32: no. 4 (October 1991), pp. 1097–101
Andrew Jackson, 'Labour as leisure – the Mirror Dinghy and DIY Sailors', *Journal of Design History* vol. 19: no. 1 (Spring 2006), pp. 57–67
Burnham Kelly, *The Prefabrication of Houses* (Cambridge, New York and London 1951)
Jüri [*sic*] Kermik, *The Luther Factory,*

*Plywood and Furniture 1877–1940* (Tallinn 2004)
B. Zorina Khan, *The Democratization of Invention: Patents and Copyrights in American Economic Development* (Cambridge 2005)
Pat Kirkham, *Charles and Ray Eames* (Cambridge, MA, 1995)
E. Vernon Knight and Meinrad Wulpi, *Veneers and Plywood* (New York 1927)
Owen Knowles, 'Veneering and the Age of Veneer: a Source and Background for *Our Mutual Friend*', *The Dickensian* 81 part 2: 406 (Summer 1985), pp. 88–96
F. Kollmann, *Furniere, Lagenhölzer und Tischerplatten* (Berlin, Göttingen and Heidelberg 1962)
F.P. Kollmann, E.W. Kuenzi and A.J. Stamm, *Principles of Wood Science and Technology II: Wood Based Materials* (Berlin, Heidelberg and New York 1975)
John W. Koning (ed.), *Forest Products Laboratory 1910–2010: Celebrating a Century of Accomplishments* (Madison, WI, 2010)
H. Koponen, *Suomen vaneriteollisuus 1893–2000 [The Finnish Plywood Industry 1893–2000]* (Helsinki 2001)
Gordon Logie, *Furniture from Machines* (London 1947)
*The London Cabinet Makers' Union Book of Prices* (London 1803, 1811, 1824 and 1836)
Brian Lutz, *Eero Saarinen: Furniture for Everyman* (New York 2012)
John F. Lutz, 'Techniques for Peeling, Slicing and Drying Veneer', USDA Forest Service Research Paper FPL-228 (Madison, WI, 1974)
R.F. Luxford, 'Fabricated Wall Panels with Plywood Coverings', FPL report R1099 (Madison, WI, February 1936)
R.F. Luxford, 'Prefabricated House System Developed by The Forest Products Laboratory', FPL report 1165 (December 1937, revised versions October 1958 and 1965)
Gary Lynch and Malcolm Gault-Williams, *Tom Blake: the Uncommon Journey of a Pioneer Waterman* (California 2001)
Charles E. MacKay, *Shavings for Breakfast: the History of Morris Furniture Glasgow* (Glasgow 2013)
Peter Mackeith and Kersten Smeds, *The Finland Pavilions: Finland at the Universal Expositions 1900–1992* (Helsinki 1992)
Christine Macleod, 'The Paradoxes of Patenting: Invention and Diffusion in 18th- and 19th-Century Britain, France and North America', *Technology and Culture* vol. 32: no. 4 (October 1991), pp. 885–910
Cecil Mallaby Firth and J.E. Quibell, with plans by J.P. Lauer, *Excavations at Saqqara: The Step Pyramid. Volume II – Plates* (Cairo 1935)
R.F. Mann, 'The Probable Trend of Aeroplane Design', *Flight* (3 January 1918), pp. 15–16
Henry Mayhew, 'Labour and the Poor. Letter LIX', *The Morning Chronicle* (4 July 1850), pp. 5–6
Jeffrey L. Meikle, *American Plastic: a Cultural History* (New Brunswick 1995)
Achim Menges, Tobias Schwinn and Oliver David Krieg (eds), *Advancing Wood Architecture: a Computational Approach* (London and New York 2017)
Louis H. Meyer, *Plywood: What It Is—What It Does* (New York 1947)
Robert C. Mikesh, *Albatros D.Va. German Fighter of World War I* (Washington, DC, 1980)
Alexander Mora, *Plywood: Its Production, Use and Properties* (London 1932)
Stephan T.A.M. Moss, *Wooden Furniture in Herculaneum* (Amsterdam 1999)
Frederick J. Myers, *Ion Exchange Coating and Plywood Resins at I.G. Farbenindustrie, Th. Goldschmidt A.G., Permutit A.G., and Chemische Werke Albert*, FIAT final report no. 715, prepared by Field Information Agency, Technical, United States Group Control Council for Germany (London 4 February 1945)
Charles A. Nelson, *History of the US Forest Products Laboratory 1910–1963* (Washington, DC, 1971)
F.H. Max Nestler, 'The Formaldehyde Problem in Wood-Based Products – An Annotated Bibliography', USDA Forest Service General Technical Report FPL-8 (Madison, WI, 1977)
Marilyn Neuhart with John Neuhart, *The Story of Eames Furniture* (Berlin 2010)
Sarah Nichols, *Aluminum by Design* (Pittsburgh and New York 2000)
Joseph L. Nicholson, 'The Plywood Plane is Here', *Forbes* vol. 46: no. 9 (1 November 1940), pp. 14–25, 31
Eliot F. Noyes, *Organic Design in Home Furnishings* (New York 1941)
Ásdís Ólafsdóttir, *Le Mobilier d'Alvar Aalto dans l'Espace et dans le Temps: La Diffusion Internationale du Design 1920–1940* (Paris 1998)
Janet Ore, 'Mobile Home Syndrome: Engineered Woods and the Making of a New Domestic Ecology in the Post-World War II Era', *Technology and Culture* vol. 52: no. 2 (April 2011), pp. 260–86
Derek Ostergard (ed.), *Bent Wood and Metal Furniture 1850–1946* (New York 1987)
Daniel Ostroff, *An Eames Anthology* (New Haven 2015)
Juhani Pallasmaa (ed.), *Alvar Aalto Furniture* (Helsinki 1984)
A.J. Panshin, E.S. Harrar, W.J. Baker, P.B. Proctor, *Forest Products, their Sources, Production, and Utilization* (New York 1962)
*Patkau Architects: Material Operations* (Princeton, NJ, 2017)
Paul David Pearson, *Alvar Aalto and the International Style* (London 1978)
Thomas D. Perry, 'Plywood Makes Better Furniture and Here's Why', *Furniture Record* vol. 52 (April 1926), pp. 40–42, 90–91
Thomas D. Perry, *Modern Plywood* (New York 1942)
Thomas D. Perry, 'Improved Methods of Making Curved Plywood', *Aero Digest* (July 1943), pp. 237, 239, 241–42
Thomas D. Perry, *Modern Wood Adhesives* (New York 1944)
Thomas D. Perry, 'Plywood is Engineered Wood', *Mechanical Engineering* (October 1952), pp. 787–96
Nikolaus Pevsner, 'The First Plywood Furniture', *Architectural Review* vol. 84: no. 501 (August 1938), pp. 75–76
Nikolaus Pevsner, 'The History of Plywood up to 1914', *Architectural Review* vol. 86: no. 514 (September 1939), pp. 129–30
Sir Richard Phillips, *A Morning's Walk from London to Kew* (London 1817)
Nicolas Pillet and Michael Sawyer, 'EUTR: Plywood Imported from China', UK National Measurement Office report prepared for the Department for Environment, Food and Rural Affairs (DEFRA) (London February 2015), https://www.gov.uk/government/uploads/system/uploads/attachment_data/file/402325/Chinese_Plywood_Research_Report.pdf (accessed 30 August 2016)
Pliny, *Natural History*, vol. 4: books 12–16, translated by H. Rackham, Loeb Classical Library 370 (Cambridge, MA, 1945)
M. Powis Bale, *Woodworking Machinery* (London 1880)
Jack Pritchard, *View From a Long Chair* (London 1984)
Nathan Reingold, 'U.S. Patent Office Records as Sources for the History of Invention and Technological Property', *Technology and Culture* vol. 1: no. 2 (Spring 1960), pp. 156–67
V.J. Rinne, *The Manufacture of Veneer and Plywood* (Kuopio 1952)
Lieut-Col B. Roustam-Bek, *Aerial Russia. The Romance of the Giant Aeroplane* (London and New York 1916)
Zöe Ryan (ed.), *Bertrand Goldberg. Architecture of Invention* (New Haven and London 2011)
Ingrid Schäfer and Valentin Zandonella, *100 Jahre Buchen – Sperrholz – Aus der Geschichte der Blomberger Holzindustrie 1893 bis 1993* (Blomberg 1993)
Eric Schatzberg, *Wings of Wood, Wings of Metal: Culture and Technical Choice in American Airplane Materials, 1914–1945* (Princeton 1999)
K. Schmidt, 'Furnier und Sperrholz', *Sperrholz* no. 6 (1933), pp. 87–89
Lisa Schrenk, *Building a Century of Progress: The Architecture of Chicago's 1933–34 World's Fair* (Minnesota 2007)
R.M. Seborg and H. O. Fleischer, *Veneer and Plywood Manufacturing Techniques and Machinery Observed in Western Germany*, FIAT final report no. 389, prepared by Field Information Agency, Technical, United States Group Control Council for Germany (London 15 October 1945)
M.L. Selbo, *Adhesive Bonding of Wood*, United States Department of Agriculture Technical Bulletin No. 1512 (Washington, DC, August 1975)
P. Morton Shand, 'Timber as a Reconstructed Material', *Architectural Review* vol. 74: no. 471 (February 1936), pp. 74–80
Andrew Shanken, *Into the Void Pacific: Building the 1939 San Francisco World's Fair* (San Francisco 2015)
C. Martin Sharp and Michael J.F. Bowyer, *Mosquito* (rev. edition, London, 1971)
Shelter Case Studies, *Shelter Projects 2013–2014* (2014), http://www.sheltercasestudies.org/shelterprojects2013-2014.html (accessed 7 July 2016)
Thomas Sheraton, *The Cabinet-Maker and Upholsterer's Drawing Book* (3rd edition, London 1802)
A.J. Stamm and R.M. Seborg, 'Forest Products Laboratory Resin-Treated, Laminated, Compressed Wood (Compreg)', FPL report 1381 (Madison, WI, 1944, revised 1955, 1960)

Standard Houses Corporation, 'Ten houses to make home ownership possible for more people', marketing publication (Chicago 1937)
P.D. Stetson, 'Mechanical Notes from America', *The Practical Mechanic's Journal* (1 April 1858), pp. 8–10
Nina Stritzler-Levine and Timo Riekko (eds), *Artek and the Aaltos* (New York 2016)
Henry Harison Suplee, 'Plywood Aeroplane Construction', *Aerial Age Weekly* (20 January 1919), pp. 945–97, 961
Colin Thom, 'Fine Veneers, Army Boots and Tinfoil: New Light on Marc Isambard Brunel's Activities in Battersea', *Construction History* vol. 25 (2010), pp. 53–67
Rob Thompson, *Manufacturing Processes for Design Professionals* (London 2007)
George W. Trayer, *Wood in Aircraft Construction*, report prepared for and published by the National Lumber Manufacturers Association (Washington, DC, 1930)
George W. Trayer, 'Data on Structural Use of Plywood from Two New Test Series', *Engineering News-Record* (9 August 1934), pp. 172–76
George W. Trayer, 'Forest Products Laboratory Prefabrication System a New Departure in All-Wood Housing', FPL report R1059 (Madison, WI, May 1935)
Marc Treib (ed.), *An Everyday Modernism: the Houses of William Wurster* (Berkeley, CA, 1995)
Pirkko Tuukkanen, *Alvar Aalto Designer* (Helsinki 2002)
Clare Vincent, 'John Henry Belter: Manufacturer of all Kinds of Fine Furniture', in Ian M.G. Quimby and Polly Anne Earl (eds), *Technological Innovation and the Decorative Arts* (Charlottesville, VA, 1974), pp. 207–34
Gerard F. Vultee, 'Fabrication of the Lockheed "Vega" Airplane-Fuselage', *SAE Technical Paper* vol. 23: no. 5 (November 1928), pp. 449–53
Shirley B. Wainwright, *Modern Plywood* (London 1927)
Julia Walter-Herrmann and Corinne Büching (eds), *FabLab: of Machines, Makers and Inventors* (Bielefeld 2013)
F.F. Wangaar and J.H. Tigelaar, *Manufacture of Plywood and Related Products in Western Germany*, FIAT final report no. 202, prepared by Field Information Agency, Technical, United States Group Control Council for Germany (London 1 October 1945)
*Wartime technological developments, a study made for the Subcommittee on war mobilization of the Committee on military affairs, United States Senate, pursuant to S. res. 107, 78th Congress, and S. res. 46, 79th Congess, authorizing a study for the possibilities of better mobilizing the national resources of the United States* (Washington, DC, May 1945)
Laura Wellesley, 'Trade in Illegal Timber: The Response in China', Chatham House report (December 2014), https://www.chathamhouse.org/sites/files/chathamhouse/field/field_document/20141210Illegal TimberChinaWellesley.pdf (accessed 30 August 2016)
Christopher Wilk, *Marcel Breuer: Furniture and Interiors* (New York 1981)
Christopher Wilk, 'Furnishing the Future: Bent wood and metal furniture, 1925–1946' in Derek Ostergard (ed.), *Bent Wood and Metal Furniture: 1850–1946* (New York 1987), pp. 121–74
Christopher Wilk, *Frank Lloyd Wright: the Kaufmann Office* (London 1993)
Sir John Gardner Wilkinson, *The Manners and Customs of the Ancient Egyptians*, new edition revised and corrected by Samuel Birch (London 1878)
Andrew Dick Wood, *Plywood of the World* (Edinburgh and London 1963)
Andrew Dick Wood and Thomas Gray Linn, *Plywoods, Their Development, Manufacture and Application* (Edinburgh and London 1942, rev. edition, 1950)
Henry Woodhouse, *Textbook of Applied Aeronautic Engineering* (New York 1920)
Harry Woodman, 'The Sikorsky Grand', *Aeroplane* (March 2004), pp. 71–87
William Wilson Wurster, 'Carquinez Heights', *California Arts and Architecture* vol. 58 (November 1941), pp. 34–42, 46
A.E. Wynn, *Design and Construction of Formwork for Concrete Structures* (London 1926, rev. edition, 1939)
John I. Zerbe, Zhiyong Cao and George B. Harpole, 'An Evolutionary History of Oriented Strandboard', US Forest Products Laboratory General Technical Report FPL-GTR-236 (Madison, WI, 2015)

## Glossary

**Bag moulding**
A process using veneers, adhesive and a flexible, impermeable bag or blanket to mould plywood by the application of fluid pressure (steam, water, air or a vacuum). Bag-moulding techniques were developed no later than the nineteenth century. They became prominent in the US from the 1930s onwards, particularly for moulding plywood aeroplane parts.

**Balsawood**
A very lightweight, strong timber from a tropical tree (*Ochroma lagopus*) native to the Americas.

**Battenboard**
Another term for blockboard.

**Biplane**
An aeroplane with two pairs of wings, one sitting above the other (see also monoplane).

**Blockboard**
A building material consisting of a core of narrow solid wooden battens joined or glued together between two plywood panels.

**Blood albumin glue**
Adhesive based on serum albumin, a component of animal blood. Compared to other organic adhesives, blood albumin has very good moisture resistance and durability.

**Box girder**
As used in early aircraft design, a series of longitudinal, horizontal and vertical solid wood or metal girders forming the hollow external frame of the fuselage, which is usually square in cross-section. Extensive wire bracing was generally required within a box girder fuselage to add strength and stiffness to the structure. The fuselage was usually covered with canvas or linen (sometimes rubberized).

**Bulkhead**
Vertical partitions that divide the hull of a ship or the fuselage of an aeroplane, providing structural support along its length.

**Casein glue**
Adhesive based on the main protein present in milk. Casein glue has good moisture resistance and durability, compared to other organic adhesives. It does not need heat to set, making it relatively easy to use and adaptable to many different applications.

**Chassis**
The base frame of a car, with its mechanism. The term can also be used more generally to refer to a frame on which other parts are mounted.

**Chipboard**
A material made from wood chips, shavings or sawdust compressed with resin or another binder to form a flat sheet. It is often coated or veneered.

**CNC**
Computer Numeric Control: the means by which a machine is operated by a computer. In a CNC lathe or router, the computer controls the cutting or shaping of a material.

**Cold-pressing**
The oldest method of producing plywood in which an assembled and glued stack of veneers are adhered to one another by being subjected to pressure, without the application of heat.

**Compound curve**
A surface that is curved in more than one direction, as seen, for example, in the shape of an egg.

**Cross-grained**
Two or more layers of veneer stacked with the grain of each layer running in an opposite direction (either at right angles, or diagonally) to that of the adjacent one.

**Cross-laminated timber (CLT)**
A material consisting of layers of solid wood bonded together with a structural adhesive. Each layer is laid at right angles to the adjacent one, resulting in great structural strength and making CLT popular for construction.

**Dirigible**
An early flying craft consisting of gas-filled bags, within a rigid frame, below which passengers travelled in a separate compartment. It is also known as an airship.

**Douglas fir**
A tall, evergreen tree of the pine family often planted for timber. Native to northwest America, it is also known as Oregon pine.

**Endmill**
A rotating cutting bit forming part of a CNC router.

**Engineered wood**
Any type of manufactured composite material consisting of layers, strands, fibres or boards of wood glued together under pressure.

**Formaldehyde**
A naturally occurring (but toxic) colourless organic compound used as the basis for synthetic chemical compounds such as industrial resins.

**Form lining**
Also known as shuttering, a mould of solid wood, plywood or metal in which concrete is set. It is part of a larger temporary structure of timber, steel or other materials known as 'formwork'.

**Fuselage**
The long body of an aeroplane, to which the wings and tail attach.

**Glulam**
An abbreviation of 'glued laminated timber': a composite material produced by gluing together laminated pieces of solid timber with the grain of all layers running lengthwise in the same direction. It is used for structural applications, especially beams.

**Grain**
The natural longitudinal arrangement of fibres in wood.

**Gusset plate**
In construction, a thick sheet used to connect beams and girders to columns and/or trusses.

**Gutta-percha**
A naturally occurring, tough and hard latex (rubber) produced from the sap of certain trees found in Malaysia.

**Hardwood**
Wood from a tree (usually deciduous and broadleaved) that bears covered seeds, such as birch, walnut, oak, ash or beech. The term does not indicate the actual hardness of the wood.

**John Bull**
A personification of the English nation, or of a typical Englishman.

**Laminated wood**
Two or more layers of wood (either solid wood or veneers) glued together. Laminated wood can be cross-grained (for example, plywood or CLT) but the term is generally used to refer to wood with the grains of all layers running in the same direction.

**Laminated veneer lumber (LVL)**
A manufactured composite material of wood veneers glued and pressed together. It is usually made with the grain of all layers running in the same direction and is generally used in load-bearing structures.

**Laminboard**
A thick compound board with a core of small wooden battens or strips, glued together at the edges and held by a wooden sheet or veneer, the grain of which is perpendicular to that of the core.

**Lath and plaster construction**
A traditional form of construction using thin strips of wood (laths), over which plaster is applied.

**Longeron**
A longitudinal structural part that runs the whole length of an aircraft fuselage.

**Lumber-core**
Another term for blockboard.

**Mahogany**
A hardwood native to tropical America (with other species, now traded as mahogany, native to Africa, India and South America). Mahogany is hugely prized in cabinetmaking for its straight grain and durability, its rich colour (often reddish) and the lustre of its finish.

**Makerspace**
A space in which amateurs and professionals share equipment, knowledge and ideas in order to make, modify or fix a range of things.

**Marine plywood**
A type of plywood, used mainly in boatbuilding, in which layers of highly durable veneer are bonded with a water-resistant adhesive or resin.

**Medium-density fibreboard (MDF)**
A type of board made from compressed wood particles or residue bonded with resin, using heat and pressure.

**Monocoque**
Literally translated as 'single shell', a structure in which a single, rigid external skin is load- or stress-bearing.

**Monoplane**
An aeroplane with a single set of wings (see also biplane).

**Off-gassing**
Of a material, emitting a chemical, often a harmful one, as a gas.

**Oriented strand board (OSB)**
A composite structural material made of flakes of wood bonded with waterproof resin under heat and pressure. Since the mid-1980s it has been widely used in construction.

**Particle board**
A board made of wood fragments, such as chips or shavings, that are bonded together with resin under heat and pressure.

**Phenol**
Carbolic acid, extracted from coal tar in the form of colourless crystals and used in the manufacture of chemicals.

***Plattenhäuser***
A German term meaning 'panel houses' and referring to prefabricated houses made from 1921 in Dresden, Germany, by the manufacturer Deutsche Werkstätten (German Workshops).

**Plywood**
A stack of thin sheets (plies) of wood (veneers), usually odd in number, glued together with the grain of each layer running perpendicular to that of the next. The cross-graining of plywood distinguishes it from other forms of laminated wood.

**Prefabricated**
Something (often a house) constructed from set of parts manufactured elsewhere, mainly in a factory.

**Resin**
A natural or synthetic semi-solid or solid substance used in adhesives, varnishes and other materials. Synthetic resins were a key component of waterproof adhesives developed from the mid 1930s.

**Roof truss**
A framework of rafters, posts and struts that supports a roof.

**Rosewood**
A strong and close-grained tropical wood, particularly valued for decorative use due to its rich colour and figurative grain patterns.

**Rotary cutter**
A lathe machine that produces a long, continuous sheet of veneer by rotating a log longitudinally against a blade.

**Scarf-joint**
A joint connecting two pieces of wood. The ends of each piece are cut in such a way that they overlap and form a continuous length.

**Semi-monocoque**
An aircraft fuselage structure that integrates a rigid shell with an internal structure, spreading stresses between the skin and the framework.

**Shelter kit**
A set of tools and construction materials, often including plywood, distributed in the aftermath of a major crisis to help people build a temporary shelter or adapt an existing one.

**Sitka spruce**
A fast-growing spruce native to the northern Pacific coast of North America, and cultivated for its strong, lightweight timber.

**Softwood**
Wood from a tree (usually coniferous and evergreen) that bears naked seeds, such as spruce, pine, fir and cedar.

**Spar**
In aircraft design, the main structural support of the wing, running the length of the wing at right angles to the fuselage and carrying the wing ribs (also known as a wing beam).

**Stressed skin**
In construction or aircraft design, an outer covering that acts as integral loadbearing support and distributes structural stresses.

**Transom**
In boatbuilding, the flat surface forming the stern of a vessel.

**Urea-formaldehyde (UF)**
A synthetic resin made by condensing urea with formaldehyde and widely used in glues and in foam insulation (UFFI). As it emits harmful gases, its use in products for domestic applications has been severely restricted or banned since the 1970s.

**Vacuum-bag moulding**
A method used to mould veneers onto curved forms. A vacuum removes all air from a sealed bag in which a veneer has been glued to a curved piece; this causes the veneer to press evenly against and adhere to the surfaces of the piece. Vacuum-bag moulding can also be used to form plywood into curved shapes, on a mould (see bag moulding).

**Veneer**
A thin sheet of wood produced by sawing, rotary cutting, peeling or slicing a log.

**Whitewood**
A generic term used to describe a number of different species of wood, including poplar, fir and spruce. In the late nineteenth century the name 'whitewood' could have an association with poor-quality timber.

**Wing beam**
Another term for spar.

**Wing rib**
The main, repeating structural element running from front to back of an aeroplane wing.

## Picture Credits

### Introduction

Fig. 1 'Stripping kauri plywood with a rotary lathe, Kennedy Mill', Australian War Memorial ART25607
Fig. 2 © McGraw-Hill
Fig. 5 © McGraw-Hill
Fig. 6 Courtesy of the Oregon Historical Society, bb015219
Fig. 7 and back cover Courtesy of the Oregon Historical Society, bb015220
Fig. 8 Courtesy of the Forest History Society
Fig. 9 Courtesy of the Oregon Historical Society, bb015222
Fig. 10 Courtesy of the Forest History Society
Fig. 11 Courtesy of the Oregon Historical Society, bb015221
Fig. 12 Courtesy of the USDA Forest Service, Forest Products Laboratory (negative: 4774 M)
Fig. 13 Courtesy of the Forest History Society

### Chapter 1

Figs 14, 16 and 17 Courtesy of National Museums Liverpool, Lady Lever Art Gallery
Fig. 18 Courtesy of Apter Fredericks
Figs 20 and 21 V&A: W.25–1969 Given by Mallett & Son Ltd
Fig. 23 Brooklyn Museum, Gift of Mrs. Ernest Vietor, 39.30. Creative Commons-BY (Photo: Brooklyn Museum, 39.30_acetate_bw.jpg)
Fig. 25 Division of Home and Community Life, National Museum of American History, Smithsonian Institution
Figs 26–28 V&A: W.22–1983
Fig. 33 Courtesy of the Department of Rare Books, Special Collections and Preservation, University of Rochester River Campus Libraries
Fig. 34 Free Library, Philadelphia, PA / Bridgeman Images
Fig. 38 V&A: B.89–2014
Fig. 39 Courtesy of The Winterthur Library: Printed Book and Periodical Collection
Fig. 40 Courtesy of Hagley Museum & Library
Fig. 41 Purchase Fund. Acc. no.: 443.1956 © 2016. Digital image, The Museum of Modern Art, New York / Scala, Florence

### Chapter 2

Fig. 42 No. 69 from Album 44: The British Antarctic Expedition, Vol. I, 1907–1909/photographs compiled by Arthur Wigram Allen. PX*D 584, a3281024. State Library of New South Wales
Fig. 44 Science Museum / Science & Society Picture Library
Fig. 46 T9.K69, The Huntington Library, San Marino, California
Figs 49 and 50 Courtesy of Hagley Museum & Library
Fig. 54 Courtesy of the Museum of Estonian Architecture
Fig. 56 Estonian Museum of Applied Art and Design
Fig. 57 V&A: W.12–2016 Given by the Shand family
Fig. 58 Pritchard Papers, University of East Anglia (PP/18/8/40/1/12)
Fig. 62 Tallinna Linnamuuseum, Tallinn: TLM _ 10014 Dr
Fig. 64 © PLA collection / Museum of London
Fig. 65 No. 69 from Album 44: The British Antarctic Expedition, Vol. I, 1907–1909/photographs compiled by Arthur Wigram Allen. PX*D 584, a3281024. State Library of New South Wales
Fig. 66 Courtesy of Sotheby's
Fig. 67 National Library of Australia, mfm X 170
Fig. 68 Photograph from the British Antarctic ("Terra Nova") Expedition (1910–1913) Album. Alexander Turnbull Library, Wellington, Aotearoa N.Z.

### Chapter 3

Fig. 69 Collections of the Grand Rapids Public Museum
Fig. 70 The University Library, University of Illinois at Urbana-Champaign
Fig. 72 V&A: 19538:2
Fig. 75 *Timber Trades Journal* (29 December 1906), p. 948. Reproduced by permission of the National Library of Scotland
Fig. 76 *Cabinet Maker and Complete House Furnisher* (5 January 1907), cover
Fig. 77 *Cabinet Maker and Complete House Furnisher* (22 February 1908), p. 314
Fig. 78 *Cabinet Maker and Complete House Furnisher* (18 March 1911), p. 383
Fig. 79 The LuEsther T. Mertz Library of The New York Botanical Garden
Figs 80 and 81 Collections of the Grand Rapids Public Museum
Fig. 82 Grand Rapids History & Special Collections, Archives, Grand Rapids Public Library, Grand Rapids, MI
Fig. 83 Courtesy of the USDA Forest Service, Forest Products Laboratory

### Chapter 4

Fig. 84 ©DR / Coll.musée de l'Air et de l'Espace-Le Bourget- Inv. Prim518
Fig. 87 Smithsonian National Air and Space Museum (NASM 72-10099)
Fig. 88 Science Museum / Science & Society Picture Library
Fig. 89 From the collection of Lewis Lupton Kaylor, Corporal, Photographic Section, Air Service, United States Army. Contributed by Alan Kaylor Cline
Fig. 91 Courtesy of the USDA Forest Service, Forest Products Laboratory (negative: 3447 M)
Fig. 92 Courtesy of the USDA Forest Service, Forest Products Laboratory (negative: 6244 M)
Fig. 93 Courtesy of the USDA Forest Service, Forest Products Laboratory (negative: M 48436 F)
Fig. 94 Courtesy of the USDA Forest Service, Forest Products Laboratory (negative: 6602 M)
Fig. 96 and front cover ©DR / Coll. musée de l'Air et de l'Espace-Le Bourget- Inv. Prim518
Fig. 98 ©Musée de l'Air et de l'Espace-Le Bourget- Inv. MC4342
Figs 99 and 100 Courtesy of the David M. Rubenstein Rare Book & Manuscript Library, Duke University
Fig. 101 Australian War Memorial E01685
Fig. 102 Courtesy of Multnomah County Library
Fig. 104 Smithsonian National Air and Space Museum (NASM 83-322)
Figs 105–108 Courtesy of Lockheed Martin
Fig. 109 Smithsonian National Air and Space Museum (NASM-00158029)
Fig. 110 Rudy Arnold Photo Collection, Smithsonian National Air and Space Museum (NASM 2004-18942)
Figs 111 and 112 Courtesy of the Forest History Society
Fig. 113 Photo: Vern C. Gorst University of Washington, Special Collections, UW29547z
Fig. 114 Courtesy of the USDA Forest Service, Forest Products Laboratory (negative: M 48697 F)
Fig. 115 Courtesy of the Forest History Society
Fig. 116 Courtesy of Northwestern University https://images.northwestern.edu/multiresimages/inu:dil-2fdd5280-4651-4efc-9120-9ef3c39b414d
Fig. 117 Courtesy of the Oregon Historical Society, bb015218
Figs 118 and 119 Courtesy of the USDA Forest Service, Forest Products Laboratory / Evergreen Air and Space Museum
Figs 120, 121 and 123 Courtesy of the de Havilland Aircraft Museum
Fig. 124 Courtesy of the Lebus Family
Fig. 125 Courtesy of the de Havilland Aircraft Museum
Figs 126 and 127 Courtesy of the Lebus Family
Fig. 128 Courtesy of the de Havilland Aircraft Museum

### Chapter 5

Fig. 129 Alvar Aalto Museum
Fig. 130 Courtesy of the Oregon History Society, bb015223
Fig. 134 Architecture and Planning Library Special Collections, University of Texas Libraries, The University of Texas at Austin
Fig. 135 © Historic England Archive
Fig. 137 V&A: W.9–1974 Given by Edgar Kaufmann, Jr © ARS, NY and DACS, London 2016
Fig. 138 Photo: Sydney W. Newbery RIBA Collections
Fig. 140 The Wolfsonian–Florida International University, Miami Beach, Florida, The Mitchell Wolfson, Jr. Collection, 85.4.90
Fig. 142 Courtesy of APA – The Engineered Wood Association
Fig. 143 Photo: Charles W. Cushman Charles Cushman Collection: Indiana University Archives (P01892)
Fig. 144 The Wolfsonian–Florida International University, Miami Beach, Florida, The Mitchell Wolfson, Jr. Collection, TD1993.45.9
Fig. 145 Photo: Gabriel Moulin APA – The Engineered Wood Association / © Moulin Studio
Figs 147 and 149 APA – The Engineered Wood Association
Fig. 150 Photo: © 2013 Christie's Images Limited. Courtesy of MAK – Austrian Museum of Applied Arts / Contemporary Art
Figs 151 and 152 New York World's Fair 1939–1940 records, Manuscripts and Archives Division, The New York Public Library, Astor, Lenox and Tilden Foundations
Figs 153 and 154 Alvar Aalto Museum
Fig. 155 National Library of Australia, N 671.05 HAR
Fig. 156 Bibliothèque nationale de France
Fig. 157 Deutsche Werkstätten / Sächsisches Staatsarchiv, Hauptstaatsarchiv Dresden (11764, Nr. F1777, negative 022091)

Fig. 158 Deutsche Werkstätten / Sächsisches Staatsarchiv, Hauptstaatsarchiv Dresden (11764, Nr. 2508)
Fig. 159 and back cover Digital Collections of National Library of Finland, http://digi.nationallibrary.fi
Fig. 160 Courtesy of the USDA Forest Service, Forest Products Laboratory (negative: M 29823 F)
Fig. 161 Courtesy of the USDA Forest Service, Forest Products Laboratory (negative: M 25983 F)
Fig. 162 Courtesy of the USDA Forest Service, Forest Products Laboratory (negative: Z M 26097 F)
Fig. 163 Courtesy of the USDA Forest Service, Forest Products Laboratory (negative: M 32420 F)
Fig. 164 Courtesy of the USDA Forest Service, Forest Products Laboratory (negative: M 33721 F)
Figs 165–172 Courtesy of the USDA Forest Service, Forest Products Laboratory (negatives: M 28745 F, M 28746 F, M 28747 F, M 28749 F, M 28750 F, M 28751 F, M 28752 F, M 28755 F)
Fig. 173 and front cover Courtesy of Jennifer Sale Crane
Fig. 174 Richard and Dion Neutra Papers, Library Special Collections, Charles E. Young Research Library, UCLA. Permissions courtesy Dion Neutra, Architect ©
Fig. 175 Photo: Julius Shulman © J. Paul Getty Trust. Getty Research Institute, Los Angeles (2004.R.10). Permissions courtesy Dion Neutra, Architect
Fig. 176 Photo: Julius Shulman. Richard and Dion Neutra Papers, Library Special Collections, Charles E. Young Research Library, UCLA. © J. Paul Getty Trust. Getty Research Institute, Los Angeles (2004.R.10). Permissions courtesy Dion Neutra, Architect
Fig. 177 Richard and Dion Neutra Papers, Library Special Collections, Charles E. Young Research Library, UCLA. Permissions courtesy Dion Neutra, Architect ©
Fig. 178 Library of Congress, Prints & Photographs Division, FSA / OWI Collection (LC-DIG-fsa-8e09028)
Fig. 179 'Plywood houses – sloping ground condition', Wurster, Bernardi and Emmons collection, Environmental Design Archives, University of California Berkeley
Fig. 180 'Suggested variations for demountable houses in Vallejo. For plywood construction', Wurster, Bernardi and Emmons collection, Environmental Design Archives, University of California Berkeley
Fig. 181 Wurster, Bernardi and Emmons collection, Environmental Design Archives, University of California Berkeley
Figs 182–186 Courtesy of the family of Bertrand Goldberg
Fig. 187 Gift of Donald Deskey, 1988-101-1515. Photo: Matt Flynn © Smithsonian Institution. © 2016. Cooper-Hewitt, Smithsonian Design Museum / Art Resource, NY / Scala, Florence

**Chapter 6**

Fig. 189 *Practical Householder* (November 1960) © www.timeincukcontent.com
Fig. 190 Courtesy of The Library of the University of California, Berkeley
Fig. 191 Rug designed by Benita Koch-Otte: Mit freundlicher Genehmigung der v. Bodelschwinghschen Stiftungen Bethel ©
Fig. 192 V&A: W.15–2014 Given by Lionel March in memory of his wife Maureen Mary Vidler. © V&A/ Courtesy of the Schindler family
Fig. 193 V&A: W.14–2005 Purchased with funds provided by the Horace W. Goldsmith Foundation © V&A/DACS 2017
Fig. 194 © DACS 2017
Fig. 195 V&A: W.41–1987 © V&A / Alvar Aalto Museum
Fig. 196 © Alvar Aalto Museum
Fig. 197 Photo: Mauno Mannelin. Artek Collection/Alvar Aalto Archive
Fig. 198 V&A: W.34–1992
Figs 199 and 200 V&A: W.12–2015 Bequeathed by John Russell Brown in memory of Gilbert and Margaret Cousland
Fig. 201 V&A: CIRC.80–1975 Given by Mr and Mrs Dennis Young
Fig. 202 V&A: W.26–1978 © V&A / Courtesy of the Summers family
Fig. 203 Courtesy Cranbrook Archives
Fig. 206 Photo: Soichi Sunami (copyright unknown). Cat. no.: IN258B.17. © 2016. Digital image, The Museum of Modern Art, New York/Scala, Florence
Fig. 207 V&A: W.31–2016 © V&A / Eames Office LLC
Fig. 208 © Eames Office LLC
Fig. 209 V&A: W.7–2017 © V&A / Eames Office LLC
Fig. 210 V&A: W.8–2017 © V&A / Courtesy of Wilde + Spieth
Fig. 211 V&A: LOAN: AMERICAN FRIENDS.713-2016. American Friends of the V&A through the generosity of Mark McDonald
Fig. 212 V&A: W.37–1992 Given by Robin Day © V&A / Courtesy of the Robin and Lucienne Day Foundation
Fig. 213 V&A: W.6–2017 Given by Michael and Mariko Whiteway together with Brain Trust Inc. © V&A / Courtesy of the Republic of Fritz Hansen
Fig. 214 V&A: W.9–2017 Given by Tommaso Fantoni © V&A / Courtesy Archivio Osvaldo Borsani
Fig. 215 V&A: W.5–2017
Fig. 216 V&A: W.25–2016 © V&A / Tange Associates
Figs 217 and 282 V&A: W.26–2016 © V&A/Courtesy of The Royal Danish Academy of Fine Arts, Schools of Architecture, Design and Conservation
Fig. 218 Photo: E. E. Allen ltd. © IWM (A 15774)
Fig. 219 Photo: E. E. Allen ltd. © IWM (A 15763)
Figs 220–222 Courtesy of Riva Historical Archive
Fig. 223 Photo: H. Holder, 1990s Courtesy of Riva Historical Archive
Fig. 224 Photo: George Phillips Courtesy of The Revs Institute for Automotive Research, Inc., Naples, Florida
Fig. 225 Photo: Eric della Faille Courtesy of The Revs Institute for Automotive Research, Inc., Naples, Florida
Figs 226–231 *Popular Mechanics* (April 1946); *Popular Mechanics* (December 1959); *Practical Householder* (June 1957); *Practical Householder* (November 1960); *Popular Mechanics* (May 1951), cover by Robert C. Korta; *Popular Science* (December 1949) *Popular Mechanics* courtesy of Hearst/Practical Householder © www.timeincukcontent.com
Figs 233 and 234 Photo: Eileen Ramsay, © PPL Media Ltd Brochure kindly loaned by Martin Egan, © Mirrorpix
Fig. 236 and back cover Photo: Warren Bolster Courtesy Concrete Wave Editions
Fig. 237 Photographer unknown Courtesy of *Thrasher* Magazine
Fig. 238 V&A: CD.19–2016
Fig. 240 Courtesy of Ann Larie Valentine

**Chapter 7**

Fig. 241 V&A: W.29–2016 © V&A / Courtesy of Opendesk
Fig. 243 Courtesy of the Forest History Society
Fig. 244 V&A: E.329–2004 Gift of the American Friends of the V&A; Gift to the American Friends by Leslie, Judith and Gabri Schreyer and Alice Schreyer Batko © V&A / Courtesy of Anna Lieber / U.S. Environmental Protection Agency
Fig. 245 Photo: Chris Granger
Fig. 246 Courtesy of the Forest History Society
Fig. 247 Photo: John Fletcher Ford From the Collection of J. F. Ford Photographs, OSU Libraries Special Collections & Archives
Fig. 248 Photo: Armin Hari
Fig. 249 © Jeremy Sutton-Hibbert / Greenpeace
Fig. 250 © Greenpeace
Fig. 251 Jasper Morrison Studio
Fig. 252 Photo: Judd Foundation Archives © Judd Foundation / ARS, NY and DACS, London 2017
Fig. 253 Institute for Advanced Architecture of Catalonia - Fab Lab Barcelona / Image courtesy of IAAC
Figs 254–259 Designers clockwise from top left: Dmitry Kutlayev for Stooland, Cartonus, Deanne Viljoen for De Steyl, Andy McDonald for Setyard, SmithMatthias, William Osman
Fig. 260 V&A: W.28–2016 (assembled) and W.29–2016 (unassembled) © V&A / Courtesy of Opendesk
Figs 261 and 262 Courtesy of Opendesk
Fig. 263 WikiHouse Foundation
Figs 264 and 265 © Facit Homes
Figs 266 and 267, front cover, and frontispiece Photo: James Dow Courtesy of Patkau Architects
Fig. 268 Endesa Pavilion by IAAC / Photo: Adriá Goula
Figs 269 and 270, and front cover © David Franck
Fig. 271 Courtesy of the USDA Forest Service, Forest Products Laboratory (negative: M 25188 F)
Figs 272 and 273 Photo: Will Pryce Courtesy of Waugh Thistleton Architects
Fig. 274 Richard McKenzie, DigitalMcK photography
Fig. 275 Courtesy of Danzer
Figs 277–281 Diagram © EDGE & LEAD. Photos clockwise from top left: © Pekka Tynkkynen / © Pekka Tynkkynen / © Emmi Keskisarja / © Pekka Tynkkynen

Front cover (bottom left) V&A: Circ. 83–1975

## Index

*Italic* page numbers refer to illustrations.

**Acknowledgments**

This book was written in conjunction with the organization of an exhibition on the same subject held at the Victoria and Albert Museum in 2017, sponsored by Made.com and supported by the American Friends of the V&A. Although my interest in this subject started long ago, a first period of focused work on it began in 2011 with a very welcome period of research in New York under the auspices of an exchange programme between the V&A and the Metropolitan Museum of Art. Morrison Heckscher, Peter Kenny and their colleagues in the American Wing, as well as staff in the Thomas J. Watson Library of the Met, were extremely hospitable. I also benefited, then and later, from a sustained period of access to the exceptional holdings of the New York Public Library, both in the General Research Division and the Science, Industry and Business Library. Here in London, the British Library and National Archives also provided fundamental materials for research. As British patents are unfortunately not currently available online, staff at the British Library's Business and IP Centre were particularly helpful in providing access to these.

The Forest Products Laboratory (Madison, Wisconsin), part of the US Forest Service, is a unique institution, which, in addition to being an active research centre, holds an excellent library of published and unpublished material on its subject, including internal papers documenting its own history of research. Librarian Julie Blankenberg has been an extremely generous correspondent and, in 2015 and 2016, host to whom I owe thanks. I am also grateful to staff at the University of Glasgow Business Archives, the Mitchell Library (Glasgow), the University of East Anglia Library (Archives Department), the Oregon Historical Society (Portland, Oregon), the Forest History Society (Durham, North Carolina), and the US National Archives (College Park, Maryland). Particular thanks are due to Madeleine Sumida for her diligent work at the latter, tracking down FTC case dockets. For undertaking work at the Library of Congress, I am especially grateful to Courtney Knapp.

Among many other organizations with research holdings consulted for this project, I am grateful to Marilyn Thompson, APA – the Engineered Wood Association; Don Shannon, Battleship Cove Museum, Fall River, Massachusetts; Anette Hellmuth, Deutsche Werkstätten, Hellerau; Mickey Anderson and Rebecca Wilson, Evergreen Museum, McMinnville, Oregon; Kevin Cook, the Museum of British Surfing; Genevieve Fong and David Hertsgaard, Eames Office; Michele Dekuiper, Mason County (Michigan) Historical Society; Mariella Di Vito and Piero Gibellini, Riva Historical Society, Milan; Chris Marino, Environmental Design Archives, UC, Berkeley; and Simon Elliott, Genie Guerard and Octavio Olvera, UCLA Library Special Collections.

Among manufacturers and designers of plywood and plywood products around the world, I am especially grateful for the help provided by: James Angel, Danzer; Bruce Bell, Facit Homes; Antti Olin, ISKU; Chris McCourt and Mark Smith, Isokon Plus; Kari Koskinen, Maija Saarinen and Peter Barnes, Koskisen; Joni Steiner, Opendesk; John and Patricia Patkau and Pete Wenger, Patkau Architects; Riccardo Sassoli, Riva; Markku Herrala, UPM; and Alastair Parvin, WikiHouse. For support of an especially useful visit to Finland, I am grateful to Pirjo Pellinen, Cultural Attaché, Embassy of Finland, London, and Tiina Paavilainen in Helsinki.

Among many experts in fields related to plywood, I am especially grateful to Jyri Kermik, University of Brighton, who generously shared his knowledge, research materials, and contacts in Estonia relating to the history of the A.M. Luther firm. For discussion on issues around the earliest history of plywood and veneer cutting I was especially fortunate to be able to discuss questions and test draft text on specialists Adam Bowett, Yannick Chastang, Barry Harwood, Peter Holmes and Geoffrey Killen. For help with specific research matters I owe thanks to: Simon Barley, John Bowen (University of York), John Burman, Daniel Charny (From Now On, and Kingston University), Martin Egan (Daily Mirror Dinghy Association), Geoffrey Goldberg, Marcus Jaka, Stefan Krebs (University of Luxembourg), Tom McCloud, Daniel Ostroff, Barbara Pisch, Erin Putalik (University of Pennsylvania), Jane Rees, Mark Resnick, Jennifer Sale Crane, Gervais Sawyer, Andrew Shanken (UC Berkeley), Nina Strizler-Levine (Bard Graduate Center) and Sarah Teasley (RCA). For her enthusiastic support of this project and deep interest in its subject, as well as her trawl of the archive and objects of the Roddis Lumber and Veneer Company, warmest thanks are owed to Jane Bradbury.

I am fortunate to work within an institution that, in partnership with the Royal College of Art, runs an MA programme in the history of design. I am grateful to Angela McShane Jones, former head of the course, and to current and former students who assisted with research: Rachel Bradford, Victoria de Lorenzo, Sophie Farrelly, Lauren Fried, Catherine Gregg, Rachel McCarthy-Yardley, Florence Maschietto, Anna Stewart and Melissa Tyler. Finally, I owe special thanks to Rachel Bradford and Miranda Vane for their work in London, and also to Johann Deurell and Denise Hagströmer for following-up Swedish research matters.

For assistance with specific research tasks, I am grateful to Julia Khokhlova and Olga Yakushenko in St Petersburg; Dagmar Lieske in Berlin; Medeya Margoshvili in Moscow; Dongmin Park in Berkeley; Lucia Savi in Italy; and Miranda Saylor in Los Angeles. For help closer to home thanks are due to: Anna Bernbaum, Dan Mifsud, Laharee Mitra, and especially to Iida Käyhkö for help with Finnish translations and Jevgenija Ravcova for help with Russian ones. Warm thanks are owed to Persephone Allen who joined the project as the 2016 Bard Graduate Center/V&A intern.

Among museum colleagues particular thanks are owed for the collegiality and generosity of Laurent Rabier, Curator of Aircraft, Musée de l'Air et de l'Espace, Paris, and to that of Ralph Steiner, Director, de Havilland Aircraft Museum, London Colney. Thanks also to: Timo Riekko, Alvar Aalto Museum; Lori Hanna Boyer and Alison Fisher, Art Institute of Chicago; Caitlin Condell, Cooper Hewitt, Smithsonian Design Museum; Christian Holmsted Olesen, Designmuseum Danmark; Dr Frank Steinbeck, Deutsches Museum, Munich; Jörg Schmalfuss, Deutsches Technikmuseum, Berlin; Marc Greuther, Jim McCabe, Meredith Long and Patrice Fisher, Henry Ford Museum; Juliet Kinchin and Paul Galloway, MoMA; and Dorothy Cochrane and Chris Moore, National Air and Space Museum (Smithsonian).

For their generosity in donating, or securing the donation of objects to the V&A especially for illustration in this book, special thanks are due to The American Friends of the V&A; Tommaso Fantoni; Martin Levy; Mark McDonald; the Shand family; and Michael and Mariko Whiteway.

At the V&A my greatest debt of gratitude is to Elizabeth Bisley. Her long-standing enthusiasm for and commitment to this subject were formalized in 2016 when she took on the role of research assistant for the project. When the opening date for the exhibition (and publication) was unexpectedly brought forward by six months, she rose to the challenge by assuming a more senior role, helping to finalize research and text for this book as well as co-curating the exhibition itself. Lizzie is an exceptional colleague and an experienced curator, academic researcher and writer; both exhibition and book have been immeasurably improved by her work. The revised schedule also led to the welcome appointment of Anna White who, as research assistant over the past year, not only undertook research for the book but also took on the onerous task of securing images and permissions for book and exhibition. Her assistance was vital to delivering this book with so many previously unpublished images.

I am very grateful to my colleagues in the Furniture, Textile and Fashion Department, especially Lesley Miller who stood in for me as head of the department for much of 2016–17; to Stephanie Wood and then Amelia Cimino for administrative help; to Leela Meinertas and Max Donnelly for specific furniture queries; to Hanne Faurby for help with translations; and to Johanna Agerman Ross and Brendan Cormier for their comments on portions of this book. I am also grateful to Linda Lloyd-Jones, Head of Exhibitions, for her support of this project; Hannah Daley, for her excellent work as Exhibitions Manager, and to other colleagues who have worked on the exhibition: Stacey Bowles, Manuela Buttiglione, Stephanie Cripps, Claire Everitt, Anna Ferrari, Ann Hayhoe, Vanessa North, Lauren Papworth and Hanaa Skalli. For their work with V&A objects in this book I am grateful to conservators Nigel Bamforth and Dana Melchar and photographers Robert Auton, Pip Barnard and Richard Davis. In the National Art Library, Jill Raymond and especially Jennifer Reeves facilitated my research. I am immensely grateful to Line Lund, Nadine Fleischer and Joni Steiner for their enthusiasm and hard work on our exhibition design; to Catherine Ince for help with Eames material; and to Bill Sherman for advice on literature and language for chapter 3. And finally, to my former colleague Michaela Zöschg, I owe gratitude for rewarding discussions regarding historical German terminology and her willingness to help at all times.

I am immensely grateful to Glenn Adamson, Edward Cooke, Chris McCourt and Sarah Medlam for reading drafts of chapters of this book. They were all exceptionally generous with their time and comments. I only regret that I could not pursue all of their pertinent suggestions. For their work on the production of this book I am indebted to Kathryn Johnson, Tom Windross and Karen Fick of V&A Publishing and, at Thames & Hudson, Andrew Sanigar, Susannah Lawson, Sarah Yates, and Roger Fawcett-Tang for their cooperative work on the design and production.

For nearly 30 years Chris McCourt and I have been discussing plywood from our very different but complementary perspectives. During that time I have benefited from his deep knowledge of the material and ways of working with it, but also from his and Lone McCourt's friendship. I owe Chris and Lone warmest thanks.

Finally, work on this book, especially the long hours required during 2016, relied on exceptional support from Carolyn Sargentson. It also benefited from her skills as a clear thinker and experienced writer. For her patience and understanding, and also that of Noah, and, at a distance, of Hannah and Sophie, and also my sister Andrea, I could not be more grateful.